WHERE STYLISTS SHOP

Regan Arts.

65 Bleecker Street
New York, NY 10012

First Regan Arts paperback edition, January 2017

Library of Congress Control Number: 2016939698

ISBN 978-1-68245-032-1

Interior design by Catherine Casalino
Cover design by Richard Ljoenes
Image credits, which constitute an extension of this copyright page, appear on page 462

Printed in the United States of America

10 9 8 7 6 5 4 3 2 1

· LOS ANGELES · LONDON · PARIS · MOSCOW · NEW ORLEANS · SHANGHAI · HONG KONG · NEW YORK · MILAN · SYDNEY · CAPE TOWN · BERLIN · LIMA · AUSTIN · BUENOS AIRES · ISTANBUL · TOKYO · TORONTO · DUBAI ·

WHERE STYLISTS SHOP

THE FASHION INSIDER'S ULTIMATE GUIDE

The Secret Source List of Designers, Stylists, Editors, Bloggers, Models, Costume Designers, Street-Style Stars, and Tastemakers

Booth Moore

Regan Arts.
NEW YORK

WH

STYL

SH

ERE

ISTS

OP

TABLE OF

CONTENTS

EUROPE

EURASIA

ASIA

MIDDLE EAST

AFRICA

AUSTRALIA

INTROD

Why write a book about shopping now?

Every day, headlines herald the death of brick-and-mortar stores. There are so many abandoned shopping centers, we now have a name for them—ghost malls. Amazon.com gets bigger by the click, and as soon as there is drone delivery, we won't ever have to leave our homes to buy anything.

But then what?

I decided to write a book about shopping now because there is still so much joy in it. It's thrilling to discover that special find or bargain on your travels that no one else at home will have, a part of the experience of creating a style uniquely yours. Whether you are treating yourself, or someone else is treating you, there's nothing quite like it. I'll never forget my friend, Heather, who, upon leaving a store with a new pair of shoes, would put them in the passenger seat of her car, box top off, so she could cast loving glances at her new beauties all the way home.

Originally, I wanted to find out where stylists shop, because they are the gatekeepers to the best clothing and accessories worn by celebrities and models on red carpets and in magazines—they are the ultimate insiders.

But when I started to think about it, I realized that everyone in the fashion industry has shopping intel. Designers, editors, retailers, models, and bloggers have it, too; in fact, anyone who loves fashion and style has it.

UCTION

Knowing the newest, the old schooliest, the hidden gems, and the unexpectedly chic is valuable currency in the fashion business. Every season that I've covered the runway shows, I stay up way too late figuring out where to shop, combining research from magazines (even the ones in French and Italian), blogs, and travel guides, with tips passed down the front row from editor to editor.

Between shows, I'd venture out and explore. Inevitably, I'd see other in-the-know colleagues treading the same path to the Marni outlet in a residential neighborhood in Milan, where you have to buzz an intercom for the creaking gate to be opened. Or, I'd spot them gawking at the stuffed animals in the sprawling, museumlike taxidermy mecca of the world in Paris.

What if you could have all the best places, and the industry secrets, in one handy guide? That's what this book is. I surveyed 175 people in the fashion industry, including celebrity stylists, designers, bloggers, editors, street-style stars, models, and store owners and asked them to share their favorite shopping destinations. I used their answers to compile a global guide with a special focus on fashion hubs New York, London, Milan, Paris, Los Angeles, and Tokyo, cutting-edge fashion destinations such as Cape Town and Seoul, and places that the style set frequents on holiday or for inspiration, such as Marrakech and Tulum.

The book tells you about the designer stores you have to visit to really understand the fashion climate of a country, as well as the stores you might never have heard about otherwise, like the best place in Paris to get Indian block-print tunics and tablecloths, or the best T.J. Maxx ($37 Marc Jacobs dresses!) outside Boston. It's the stores you have to see IRL because they are just fun, such as

INTROD

Bedrock in Tokyo, which can only be accessed through the Forbidden Fruit café; the Doota mall in Seoul where you can shop for the latest teeny-bopper fashion twenty-four hours a day; and Mall of the Emirates, which has its own indoor ski slope.

Although this guide is devoted largely to brick-and-mortar stores around the world, the thrill of the hunt and the find can be experienced online, too, if you know where to look, which is why I've included Internet tips—from the best Etsy shop to find traditional boro-style Japanese clothing to a fantastic resource for discovering the hottest new African designers.

Not a week goes by when I don't ask a total stranger, "Where did you get that?" Recently, it was the lady pouring my iced coffee on Third Street in Los Angeles who was wearing a fabulous pair of gold nameplate earrings that spelled out BONITA. She told me they came from the Slauson Super Mall. I went the next weekend and bought my own. They were made by a woman named Boss Lady for $100 in less than two hours, and packaged in a robin's-egg-blue bag as if they were from Tiffany & Co.

At its best, shopping is about discovery, and there's no better way to get to know a city than by hitting the stores. You can find out so much about a place through its local designers, its markets, and its favorite chains. The things you come home with create a scrapbook of your trip, which you can relive every time you wear them. Done over a lifetime, shopping is a collection of experiences that informs your fashion sense. My style has been influenced by trying to dress like TV character "Murphy Brown" when I was a teenager, using Ralph Lauren pieces

UCTION

scored at one of the label's first outlets near my parents' house in Manchester, Vermont; by the Native American jewelry I collected on multiple trips to the Southwest; by the sparkly socks amassed on visits to the Tabio store in Paris during fashion week; and by my desire to mimic the style of my California rock 'n' roll idols Stevie Nicks and Belinda Carlisle, first using treasures scored at vintage stores in New York City, where I grew up, and eventually in Los Angeles, where I live now.

Shopping is about the thrill of the hunt. I'll never forget, in the days before the Internet, calling Lord & Taylor store after Lord & Taylor store up and down the Eastern seaboard, looking for a pair of pink silk shantung Enzo Angiolini slides in my size. I finally found a pair, after an entire Saturday afternoon on the phone, and made the drive all the way to Paramus, New Jersey, just to pick them up. I couldn't wait to wear the shocking pink shoes and tell everyone the lengths I had gone to find them. Moral of the story? No serious shopping conquest is really over unless, and until, you have scored. And then, there's nothing better than showing it off.

Everyone has a shopping story.

Happy hunting.

FREE
CITY

NORTH AMERICA

UNITED STATES
CANADA

LOVE ADORNED

NEW YORK

NEW YORK

THE MAJORS

ABC Carpet & Home

This mecca for home design, tabletop, and apothecary items bills itself as a "three-dimensional living magazine and interactive museum." The original New York location also carries quirky gifts, such as Macon & Lesquoy embroidered pins, flowy dresses by Ryan Roche, Giada Forte, and Vlas Blomme, metallic clutches by Tracey Tanner, delicate jewelry by Sweet Pea and Elisa Solomon, and chakra-balancing bracelets by Tiny Om. You might see fashion designer Mara Hoffman wandering the floor, searching for inspiration: "I feel like I'm shopping in a hundred different countries during just one visit," she says. Grab lunch at one of Jean Georges Vongerichten's on-site restaurants, ABC Kitchen or ABC Cocina.

888 Broadway, New York, NY 10003, +1-212-473-3000, abchome.com.

Barneys New York

The Madison Avenue flagship showcases the edgy boho mix that Barneys is known for. The collection includes bags by Goyard, Loewe, and Céline, jewelry from Irene Neuwirth, Jennifer Meyer, and Sidney Garber, and an unparalleled collection of clothes by Dries Van Noten, Azzedine Alaïa, Dolce & Gabbana, Narciso Rodriguez, as well as contemporary labels like Ulla Johnson, Isabel Marant, Raquel Allegra, and Pas de Calais. Don't miss lunch at Freds. The Palm Beach shrimp salad is designer Joseph Altuzarra's favorite, and jewelry designer Meyer splurges on the Robiola with truffle oil. There's also a new Chelsea location that's worth checking out.

660 Madison Ave., New York, NY 10065, +1-212-826-8900, barneys.com, and other locations.

Bergdorf Goodman

The grande dame of American department stores, Bergdorf Goodman sits on the site once occupied by the Cornelius Vanderbilt II mansion. Inside, you'll find every luxury label on the planet (Dries Van Noten, Gucci, Oscar de la Renta, Altuzarra, Libertine, to name just a few), one of the world's best women's shoe departments, and fab finds from emerging labels. Personal note: I bought my first pair of high heels here as a teenager, at the now-defunct Delman shoe salon. Today, the second-floor shoe department is not to be missed, with fancy footwear from Chanel, Aquazzura, Roger Vivier, Christian Louboutin, and more. "The label whore in me continues to go back to Bergdorf for my fancy footwear. Whether it's a fancy Valentino or a platform from Stella McCartney, it's always the best. And, if you can hold out, their sales are beyond," says fashion editor Sasha Charnin Morrison. Dozens of our stylish shoppers cited it as a favorite. "It's windowless and cozy, even a little bit cramped, but the edit of the shoes is flawless. I basically want to live there," says stylist Kemal Harris. Enjoy a Gotham salad, a glass of champagne, and views of Central Park at the Kelly Wearstler–designed BG Restaurant on the top floor, which also boasts an extensive collection of home accessories and gifts. "They have this really cool section of vintage objects and barware that I'm obsessed with, and don't even get me started on their room of ornaments during the holidays." says *Empire* costume designer Paolo Nieddu. The men's store is across the street.

754 Fifth Ave., New York, NY 10019, +1-888-774-2424, bergdorfgoodman.com.

Bloomingdale's

From hoopskirts (that's what the Bloomingdale brothers got their start selling in the 1860s) to the iconic Bloomie's bikini underwear that made the store a tourist attraction starting in the 1970s, Bloomingdale's is a classic. The 59th Street flagship can't be beat, especially for its window displays and in-store boutiques featuring pop culture merchandise, whether souvenirs from the movie *Star Wars* or the Broadway musical *Hamilton*. But the place deserves high-fashion props, too. "Often when I go to Forty Carrots for fro-yo, I get sucked into the designer floor; I've found that they tend to have the best Chanel shoe sales, because few people actually frequent Bloomingdale's for its selection of Chanel," says Man Repeller's Leandra Medine.

1000 Third Ave., New York, NY 10022, +1-212-705-2000, bloomingdales.com, and other locations.

Dover Street Market

Located in a seven-story Beaux Arts building sans sign on the corner of Lexington and 30th Street near New York's Curry Hill, this is the only stateside location of Japanese designer Rei Kawakubo's men's and women's avant-garde-fashion superstore. Inside, you'll find Comme des Garçons and other labels under its umbrella, including Play, Black, Shirt, and Junya Watanabe, as well as an edited mix of high-end labels (Simone Rocha, Gucci, J.W. Anderson, Rick Owens, Gosha Rubchinskiy, Vetements, Sacai) and streetwear (Supreme, Facetasm, Visvim, Hood by Air). The interior is equally inspiring, from the colorful installation by the mother of yarn bombing, Magda Sayeg, to the "Biotopological Scale-Juggling Escalator," a tunnel-shaped stairway designed by visionary architect Madeline Gins that connects the second and third floors. "One of the best curated stores in the world, DSM mixes young street-skate brands like Alltimers with the heavy hitters like Louis Vuitton," says Norstrom's head of creative projects, Olivia Kim. "I grab lunch at Rose Bakery on the ground floor, then take the elevator up and circle each of the seven floors," says accessories designer Sally Perrin. "It's small enough not to feel overwhelmed by the selection; the pieces are unique and avant-garde, so I always feel like I've come away with a piece of wearable art." "I love the museum-y feel of all the different floors," says retailer/designer Ann Mashburn, adding, "the staff is so incredibly pleasant and approachable, especially for such an over-the-top fashiony place, and I love the Japanese toilets."

160 Lexington Ave., New York, NY 10016, +1-646-837-7750, shop.doverstreetmarket .com/us, and other locations.

Saks Fifth Avenue

The first Saks opened in 1924 between 49th and 50th streets on upper Fifth Avenue in what was at the time primarily a residential neighborhood. Now, it has grown into an international empire of stores. The flagship is already costume designer Jenn Rogien's go-to for "a constantly evolving assortment," and come 2018, it will have even more to offer, after a major renovation that will move the beauty department to the second floor, and enhance it with a brow bar, 16 spa treatment rooms, and a flower shop. There will be a high jewelry vault in the basement, a replica of Coco Chanel's apartment upstairs, and the first US outpost of Paris' L'Avenue restaurant with terrace views of Rockefeller Center and St. Patrick's Cathedral. Add to that the already world-famous shoe department with its own zip code, 10022-SHOE, and Saks is shaping up to be the new luxury standard. Designer Mary Alice Haney praises the salespeople as tops for pulling special pieces, "if you are looking for pieces for an event and don't want to worry about wearing the same thing as someone else." 'Nuff said.

611 Fifth Ave., New York, NY 10022-SHOE, +1-212-753-4000, saksfifthavenue.com, and other locations.

SOHO

Alice and Olivia

Stacey Bendet's New York–based contemporary clothing label is beloved by Gwyneth Paltrow, Katy Perry, Dakota Fanning, and other celebs for its girlish print dresses and blouses, art and pop cultural collabs, and charitable initiatives. Recent collections have been inspired by The Grateful Dead (Bendet's husband, Eric Eisner, is producing a Grateful Dead documentary with Martin Scorsese) and the artist Jean-Michel Basquiat.

98 Greene St., New York, NY 10012, +1-646-790-8030, aliceolivia.com, and additional locations.

De Vera

This store slash gallery boasts a finely curated selection of Venetian glass, ivory carvings, and jewelry—whether its Georgian brooches or Sardinian coral pendants. It's Tory Burch's go-to for "exquisite antique jewelry and the most interesting collection of objets d'art." "Everything from Japanese lacquer to Roman ephemera is available. It's truly a jewel box of a store," says shoe designer Paul Andrew. Joseph Altuzarra calls it "a treasure trove," and it is shoe designer Brian Atwood's favorite place for gifts.

1 Crosby St., New York, NY 10013, +1-212-625-0838, deveraobjects.com.

Gentle Monster

We challenge you to walk out of the flagship of this young Korean eyewear brand without a pair of sunglasses. The immersive space with rotating art installations is so calm and Zen-like, you'll want to stay and try on every pair of confetti-flecked acetate cat-eye, mirrored round, and goggle-style sunnies (and then take selfies). It doesn't hurt that the brand has collaborations with cool-kid labels such as Opening Ceremony, Tome, and Hood by Air, and most frames are less than $300.

79 Grand St., New York, NY 10013, +1-646-928-1694, en.gentlemonster.com, and other locations.

Journelle

It's rare to find a lingerie store that focuses on the tried-and-true brands (Chantelle, Eberjey, La Perla) as well as up-and-comers (Le Petit Trou, Paloma Casile), but Journelle is that store. "Part of the fun of being a woman is being able to wear something supersecret and sexy under a suit and feel great about it," says accessories designer Aurora James. "A new pair of undies or bra is a pick-me-up. Journelle has a great selection of everything from cute panties to seductive lingerie at a great cross section of prices."

125 Mercer St., New York, NY 10012, +1-212-255-7803, journelle.com, and additional locations.

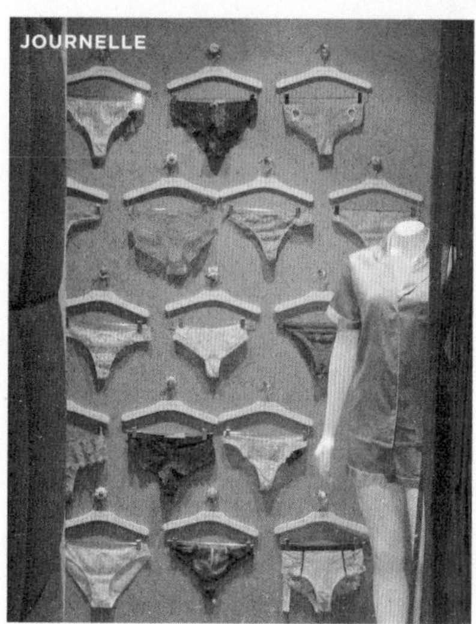
JOURNELLE

Kirna Zabête

This boutique, started in 1999, helped pioneer high fashion in SoHo. Graphic displays, neon signs, and colorful chandeliers lend a pop art sensibility to the 10,000-square-foot store, which offers a whimsical edit of pieces both super-high-end (Céline, Givenchy, Gucci, Valentino, Fendi) and contemporary cool (Frame Denim, Zimmerman, Piamita, Mira Mikati, Ellery, Sarah's Bags, Yazbukey). "Owner Beth Buccini has an impeccable eye," says fashion insider Alina Cho. "She always seems to buy that dress, shoe, or bag I never knew I wanted but suddenly can't live without. . . . I can find established designers like Gucci and Chloé as easily as I can Rosie Assoulin and Isa Arfen."

477 Broome St., New York, NY 10013, +1-212-941-9656, kirnazabete.com.

Odin New York

Casual-cool menswear by Comme des Garçons Shirt, Duckie Brown, Acne Studios, Won Hundred, Engineered Garments, Common Projects, and more, plus basics and fragrance by Odin's in-house label. "A small shop but very well curated," says Sabah founder Mickey Ashmore. "Feels more like my closet than a store," says fashion editor/TV host Joe Zee.

161 Grand St., New York, NY 10013, +1-212-966-0026, odinnewyork.com, and an additional location in the East Village.

Patron of the New

"For a serious fashion fix, the style here is bold and brash with an eye for the avant-garde," says Hong Kong–based fashion journalist and blogger Divia Harilela. Inside this darkly romantic boutique with a Parisian vibe, you'll find second-skin minidresses by Balmain and Alexandre Vauthier, blinged-out sneakers by Buscemi, harem shorts by DRKSHDW, Fear of God bomber jackets, Unravel destroyed knits, Zilla handbags made out of artificial sponges, and other goodies. Men's and women's.

151 Franklin St., New York, NY 10013, +1-212-966-7144, patronofthenew.us.

Rachel Comey

Comey's namesake label, which began as menswear, grew out of the New York downtown arts scene in the early 2000s. Her collections are a favorite

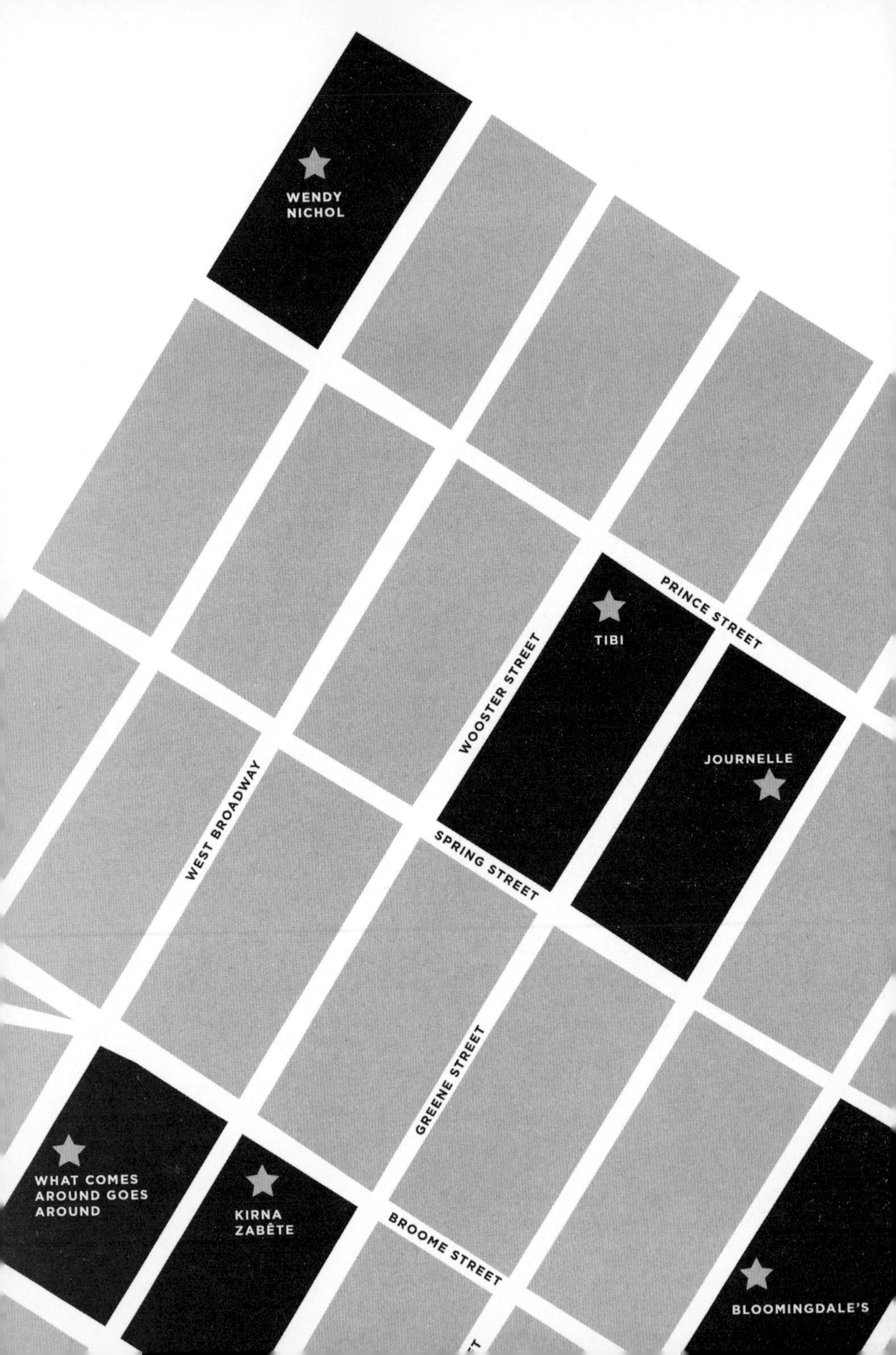
WENDY NICHOL
PRINCE STREET
TIBI
WOOSTER STREET
JOURNELLE
WEST BROADWAY
SPRING STREET
GREENE STREET
WHAT COMES AROUND GOES AROUND
KIRNA ZABÊTE
BROOME STREET
BLOOMINGDALE'S

SOHO

NEW YORK

WEST HOUSTON STREET

BROADWAY

JILL PLATNER

DO KHAM

RACHEL COMEY

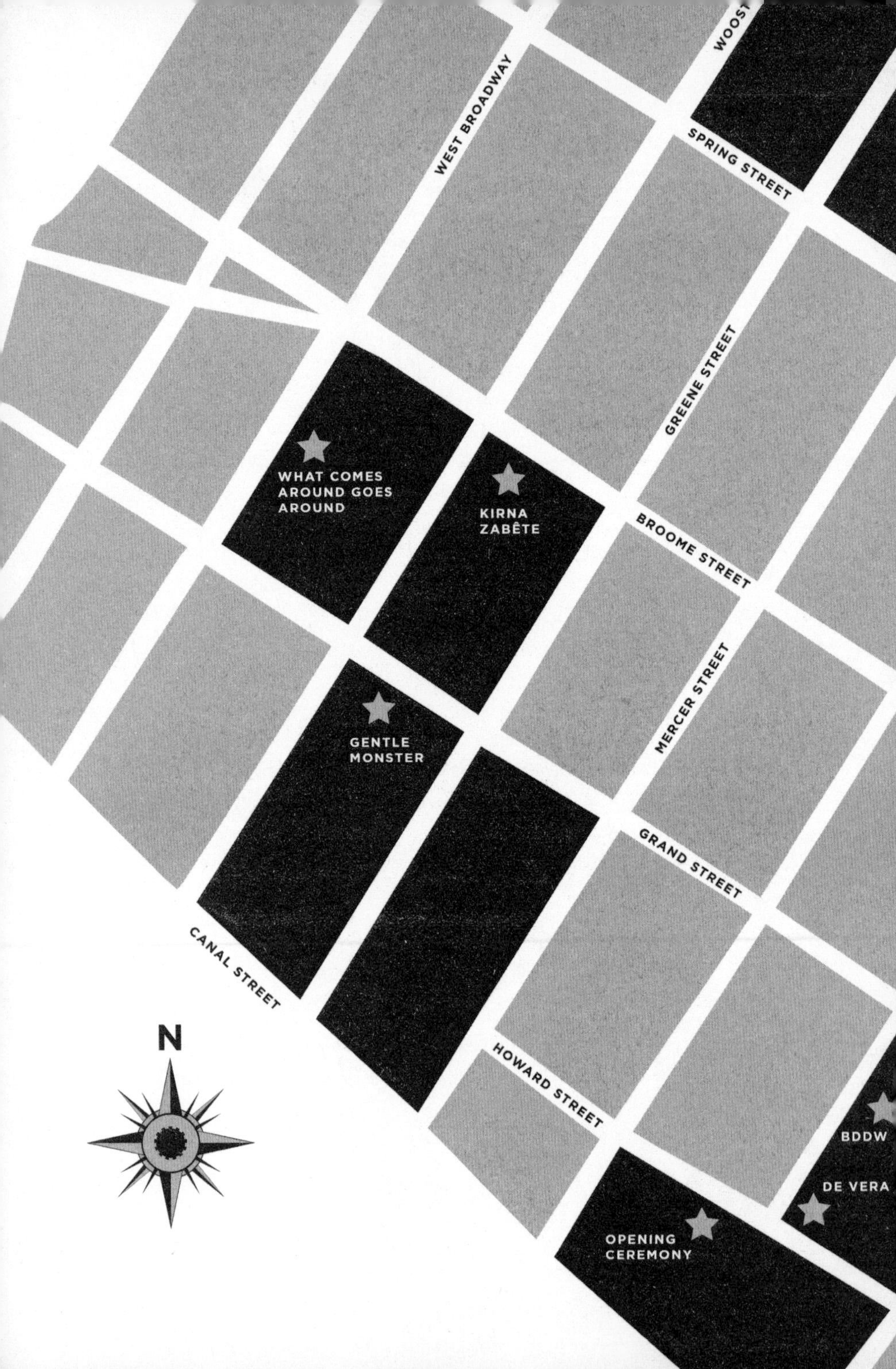
WOOST
WEST BROADWAY
SPRING STREET
GREENE STREET
WHAT COMES
AROUND GOES
AROUND
KIRNA
ZABÊTE
BROOME STREET
MERCER STREET
GENTLE
MONSTER
GRAND STREET
CANAL STREET
N
HOWARD STREET
BDDW
DE VERA
OPENING
CEREMONY

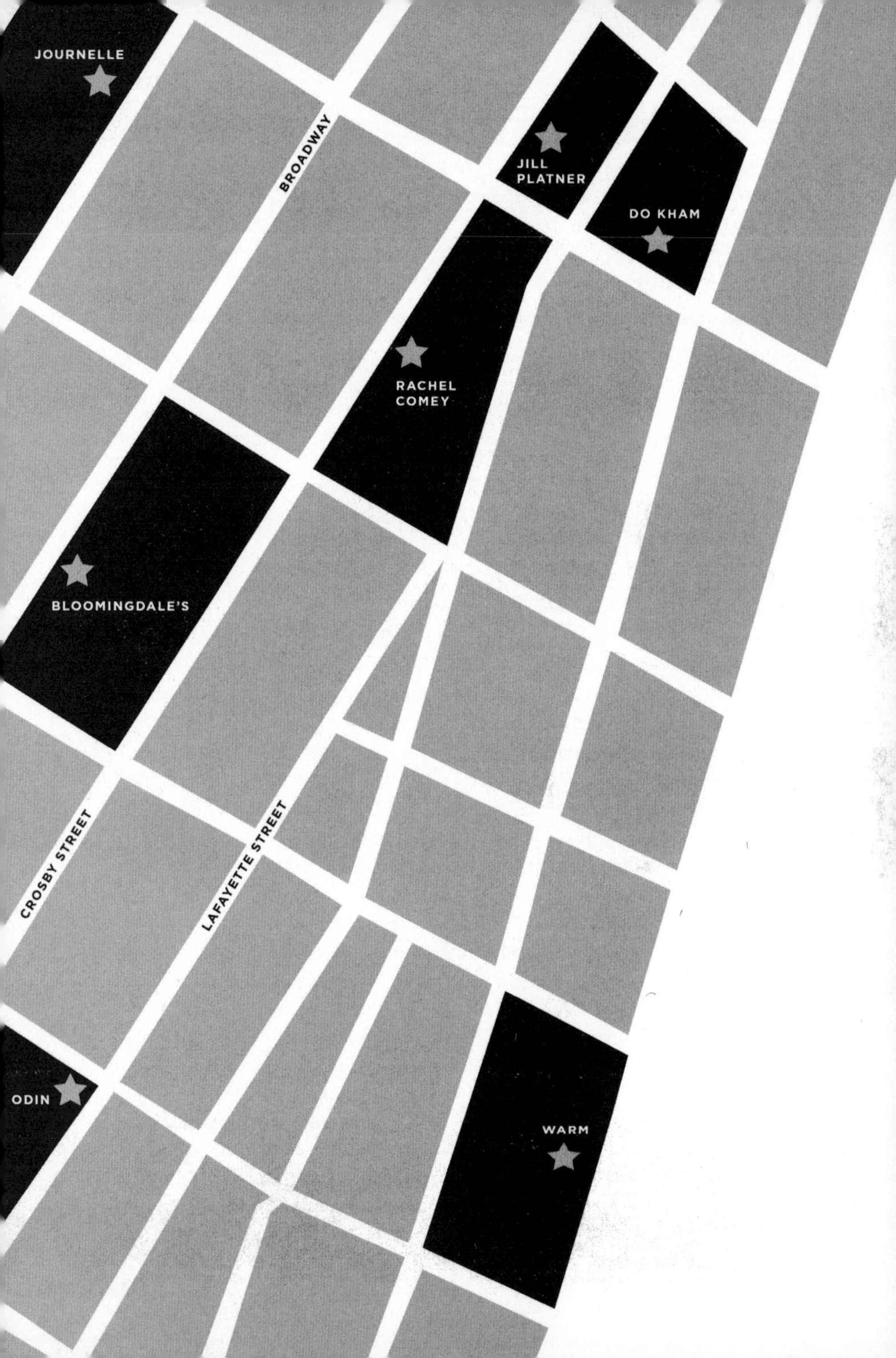
JOURNELLE
BROADWAY
JILL PLATNER
DO KHAM
RACHEL COMEY
BLOOMINGDALE'S
CROSBY STREET
LAFAYETTE STREET
ODIN
WARM

RACHEL COMEY

with Rashida Jones, Taylor Schilling, and others for their arty textiles (foam, linen, pebble, crochet), modern silhouettes, and covetable footwear. Comey and her partner Sean Carmody collaborated with Brooklyn-based architect Elizabeth Roberts and San Francisco–based interior designer Charles de Lisle on the spare design of her store with a wood beam ceiling and skylight to showcase denim culottes, drapey trench coats, and chunky wood-soled sandals and boots.

95 Crosby St., New York, NY 10012, +1-212-334-0455, rachelcomey.com, and an additional location in Los Angeles.

Rebecca Minkoff

In 2004, Rebecca Minkoff's first runway show was taped as a plotline for the TV shows *Laguna Beach* and *The Hills*, but it wasn't until 2005, when she debuted her "Morning After Bag," that things really took off. A satchel designed to be small enough for a night on the town but large enough to carry a change of clothes, the style attracted a celebrity following that included Jessica Alba and Reese Witherspoon. Now, Minkoff has a full-fledged collection of clothing and accessories, loosely inspired every season by rock 'n' roll. Several of her boutiques, including this one, are "wired" for millennial-friendly shopping, with touchable video walls and digitized dressing room experiences.

96 Greene St., New York, NY 10012, +1-212-677-7883, rebeccaminkoff.com, and additional locations.

RACHEL COMEY
NYC LOCAL FAVES

Rachel Comey is a New York-based fashion designer whose career kicked off with a collaboration with the band Gogol Bordello, earning her a place in the 2001 Whitney Biennial. Her namesake women's label, which launched in 2004, is sold at more than a hundred high-end boutiques and stores in sixteen countries as well as stand-alone stores in New York and Los Angeles.

PEARL RIVER in NYC was always a favorite for home items and party decorations (it's online now). **HOUSING WORKS** for old books. **ESSEX CARD SHOP ON AVENUE A** for Le Pens. There are some old bra and underwear shops on lower **ORCHARD STREET** that are still there and fun for surprising negligees or undergarments. For me, the search is as thrilling as the find.

I love the **FLEA MARKET ON 26TH STREET**. I know it's been reduced to one open lot, but there are still some great vendors there. I love our store on Crosby Street. Crosby Street has so many great stores, so if you are looking for locally designed and manufactured productions, then a visit to Crosby Street is a must. **JILL PLATNER** on Crosby north of Prince is a great jewelry designer; just below, is us and **TESS GIBERSON**. Then heading south you eventually get to **BDDW**, such beautiful furniture in an epic storefront.

My friend Leanne just turned me on to the tin plates at the **FRICK COLLECTION**. Such a beautiful alternative to disposable plates or carrying your heavy ceramics outside for a picnic. While uptown, a visit to the bookstore **ALBERTINE** at the French Embassy is a secret must-visit spot!

PEARL RIVER MART, PearlRiver.com.

HOUSING WORKS BOOKSTORE CAFÉ, 126 Crosby St, New York, NY 10012, +1-212-334-3324, housingworks.org.

ESSEX CARD SHOP, 39 Avenue A, New York, NY 10009, +1-212-228-7740.

CHELSEA FLEA MARKET, Uptown Side of West 25th Street between Broadway and Sixth Avenue, NY 10010.

RACHEL COMEY, 95 Crosby St, New York, NY 10012, +1-212-334-0455, rachelcomey.com.

JILL PLATNER, 113 Crosby St, New York, NY 10012, +1-212-324-1298, jillplatner.com.

TESS GIBERSON, 97 Crosby St, New York, NY 10012, +1-646-998-4391, tessgiberson.com.

BDDW, 5 Crosby St, New York, NY 10013, +1-212-625-1230, bddw.com.

THE FRICK COLLECTION, 1 East 70th Street New York, NY 10021, +1-212-288-0700, frick.org.

ALBERTINE, 972 Fifth Avenue (at 79th Street), New York, NY 10075, +1-212-650-0070, albertine.com.

ONLINE SHOPPING TIP

"I like Farfetch.com because you get a variety of styles and designer pieces that are not commonly found in other stores," says stylist/designer Maryam Malakpour. "They have about 400 boutiques all around the world that are subscribed to Farfetch.com, which gives more variety and extensive options." Raven Kauffman agrees: "I just love being able to shop every amazing boutique around the world at midnight from my iPad. It's such an indulgence."

Saturdays NYC

"For guys, this is such a cool spot," says actress, blogger, and model Christina Caradona of the New York–based board-short and surf lifestyle brand. "They have this little outdoor area and a coffee shop in the store—I used to get coffee there all the time because the guys were so attractive."

17 Perry Street, New York, New York 10014, +1-347-246-5830, saturdaysnyc.com, and additional locations.

Tibi

Flagship for Amy Smilovic's relaxed, feminine label, a favorite with street-style stars such as Leandra Medine. Smilovic's Instagram-friendly designs feature dramatic ties, back vents, and artful ruffles. You can also thank her for helping to kick off the off-the-shoulder trend.

120 Wooster St., New York, NY 10012, +1-212-226-5852, tibi.com.

Wendy Nichol

Silk dusters, lace jumpers, leather bullet bags, and pavé diamond "middle finger" rings for the chic Goth. "I'm completely obsessed with this designer and her entire existence," says stylist Kemal Harris. "One of my clients told me she's an actual witch! Her collections are very feminine and wearable, despite being mostly produced in all-black silk and leather. Her jewelry is to die for, and if you are in need of a crown made of patent leather, trust me, she's designed the perfect one."

147 Sullivan St., New York, NY 10012, +1-212-431-4171, wendynicholnyc.com, and an additional location in Nolita.

What Goes Around Comes Around

Collectible vintage from the 1890s to the 1990s, including Chanel bags galore, concert tees, Levi's, and more. "Always offers something I must have, whether for personal use or inspiration for my collections," says A.L.C. designer Andrea Lieberman. The original location in SoHo is the best.

351 West Broadway, New York, NY 10013, +1-212-343-1225, whatgoesaroundnyc.com, and additional locations.

LOWER EAST SIDE, NOLITA, EAST VILLAGE

Anna Sheffield

Tucked away next door to a Chinese-menu printing shop on the Lower East Side is this hidden gem full of gems. "She basically invented the concept of stacking rings and then took it a step further with curved nesting rings that fit snugly against raw diamonds and triple-gem pyramid rings," says stylist Kemal Harris. "Where else can you get an eternity band of black diamonds, the ultimate example of inconspicuous luxury, for $500?"

47 Orchard St., New York, NY 10002, +1-212-925-7010, annasheffield.com.

DEAR: Rivington

"So, so inspiring," says Valery Demure. "Beautiful clothing, vintage Comme des Garçons, Junya Watanabe, Yohji Yamamoto, etc. Handbags, socks, jewelry, headpieces. They create the most beautiful collection downstairs with homewares, furniture, ceramics, handmade dolls, art, illustrations. It's owned by a supercool Korean couple with a gorgeous dog—an English bull terrier called Dumbo."

37 Great Jones St., New York, NY 10012, +1-212-673-3494, dearrivington.com.

Dö Kham

A Tibetan emporium in the heart of Nolita. "Very jet-set boho style," says Catherine Ryu, creative director of Citizens of Humanity. "They even sell bracelets blessed by the Dalai Lama. I've been frequenting this shop since the '90s. It's my go-to place for beachy tunics that I wear on vacation or in the heat of summer, in an array of gorgeous colors! The owner, Phelgye [Kelden], is a kind and delightful man filled with a wealth of knowledge about Tibet." "I always find something, whether it's a piece of jewelry or an unusual caftan that I never would have noticed outside the confines of the shop and am often resistant to purchase but always end up wearing in spades," says Leandra Medine.

51 Prince St., New York, NY 10012, +1-212-966-2404, dokham.com.

John Derian

Three boutiques in a row, this lifestyle fantasyland sells Derian's signature plates, plaques, and paperweights decoupaged with letters, insects, and flowers. You'll also find furniture, Moroccan poufs, blankets, scarves,

Astier de Villatte ceramics, incense and candles, colorful paper lanterns, and more. "My go-to for gifts," says accessories designer Lizzie Fortunato. "There is always something to discover," says Moscow-based textile designer Olya Thompson. "An unusual light fixture, a fringed Moroccan bath towel in that perfect baby-coral color, a birthday hat with a pinup beauty on top. . . . Everything I have ever bought here I absolutely cherish."

6 E. 2nd St., New York, NY 10003, +1-212-677-3917, johnderian.com.

Love Adorned

In two decades, traveler and collector Lori Leven has built her small tattoo, piercing, and jewelry shop into a trio of lifestyle boutiques selling jewelry, crystals, and trinkets from India, Indonesia, Japan, and other countries. Also featured are *shibori* textiles, fringed moccasins, dream catchers, planters, and other housewares. She has pieces for men and women, and alternative bridal options, too. No surprise that boho designers Ulla Johnson and Mara Hoffman are devoted fans. The Elizabeth Street store is the flagship. "I die for all the jewelry in this store," says Olivia Kim. "She has such a great eye for mixing the precious with vintage and the store has a modern bohemian feel."

269 Elizabeth St., New York, NY 10012, +1-212-431-5683, loveadorned.com, and additional locations.

Maryam Nassir Zadeh

Launched in 2008, Zadeh's art-gallery-like boutique on the Lower East Side specializes in haute minimalism and fresh indie designers. "A true incubator of young and important talent—it's almost like you get to see the next generation of fashion hanging in a store," says Leandra Medine. You'll find conceptual designs by Jacquemus, Bless, Jesse Kamm, and Dusan alongside accessories from Rochas, jewelry by Sophie Buhai, and the popular in-house line of wide-leg pants, cotton dresses, block-heel pumps, sandals, and other basics.

123 Norfolk St., New York, NY 10002, +1-212-673-6405, mnzstore.com.

No Relation Vintage

This secondhand store with budget prices "is always our final stop at the end of a long workday in the city," says jewelry designer Gabriela Artigas. "We love to unwind by browsing through the endless racks of everything." The store is part of the L Train Vintage family.

204 First Ave., New York, NY 10009, +1-212-228-5201, ltrainvintage.com.

Opening Ceremony

Founded by California natives Carol Lim and Humberto Leon in 2002, Opening Ceremony was conceived as a shopping version of the Olympics, featuring emerging designers from a different country each year alongside up-and-coming American labels such as Proenza Schouler, Rodarte, and Alexander Wang. The idea was to bring the magic of travel and discovery to local customers. Now with stores in L.A., London, and Tokyo, Lim and Leon can be credited with fueling collaboration fever in fashion and helping a younger generation discover heritage brands such as Pendleton, Levi's, and Reyn Spooner. "All Opening Ceremony stores have a creative architectural solution to the use of space," says stylist/designer Maryam Malakpour. Lim and Leon, who design their own in-house label as well as LVMH-owned luxury label Kenzo, are known for collaborating with Spike Jonze, Terence Koh, Chloë Sevigny, and other creatives on fashion shows, installations, and product ranges.

35 Howard St., New York, NY 10013, +1-212-219-2688, openingceremony.com, and additional locations.

Ritual Vintage

Chloë Sevigny loves this space for "Victorian, Edwardian, 1970s Saint Laurent," and everything in between. Bonus? "They also have a trick mirror—a tall, skinny mirror," she says.

377 Broome St., New York, NY 10013, +1-212-966-4142, ritualvintage.com.

The Sabah Dealer

The place to get former hedge funder Mickey Ashmore's comfy-chic, handmade-in-Turkey leather espadrilles in a rainbow of colors. He'll even serve you a cup of tea while you find your perfect size. Call or email for hours.

Sabah House, 211 E. 12th St., New York, NY 10003, +1-646-864-0790, sabah.am.

Timbuktu

"One of my favorite stores in Manhattan is this Turkish and Moroccan importer," says menswear retailer Josh Peskowitz. "I've bought clothes, home goods and textiles from them constantly over the years. It's by no means a fashion store, but I've definitely worn a bunch of stuff I've bought there to Milan and Paris Fashion Week."

45 Second Ave., New York, NY 10003, +1-212-473-4955.

Tokio 7

"I'm a vintage hound, and this is probably my favorite place," Chloë Sevigny says of this secondhand spot on East 7th Street where she's bought and sold many a piece. Just don't go on a Saturday afternoon; it gets so crowded inside that it's hard to see anything!

83 E. 7th St, New York, NY 10003, +1-212-353-8443, tokio7.net.

United Nude

The only US store for the architectural footwear brand known for its injection-molded and carbon-fiber heels designed by creative director Rem D. Koolhaas (not to be confused with his architect uncle Rem Koolhaas). Lady Gaga, Kim Kardashian, and Solange Knowles are fans of the alien-looking styles created in collaboration with Dutch fashion designer Iris van Herpen. United Nude's core collection includes more down-to-earth elastic fabric booties and Möbius carved-out heels. The store's darkly lit interior, with shoes mounted in glowing cubbies, adds to the allure.

25 Bond St., New York, NY 10012, +1-212-420-6000, unitednude.com, and additional locations.

Warm

It's always summer at Warm, which was opened by the "urban hippie" husband-and-wife team Winnie Beattie and Rob Magnotta. Specializing in the "French girl goes to Costa Rica" look, they stock designers such as Isabel Marant, the Elder Statesman, Heidi Merrick, Roseanna, Giada Forte, Mara Hoffman, and NSF, as well as their own in-house label of breezy dresses and tunics, and a Warm fragrance that smells like a day at the beach. "Built on the premise of warm people, warm places, and warm things, this shop offers the best of the best for the refined, beach-loving, chic yet bohemian girl," says stylist Cristina Ehrlich. The store features men's, women's and children's clothing, photography, books, home accessories, and more.

181 Mott St., New York, NY 10012, +1-212-925-1200, warmny.com.

MEATPACKING DISTRICT, CHELSEA

Artists & Fleas

"At Chelsea Market, I always make a pit stop at Pamela Barsky's booth for pouches with witty quotes and sayings on them," says Jacey Duprie, creator of Damsel in Dior, of this artist, designer, and vintage market held daily. "They make for wonderful gifts and I never leave without a smile on my face and pouch in my hand."

Chelsea Market, 88 Tenth Ave., New York, NY, 10011, artistsandfleas.com, and additional locations.

Jeffrey

One of the first to open a retail boutique in the Meatpacking District, Atlanta transplant Jeffrey Kalinsky helped turn the area into a trendy hot spot. Open since 1999, the boutique stocks men's and women's designer labels, like Prada, Gucci, Valentino, and Sacai, and one of the best selections of shoes in the city, always with plenty of exclusives. "Filled with inspiration," says Alice and Olivia designer Stacey Bendet.

449 W. 14th St., New York, NY 10014, +1-212-206-1272, jeffreynewyork.com.

Story

"Point of view of a magazine, changes like a gallery, sells things like a store." That's how founder Rachel Shechtman describes her ever-changing, experiential retail space. Every four to eight weeks, there's a complete overhaul of theme, design, and inventory, so "if you visit NYC a few times in an year, the store will be completely visually different each time," says stylist and Newbark designer Maryam Malakpour. "You can find clothing, decor, accessories, et cetera." Past "stories" have curated merchandise around themes of "love," "Made in America," and "wellness."

144 Tenth Ave., New York, NY 10011, +1-212-242-4853, thisisstory.com.

Urban Zen

Globally inspired clothing, accessories, and home furnishings supporting Donna Karan's charitable Urban Zen Foundation. "For cashmere, it is the perfect shop," says fashion industry consultant Fern Mallis. "Plus they also sell beautiful handmade jewelry and decor from artisans around the world."

705 Greenwich St., New York, NY 10014, +1-212-206-3999, urbanzen.com, and additional locations.

SOUTH STREET SEAPORT

Brother Vellies

"Aurora James's eclectic and elegant store sets a new standard for luxury," says Studio 189 cofounder Abrima Erwiah. The store features her full range of magical shoes and handbags handmade in Kenya, Morocco, and South Africa with handwoven details from Burkina Faso.

4 Fulton St., New York, NY 10038, +1-212-480-8869.

UNION SQUARE/FLATIRON/WEST 30s

AEO & Aerie

The lingerie sub-brand of casual clothing chain American Eagle Outfitters, which has more than a hundred locations (both stand-alone and inside

AEO stores) throughout the US and Canada, is worth checking out. You can pick up cute underwear at very reasonable prices. "I feel very old when I go in there because there are tweens in the store," says designer Rebecca Minkoff, "but the underwear is great. They make the best boy shorts—I stock up on twelve pairs for like $35."
19 Union Square West, New York, NY 10003, +1-212-645-2086, ae.com, and additional locations.

Aritzia

Canadian clothing chain with its own in-house brands of minimalist and boho-inspired attire that can hold its own against the high-end Marni, Mansur Gavriel, Maryam Nassir Zadeh, and Céline accessories you may already have (or want to have) in your closet. Look for washed-indigo cross-back dresses; textural cotton culottes; wrap-front jumpsuits; elongated, split-side rib-knit sleeveless sweaters; fringed kimono jackets; and lace-inset festival blouses plus denim by Citizens of Humanity and Frame, leather jackets by Mackage, and more. Most pieces are less than $300. Although there are stores across the US and Canada, the 8,000-square-foot Flatiron flagship is one of their best.
89 Fifth Ave., New York, NY, 10003, +1-212-462-1095, aritzia.com, and additional locations.

Bandier

Workout wear too fashionable to stay in the gym by Sundry, Spiritual Gangster, Michi, Koral, Mackage, APL, and more. "I stop in every time I'm in New York City," says blogger/socialite NJ Goldston. "You gotta love the pulsing music and the knowledgeable fitness staff."
164 Fifth Ave., New York, NY 10011, +1-646-360-3345, bandier.com, and additional locations.

Elegance Hosiery

A true hidden gem, this hosiery and sock place is in Penn Station near the Amtrak. Great for metallic socks and patterned stockings from Europe. "Every time I pass through there, I stock up on fishnets and interesting hosiery," says designer/personal shopper Raven Kauffman. "Not white glove service, mind you, but a great selection that I have never seen anywhere else. I always buy the micro-fishnets, which are the absolute best."
One Penn Plaza, New York, NY 10119, +1-212-736-5306.

Marlene Wetherell

Vintage Yves Saint Laurent gypsy blouses, Dior turbans, and a Teal Traina serape-stripe halter dress are just a few of the fabulous finds to be snapped up here. "My best-kept secret . . . until now," says blogger Lainy Hedaya. Paris-based handbag designer Olympia Le-Tan shops the store online at www.1dibs.com.

40 W. 25th St., Gallery 210, New York, NY 10010, +1-917-225-0662, marlenewetherell.com.

New York Vintage

The hands-down favorite of stylish shoppers (stylist and designer Rachel Zoe, jewelry designer Kara Ross, fashion tech entrepreneur Alexandra Wilkis Wilson) for high-end vintage by Chanel, Emilio Pucci, Giorgio di Sant'Angelo, Holly Harp, Zandra Rhodes, and more. "I adore the owner, Shannon Hoey—she has a true passion for vintage and it shows," says Zoe. "I can spend a whole day in her store looking through evening gowns from all of my favorite designers." What do first lady Michelle Obama's vintage Norman Norell dress, Sarah Jessica Parker's *Sex and the City* bird-shaped wedding headpiece, and the 1920s showgirl costumes in *Boardwalk Empire* have in common? They all came from this place, which also has a rental-only archive for costume designers and stylists.

117 W. 25th St., New York, NY 10001, +1-212-647-1107, newyorkvintage.com.

The Strand

New York's most iconic bookstore, opened in 1927, boasts eighteen miles of new and used books, and is an endless source of inspiration for designers. "I never walk out without something in my hand," says Jeremy Scott. French designer Olympia Le-Tan, who reimagines classic book covers as handbags and accessories, also counts this as one of her favorite haunts. "My favorite place to get lost," says shoe designer Isa Tapia. "Also, the basement is full of hidden gems. . . . once I found Isaac Mizrahi comic books there."

828 Broadway, New York, NY 10003, +1-212-473-1452, strandbooks.com.

ONLINE SHOPPING TIP

"I love the Muzungu Sisters website (muzungusisters.com)," says Leandra Medine of the London-based, globally inspired collection. "I'm a big fan of their straw totes, velvet bolero jackets, and beaded jewelry and belts of which they have plenty. I have also recently really taken to an L.A. site called Lisa Says Gah (lisasaysgah.com)," she says of the multi-label online retailer. "Reminds me a lot of Maryam Nassir Zadeh, but has its own sort of subversive West Coast vibe of maximalism even though it is very minimalist."

UPPER EAST SIDE and UPPER WEST SIDE

Aquazzura

The first US location for the Florentine shoe brand designed by Edgardo Osorio. The fringed "Wild Thing" sandals, lace-up suede "Belgravia" flats, and cutout "Sexy Thing" sandals have made fans of Moda Operandi founder Lauren Santo Domingo, Her Royal Highness Beatrice of York, and Leandra Medine.

939 Madison Ave., New York, NY 10021, +1-347-328-0080, aquazzura.com, and additional locations.

Fivestory

This multi-brand boutique occupying a jewel box of a town house on East 69th Street has cocktail frocks, whimsical clutch purses, and strappy sandals for Park Avenue princesses, by Rosie Assoulin, Monse, Mary Katrantzou, Edie Parker, Charlotte Olympia, Paul Andrew, and more. There's also a fun selection of jewelry, including emoji-inspired studs by Alison Lou and silk thread Les Bonbons earrings by Rebecca de Ravenel. "An intimate shopping experience with a great point of view," says accessories designer Karen Erickson.

18 E. 69th St., New York, NY 10021, +1-212-288-1338, fivestoryny.com.

AQUAZZURA

Gianvito Rossi

The only stateside boutique for the Italian footwear designer known for his sexy leather and PVC pumps, and velvety-soft suede sandals with comfortable block heels.

963 Madison Ave., New York, NY 10021, +1-646-869-0201, gianvitorossi.com, and additional locations.

Hayward House

You will want to move into the second-story Hayward flagship in the palatial Grosvenor Atterbury mansion. Here, Marin Hopper (daughter of Dennis) sells her line of chic, made-in–New York handbags and accessories inspired by Hollywood

ONLINE SHOPPING TIP

"I love Net-A-Porter.com for the one-stop shopping and, of course, same day delivery in Manhattan," says accessories designer Lee Savage. "I also love SSENSE.com, which always has a cool edit of edgier styles."

royalty such as agent Leland Hayward and fashion icon Slim Keith. The store's wood-paneled interior, gold-etched ceiling, and fretwork fireplace are not to be believed.

131 E. 70th St., New York, NY 10021, +1-212-585-1712, haywardluxury.com.

Neue Galerie Gift Shop

"I adore the artists of the Viennese Secession and their influence on both fashion and decorative arts and textiles," says designer/personal shopper Raven Kauffman. "You can pick up a fabulous caftan here in the spirit of Koloman Moser, Klimt's painting smock, or even a pair of fingerless gloves and a beautiful cashmere scarf. Great for unique gifts."

1048 Fifth Ave., New York, NY 10028, +1-212-628-6200, neuegalerie.org.

Norma Kamali

The quintessential New York designer, Kamali has been in business nearly fifty years and is still going strong. She's an innovator for her jersey sportswear, sweatshirt dresses, sleeping bag coats, and sophisticated swimwear (she designed the red one-piece bathing suit worn by Farrah Fawcett in the iconic 1976 poster). Kamali's flagship boutique also has an organic café.

11 W. 56th St., New York, NY 10019, +1-212-957-9797, normakamali.com.

Proenza Schouler

Flagship store for designer darlings Jack McCollough and Lazaro Hernandez featuring two floors of clothing, shoes, and handbags. Steel shelves, exposed wood beams, and an indoor cactus garden add to the modern and architectural vibe.

822 Madison Ave., New York, NY 10065, +1-212-585-3200, proenzaschouler.com, and additional locations.

Sanjay Kasliwal

For nine generations, the Kasliwal family has been handcrafting jewelry, a lineage that can be traced back to India and the crafting of megawatt bling for the maharajas of the Mughal empire. The selection here blends the old (an enameled band ring) with the new (a yellow gold bubble ring).

971 Madison Ave., New York, NY 10021, +1-212-988-1511, sanjaykasliwal.com, and additional locations.

Tory Burch

The New York designer has transformed a small collection of tunics made at her kitchen table into a lifestyle empire, with this 8,000-square-foot Madison Avenue townhouse flagship as its crown jewel. Browse and buy Burch's entire retro-feminine collection.

797 Madison Ave, New York, NY 10065, +1-212-510-8371, and additional locations, toryburch.com.

FINANCIAL DISTRICT

Century 21

A NYC icon for more than fifty years, this discount department store is the mack daddy of off-price designer retail. Although there are now several stores, the original in the Financial District is the one to hit for deals and steals from Rick Owens, Saint Laurent, Givenchy, Jimmy Choo, Giorgio Armani, and more. "You can find some insane bargains on designer pieces, especially during their semiannual sales. And the designer shoe game is serious," says costume designer Jenn Rogien,

22 Cortlandt St., New York, NY 10007, +1-212-227-9092, c21stores.com, and additional locations.

BROOKLYN

Bird

Jen Mankins's boutiques are worth crossing the river for. You'll find printed dresses and coats by Dries Van Noten, Maria Cornejo, and Marni; pants and clogs by Rachel Comey; bags by Mansur Gavriel, Building Block, and Lizzie Fortunato; and more. The Williamsburg location is the largest; there is also one in Cobble Hill and one in Park Slope (the original, open since 2004).

203 Grand St., Brooklyn, NY 11211, +1-718-388-1655, shopbird.com, and additional locations.

Brooklyn Flea Market

Starting the first weekend in April and running through November, the market takes place outdoors: Saturdays in Fort

JENN ROGIEN

SHOP BROOKLYN LIKE HBO'S *GIRLS*

Emmy-nominated costume designer Jenn Rogien is behind the personality-print blouses and onesies, folksy maxi dresses, and jeweled barrettes worn by the characters on Lena Dunham's Girls. *And when it comes to research, there's no place like home. (Jenn is also responsible for outfitting the prison population in the Netflix series* Orange Is the New Black.*)*

There's a Tibetan store in Fort Greene that has the best jewelry: **21 TARA** on Myrtle Avenue. It not only has a great selection of Tibetan and Nepalese pieces but also delicate gold and silver pieces that are very much contemporary. Cool textiles and clothes also make it worth stopping in.

I also love **PEOPLE OF 2MORROW** in Greenpoint. It's a hybrid of amazing things: vintage, gift, home goods, young jewelry designers, all pulled together in a bright, airy cool space. I've done quite a bit of shopping for the "Girls" here over the years.

I love **OAK** in Williamsburg for a bit of personal shopping or for dressing an aggressively casual character. Oak's pieces are cool, casual, and worth living in. I try to drop in whenever we shoot in the neighborhood.

URBAN JUNGLE might be my favorite thrift warehouse in Brooklyn. It's part of the L Train Vintage family. Urban Jungle is massive and full of amazing finds. We've shopped with them fairly regularly for flashbacks on *Orange Is the New Black.* Most recently my team and I bought bags and bags of '90s clothes for a pilot we were working on. I'm looking forward to stopping in when we head back for our final season of *Girls*.

21 TARA, 388 Myrtle Ave., Brooklyn, NY 11205, +1-347-916-0045.

PEOPLE OF 2MORROW, 65 Franklin St., Brooklyn, NY 11222, +1-718-383-4402, peopleof2morrow.com.

OAK, 55 Nassau Ave., Brooklyn, NY 11222, +1-718-782-0521, oaknyc.com, and additional locations.

URBAN JUNGLE, 118 Knickerbocker Ave., Brooklyn, NY 11237, +1-718-381-8510, ltrainvintage.com.

ONLINE SHOPPING TIP

"I like to visit New York's **CapBeauty.com** for nontoxic beauty products," says Shiva Rose, who has her own line of skincare at **ShivaRose.com**. "I also love Mountain Rose Herbs (mountainroseherbs.com) for teas and oils."

Greene and Sundays in DUMBO. Our stylish shoppers prefer the Fort Greene location, in a schoolyard on leafy Lafayette Avenue, where 150 vendors sell a mix of old (vintage jean jackets, Bakelite jewelry, and Indian dresses) and only-in-Brooklyn new (palmistry-inspired stud earring sets, grandpa cardigans for babies, and bicycle paintings). "Great food and offbeat treasures," says fashion designer Ulla Johnson, who lives in the neighborhood. Local food offerings include Ramen Burger, Red Hook Lobster Pound, and the Good Batch cookies.

176 Lafayette Ave., Brooklyn, NY 11238, +1-718-928-6603, brooklynflea.com.

Catbird

Founded in 2004, this gem of a store features delicate jewelry such as first knuckle rings and ear climbers made in house, alongside paper items by Rifle, trays by John Derian, candles, and apothecary items.

219 Bedford Ave., Brooklyn, NY 11211, +1-718-599-3457, catbirdnyc.com.

Concrete & Water

Cute lifestyle boutique with a mix of local and international labels (Sea, A.P.C., Ganni), plus quirky accessories (taco-shaped lapel pins by Pintrill, cork-heel pumps by Anne Thomas, clutches by Lizzie Fortunato). A back patio with a ping-pong table invites hanging out in the warmer months.

485 Driggs Ave., Brooklyn, NY 11211, +1-917-909-1828, concreteandwater.com.

CONCRETE & WATER

OROBORO

Electric Feathers

"I always visit for pants or dresses by the visionary designer Leana Zuniga," says actress/blogger/beauty entrepreneur Shiva Rose of the Brooklyn-based designer's flagship. It features versatile garments such as her signature Infinite Rope dress, which can be rolled up, tucked in a knapsack, and unfurled for ease when traveling and her Infinite Bandeau, which can be worn as a top, scarf, belt, or headdress.

60 Broadway, Brooklyn, NY 11249, +1-347-227-7023, electricfeathers.com.

Oroboro

Boho duds by Ulla Johnson, Electric Feathers, Ryan Roche, 69 denim, Rachel Craven, Ace & Jig, and other designers, alongside shoes by Brother Vellies, A Détacher, and Dieppa Restrepo, apothecary items by Brooklyn Beach, Fig & Yarrow, plus textiles and wall hangings, and ceramics. "The buyer, April, has such incredible and original taste," says Shiva Rose. "It's sort of my home away from home," says Brother Vellies designer Aurora James, who suggests ducking into Sprout Home around the corner for flowers, and Devoción across the street for a latte.

326 Wythe Ave., Brooklyn, NY 11249, +1-718-388-4884, oroborostore.com.

WASHINGTON

DISTRICT OF COLUMBIA

Hu's Wear and Hu's Shoes

Within one block of each other, Hu's Shoes and Hu's Wear feature designer ready-to-wear, footwear, handbags, and accessories by Kenzo, Erdem, Chloé, Isabel Marant, Valentino, Jerome Dreyfuss, and more.

3005 and 2906 M St. NW, Washington, DC 20007, +1-202-342 0202, husonline.com.

National Museum of the American Indian

"My favorite gift shop in the world," says retailer Josh Peskowitz. "They work with so many artisans, and I've bought jewelry and home goods that I use all the time. Both as reference and just to wear. The food court there is also terrific. They have the stalls set up by region. Great Plains cooking here, Pacific Northwest cooking there."

4th St., and Independence Ave. SW, Washington, DC 20560, nmai.si.edu.

RELISH

Relish

"An artfully chosen array of well-known labels such as Marni, Aspesi, and Marc Jacobs, but also lesser-known ones, eclectic brands such as Sacai and Simone Rocha," says *Washington Post* fashion editor Robin Givhan. "It's the very personal point of view of owner Nancy Pearlstein."

3312 Cady's Alley NW, Washington, DC 20007, +1-202-333-5343, relishdc.com.

Salt and Sundry

"For housewares and hostess gifts, Salt and Sundry in Union Market is a delight. It's got craft cocktail mixers, Turkish towels, hand-carved furniture, and jewelry," Robin Givhan says.

1309 5th St. NE, Washington, DC 20002, +1-202-556-1866, shopsaltandsundry .com, and an additional location in Logan Circle.

FREEPORT

MAINE

L.L. Bean

"I don't think I would ever classify myself as a preppy guy, but I love the classic, all-American L.L. Bean flagship," says fashion editor/TV host Joe Zee. "First of all, it is open twenty-four hours(!), but I also think it's because where I grew up the must-have items in high school were always the L.L. Bean sweaters and 'duck boots.' And the fact that you can buy those here along with a shotgun case is so authentic."

95 Main St., Freeport, ME 04032, +1-877-755-2326, llbean.com, and additional locations.

L.L. BEAN

WOODSTOCK

VERMONT

Who Is Sylvia?

"Every summer we go to Woodstock, Vermont, to see family," says L.A.–based jewelry designer Sonia Boyajian. "It's a very charming, classic New England town with covered bridges and old-world charm. There is a tiny vintage shop there called Who is Sylvia? and it's by far my favorite destination to visit. You can get anything from beautiful vintage clothing to hand-embroidered tablecloths, stunning hats, and even some children's clothing."

26 Central St., Woodstock, VT 05091, +1-802-457-1110.

WESTON

VERMONT

The Vermont Country Store

Open since 1946, you can still spend hours browsing at this ultimate general store. There's everything from Lanz of Salzburg flannel nightgowns and made-in-Vermont Darn Tough socks to Tangee color-changing lipstick and Vermont maple syrup. The Weston location also has the Bryant House restaurant, which serves such tavern classics as Vermont cheddar cheese soup.

657 Main St., Weston, VT 05161, +1-802-824-3184, vermontcountrystore.com, and an additional location in Rockingham.

VERMONT COUNTRY STORE

BOSTON

MASSACHUSETTS

Ball and Buck

This menswear shop with hunting-inspired apparel is on lad-mag top lists. It stocks rugged-yet-refined apparel, all made in the USA, plus oyster knives, wallets, belts, and vintage *Playboy* magazines. There's a barbershop, too.

144B Newbury St., Boston, MA 02116, +1-617-262-1776, ballandbuck.com.

Bobby From Boston

Bobby Garnett was a vintage clothing pioneer when he founded his Provincetown store in 1974 (it moved to the South End in 1995). Over the years, he sold vintage menswear to the design teams at Marc Jacobs, Ralph Lauren, J. Crew, and more, and assembled a museum-worthy collection of pleated pants, two-tone shoes, and workwear, with corresponding, historically accurate props, dating back to the 1930s. Garnett, who also provided costumes for dozens of films, died in May 2016, but his legacy continues.

19 Thayer St., Boston, MA 02118, +1-617-423-9299, bobby-from-boston.com.

Bodega

"A store that left a great impact on me," says journalist and author Susana Martinez Vidal, about Bodega, "It's hidden behind an actual bodega that sells sodas, water, and snacks on a small street off the commercial thoroughfare. The store is only accessible to those who know its secret. The bodega looks old and unkempt, but a marvelous store appears suddenly behind a Snapple vending machine, which in fact is a sliding door." Inside, you'll find rare and stylish sneakers, plus amazing menswear from Garbstore,

A.P.C., Norse Projects, Woolrich, and more.

6 Clearway St., Boston, MA 02115, shop.bdgastore.com.

Castanet

Building on the legacy of beloved Boston consignment store The Closet, Castanet took over the space in the spring of 2016, and is the place to go for gently used clothing, handbags, and shoes by Chanel, Isabel Marant, Balenciaga, The Row, Marni, and more.

175 Newbury St., second fl., Boston, MA 02116, +1-617-536-1919, shopcastanet.com.

December Thieves

Stop by this local fave for limited-run jewelry, including stackable rings and earthy, crystal-adorned necklaces, modern-looking bags, arty home decor, and fun men's accessories.

88 Charles St., Boston, MA 02114, +1-617-982-6802, decemberthieves.com.

Dress

The boutique is named after the one piece of clothing every woman probably has in her wardrobe, the little black dress, but it sells much more, including denim by M.i.h Jeans, Lizzie Fortunato jewelry, Rachel Comey tops, and Ulla Johnson wraps.

70 Charles St., Boston, MA 02114, +1-617- 248-9910, dressboston.com.

Riccardi

This edgy, bi-level Newbury Street boutique stocks all the major designers for men and women, including Kenzo, Moschino, Comme des Garçons Play, Neil Barrett, Thom Browne, Valentino, and Givenchy.

116 Newbury St., Boston, MA 02116, +1-617-266-3158, riccardiboston.com.

Serenella

Credited with introducing Emilio Pucci, Romeo Gigli, and other high-end designers to Boston back in the day, Serenella has been at the cutting edge of fashion since opening in 1980. The two boutiques (in Boston and Nantucket) feature an array of luxury designers, including old standbys Agnona, Bottega Veneta, Dolce & Gabbana, Loewe, and Roberto Cavalli, and members of the new guard, including Lisa Marie Fernandez, Rosie Assoulin, and Roksanda.

134 Newbury St., Boston, MA 02116, +1-617-262-5568, serenella-boston.com.

Twentieth Century Limited

A hidden gem full of vintage costume jewelry gems, this Beacon Hill basement store stocks sparklers by Miriam Haskell, Trifari, Dior, Georg Jensen, Kenneth Jay Lane, Oscar de la Renta, and more.

73 Charles St., Boston, MA 02114, +1-617-742-1031, boston-vintagejewelry.com.

FARAN KRENTCIL

BOSTON SECRETS

Boston-bred Faran Krentcil is a contributing editor at ELLE.com and Yahoo News. She is the founding editor of Fashionista.com and served as NYLON's first-ever digital director. Last year, she illustrated her first book, The Craft, *by rock stylist Lou Teasdale.*

In Boston, I always visit **THE GARMENT DISTRICT,** a bonkers clubhouse for club kids, vintage lovers, and deadstock denim junkies. Think: If Patricia Field had four floors of retail.

SUDO SHOES is the only cruelty-free shoe store in the Boston area, with good weatherproof options and a full selection of vegan Doc Martens!

Where college girls go to scope potential dates, **CONCEPTS** has hard-to-find collaborations from A Bathing Ape + Adidas, and Rihanna's Fenty line.

Now that Boston's beloved Filene's Basement has bit the dust, Framingham, Massachusetts-based **TJ MAXX** is the hometown discount store to visit for crazy deals on designer clothes. The one on Route 4/225 in Bedford is the one you want. It's the unofficial flagship with designer stuff.

I love to buy custom-made embroidered moccasins and loafers online at Boston-based **ARTEMIS DESIGN** CO.—cuter than Gucci, I swear.

THE GARMENT DISTRICT, 200 Broadway, Cambridge, MA 02139, +1-617- 876-5230, garmentdistrict.com.

SUDO SHOES, 1771 Massachusetts Ave., Cambridge, MA 02140, +1-617- 354-1771, sudoshoes.com.

CONCEPTS, The Atrium, 37 Brattle St., Cambridge, MA 02138, +1-617- 204-2104, cncpts.com.

TJ MAXX, 297 Great Rd, Bedford, MA 01730, (781) 275-8864, tjmaxx.com.

ARTEMIS DESIGN, Artemisdesignco.com.

FREE CITY

LOS ANGELES

CALIFORNIA

THE MAJORS

Neiman Marcus

The Beverly Hills outpost of Neiman Marcus has a secret weapon, and that's Catherine Bloom, a personal shopper so renowned, her bosses built her "Bloom's Room" to cater to stylists and celebs. "My two big secrets in Los Angeles are the amazing personal shoppers Catherine Bloom at Neiman's and Tony Ferreira at Saks," says Haney designer Mary Alice Haney. "If I had the resources, Catherine is the only person I would shop with," says Rodarte's Kate Mulleavy. Our stylish shoppers also praise the store's Mariposa restaurant and its irresistible warm popovers.
9700 Wilshire Blvd., Beverly Hills, CA 90212, +1-310-550-5900, neimanmarcus.com, and additional locations.

Maxfield

Temple to dark and decadent high fashion in the land of sunshine since its opening in 1969, Maxfield combines the latest from Chanel, Givenchy, Balmain, Saint Laurent, Alaïa, and Isabel Marant, with accessories by Céline and Gucci, jewelry by Lisa Eisner, vintage Hermès bags, and Cartier baubles. Not only did founder Tommy Perse define a new, largely all-black aesthetic for L.A., he also gave many designers a launch pad in the US, including Rick Owens, Giorgio Armani, Yohji Yamamoto, and Comme des Garçons's Rei Kawakubo. Crazy-expensive jeans and leather jackets by Japanese designers abound, as do cashmere sweaters as thick as blankets, for warding off that California coastal chill. "Push open the glass doors and get ready to find anything from a taxidermy chicken to an overnight bag to the most beautiful dress you've ever seen," says interior designer Brigette Romanek, "and sometimes they have vintage Kelly bags or a Cartier bangle from the '70s. They have the best of everything." "My go-to source for special pieces since my days as a bicoastal stylist," says designer Andrea Lieberman. "Added bonus: Gracias Madre is on the same block." "The first time I shopped there, it was the late '80s. I came home flush from a modeling gig in Paris and went to Maxfield," says handbag designer Kendall Conrad. "They offered me champagne while I shopped and I thought that was so cool. I bought an incredible Thierry Mugler dress that had a sheer black front with flames covering the chest. I thought Maxfield was out of *Scruples*." You can also browse cases of antique erotica, skulls, and other offbeat ephemera.

8825 Melrose Ave., West Hollywood, CA 90069, +1-310-274-8800, maxfieldla.com, and additional locations.

BEVERLY HILLS

Alo Yoga

Gigi and Bella Hadid, Kendall Jenner, and Hailey Baldwin wear this brand's moto and goddess leggings in the studio and on the street. "This is the new face of retail," says blogger/socialite NJ Goldston. "It's a wonderful mix of perfectly curated and spectacularly merchandised athletic apparel with everything from an open-air coffee and juice bar to a rooftop yoga studio and event space. You won't want to leave." Another reason to stop in? Stumptown coffee, cold-pressed Raw Juicery juice, and local, sustainable bites by Café Gratitude.

370 N. Canon Dr., Beverly Hills, CA 90210, +1-310-295-1860, aloyoga.com.

Beverly Hills Hotel Gift Shop

This fabulous hotel gift shop routinely collaborates with designers on stylish items inspired by the famed Pink Palace, including Charlotte Olympia's Charlotte Dellal and milliner Stephen Jones. "I could spend a day and $1,000 in the gift shop of the Beverly Hills Hotel just poring over all the pink-and-white striped and palm-tree-covered tchotchkes," says San Francisco–based fashion retailer Emily Holt. "I've always loved the gift shop at the Beverly Hills Hotel! #thinkpink!" says accessories designer Sally Perrin.

9641 Sunset Blvd., Beverly Hills, CA 90210, +1-310-276-2251, dorchestercollection.com.

Lily et Cie

A vintage store even an Oscar nominee would love, with rare pieces from the 1920s to the 1990s. This super-high-end spot is "a gem on epic levels," says A.L.C. designer Andrea Lieberman. "[Owner] Rita Watnick has the most incredible collection of vintage I have ever seen."

9044 Burton Way, Beverly Hills, CA 90211, +1-310-724-5759.

Mameg

Hidden behind the Maison Martin Margiela store, Sonia Eram's chic spot stocks arty clothing and accessories by Jil Sander, Hussein Chalayan, and more. "It's a very intimate shopping experience. On most afternoons clients are offered a glass of champagne and some Persian sweets while they look around," says jewelry designer Sonia Boyajian.

9970 S. Santa Monica Blvd., Beverly Hills, CA 90212, +1-310-556-2600, mameg.com.

Maxfield Bleu

Love to shop at Maxfield but don't have the budget? Our stylish shoppers' secret is Maxfield Bleu, the sale shop for Maxfield, which has past-season goodies by all the top brands at up to 70 percent off.

301 N. Canon Dr., Beverly Hills, CA 90210, +1-310-275-7007, maxfieldla.com.

Nadine Krakov Collection

An antique jewelry store in the heart of Beverly Hills. "The couple that owns the business have become friends," says Brigette Romanek. "I sit with them and try on antique and new jewels. They have every high-end jewelry brand and can give you the history of each piece. Nadine knows me better than I know myself. She calls me when she has a piece that she thinks I'd like. She hasn't missed once in the past ten years."

191 S. Beverly Dr., Beverly Hills, CA 90212, +1-310-860-9991, beverlyhillsjewelry.net, and an additional location on Canon Drive.

Tom Ford

The designer's namesake label may be based in London, but his spiritual home is in L.A., where his Rodeo Drive store is a hangout for friends and fans who come by to drop serious cash or to just say hi to their favorite salespeople. Ford has outfitted Daniel Craig as James Bond; dressed a constellation of stars, including Justin Timberlake, Gwyneth Paltrow, and Julianne Moore, for stage and red carpets; and been the subject of a Jay Z song. He's also directed two films. While his menswear may be deeply rooted in Savile Row tradition, his womenswear, with its myriad cinematic and pop culture references, looks very at home in L.A. In this two-level store, you'll find Ford's fragrances, accessories, and men's and women's collections, as well as the kind of over-the-top luxe pieces, like a $98,000 crocodile minidress, that make Beverly Hills what it is.

346 N. Rodeo Dr., Beverly Hills, CA 90210, +1-310-270-9440, tomford.com, and additional locations.

WEST HOLLYWOOD/MELROSE PLACE/MELROSE

The Apartment by the Line

Vanessa Traina Snow, designer muse and stylish daughter of novelist Danielle Steel, opened her first home-as-store concept Apartment by the Line in New York's SoHo, but we prefer the airy, light-filled Los Angeles location on Melrose Place. "You want to move right in," Louise Roe says of the store, which takes the retail trend of curation to a new level, with absolutely everything for sale, from the $50,500 Helmut Newton photograph hanging on the wall to the $895 pair of exclusive alligator Alexandra Knight Birkenstocks in the walk-in closet to the $8 Morihata charcoal toothbrush on the bathroom sink. "The epitome of great taste," says fashion editor/TV host Joe Zee. "Like walking into one of the chicest apartments you have ever seen," says stylist and designer Maryam Malakpour.

8463 Melrose Place, second fl., Los Angeles, CA. 90069, +1-323-746-5056, theline.com, and an additional location in New York.

Curve

Nevena Borissova was a retail pioneer when she opened her first store on Robertson Boulevard in 1997, before the stretch became hot, and now her empire has extended to other locations in L.A. and the rest of the country. Throughout, she's catered to women looking for a

ONLINE SHOPPING TIP

"I love sites like **Eyebobs.com** for their velvet readers, which I give out as gifts all the time, **Zerouv.com** for sunglasses, and **APL.com** for metallic knit sneakers (full disclosure, my sons run the company)," says NJ Goldston. "**Yoox.com** is the only one I know who carries French designer Marie Beltrami's mouse rings. You stack them on every finger. I met the designer at a party in Paris, she took a ring off her hand and insisted I take it—I'd never met her! I also love **Ashlynd.com** for clutches that are completely whimsical. At very social media-savvy parties, I always grab my chalkboard clutch from her and write the hashtag of the night. It's such an icebreaker."

well-edited selection of the newest labels, including J.W. Anderson, Baja East, Co, Ellery, Mugler, and more.

154 N. Robertson Blvd., Los Angeles, CA 90048, +1-310-360-3008, shopcurve.com, and additional locations.

Decades

Cameron Silver may have migrated to the East Coast to be fashion director of H by Halston for QVC, but back at home, Decades still sets the bar for upscale vintage in Los Angeles. The boutique opened in 1997, and helped introduce vintage to the red carpet, dressing stars such as Julia Roberts, Renée Zellweger, and Chloë Sevigny. Upstairs is the primo stuff; downstairs, you'll find more recent designer pieces, and the famous twice-annual shoe sale.

8214 Melrose Ave., Los Angeles, CA 90046, +1-323-655-1960, decadesinc.com.

The Elder Statesman

Located in a converted bungalow, the home base for L.A. designer Greg Chait's ultra-luxe boho cashmere label sells supersoft cashmere Baja hoodies, palm tree intarsia sweaters, tie-dyed sweatpants, striped blankets, teddy bears, and more.

607 Huntley Dr., West Hollywood, CA 90069, +1-424-288-4221, elder-statesman.com.

Elodie K.

Resorty, whimsical boutique located next to Alfred Coffee, with shoes by Aquazurra, Sophia Webster, and Ancient Greek Sandals; denim by Seafarer; beachwear by Lisa Marie Fernandez and Camilla; and more. "Every time I come in, I discover great new European labels, unavailable anywhere else in L.A.," says blogger Anabelle Fleur. "Elodie K. was probably one of the first places to carry Dodo Bar Or's stunning hand-embroidered separates and Paula Cademartori's statement-making bags." Owner Elodie Khayat has her own collection of jewelry, including body chains, hand chains, and earrings.

8428 Melrose Place, West Hollywood, CA 90069, +1-323-658-5060, elodiek.com.

Gabriela Artigas

Stop by this charming store to shop tusk earrings, chain rings, star-shaped barrettes, and other pieces by the L.A.–based sister act Gabriela and Tere Artigas, who started their brand in 2003. Since then, their everyday statement jewelry has found favor with the likes of Tyra Banks, Emma Roberts, Chelsea Handler, and Carey Mulligan.

370 N. La Cienega Blvd. #1, Los Angeles, CA 90048, +1-310-360-0796, gabrielaartigas.com.

IRENE NEUWIRTH

Indigo Seas

"For the last thirty years or so I've loved this divine shop by Lynn Von Kersting, who also owns the two Ivy restaurants in Los Angeles," says Libertine fashion designer Johnson Hartig. "Lynn has one of the most sophisticated and clever eyes in the business and curates such a fantastic selection of her own upholstered furniture and quirky, divine objets in a delightful way. I remember when Michael Smith, the decorator, worked there as Lynn's assistant in the 1980s, and he has kind of adopted Lynn's best attributes in his own design work."

123 N. Robertson Blvd., Los Angeles, CA 90048, +1-310-550-8758, indigoseas.us.

Irene Neuwirth

The Venice, California–based jewelry designer is known for carefully balanced constructions of bold, rough-cut, and semiprecious stones. She upped the retail game with her first store, an impressive mix of whimsical chic and at-home L.A. ease. Jewelry is displayed in glass cases with dioramas designed by local artist Clare Crespo. Tiny pieces are draped on birds, flowers, and butterflies fashioned out of cashmere, snakeskin, and suede. A pink velvet couch and a pair of shearling chairs set up in front of a fireplace and bookshelves filled with volumes on everything from the artist Elizabeth Peyton to Audubon animals encourage shoppers to stay awhile.

8458 Melrose Place, West Hollywood, CA 90069, +1-323-285-2000, ireneneuwirth.com.

Isabel Marant

Sure, the French designer has other stores—in Paris, New York, Tokyo, etc.—but the L.A. location is her most inspiring, thanks to the cactus garden out front and the artist-studio feel inside. Both her runway and Étoile brands are sold here, along with her coveted accessories.

8454 Melrose Place, Los Angeles, CA 90069, +1-323-651-1493, isabelmarant .com, and additional locations.

Jenni Kayne

The L.A. designer has earned fans near and far for her relaxed-yet-polished pieces that mix masculine and feminine elements: dotted swiss boyfriend shirts, crepe slim pants, twill military jackets, and beach-appropriate sweater coats. She has her own line of shoes, too, including her signature much-imitated d'Orsay flats. You'll also find handbags by Mansur Gavriel and jewelry by Sophie Bille Brahe. "So chic and well curated," says stylist Ilaria Urbinati. "She has beautiful taste." Check out Kayne's lifestyle blog Rip and Tan, which features recipes, entertaining tips, and interviews.

614 N. Almont Dr., West Hollywood, CA 90069, +1-310-860-0123, jennikayne.com, and additional locations.

Nasty Gal

Ground zero for #GirlBoss Sophia Amoruso, the Melrose flagship features a mix of trendy apparel, shoes, accessories, and intimates. You'll find lace-up tops, ruffled rompers, leather minis from the Nasty Gal brand alongside other labels, including Jeffrey Campbell, Vans, and For Love & Lemons, plus vintage bags and jewelry from Louis Vuitton and Chanel. There's a magazine nook with tech gifts and a few vinyl records for sale, including one by Betty Davis, whose funk song "Nasty Gal" inspired the brand's name.

8115 Melrose Ave., Los Angeles, CA, 90046, +1-323-658-1010, nastygal.com, and an additional location in Santa Monica.

The Office of Angela Scott

The Santa Barbara designer's menswear-inspired footwear for women includes black-and-navy striped oxfords with chunky heels, black patent leather platform kiltie loafers, chocolate suede cutout flat booties with perforated details, black-and-white deco-inspired derby oxfords, priced from $195 to $625. Scott's shoes have been worn by Cate Blanchett, Julia Roberts, Ellen DeGeneres, and Taylor Swift. There are select styles for men, too.

7975 Melrose Ave., Los Angeles, CA 90046, +1-323-424-7796, theofficeofangelascott.com.

REFORMATION

Reformation

Founder Yael Aflalo has caused a sensation with her reworked vintage garments, which are not only eco-friendly but also sexy enough to make fans of the model crowd, including Lily Aldridge, Rosie Huntington-Whiteley, Karlie Kloss, and others. Popular styles include thigh-high-slit maxi dresses, open-back jumpsuits, and off-shoulder blouses, and most items top out at $300. "My favorite affordable shop," says stylist Ilaria Urbinati. "I shop there an embarrassing amount (and on their site, too). And, like, where in the hell was this store when I was in my 20s? I love that the clothes are all about being eco and ethically made, but they're actually sexy, cool-girl clothes, nothing granola about them." In addition to the in-house label, the store stocks vintage denim, accessories by Monserat De Lucca, B-Low the Belt, and more.

8253 Melrose Ave., Los Angeles, CA 90048, +1-323-852-0005, thereformation .com, and additional locations.

Reservoir

The concept of New York City transplants Aliza Neidich and Alissa Jacob, Reservoir features a mix of clothing, accessories, and home goods with an easy sophistication made for L.A., including Ryan Roche hand-knit sweaters, Denis Colomb linen dresses, Ellery sleek crepe dresses and tops, Re/Done denim, MadeWorn tees, Newbark slides, and Wendy Nichol fringed leather bucket bags. Home furnishings and gift items have a handmade modern vibe.

154 S. Robertson Blvd., Los Angeles, CA 90048 +1-323-300-5309, reservoir-la.com.

Ron Herman at Fred Segal

As a young entrepreneur in the early 1960s, Fred Segal unleashed the first wave of designer denim mania (when jeans were retailing for $3.98, he priced his at $19.95) and promptly had customers lining up around the block. What made him a true retail visionary, though, was pioneering the shop-in-shop concept that is now standard practice in department stores. Segal served as the original savvy landlord, clustering a collection of cutting-edge, independent retailers inside his ivy-covered walls on Melrose, starting in 1965. With their ability to spot the next big thing, his deputized curators of cool—Ron Herman chief among them—helped establish the Fred Segal center as a retail must-visit (and as a de facto extension of the wardrobe departments for many a fashion-influencing TV show, *Melrose Place* and *Friends* among them). Ron Herman carries the torch for SoCal style at his men's and women's stores at Melrose Center (and in other locations around Southern California and in Japan), where you'll find everything for the L.A. look from must-have denim, rocker T-shirts, and swim trunks to breezy dresses; patchwork men's jackets by Junya Watanabe; hoodies by Solca; diver-print button-down shirts by Portuguese Flannel; and more.

8100 Melrose Ave., Los Angeles, CA 90046, +1-323-651-4129, ronherman.com, and additional locations.

Roseark

This converted West Hollywood bungalow is a gallery of must-have high-end jewelry, accessories, and art from around the world. It's full of unique discoveries such as a Dagmar Zaragoza hand-embroidered fabric collar and porcelain bead scarves from Guatemala, Amedeo's edgy cameo rings, Daniela Villegas's butterfly fish earrings, Elisabeth Bell Jewelry shark tooth ear climbers, Victorian estate pieces that have been tweaked by in-house artisans, and more. Prices start at $25.

1111 N. Crescent Heights Blvd., West Hollywood, CA 90046, +1-310-395-6706, roseark.com.

RTH

Designer René Holguin has two neighboring stores on La Cienega Boulevard devoted to his label RTH. With rotating art displays, talisman-like handcrafted

ONLINE SHOPPING TIP

Jeweler Irene Neuwirth recommends matchesfashion.com for clothes. "I feel like they have a better curated shopping experience than others," and ylang23.com for jewels (including her own). She likes boho-inspired L.A.-based brand Doen Collective, too, at shopdoen.com. Also based in L.A., dreslyn.com has a nice curation of contemporary labels. For vintage, Neuwirth, like most every other contributor in this book, singles out 1stdibs.com.

leather jewelry, handmade apothecary items, and the scent of piñon incense in the air, they are like upscale souvenir shops. Holguin's unisex collection isn't sold online, so you have to go to his shops to procure his twist on the classic navy blazer, or the cult-favorite drop-crotch jeans. "Japan-meets–Ralph Lauren in Los Angeles," says stylist Amanda Ross. "Familiar yet wholly original," says Lori Leven, the founder of Love Adorned. "His refined eye brings you items that other retail stores will say they discovered a year later." "And the fragrance and the body oil . . . it is all made with care and so, so cool," says stylist Sarah Schussheim. Experiential retail at its best.

529 and 537 N. La Cienega Blvd., West Hollywood, CA, 90048, +1-310-289-7911, rthshop.com.

Sielian's Vintage Apparel

"Every stylist comes here," says stylist Jen Rade, which is why Miley Cyrus, Kim Kardashian, Katy Perry, and others have worn vintage sourced from this West Hollywood gem, which stocks cocktail frocks and more by Jean Paul Gaultier, Thierry Mugler, Oscar de la Renta, James Galanos, and Gianfranco Ferré.

8629½ Melrose Ave., West Hollywood, CA 90069, +1-310-246-9595, sieliansvintageapparel.com.

Ten Over Six

Accessory-obsessed cool girls head to this airy, all-white space for offbeat items by fashion-insider favorites like Rachel Comey, No. 6, Marlow Goods, and Thierry Lasry. "My wildcard store," says Brigette Romanek. "They carry really unique bags, clothes, shoes, and jewelry. I find things here that I won't find everywhere else."

8425 Melrose Ave., Los Angeles, CA, 90069, +1-323-330-9355, shop.tenover6.com.

The Row

First retail store for The Row, the stealth-wealth luxury brand created in 2006 by former child stars Mary-Kate and Ashley Olsen. The residential-style space features furniture sourced from local purveyors JF Chen, Galerie Half, and Thomas Hayes Gallery, paintings by artists John Tweddle, Sergej Jensen, and vintage jewelry and objects—all of it for sale. There are also Manolo Blahnik shoes and Sidney Garber jewelry. "It's so beautifully appointed and designed, it feels a little like being in a live-in museum," says Refinery29's Christene Barberich. "I want everything, all the time, including the furniture that's for sale," says interior designer Brigette Romanek. "The sweaters are 'forever' items; they get more cozy with time. The leather leggings, the dresses! When I wear their clothes, I feel empowered."

8440 Melrose Place, Los Angeles, CA 90069, +1-310-853-1900, therow.com, and an additional location in New York City.

Violet Grey

Expertly curated beauty boutique with the best products by Charlotte Tilbury, Tom Ford, Giorgio Armani, Le Mer, RGB, Root Vanish, and more, tested and approved by top Hollywood makeup artists, hairstylists, and celebrities. Check out the website's Violet Files section for celebrity profiles and beauty routines, expert beauty lessons, and how-tos.

8452 Melrose Place, Los Angeles, CA 90069, +1-323-782-9700, violetgrey.com.

Wasteland

It's Coachella year-round at this Melrose Avenue institution, which has a large, on-trend collection of vintage clothing for men and women that won't break the bank; denim cutoffs and overalls start at $32, Mexican blouses at $22, and Lurex hippie skirts at $28. There is more serious stuff, too, including I. Magnin cocktail coats and sequin cocktail dresses. "If you really look, you can find great stuff like '90s Helmut Lang, Prada, and Comme des Garçons," says designer Rosetta Getty. Bonus: You might run into Chloë Sevigny; she has said that this is her favorite store in L.A.

7428 Melrose Ave., Los Angeles, CA 90046, +1-323-653-3028, shopwasteland .com, and additional locations.

Zero Maria Cornejo

Maria Cornejo may be a New York–based designer (and have her original store there), but we prefer to shop her relaxed draped dresses, cocoon coats, and jumpsuits in geometric-inspired cuts at the light-filled L.A. outpost. Cornejo's demo is artsy and intellectual; her aesthetic, minimalist, feminine, and friendly. Is it any wonder that former First Lady Michelle Obama, actor Tilda Swinton, and artist Cindy Sherman are fans?

8408 Melrose Place, Los Angeles, CA 90069 +1-323-782-4915, zeromariacornejo.com, and an additional location in New York.

BEVERLY BOULEVARD and THIRD STREET

Anine Bing

Why not go straight to the source for the army jackets, leather biker pants, tassel minidresses, vintage-looking "Los Angeles" tees, and lace bralets that have earned a cultlike following among the young Hollywood set, including Kendall Jenner, Rosie Huntington-Whiteley, Kate Bosworth, and Jessica Alba? This is Danish model-turned-designer (and L.A. transplant) Bing's hometown flagship.

8128 W. Third St., Los Angeles CA, 90048, +1-323-424-3165, aninebing.com, and additional locations.

Elaine Kim

The L.A. designer creates timeless classics (lace blazers, silk bombers, linen pants, pencil skirts) as well as custom-made garments. Her styling services are available on-site or via Skype. "I wear a lot of slouchy suits, and Elaine makes them for me in whatever color I want," says stylist Ilaria Urbinati. "It feels very old school to have my suits made."

8373 W. 3rd St., Los Angeles, CA 90048, +1-323-937-0355, elainekim.com.

George Esquivel

The L.A. shoemaker and his band of craftsmen have been hand-cobbling high-end shoes for a who's who of the well-heeled, including rock stars, NBA players, politicians, and Hollywood heavyweights, for more than a decade. His signature wing tips and boots are made from high-quality European leathers that are pebbled, painted, sunbaked, or pummeled into laid-back luxe. His appointment-only studio has plenty of pairs to try on and buy on the spot, and he takes custom orders, too. The shoes are made about an hour south of L.A. at Esquivel's Buena Park workshop.

8309 W. 3rd St., Los Angeles, CA 90048, +1-714-670-2200, esquivelshoes.com.

L.A. Eyeworks

An institution for creative peoples' creative frames since 1979, L.A. Eyeworks breaks the mold with its whimsical designs, and with its store windows that are a messaging platform for political discussion (and a good pun). Since 1981, the brand's portrait ad campaign, photographed

HOW TO SHOP FOR RETRO FASHION ONLINE

The Los Angeles-based burlesque dancer and style icon is a vintage connoisseur and collector. Her high-end striptease act has been performed to sold-out crowds around the world.

I grew up watching classic films because my mother loved them, and that's where my obsession with retro glamour comes from. As a little girl, I especially loved those big Technicolor musicals starring Betty Grable, Carmen Miranda, and Rita Hayworth, and so 1940s era style has always been the dearest to me. I think it was the most glamorous time for both beauty and fashion, and many of the silhouettes are still chic and easy to wear today. I have a "code" that I rarely stray from, and it's all rooted in my childhood fantasies about growing up to be like the movie stars of the 1940s.

I like to get my swimsuits at **PINUPGIRL-CLOTHING.COM** They fit well and are made with nice luxurious satin Lycra that gives that glamorous retro shape, plus they're made in a broad range of sizes and look fantastic on every woman.

I like **LENAHOSCHEK.COM** for well-made retro style skirts and sweaters. I also love wearing pieces from their dirndl collection.

THE DEPOP MARKETPLACE APP, depop.com, is like Instagram for shopping, lots of glamour girls and fashion bloggers sell their things on it. I sell my own vintage clothes, jewelry, and samples from my lingerie collection, too.

WHEELSANDDOLLBABY.COM is great for cardigans and pencil skirts.

SECRETSINLACE.COM is a go-to for authentic fully fashioned seamed stockings with French and Euro heels. These are for the next-level stocking aficionado, made on the same machines as they were in the 1940s and '50s. Once you feel the difference of fully fashioned stockings, you can't go back to modern Lycra stockings. It's like becoming part of an elite club.

I like **BARENECCESSITIES.COM** for everything lingerie, they carry a vast selection of brands and a wide variety of sizes. I aways send fans there to get my lingerie brand because they stock all the larger sizes, whereas many

by Greg Gorman, has featured more than 200 cultural provocateurs (Grace Jones, Andy Warhol, Joey Arias, and Debbie Harry, to name just a few), anchored by the brand's tagline: "A face is like a work of art. It deserves a great frame." "It's my candy store," fashion journalist/retailer Rose Apodaca says of the Beverly Boulevard space, designed by L.A. architect Neil Denari.

7386 Beverly Blvd., Los Angeles, CA 90036, +1-323-931-7795, laeyeworks.com, and an additional location on Melrose Ave.

Mister Freedom

A brick building houses the retail space and design studio created by French expat Christophe Loiron in 1990. Clothing spans the late 1800s to the 1970s from around the world, but Loiron specializes in men's rugged US and European vintage. "A denim lover's dream," says designer Andrea Lieberman. Loiron also designs a handful of his own vintage-inspired collections in the style of the American frontier, the Mexican Revolution, and 1950s California. This is one of French designer Isabel Marant's favorite L.A. haunts. Emily Current and Meritt Elliott are also devotees.

7161 Beverly Blvd, Los Angeles, CA 90036, +1-323-653-2014, misterfreedom.com.

Noodle Stories

This is L.A.'s top destination for clothing and accessories by interesting, intellectual designers such as Sacai, Martin Margiela, Issey Miyake, Anti-past, Pas de Calais, Sofie D'Hoore, Y's, and more. Two doors down, the NS Temp store currently features men's and women's Comme des Garçons, plus selections from CDG Black, Tricot Comme des Garçons, and Junya Watanabe.

8323 W. 3rd St., Los Angeles, CA 90048, +1-323-651-1782, noodlestories.com.

Regency Jewelry Co.

The store offers expert jewelry repair and several cases of tempting vintage pieces, including Southwestern squash blossom necklaces, and Elsa Peretti originals. "Many years ago, I bought myself a garnet and gold princess ring from a 75 percent–off tray," says WhoWhatWear's Hillary Kerr. "The craftsmanship is amazing, and the price was almost criminally affordable. It makes me feel like a 1940s dame in all the right ways." Personal note: I, too, have found great vintage pieces there, including a 1950s-era aurora borealis cocktail bracelet.

8129 W. 3rd St., Los Angeles, CA 90048, +1-323-655-2573, regencyjewelry.com.

Re-Mix Vintage Shoes

Fashion insider Liz Goldwyn and other retronauts hit this store for deadstock vintage shoes and reproductions of styles from the 1920s to the 1970s, including ankle-strap platforms and perforated lace-ups. It has men's shoes, too.

7384 Beverly Blvd., Los Angeles, CA 90036, +1-323-936-6210, remixvintageshoes.com.

Scent Bar

This olfactory heaven is set up like a bar, allowing shoppers to try on fragrances while they enjoy coffee or prosecco and features hard-to-find brands from around the globe such as Escentric Molecules, Ex Nihilo, 10 Corso Como, Altaia, and Mancera. "Best in L.A. for niche fragrances and candles," says fashion journalist and consultant Melissa Magsaysay.

7405 Beverly Blvd., Los Angeles, CA 90036, +1-323-782-8300, luckyscent.com.

Scout

"Best selection of vintage clothing at affordable prices," says stylist and designer Maryam Malakpour. "Joey [Grana], the owner, has incredible taste and I have been following his handpicks for more than ten years. I found two Valentino Couture silk blouses there that I love." Other stylish shoppers praise the collection of '90s and minimalist clothing. "Exactly the type of vintage shopping I like to do," says retailer Lori Leven. "A super-tight edit of pieces you aren't sure are contemporary or vintage when you pick them up."

8021 Melrose Ave., Los Angeles, CA 90046, +1-323-461-1530, scoutla.net.

Shabon

"One of my favorite vintage stores in L.A.," Nicole Richie says of this just-right-sized spot with wares spanning from the Victorian era to the '90s, where she nabbed one of her all-time-greatest finds, a vintage YSL oversized coat.

7617 Beverly Blvd, Los Angeles, CA 90036, +1-323-692-0061, shabonla.com.

LA BREA

A + R Store

Global design, edited by fashion journalist and author Rose Apodaca and her husband, Andy Griffith (no, not that Andy Griffith). This inspirational showroom for modern furniture, lighting, and rug design also has plenty of grab-and-go gifts and toys, including safety pin earrings, animal head pins, digital wristwatches, and other tempting baubles.

171 S. La Brea Ave., Los Angeles, CA 90036, +1-323-692-0086, aplusrstore.com.

Aether

L.A.–based brand of men's and women's performance gear and off-duty athleisure for mountain, motorcycle, gym, or street. The flagship on La Brea Avenue has a walk-in freezer, chilled to 9 degrees Fahrenheit for coat testing, and a curated selection of "man toys," including a $19,850 Ducati motorcycle, a $1,500 electric skateboard, a $2,000 folding kayak, a $174 ax, and books on subjects such as subterranean London and container architecture.

161 S. La Brea Ave., Los Angeles, CA 90036, +1-323-746-5147, aetherapparel.com, and additional locations.

American Rag Cie

Southern California high-low style and culture in all its glory—vintage mixed with denim and workwear, contemporary clothing and streetwear, plus books, DVDs, and housewares, and a see-and-be-seen sidewalk café. American Rag is really three stores in one. The main shop features designer clothing and shoes alongside a superbly edited selection of vintage clothing and accessories. The denim bar has workwear and denim (Denham, Levi's Made & Crafted, Current Elliott, Mother), and the housewares store features outdoor furniture, glassware, and accessories with a French Mediterranean twist to match the restaurant's menu. "The best omelets," says Nicole Richie.

150 S. La Brea Ave., Los Angeles, CA 90036, +1-323-935-3154, americanrag.com, and an additional location in Newport Beach.

Rick Owens

The visonary designer who started his Goth luxe brand in L.A. in 1994, comes full circle with his L.A. store. Located on a seedy stretch of La Brea Avenue, it's just down the street from the Plaza Salon, a drag bar where he spent many a late night, including one when he met "a shriveled little man" on the dance floor who turned out to be his hero, Iggy Pop. The 5,200-square-foot concrete-floor space has a water tank that releases slow-motion bubbles and a wall that emits fog every five minutes. Featured inside? Owens's entire glamorous, gritty universe, including women's knitwear and T-shirts in his signature drapey silhouettes; sports-infused menswear, shoes, and accessories; the simple benches and tables he designs; and jewelry designed by his muse and wife, Michele Lamy.

819 N. La Brea Ave., Los Angeles, CA 90038, +1-323-931-4960, rickowens.eu, and additional locations.

The Way We Wore

Doris Raymond's vintage gold mine is the best combination of accessible (a $25 boho belt) and aspirational (a $9,500 1950s Givenchy gown), which is why it's a hit with designers, stylists, and tastemakers alike. Personal note: I once took fashion collector Iris Apfel on a shopping trip there and she had a field day. "You could stumble upon anything from a Madame Grès gown to original Yves Saint Laurent Rive Gauche culottes," says fashion journalist Christina Binkley. "If you're a design professional, she might even let you peek into her archives next door—that's really special." Raymond has been called "the godmother of fashion inspiration"; she even starred in her own docuseries on the Smithsonian Channel, *L.A. Frock Stars*.

334 S. La Brea Ave., Los Angeles, CA 90036, +1-323-937-0878, thewaywewore.com.

Union

A source for hard-to-find menswear labels from around the world, including Christopher Kane, Gosha Rubchinskiy, Raf Simons, Visvim, and Ganryu.

110 S. La Brea Ave., Los Angeles, CA 90036, +1-323-549-6950, store.unionlosangeles.com.

HOLLYWOOD

Des Kohan

A trend forecaster for brands such as Prada and Gucci before opening her boutique in 2005, Desiree Kohan has built her business on her ability to teach clients how to incorporate clothing by avant-garde local and European designers—Juan Carlos Obando, Dusan, Damir Doma, Hussein Chalayan, etc.—into their everyday wardrobe. She also has a great eye for modern-yet-organic jewelry by Annie Costello Brown, Gabriela Artigas, and Aesa. "I know that I can walk in there at any time and emerge with a complete outfit that feels unique, elegant, timeless, and effortlessly chic," says designer/personal shopper Raven Kauffman. "I love the vibe there. You always feel like you are their most important client, no matter how often you go or how much you spend."

671 Cloverdale Ave., Los Angeles, CA 90036, +1-323-857-0200, deskohan.com.

Free City Supershop

Nina Garduno's hippie chic–meets–pop art–meets–commune store/gallery is L.A.'s antidote to cookie-cutter fashion. You'll browse unisex T-shirts, sweatshirts, sweatpants, and phone cases hand-printed with doves, rainbows, bicycles, and other feel-good graphics, and slogans such as COLOR AND SOUND, ARTISTS WANTED, and LIFE NATURE LOVE. There's a different theme each year, and the store also sells patchouli perfume, brown bread, ceramic pots, and books on subjects as diverse as Corita Kent and Yoko Ono.

1139 N. Highland Ave., Los Angeles, CA 90038 +1-323-461-2226, freecitysupershop .com, and additional locations.

Just One Eye

Part boutique, part art gallery, Just One Eye is the brainchild of Paola Russo, former fashion director of Maxfield. Expect the unexpected when you walk inside the art deco building in which tycoon Howard Hughes once ran his business empire, from a $65,000 Marilyn Minter print to a $12,500 Ulysses Tier 1 survival kit designed by the store and filled with supplies to get through a disaster (yes, really). In the men's and women's clothing departments, offerings run the gamut from minidresses by Anthony Vaccarello and rabbit ear headbands by Maison Michel to streetwear by Off-White and sneakers by Y-3. The store is also known for its quirky collaborations; one paired The Row and artist Damien Hirst, which resulted in Nile crocodile backpacks festooned with colorful pills and polka dots and priced at an astronomical $55,000. "Beautiful just to visit," says Hong Kong–based fashion journalist Divia Harilela.

"It's in an odd location and the storefront isn't a typical one. They needed to make it a destination, and they have, first of all by having an unusual space, and decor by Blackman Cruz, one of the best furniture stores ever created," says interior designer Brigette Romanek. "You'll have a unique shopping experience."

7000 Romaine St., Los Angeles, CA 90038, +1-323-969-9129, justoneeye.com.

Lost & Found

This string of five storefronts on Yucca Street in Hollywood is a one-stop shop for the laid-back L.A. lifestyle, with items for men, women, and kids; and an impeccable selection of boho dresses and blouses by Ulla Johnson, Nili Lotan, and Burning Torch, Local indigo jackets, Closed denim, B'Sbee shirts, furniture and other items for the home, such as maple cutting boards, Wallace Sewell throws, Studio One selvedge baskets, and more.

6320 Yucca St., Los Angeles, CA 90028, +1-323-856-5872, lostandfoundshop.com, and an additional location in Santa Monica.

Sonia Boyajian

L.A. jewelry designer known for kinetic-looking earrings and sculptural necklaces made of mismatched beads, candy-colored crystals, and fish-shaped pendants. Boyajian's studio/ store is a jewelry fantasyland, with pieces hanging on the walls, spilling from drawers, and coming together on her worktable (she makes it all by hand, from setting stones to twisting wires). Boyajian has collaborated with several designers over the years on jewelry for runway collections, including

Ulla Johnson, Peter Copping for Nina Ricci, and Bernhard Wilhelm, and will happily collaborate with customers to make custom pieces.

1947 N. Cahuenga Blvd., Ste. 102, Los Angeles, CA 90068, +1-323-325-1222, soniabstyle.com. By appointment.

The Supply Sergeant

Established in 1946, this regional chain is the go-to for Hollywood studios looking to outfit casts and backup dancers in military gear. You'll find American military uniforms from the Vietnam War, foreign uniforms, and the kind of camping and survival gear people snap up for the Coachella music festival. Costume designer Arianne Phillips singles out the Hollywood Boulevard location, across from the Musso & Frank Grill.

6664 Hollywood Blvd., Hollywood, CA 90028, +1-323-463-4730, supplysergeantstores.com, and an additional location in Burbank.

SILVER LAKE/LOS FELIZ/ECHO PARK

Broome Street General Store

"Cozy, a little folksy, and has great stuff for your home," says Tere Artigas, who handles sales and press for her sister Gabriela Artigas's jewelry line. "Sells the kind of pieces that you would expect to find in a cold-weather beach house in Northern California, plus they make really good coffee and chocolate cookies."

2912 Rowena Ave., Los Angeles, CA 90039, +1-323-570-0405, broomestgeneral.com.

Clare V.

Hometown handbag designer Clare Vivier's first store helped put Silver Lake on the fashion map. Her colorful leather accessories marry French chic and minimalist L.A. cool. You'll find all her colorful bags here, including the Karlie Kloss–approved Sandrine duffle, totes, belt bags, and clutches, along with her tees and sweatshirts emblazoned with French phrases, sunglasses made in collaboration with Garrett Leight, and jewelry by L.A. local Annie Costello Brown. "One of those places I can't drive by without stopping," says fashion journalist Christina Binkley. "Her bags are great quality for the price, and she single-handedly transformed my evening-bag experience with her fold-over pockets. If I don't buy a bag, I can always grab one of her fun 'Merci Beaucoup' matchbooks—they're cheery and they're free!"

3339 W. Sunset Blvd., Los Angeles, CA 90026, +1-323-665-2476, clarev.com, and additional locations.

Lake

Cute boutique offering sunny, colorful boho styles from Ace & Jig, Maison Scotch, Matta, Humanoid, Isabel Marant Étoile, Iro, and Ulla Johnson, alongside Petit Bateau T-shirts and Jerome Dreyfuss bags, plus throw pillows, objets, and perfumes. Grab a coffee at L.A. Mill two doors down.

1618½ Silver Lake Blvd., Los Angeles, CA 90026, +1-323-664-6522, lakeboutique.com.

Mohawk General Store

Started by husband-and-wife team Kevin and Bo Carney, this spare but warm boutique is the cornerstone of the Sunset Junction retail scene, offering arty, minimalist clothing and accessories from a mix of local (Jesse Kamm, Raquel Allegra, Building Block, Black Crane), national (Apiece Apart, Engineered Garments, Rachel Comey, Mansur Gavriel), and international brands (Lemaire, Carven, A Détacher, Comme des Garçons, Dries Van Noten). The boutique also sells mid-century furniture, vinyl records, design books, and apothecary items. Stylist Jessica de Ruiter is a regular, and Nasty Gal's Sophia Amoruso likes to stop by after brunch at Cafe Stella. The men's store next door has elevated basics by Engineered Garments, Dries Van Noten, Gitman Bros., and more.

4011 W. Sunset Blvd., Los Angeles, CA 90029, +1-323-669-1601, mohawkgeneralstore.com., and an additional location in Pasadena.

Steven Alan Outpost

This is the permanent sale outpost for the chain of boutiques offering well-made, often American-manufactured men's and women's clothing from Apolis, RRL, Our Legacy, Rachel Comey, and more, with a smattering of Isabel Marant, A.P.C., Acne, and Apiece Apart. "A great place to buy all the women's and menswear of Steven Alan's regular stores, at discount," says fashion journalist Christina Binkley. "I never know what I'll find there—could be a snuggly sweater for my husband, or socks for myself, or a blouse."

1937½ Hillhurst Ave., Los Angeles, CA 90027, +1-323-667-9500, stevenalan.com.

Tavin

Opened in 2009 in Echo Park, Erin Tavin's vintage goldmine carries clothing from Victorian-era pieces to present day. There's also a strong collection of 1960s and '70s pieces, including Indian and Afghan dresses. Most items are in the $200-and-up range, though there is an "under $100" section.

1543 Echo Park Ave., Los Angeles, CA 90026, +1-213-482-5832, tavinboutique .com.

Few designers are as closely tied to California as Kate and Laura Mulleavy of Rodarte. The sisters started their label in 2005 out of their parents' Pasadena guesthouse. Since then, they've designed costumes for the film Black Swan*, dressed celebrities for the red carpet (including Dakota Fanning, Kirsten Dunst, and Katy Perry), and won numerous awards for their multilayered runway collections, spun from memories of trips to the Redwood National Park, the Santa Cruz boardwalk, and Caffe Trieste in San Francisco's North Beach. More than a decade later, the Mulleavys still live together in Pasadena. Here are their shopping favorites in their 'hood.*

Laura: For vintage, Carmen Hawk, who used to be the designer of Jovovich-Hawk. Her store, **AVALON VINTAGE** in Eagle Rock, is amazing. She also has the best Instagram page.

Kate: It was our dad's birthday, and up on the wall were these mushroom candles from the 1970s. We had to get them because (a) our dad is a mushroom guy, and (b) he loves candles. Basically, Carmen has great stuff that always has a story.

Laura: We grew up going to the **HUNTINGTON LIBRARY GIFT SHOP** because our grandmother was a docent. Over the years, we discovered how much better it is than other museum gift shops. The **NORTON SIMON MUSEUM** also has a great bookstore.

Kate: They sell you bottles of wine and you can go sit outside. It's like being in Europe. I got my favorite jean jacket at **VIRGIL NORMAL,** which is owned by our friend stylist Shirley Kurata. My favorite bookstore in L.A. is **CARAVAN BOOK STORE.** It's right near the Biltmore Hotel downtown. It's a little jewel box specializing in Western America books, from Jack Keruoac to westward expansion.

AVALON VINTAGE, 106 North Ave. 56, Los Angeles, CA 90042, +1-323-309-7717.

VIRGIL NORMAL, 4157 Normal Ave., Los Angeles, CA 90029, +1-323-741-8489, virgilnormal.com.

THE HUNTINGTON STORE, 1151 Oxford Rd., San Marino, CA 91108, +1-626-405-2142, thehuntingtonstore.org.

NORTON SIMON MUSEUM STORE, 411 W. Colorado Blvd., Pasadena, CA 91105, +1-626-449-6840, store.nortonsimon.org.

CARAVAN BOOK STORE, 550 S. Grand Ave., Los Angeles, CA 90071,

PASADENA/DOWNTOWN/EAST OF DOWNTOWN

Acne Studios

Acne (an acronym for Ambition to Create Novel Expression) was founded in 1996 in Stockholm by musician-turned-fashion designer Jonny Johansson. The brand has boutiques around the world—but the L.A. outpost is special. Opened in 2013 in the historic art deco Eastern Columbia Building on Broadway, it helped cement the gentrification of downtown L.A. and draw other high-end retailers to the neighborhood. "My go-to for everything," says blogger Chriselle Lim of this hipster haven, with denim, cool boots, and coats. "They are connected to iL caffe, which is a great spot to pick up my daily coffee and/or to have a meeting. They also have a very cute floral shop right across the street that just opened up. One-stop shop!"

855 S. Broadway, Los Angeles, +1-213-243-0960, acnestudios.com, and additional locations.

Alchemy Works

A retail, gallery, and events space with the added bonus of a Warby Parker showroom. You'll find everything from Will Adler photographs and boards by Almond Surfboards to Miansai bracelets and Martiniano shoes. Owned by Raan Parton (cofounder of Apolis, below) and his wife, Lindsay.

826 E. 3rd St., Los Angeles, CA 90013, +1-323-487-1497, alchemyworks.us.

Apolis

The new uniform of the creative class, Apolis's relaxed menswear includes indigo-dyed boiled-wool blazers, slim-cut cotton canvas utility pants, and washed oxford button-downs with do-gooder appeal. L.A.–based founders —and brothers—Raan and Shea Parton scour the globe for artisanal manufacturers to produce their designs using the highest social and environmental standards. "They have simple styles mainly for men, but much of it could be labeled unisex," says costume designer and author Tracy Tynan. "Some terrific indigo-dyed items like a soft, cozy alpaca cardigan." This is their flagship, located in downtown L.A.'s trendy Arts District.

806 E. 3rd St., Los Angeles, CA 90013, +1-213-613-9626, apolisglobal.com, and an additional location in New York City.

Building Block

The West Coast's cool-girl leathergoods brand opened its first store in downtown L.A.'s burgeoning Chinatown in 2016, showcasing its full range of industrial design–minded accessories. The store's design was inspired by the seminal 1934 Museum of Modern Art exhibition,

"Machine Age," which put industrially designed objects like springs, ball bearings, and propellers in the context of an art museum. Bags hang from oversized springs on the walls, and sit on beds of foam balls in planters.

970 N. Broadway, Los Angeles 90012, +1-323-803-3420 building-block.com.

Casa Bernal

Located on Olvera Street, known as the birthplace of the city, where a Mexican marketplace re-creates old Los Angeles with structures, painted stalls, street vendors, cafés, restaurants, and gift shops.

Casa Bernal has been open since 1944, selling embroidered Mexican blouses, charro suits, handblown glassware, serapes, blankets, paper flowers, baskets, and more. This is accessories designer Sally Perrin's go-to for traditional Mexican clothing.

W-23 Olvera St., Los Angeles, CA 90012, +1-213-687-4568, casabernalstore.com.

Daiso Japan

Japanese version of a dollar store, with 8,000 square feet of goodies for the home, bath, and closet, many priced at about $1.50 each. "So fun to wander through and pick up everything from my favorite green tea to toilet scrubbers and makeup sponges," says fashion journalist Melissa Magsaysay. "The brightly lit environment and the shelves packed with colorful products in adorable packaging is a sensory overload in the best way imaginable." There are numerous locations in the L.A. area alone; this one in Little Tokyo is well worth browsing.

333 S. Alameda St., at the Little Tokyo Galleria, Los Angeles, CA 90013, +1-213-265-7821, daisoglobal.com, and additional locations.

Replika Vintage

"The guy that runs it has an incredible eye," says costume designer and author Tracy Tynan. "Not cheap but everything is in mint condition. Recently, I got a wonderful Dior chiffon camouflage skirt there, cut on the bias."

1812 N. Broadway, Los Angeles, CA 90031, by appointment at +1-323-251-7613, replikavintage.com.

Shareen

Chic downtown warehouse of vintage goodness curated by former fashion editor, model scout, and actor Shareen Mitchell, who got her start at the Melrose Trading Post. A treasure trove of restored and reconstructed dresses, leather coats, tutus, and sequin jackets on racks organized by decade (1940s through the 1990s) or theme (ethnic, pantsuits, etc.), with alterations available on-site.

"It feels like a secret society for cool girls and vintage lovers," says designer Erin Fetherston. "A great resource for design inspiration and cool vintage finds," says *Mad Men* costume designer Janie Bryant. Mitchell has since opened a second store in New York City, launched a line of bridal, evening, and ready-to-wear pieces, and starred in a reality TV series, *Dresscue Me*.

1721 N. Spring St., Los Angeles, CA 90012, +1-323-276-6226, shareen.com.

Slauson Super Mall

This indoor mall is an L.A. experience, featuring a variety of vendors selling trucker caps emblazoned with sports teams, neighborhoods, bejeweled mustaches, spikes, and horns; tube socks; lace thongs; hair extensions; sneakers shrink-wrapped for safe keeping; and screen print while-you-wait NWA and Cali T-shirts. Don't miss the lady with soaps that look like slices of cake, or TF Jewelry, where you should ask for Boss Lady. She can make you a custom gold nameplate necklace or earrings for about $100 in two to three hours, and will even wrap it in robin's egg blue packaging like that other Tiffany.

1600 W Slauson Ave, Los Angeles, CA 90047, +1-323-778-6055, slausonsupermallinc.com.

St. Vincent de Paul

"A huge thrift store with a mix of clothes, furniture, paintings, and appliances. I find weird and great things here—I might come out with a dress and a couch," says Brigette Romanek.

210 N. Avenue 21, Los Angeles, CA 90031, +1-323-224-6280, svdpla.org.

SANTA MONICA/BRENTWOOD/ PACIFIC PALISADES/MALIBU

Becker Surfboards

This iconic surf-shop chainlet is a favorite for bikinis, flip-flops, Baja hoodies, and beach cardigans. The Malibu outpost is a good place to stop after a morning riding the waves or lounging on the sand. "I can do some serious damage here," says Chrome Hearts cofounder Laurie Lynn Stark. "I buy weird socks and flip-flops, and squeeze into some cheap bathing suits. I love it."

23755 Malibu Rd., Malibu, CA 90265, +1-310-456-7155, beckersurf.com, and an additional location in Hermosa Beach.

Brentwood Country Mart

This outdoor shopping center is a quintessential L.A. experience. "One of my favorite places to spend an afternoon," says jewelry designer Jennifer Meyer. "My family and I love to eat at Farmshop, and it also has a delicious selection of groceries to bring home for dinner. Broken English has

HIDDEN TREASURES

the most unique jewelry selection. Poppy Store has my favorite selection of children's clothes. I love stopping by Jenni Kayne for clothes, accessories, and home goods. Sugar Paper is my go-to for all things stationery, plus it has the sweetest little gifts. We usually finish the day with a treat from Sweet Rose Creamery—it has such fresh and creative flavors, and vegan ones, too!"

225 26th St., Santa Monica, CA 90402, +1-310-451-9877, brentwoodcountrymart.com.

Elu

"Elu has a clear, intentional point of view and understated, casual elegance," says Dreslyn.com owner Brooke Taylor Corcia of the Malibu outpost of this chainlet, featuring low-key luxe by Guidi, Uma Wang, Henry Beguilin, Rick Owens, and Vetements.

3824 Cross Creek Rd., Malibu, CA +1-310-317-6177, elubycn.com, and additional locations.

Elyse Walker

Beachy casual with a metropolitan edge, this 6,500-square-foot store has everything a woman needs to take her from carpooling (Isabel Marant jackets, Raquel Allegra sweaters, Frame Denim jeans) to a business meeting (Stella McCartney suits, Chloé separates) to a museum gala (Givenchy and J. Mendel gowns). Owner Elyse Walker, whose family was in the shoe business, puts a huge focus on accessories, including bags by Givenchy, Proenza Schouler, and Balenciaga and shoes by Gianvito Rossi and Golden Goose. "A little pocket of high fashion in the Palisades," says stylist Elizabeth Stewart.

15306 Antioch St., Pacific Palisades, CA, 90272, +1-310-230-8882, elysewalker.com, and an additional location in Newport Beach.

Hidden Treasures

There's nothing hidden about this place. Located in a house kitted out to resemble a pirate ship, it's complete with a steering wheel on the balcony and a mermaid statue and life preserver out front. The bounty inside ranges from colorful rave wigs to band T-shirts to Mexican embroidered dresses to an antique diving helmet. You can get lost for hours trying on things. A must-see, this is where Rodarte's Kate Mulleavy found her favorite vintage T-shirt of all time, with a picture of Barbra Streisand from *Hello, Dolly!* airbrushed on the back. "It's my favorite thing ever and it was under $50," she says.

154 S. Topanga Canyon Blvd., Topanga, CA 90290, +1-310-455-2998, hiddentreasurestopanga.com.

James Perse

Perhaps the most enjoyable of all of Perse's stores, the Malibu Lumber Yard outpost suits his upscale laid-back beach-luxe lifestyle brand to a tee, with its outdoor lounge chairs and a pool table. Inside, you'll find the full range of the brand's surf 'n' sand–inspired colored jersey and French terry separates, linen shorts and pants, plus furniture and home goods, bikes, and boards. Perse is the son of Maxfield founder Tommy Perse, who brought the all-black look to L.A. The two couldn't be more different, except when it comes to retail know-how.

3939 Cross Creek Rd. Ste. E-100, Malibu, CA 90265, +1-310-469-6030, jamesperse.com, and additional locations.

CULVER CITY/VENICE

Arcana: Books on the Arts

This high-end purveyor of fine art, fashion, photography, and film books is a must-visit for creatives, including Bottega Veneta designer Tomas Maier. It's not cheap, but you can find lots of first editions, including *Black Panthers 1968, Calder Jewelry,* and other eclectic items, such as a 1992 edition of Paris *Vogue* edited by the Dalai Lama. "A great source of inspiration," says accessories designer Sally Perrin. The store will ship books for you, so when you arrive home, a gift will be waiting for you, Maier says.

8675 Washington Blvd., Culver City, CA 90232, +1-310-458-1499, arcanabooks.com.

ARI SETH COHEN

RETRO ROW IN LONG BEACH

Ari Seth Cohen is the street-style photographer and creator of Advanced Style, a blog that's been documenting the fashion and style of the over-60 set since 2008. He's also the author of two books based on the blog: Advanced Style *(2012) and* Advanced Style: Older & Wiser *(2016) as well as a documentary released in 2014.*

Kathleen Schaaf's 4th Street Shop, **MEOW** always has a rack of patterned tuxedo jackets ripe for the picking. **IN RETROPSECT** has great mod and midcentury furniture, clothing, and collectibles. I always find an old Charles Schulz book or '70s embroidered pillow. My favorite pin and sliver-flecked armchair come from there. One of the best gift stores I have ever seen stocked to the brim with collections of old glassware, trophies, kitschy elves and ornaments, globes, ceramic dogs, classic board games, and treasures is **PAST AND PRESENT RETROADA.** During Christmas they have stacks of Technicolor vintage ornaments in their original packing!

MEOW, 2210 E 4th St., Long Beach, CA 90814, +1-562-438-8990, Meowvintage.com.

IN RETROSPECT, 2122 E 4th St., Long Beach, CA 90814, +1-562-433-6600, inretrospect.com.

PAST AND PRESENT RETROADA, 2001 E 4th St., Long Beach, CA 90814-1001, +1-562-434-6464.

Garrett Leight California Optical

Leight, whose father, Larry, founded Oliver Peoples in 1987, struck out on his own in 2009, opening this store in Venice Beach. His geek-chic and retro-inspired frames (each one is named after a Venice street), are a hit with Kendall Jenner, Kristen Stewart, Emily Ratajkowski, Garance Doré, and Johnny Depp. He has collaborated on frames with indie labels Want Les Essentiels, and Mark McNairy. The brand also publishes a pretty cool biannual magazine, *Spectacle*, that covers music, food, and culture.

1423 Abbot Kinney Blvd., Venice, CA 90291, +1-310-392-3400, garrettleight .com, and additional locations.

General Store

Vintage clothes, textiles, handmade espadrilles, macramé market totes, handmade ceramic cactus sculptures, brass incense burners, wooden baby rattles, and more things you didn't know you needed, all with a modern sensibility. It's hard to come out of this place empty-handed. Personal note: Last time, I bought a wood surf-wave nesting puzzle that sits on the mantel in my living room. There's also a location in San Francisco.

1801 Lincoln Blvd., Venice, CA 90291, +1-310-751-6393, shop-generalstore.com, and an additional location in San Francisco.

Govinda's International Imports

"My happy place for a peaceful lunch and authentic wares is the vegetarian restaurant and general store located within the Hare Krishna Cultural Center," says fashion consultant Victoria Brynner. Affordably priced tunics, saris, wrap skirts, colorful clutch bags, bangles, incense, pillows, and more abound at this authentic Indian shopping emporium that's been drawing the fashion crowd and celebrities to the West L.A. Hare Krishna temple since 1982.

3764 Watseka Ave., Los Angeles, CA 90034, +1-310-204-3263.

Heist

Stylish boutique with a boho bent, featuring low-key clothing and accessories by Nili Lotan, Giada Forte, Isabel Marant, Jerome Dreyfuss, Ulla Johnson, Closed, Mes Demoiselles, K. Jacques, Golden Goose. "Our favorite designers and the friendliest staff," say stylists and designers Emily Current and Meritt Elliott.

1100 Abbot Kinney Blvd., Venice, CA 90291, +1-310-450-6531, shopheist.com.

Kendall Conrad

The former fashion model's down-to-earth, SoCal-Euro-inspired accessories line features handbags, leather bracelets, and sandals in luxe materials and muted colors, plus organic-shaped sterling silver and brass jewelry. One of her best-sellers is a a zip-around pouch with tassel details that can hold an iPhone and also has slots for credit cards or cash. It comes in leather, alligator, or snakeskin. "Everything she carries is artisanal, handmade, timeless, and made in the USA," says Figue designer Stephanie Von Watzdorf of the L.A.–based talent.

1121 Abbot Kinney Blvd., Venice, CA 90291, +1-310-399-1333, kendallconraddesign .com, and additional locations.

Le Magazyn

Bringing the best of Bossa to L.A., this is a treasure trove of bags, shoes, jewelry, clothing, furniture, home goods, and art, from a range of international designers, mostly from Brazil and made by hand. Think macramé sandals and laborodite earrings.

904 Pacific Ave., Venice, CA 90291, +1-310-450-5333, lemagazyn.com.

LFrank

Earthy, elegant jewelry and lingerie by California native Liseanne Frankfurt. Lapis feather earrings, tourmaline pendant necklaces, multicolored tourmaline cigar band rings, luscious silk kimonos, and slip dresses: This is the stuff boho boudoir dreams are made of.

226 Main St., Venice, CA 90291, +1-310-452-0771, lfrankjewelry.com.

Magasin

Josh Peskowitz, the former men's fashion director of Bloomingdale's, settled on L.A. for his first independent retail venture, a 1,500-square-foot store in Culver City's Platform development (where you'll also find Linda Farrow and Aesop). The boutique features a strong mix of upscale international labels selling Peskowitz's interpretation of the men's creative-casual wardrobe, including unstructured Camoshita jackets, garment-dyed polos from Massimo Alba, cashmere T-shirts from Naadam, handmade slipper-like leather shoes by Feit, bucket hats and totes by Monitaly.

8810 Washington Blvd., Culver City, CA 90232, +1-213-458-8424.

Strange Invisible Perfumes

Venice-based natural fragrance house that uses botanical essences to create transporting scents, such as Ojai and Magazine Street, plus perfumes inspired by your zodiac sign. "I am never without their incredible botanical perfume, or any number of the excellent brands of skincare that they offer, especially May Lindstrom's line, or a flower remedy from Alexis Smart Flower Remedies," says jewelry designer Liseanne Frankfurt.

1138 Abbot Kinney Blvd., Venice, CA 90291, +1-310-314.1505, siperfumes.com.

NEWPORT BEACH/LONG BEACH

A'Maree's

A fashion force forty miles south of L.A., this waterfront Newport Harbor space invites comparisons to Peggy Guggenheim's palazzo in Venice, Italy. Boasting soaring arched windows and portholes in the floor that allow views of the fish swimming below, it even has its own boat slip for those who want to dock and shop. The modernist building was designed in 1961 by Pasadena architects Thornton Ladd and John Kelsey, who would go on to design the Norton Simon Museum. As yachts float by, sunlight pours over cases of sparkling jewelry. Racks are filled with jackets and shorts by The Row, fringed jeans by Chloé, lace-trimmed T-shirts by Sacai, oversized shirts by Junya Watanabe, and wispy Dosa dresses. The business began in 1976 as a labor of love for family matriarch Nancy Brown. Now, Brown's three daughters—Dawn Klohs, Denise Schaefer, and Apryl Schaefer—run the show. "One of the finest boutiques ever," says stylist Jessica de Ruiter. "The candles, the sunglasses, jewelry, of course," says jewelry designer Irene Neuwirth. "And the clothing and books and . . . the list goes on. I love Denise and Dawn! I feel like I'm on vacation when I'm sitting and having a deliciously healthy lunch and a coffee in their gorgeous kitchen." There's also a sale shop on Balboa Island.

2241 West Coast Hwy., Newport Beach, CA 92663, +1-949-642-4423, amarees.com.

SPECIAL EVENTS/SERVICES

A Current Affair

This twice-yearly pop-up vintage marketplace is a must-shop for designers and vintage aficionados, including Alice and Olivia's Stacey Bendet, Figue's Stephanie von Watzdorf, and A.L.C.'s Andrea Lieberman, who says, "I wish they would pop up more often." "My girlfriends and I turn it into a half-day adventure," says Nicole Richie. More than sixty vendors, and events in L.A. and Brooklyn. Co-founded by Joey Grana, owner of vintage boutique Scout.

Itsacurrentaffair.com.

DTLA Custom

This group of artists will personalize any leather good in your closet, from a Louis Vuitton tote to a pair of Minnetonka baby moccasins. They'll hand-paint stripes, initials, palm trees,

HEATHER JOHN FOGARTY

WEEKEND SHOPPING IN OJAI

As a Bay Area native, and a freelance fashion and food writer for Los Angeles *magazine, the* Los Angeles Times, *and other publications, Heather John Fogarty has shopped her way up and down the California coast.*

I'm obsessed with **IN THE FIELD**! I want everything in the store, from the moose antlers to the home stuff—Rachel Craven linens, local ceramics, vintage surfboards. The clothing edit is heaven—chic and easy pieces from Ulla Johnson, Imogene & Willie, and Beatrice Valenzuela, and Agnes Baddoo handbags—exactly what you want to be wearing around town. Laid-back, modern boho at its best. There are great men's T-shirts, too.

I love **SUMMER CAMP** for housewares, and I kind of "need" some of the Bernscott Pottery ceramics by Ojai artist Karen Scott. Great vintage Southwestern rugs and throws, and reclaimed wood frames. They have a lot of vintage/flea market finds and soy candles, tongue-in-cheek Ojai Nightlife T-shirts, that kind of thing.

Another place that's good for home stuff is **DEKOR & CO.** Really beautiful selection of Swedish beauty products, Moroccan rugs, Danish modern furniture, and artisanal teas.

IN THE FIELD, 730 E. Ojai Ave., Ojai, CA 93023, +1-310-403-4292, inthefieldojai.com.

SUMMER CAMP, 1020 W. Ojai Ave., Ojai, CA 93023, +1-805-861-7109, shopsummercamp.com.

DEKOR & CO., 105 S. Montgomery St., Ojai, CA 93023, +1-805-272-8675, dekorandco.com.

lipsticks, pet portraits, cartoon characters, or more on any leather surface, starting at $175.

+1-310-935-0477, dtlacustom.com.

Echo Park Craft Fair

Not your traditional craft fair. This twice-yearly indie marketplace founded by designers Beatrice Valenzuela and Rachel Craven in 2009 features vendors who also sell their wares at boutiques such as Mohawk General Store in Los Feliz and Bird in Brooklyn. Typically, you'll find jewelry by Annie Costello Brown, Dream Collective, and Gabriela Artigas, leather totes by Agnes Baddoo, embroidered jeans by Bliss and Mischief, and gauzy dresses by Doen. The event has helped shape the made-in-L.A. aesthetic associated with the creative communities of Los Feliz, Echo Park, and Silver Lake that has been embraced around the world.

Echoparkcraftfair.com.

Long Beach Antique Market

"Super-expansive, with hundreds of vendors and an incredibly eclectic mix of furniture, clothing, and collectibles," says Brother Vellies designer Aurora James. "Because it's a little ways outside of downtown L.A., it's slightly less frequented than the Rose Bowl, which ups your chances of scoring that hidden treasure." "The Rose Bowl Flea is more famous," says *Tomboy Style* author Lizzie Garrett Mettler, "but there are more deals to be had in Long Beach. I like to pop into Number Nine afterward for a great bowl of pho."

Third Sunday of every month.

4901 E. Conant St., Long Beach, CA 90808, +1-323-655-5703, longbeachantiquemarket.com.

Melrose Trading Post

Small but mighty, this weekly open-air flea market in the parking lot of Fairfax High School in the heart of L.A.'s

ONLINE SHOPPING TIP

"There is this website/blog called Love The Edit (lovetheedit.com) that makes navigating Amazon easy and actually chic!" says L.A.-based fashion journalist/consultant Melissa Magsaysay. "We all use Amazon for paper towels and dog food reorders, but there is a lot of fashion and accessories to be had and often at better prices. For me, the biggest draw for buying clothing or accessories on Amazon is how quickly it can arrive, because I am the most impatient person, particularly when having to wait for something I want to wear right away."

Melrose shopping district offers a vintage fix for stylist/designer Maryam Malakpour, jewelry designer Daniela Villegas, and other stylish shoppers. "Small but good quality, great for finding cool dresses for every day, very accessible and easy," says Villegas. Canadian model-turned-blogger Elizabeth Minett hits the textile stand that sells "exquisite hand-dyed prints from Mali."

7850 Melrose Ave., Los Angeles, CA 90046, +1-323-655-7679, melrosetradingpost.org.

Rose Bowl Flea Market

One of the world's best, this monthly market with more than 2,500 vendors is regular stop for designers, stylists, and fashion lovers from as far away as China and Japan. "You have to get there at 7 a.m., and you couldn't go through the whole thing in a day if you tried," says blogger Shea Marie. "You can find everything from handmade furniture, furs, vintage jewelry, and amazing vintage designer finds. One of my favorite finds was a vintage Escada star-studded belt." "There are endless options for everything you need or don't need in your closet," says designer Anine Bing. Stylist Tara Swennen goes monthly, TV fashion personality Joe Zee shows up early for midcentury furniture, and The Great designers Emily Current and Meritt Elliott scour the vendors for vintage denim, tees and Victorian dresses. This is where stylist B Åkerlund scored her single best shopping find of all time: *a life-size Andy Warhol doll.*

Second Sunday monthly, 1001 Rose Bowl Dr., Pasadena, CA 91103, +1-626-577-3100, rgcshows.com/rosebowl.

Vintage Fashion Expo

Twice-yearly haunt for vintage hounds in Los Angeles and San Francisco, featuring more than fifty dealers from around the country. Rachel Zoe, Who What Wear's Hillary Kerr, Liz Goldwyn, and Dita Von Teese are all devotees. "I have found so many unbelievable pieces, one being an amazing Oscar de la Renta, all black, chantilly lace couture cocktail dress," Zoe says. "I also found my Chanel briefcase there, which is one of my most treasured pieces."

Vintageexpo.com.

CALIFORNIA

SANTA BARBARA

Wendy Foster

Wendy Foster brought designer fashion to Santa Barbara in the 1970s and her lifestyle shop (near San Ysidro Ranch) is worth a stop anytime you're nearby for inspired, relaxed-yet-elegant pieces. Foster's retail empire, which she owns with her husband, at Pierre Lafond, also includes two vineyards, a bistro, a gourmet market, a home accessories store upstairs, and three other area clothing boutiques. (Designer Jenni Kayne singles out the Pierre Lafond store in the same complex, for "a really eclectic and inspiring assortment of home goods, such as well-designed baskets and cutting boards.")

516 San Ysidro Road, Santa Barbara CA 93108, +1-805-565-1506, wendyfoster.com.

PALM SPRINGS/PALM DESERT

Desert Hills Premium Outlets

A must-stop on the way to or from the desert, this outlet mall has everything, from the tip-top (Prada, Saint Laurent, Gucci, Valentino, Jimmy Choo, Etro, Marni) to Barneys New York, James Perse, J. Crew, Maje, Rag & Bone, Wolford, and more. Personal note: Some of my best shopping scores of all time have come from here, including a pair of Manolo Blahnik pink crocodile slingbacks I got for less than $500, and a Prada peacock-feather-covered, straight-from-the-runway hat I snapped up for about $300.

48400 Seminole Dr., Cabazon, CA 92230, +1-951-849-6641, premiumoutlets.com/outlet/desert-hills.

The Fine Art of Design

When Louis Vuitton hosted its cruise show in Palm Springs in 2015, fashionable guests such as blogger Susie Bubble found their way to this Palm Desert vintage clothing must-see while they were in town. Bubble nabbed a vintage Courrèges jacket here, and I found a fabulous rainbow-striped dress. "I have found some true gems here, an Oscar de la Renta lace blouse, an amazing velvet and taffeta gown from the '80s," says jewelry designer Liseanne Frankfurt, who grew up in Palm Springs.

73717 Hwy. 111, Palm Desert, CA 92260, +1-760-565-7388, thefineartofdesign.com.

TRINA TURK

PALM SPRINGS

L.A. designer Trina Turk has been the unofficial fashion ambassador for Palm Springs for almost as long as she's been in the business (since 1995). She's a lover of the area's midcentury aesthetic, which inspires her California resort-chic label, and its architecture (her gleaming 1936 "Ship of the Desert" weekend home has been photographed numerous times for magazines and is the brand's spiritual home).

Turk opened her first store in Palm Springs in 2002. Housed in a low-slung, glass-walled 1960s Albert Frey building, it's become a destination for stylish travelers, and has expanded to three storefronts carrying womenswear, home goods, and the Mr. Turk collection.

There are so many local gems in Palm Springs. One of my favorites is **BON VIVANT**, which has decorative accessories for the home, great vintage jewelry and, occasionally, furniture. I love Patrick and James, the proprietors, their knowledge of their vintage finds, and their enthusiasm for seeing their finds go to a good home. I would not want to describe this store as cheap, because it's not. But chic, yes—due to Patrick's amazing eye for the beautiful and the whimsical. He scours flea markets, estate sales, and church bazaars for an unrivaled selection of decorative objects for your home at very reasonable prices. **MODERNWAY** has mostly midcentury furniture, with a special love for the outrageousness and color of the 1970s. **HEDGE** in Cathedral City is a serene, graphic, and modern point of view on how to decorate your home with mostly vintage furnishings and objects. And, of course, **TRINA TURK** and **MR. TURK**! A visit to Palm Springs is not complete without a stop here.

BON VIVANT, 766 N. Palm Canyon Dr., Palm Springs, CA 92262, +1-760-534-3197, gmcb.com.

MODERNWAY, 745 N. Palm Canyon Dr., Palm Springs, CA 92262, +1-760-320-5455, psmodernway.com.

HEDGE, 68-929 Perez Rd., Cathedral City, CA 92234, +1-760-770-0090, hedgepalmsprings.com.

TRINA TURK PALM SPRINGS, 891 N. Palm Canyon Dr., Palm Springs, CA 92262, +1-760-416-2856, trinaturk.com.

METIER

SAN FRANCISCO

HAYES VALLEY

Azalea

Denim-heavy store features trendy crop tops, high-low dresses, and culottes from Alexander Wang, Ksubi, and Iro, as well as in-house label Azalea—which is priced at less than $100—also menswear from John Elliott, Stampd, and more. Don't miss sister store Rand and Statler, next door to the Hayes Street location, offering edgier, higher-priced labels such as Acne, A.L.C., Comme des Garçons Play, and Anine Bing.

411 Hayes St., San Francisco, CA 94102, +1-415-861-9888, and 956 Valencia St., San Francisco, CA 94102, +1-415-682-6988, azaleasf.com.

Bell'occhio

The chicest general store you'll ever come across, Bell'occhio translates to "beautiful eye" in Italian. "From the eighteeth-century French jewelry in its original boxes to vintage commemorative French Liberation ribbons, owner Claudia Schwartz's shop has some amazing finds," San Francisco–based model, fashion journalist, and couture collector Tatiana Sorokko says. "Scented Armenian burning papers, unique handmade stationery items, and carrot-shaped paper packages of *amandes au chocolat* are just a few items I love." Also a favorite of Martha Stewart's, it's a one-stop shop for gifts, with many things under $100.

10 Brady St., San Francisco, CA 94103, +1-415-864-4048, bellocchio.com.

Metier

Estate pieces mingle with gems by contemporary masters at Metier, a gem of a store, with midnight-blue walls artfully leafed with gold, and a curated collection of new and vintage jewelry and accessories. The owners seek out unique designers, such as Gabriella Kiss and Montréal-based Arielle de Pinto, who treats metal like fabric, crocheting sterling silver and gold vermeil into lacy chain-mail-like adornments. Pieces start at $50.

546 Laguna St., San Francisco, CA 94102, +1-415-590-2998, metiersf.com.

Modern Appealing Clothing (MAC)

"A San Francisco institution," says San Francisco–based retailer Emily Holt. "They've been around for thirty-five years and are the authority on avant-garde designers from places like Japan and Belgium. They're unafraid of wacky, which, in its own way, is very San Francisco." Men's and women's clothing by Dries Van Noten, Sofie D'Hoore, Tricot Comme des Garçons, Noir Kei Ninomiya, and Walter Van Beirendonck.

387 Grove St., San Francisco, CA 94102, +1-415-863-3011, modernappealingclothing .com, and an additional location in Dogpatch.

Reliquary

This is one of San Francisco designer Erica Tanov's local favorites, "a curiosity shop of sorts, featuring vintage and new women's clothing, jewelry, and folk art." You'll find comfy basics by CP Shades alongside vintage American, French, and Japanese workwear, Southwestern and Tuareg jewelry, and RTH leather totes.

544 Hayes St., San Francisco, CA 94102, +1-415-431-4000, reliquarysf.com.

THE MISSION

Anaïse

Great selection of hard-to-find, cool-girl labels from the US (Jasmin Shokrian, Dosa, Co) and abroad (Carven, Hache, Chalayan, Vanessa Bruno), with anti-It bags by Eatable of Many Orders and Isaac Reina.

3686 20th St., San Francisco, CA 94110, +1-408-807-9379, shopanaise.com.

Gravel & Gold

Women-owned design collective that makes whimsical, print-centric housewares (boob-print towels, anyone?) and casual clothing. The store also stocks artsy fun jewelry by Dream Collective and Annie Costello Brown, notebooks, pottery, incense, and more by indie makers.

3266 21st St., San Francisco, CA 94110, +1-415-552-0112, gravelandgold.com.

Le Point

Spare concept space opened by stylist Pauline Montupet to showcase classic-cool labels such as Clare Vivier, Ryan Roche, Opening Ceremony, Lemlem, and Creatures of Comfort.

301 Valencia St., San Francisco, CA 94103, +1-415-400-4275, shoplepoint.com.

Mira Mira

Small boutique selling next-gen indie designers with a boho sensibility, including Polder (from France), Rodebjer (from New York), and Ottod'ame (from Italy). This is where you'll find kimono jackets, diaphanous dresses, and high-waist pants from the next Isabel Marants.

3292 22nd St., San Francisco, CA 94110, +1-415-648-6513, miramirasf.com.

BELL'OCCHIO

Small Trade Company

Matt Dick's design atelier above the Heath Ceramics flagship in the Mission District produces Japanese-inspired aprons and other workwear, bags, and *shibori*-dyed apparel. He has collaborated with Levi's, Blue Bottle Coffee, and Commune Design on products.

550 Florida St., Ste. D, San Francisco, CA 94110, +1-415-570-1019, smalltradecompany.com.

Voyager

A concept store for men and women with a Japanese vibe, it stocks minimalist clothing by Priory, Shaina Mote, Black Crane, WayWay, Metier, and others; arty Scandinavian textile-driven styles by Dusen Dusen and Henrik Vibskov, plus Hobonichi notebooks, gifts, and decorative objects.

365 Valencia St., San Francisco, CA 94110, +1-415-795-1748, thevoyagershop.com, and an additional location in downtown Los Angeles.

NORTH BEACH

Al's Attire

A taste of couture in North Beach. This mom-and-pop bespoke clothing and accessories store can make everything from patchwork leather boots to seersucker suits. "A favorite for custom-made footwear," says model and fashion journalist Tatiana Sorokko. "I first met [owner] Al Ribaya in 2008, when I had the idea to make flat sandals with burnt ostrich feathers, just like the adornment of Ralph Rucci's chiffon evening gown that I wanted to wear for the gala opening of the San Francisco Opera." Shoes are built around a wooden last made for each customer's feet.

1300 Grant Ave., San Francisco, CA 94133, +1-415-693-9900, alsattire.com.

City Lights

The independent bookstore founded in 1953 by Lawrence Ferlinghetti, published Allen Ginsberg's *Howl* in 1956, inspiring a generation of nonconformist youth and propelling the Beats into international consciousness. A copy of *Howl* from here is the consummate San Francisco souvenir.

261 Columbus Ave., San Francisco, CA 94133, +1-415-362-8193, citylights.com.

PACIFIC HEIGHTS

March

"Next-level home store filled with the most wonderful pottery, enamelware, ridiculously luxurious knives and wooden utensils, hand-painted glassware, and beyond-beautiful packaged pantry goods like olive oil, marmalade, and almond butter," says Emily Holt. "Stocks some of the most amazing ceramics, wood, and leather products you could ever imagine," says fashion designer Mara Hoffman. Think spatterware, copper teakettles, and haute aprons.

3075 Sacramento St., San Francisco, CA 94115, +1-415-931-7433, marchsf.com.

PRESIDIO HEIGHTS

Betty Lin

Chic and cheerful cropped flare pants by Suno and Marni, ruffled blouses by Ellery, jumpsuits by Rachel Comey and Nili Lotan, and more.

3625 Sacramento St., San Francisco, CA, 94118, +1-415-345-8688, shopbettylin.com.

TENDERLOIN

Hero Shop

A highly curated fashion and lifestyle concept store created by former *Vogue* editor Emily Holt, it stocks women's ready-to-wear and accessories plus home, lifestyle, and tech items from established designers and local West Coast brands. Labels include Creatures of the Wind, Adam Lippes, Sophie Buhai, Myriam Schaefer, Paul Andrew, Vans, Stevie Howell, Future Glory, and Lola Fenhirst.

982 Post Street, San Francisco, California 94121, +1-917-539-1562, hero-shop-sf .myshopify.com.

HERO SHOP

JayJeffers

Vintage and made-to-order home furnishings and accessories housed in a 1910 San Francisco warehouse in the newly trending Tenderloin neighborhood. Penguin cocktail shakers, tuxedo-inspired lighters, design books, candles, acrylic trays, woven leather totes, and more.

1035 Post St., San Francisco, CA 94109, +1-415-440-7300, jayjeffers-thestore.com.

In Fiore

Old-world-style apothecary with a cultlike following. Since 1999, owner and founder Julie Elliott has drawn on the power of flowers to create her range of body balms (try the Bois de Rose), face serums, and solid perfumes.

2044 Fillmore St., San Francisco, CA 94115, +1-415-563-5000, infiore.net.

FINANCIAL DISTRICT

Lang Antique & Estate Jewelry

Fine antique and estate jewelry, from Georgian period to contemporary styles. “I don’t know why anyone would shop for fine jewelry anywhere else,” says editor-turned-retailer Emily

Holt. "They have amazing Victorian pieces and it's possible to find a ring for under $500."

309 Sutter St., San Francisco, CA 94108, +1-415-982-2213, langantiques.com.

NOE VALLEY

MAAS & Stacks

Owner Otto Zoell stocks high-concept menswear by labels such as Craig Green, J.W. Anderson, and Gosha Rubchinskiy, as well as subversive streetwear brands like Brain Dead.

2128 Market St., San Francisco, CA 94114, +1-415-678-5629, maasandstacks.com.

Mill Mercantile

Founded in 2012 as the women's counterpart to San Francisco's menswear stalwart Unionmade, this store specializes in tomboy-chic jeans by Raleigh Denim, culottes by Black Crane, popover dresses by Samuji, striped shirts by Saint James, beauty items by Aesop, and a handful of exclusives, such as indigo-dyed Tretorn sneakers.

3751 24th St., San Francisco, CA 94114, +1-415-401-8920, millmercantile.com.

ONLINE SHOPPING TIP

"I buy Everlane religiously," says Emily Holt of the online retailer everlane.com. "It's such an easy purchase because it's reasonably priced ($18 to $200 for ready-to-wear), I know the clothes are responsibly made, the designs are basic enough to wear every day but not boring, and their user experience is easy and friendly. And, because things often sell out, there's that crucial sense of urgency. But most of all, it's a SF brand so I get a little jolt of hometown pride and satisfaction with each purchase." Stylist Jen Rade agrees. "Their modern point loafers, I wear every day. If they stopped making them, I don't know what I would do. I'd have to become a dairy farmer."

HAIGHT-ASHBURY

Relic Vintage

A vintage store in the center of Haight-Ashbury with a focus on the 1920s to the 1960s. This is where vintage connoisseur Dita Von Teese found her best vintage score in twenty-five years of collecting, a 1954 Christian Dior New Look three-piece tweed skirt suit, with the Christian Dior Paris label bearing the red serial numbers. "It's silk-lined, with garters attached to the blouse. It was like a mirage when I saw it!" says Von Teese. "The owner said, 'I have something in the back you might be interested in.'" The lesson? Always ask what's in the back.

1605 Haight St., San Francisco, CA 94117, +1-415-255-7460, relicvintagesf.com.

CASTRO

Sui Generis

Sui Generis—its name comes from the Latin expression meaning "of its own kind"—is a consignment store that puts as much emphasis on menswear as womenswear, with separate locations dedicated to each. "A treasure in the heart of the Castro," says famed dandy Patrick McDonald of the men's location. "You can find fabulous pieces from Jean Paul Gaultier, Alexander McQueen, and Ralph Lauren, gently worn."

Women's, 2147 Union St., San Francisco, CA 94123, +1-415-800-7584.

Men's, 2231 Market St., San Francisco, CA 94114, +1-415-437-2231, suigenerisconsignment.com.

PRESIDIO

Susan

Owner Susan Foslien is the grande dame of San Francisco fashion retail, known for her early championing of such labels as Comme des Garçons, Rodarte, and Barbara Tfank. The store doesn't have a website, so you have to visit to see what's new from Vetements, Yang Li, and Simone Rocha. Don't miss Foslien's contemporary fashion space Grocery Store next door.

Susan, 3685 Sacramento St., San Francisco, CA 94118, +1-415-922-3685.

Grocery Store, 3687 Sacramento St., San Francisco, CA 94118, +1-415-928-3615.

ERICA TANOV

THE BAY AREA

Erica Tanov is the consummate earthy-chic Bay Area designer. A California native, Tanov launched her namesake collection in 1990. Her earliest pieces—seamed slips and chemises—reflected her dedication to fine fabrics, construction, and subtle details. Tanov opened her first retail store in 1994 in the Berkeley building where her grandfather once ran his laundry business. Her store sells raw-edge linen dresses, tie-dyed silk blouses, damask maxi skirts, and more.

Right down the street from my studio in Berkeley, **FAR & FEW** has an eclectic mix of vintage clothing, home furnishings, and jewelry. It's a good place to dig and find a treasure. **TAIL OF THE YAK** is a Berkeley institution and a must go-to when visiting the Bay Area. It has a fantastic assortment of bibelots and unusual objects, vintage and new, and a gorgeous selection of estate jewelry.

In Oakland, **TEMESCAL ALLEYS** is an indie shopping enclave where you'll find eighteen locally owned specialty shops, some with their own workspace. My favorite is **HOMESTEAD APOTHECARY**, which has the best selection of tinctures, herbs, fragrances for healing, and beauty products. On Piedmont Avenue, **MERCY VINTAGE** is a nicely edited, supercool high-end designer vintage clothing and accessories store.

My family has a cabin in Soda Springs and while my time spent there isn't usually for shopping, there is, surprisingly, a great store in nearby Truckee tucked among some touristy, not-so-appealing shops. **BESPOKE** has a nice "general store" feel. It's casual, earthy, and masculine. I especially like the pocketknife collection, both vintage and new.

ERICA TANOV, 1827 4th St., Berkeley, CA 94710, +1-510-849-3331, ericatanov.com, and an additional location in Marin.

FAR & FEW, 1643 San Pablo Ave., Berkeley, CA 94702, +1-707-490-6665.

TAIL OF THE YAK, 2632 Ashby Ave., Berkeley, CA 94705, +1-510-841-9891.

TEMESCAL ALLEYS, 49th St. between Telegraph Ave. and Clarke St., Oakland, CA 94609, temescalalleys.com.

HOMESTEAD APOTHECARY, 486 49th St. #C, Oakland, CA 94609, +1-510-541-5225, homesteadapothecary.com.

MERCY VINTAGE, 4188 Piedmont Ave., Oakland, CA 94611, +1-510-654-5599, mercyvintage.com.

BESPOKE, 10130 Donner Pass Rd., Truckee, CA 96161, +1-530-582-5500, bespoketruckee.com.

FISHERMAN'S WHARF

Art Attack SF

"Such a cool place, the art is all created by talented local artists," says shoe designer Sophia Webster. "I bought a piece there titled *Hello Frida*, by an artist named María Motta. It's a print of Hello Kitty dressed as one of my favorite artists, Frida Kahlo. It makes me so happy to have it hanging next to my desk in my studio."

2722A Hyde St., San Francisco, CA 94109, +1-415-814-3136, artattacksf.com.

Helpers House of Couture

This 100 percent for-charity, by-appointment-only boutique is run by San Francisco style icon Joy Venturini Bianchi. It features several rooms of couture, men's apparel, and jewelry, plus one room where everything is less than $100. There's also a second, more affordable boutique, Helpers Homes Bazaar.

Art Attack SF, 2626 Fulton St., San Francisco, CA 94118, +1-415-609-0658. Helpers Homes Bazaar, 900 North Point St., San Francisco, CA 94109, +1-415-441-0779.

INNER/OUTER RICHMOND

Legion of Honor Museum Store

"Museum shops are always a good idea," says designer Ulla Johnson, who praises the Legion of Honor's for unusual items and one-of-a kind gifts. "Related to an exhibition of royal Hawaiian featherwork, they had the most beautiful necklaces

ONLINE SHOPPING TIP

"Totokaelo.com does a terrific job with their online store," says fashion consultant Libby Callaway. "They integrate customers' comments and questions in a way that I have never seen on another site; basically, they post and answer folks' questions in the info section beside the garment or accessory. I love that."

made from red and white swallow feathers, all sewn meticulously by hand," she says. "You would have to travel around the world and wait weeks for an opportunity to find such a rare and almost extinct art form."

Lincoln Park, 100 34th Ave., San Francisco, CA 94121, +1-415-750-3677, shop.famsf.org.

Park Life

Started in 2006 by Jamie Alexander and Derek Song, Park Life features art and design products culled from all over the world, including witty T-shirts, skateboard decks, tea towels, David Bowie tribute pins, books, paper goods, and original art.

220 Clement St., San Francisco, CA 94118, +1-415-386-7275, parklifestore-webstore.com.

UNION SQUARE/CHINATOWN

Neiman Marcus

The Union Square flagship is worth a stop for its interior alone. The building was constructed in 1983 by architect Philip Johnson, who preserved the remarkable stained-glass rotunda from the old City of Paris department store that once stood on the same corner, turning it into a restaurant that's become a ladies-who-lunch, San Francisco tradition. "There's nothing like having a fancy little tea at the Rotunda inside of Neiman Marcus. The view is incredible," says Nasty Gal founder Sophia Amoruso. "There's definitely an old-school glamour to it," adds designer Erin Fetherston. "I love that it has a history and they maintained it," stylist George Kotsiopoulos adds.

150 Stockton St., San Francisco, CA 94108, +1-415-362-3900, neimanmarcus.com, and additional locations.

ONLINE SHOPPING TIP

"Flora and Henri (floraandhenri.com), a Seattle-based company, has been my favorite children's brand for years," says Olya Thompson. "They have a rare delicate palette that underscores children's natural, unaffected charm. Dresses of restrained, sweet beauty, perfect and extremely practical cashmere cardigans of camel, seafoam green, and buff shades. There are great paper-thin cotton long sleeve T-shirts. Pepe shoes and Derek Rose batiste pajamas are also found on the site."

NEIMAN MARCUS

Old Shanghai

This is a cut above other Chinatown stores, with sophisticated traditional Chinese wares, including floral cheongsam and beaded evening purses, hanging lanterns, silk fans, and a line of contemporary home and fashion goods (think bamboo dishware, silk pillows, printed scarves, and jewelry rolls), all at reasonable prices.
645 Grant Ave., San Francisco, CA 94108, +1-415-986-1222, oldshanghaionline.com.

Torso Vintages

This museum-like collection of vintage is beloved by stylish shoppers (Alice and Olivia's Stacey Bendet, jewelry designer Kara Ross) and well-heeled celebrities (Victoria Beckham, M.I.A., Lenny Kravitz). You'll find Dior pieces in the four figures, as well as old I. Magnin styles, colorful furs, and affordable sunglasses, turbans, beaded clutches, and enamel compacts.
272 Sutter St., San Francisco, CA 94108, +1-415-391-3166, torsovintages.com.

ONLINE SHOPPING TIP

With the launch of Olivia Kim's new shop-in-shop boutiques SPACE at select Nordstrom stores, the retail stalwart is introducing up-and-coming designers as well as more established brands that aren't necessarily traditional department store staples. SPACE also lives online at shop.nordstrom.com/c/space-shop-all, where you can find edgy items from Comme des Garçons, Simone Rocha, Vetements, Brother Vellies, and more.

Wilkes Bashford

Luxury clothier and menswear icon Wilkes Bashford changed San Francisco's style landscape when he opened his men's store in 1966. He brought Ralph Lauren, Giorgio Armani, and other designers to the area for the first time. Bashford promoted a "bold conservative" look, educating shoppers about how to wear Brioni and Versace suits; he eventually added a strong womenswear selection. In 2009, the company invested millions of dollars in a remodel of the store's seven-story town house on Sutter Street. A charming figure, Bashford lunched with legendary newspaper columnist Herb Caen and former San Francisco Mayor (and avowed fashion enthusiast) Willie Brown every Friday for years.

375 Sutter St., San Francisco, CA 94108, +1-415-986-4380, wilkesbashford .mitchellstores.com, and an additional location in Palo Alto.

SEATTLE

BALLARD

Horseshoe

Clothing and accessories with a nod to Americana style (dresses by Prairie Underground, earmuffs by Pendleton, boots by Frye).

5344 Ballard Ave. NW, Seattle, WA 98107, +1-206-547-9639, shophorseshoe.com.

Lucca Great Finds

The name says it all. Lucca carries ceramics by Astier de Villatte, embroidered pillows and accessories by Brooklyn's Coral & Tusk, Mariage Frères teas, and custom cards.

5332 Ballard Ave. NW, Seattle, WA 98107, +1-206-782-7337, luccagreatfinds.com.

Prism

Modern arty jewelry, clothing, and objets (marble necklaces by RillRill, Wonders of Washington patches, solar-powered watches, Lulu Organics hair powder, and the like).

5208 Ballard Ave. NW, Seattle, WA 98107, +1-206-402-4706, templeofcairo.com/prism.

FREMONT

Atlas Clothing

"I've found amazing old Betsey Johnson dresses, Michael Jordan T-shirts, Levi's jean shorts, and other awesomeness here each and every time," says Nordstrom VP of Creative Projects Olivia Kim.

3509 Fremont Place N., Ste. 200, Seattle, WA 98103, +1-206-323-0960.

Essenza

Owned by Becky Buford, this jewelry and apothecary shop has delicate earrings by Rockstella and Tai and fragrances by Parfums DelRae, Miller et Bertaux, and others.

615 N. 35th St., Seattle, WA 98103, +1-206-547-4895, essenza-inc.com.

Fremont Vintage Mall

Dozens of vendors under one roof selling vintage clothing, accessories, home furnishings, vinyl, Pyrex, old sports jerseys, taxidermic animals, and more. Olivia Kim loves coming here on Sunday afternoons on her way to the Fremont flea market.

3419 Fremont Place N., Seattle, WA 98103, +1-206-329-4460, fremontvintagemall.com.

Les Amis

Also owned by Essenza's Becky Buford, this darling boutique has a French country vibe, with Isabel Marant, Rachel Comey, Dosa, and Giada Forte clothing.

3420 Evanston Ave. N., Seattle, WA 98103, +1-206-632-2877, lesamis-inc.com.

DOWNTOWN/CAPITOL HILL

Nordstrom

The flagship of the department store chain has a wider selection than most Nordstrom stores, including top-of-the-line styles by Chanel, Chloé, and more.

500 Pine St., Seattle, WA 98101, +1-206-628-2111, shop.nordstrom.com, and additional locations.

Filson

"Seattle is home to heritage outdoor outfitter Filson. They still manufacture a large number of their products here in town," says Olivia Kim. The 6,000-square-foot-flagship features limited-edition items not available anywhere else.

1741 First Ave. S., Seattle, WA 98134, +1-206-622-3147, filson.com, and additional locations.

Totokaelo

This tranquil, all-white concept store dedicated to avant-garde designers—think Black Crane, Lemaire, Comme des Garçons, Dries Van Noten, Acne, Marni, and Rick Owens—is on the rise. It has expanded its floor space twice over the past thirteen years, and recently opened a New York City location. The men's, women's, and home collections are outstanding, and they dive deep into labels not always well represented in the US, including Haider Ackermann, Our Legacy, and Ann Demeulemeester.

1523 Tenth Ave., Seattle, WA 98122, +1-206-623-3582, totokaelo.com, and an additional location in New York City.

OLIVIA KIM

WASHINGTON

As director of creative projects for Nordstrom, it's Seattle-bred Olivia Kim's job to curate cool for the department store's themed Pop-In shops, whether she's discovering made-in-Africa antelope fur shoes by Brother Vellies in New York or calling on downtown L.A. design destination Poketo for quirky home products. Here are her favorite spots in her adopted hometown.

The **FRYE ART MUSEUM SHOP** has a unique and curated collection of gifts, objects, and art from local Seattle- and Washington-based artists with a superclean aesthetic.

I absolutely love **PIKE PLACE MARKET**, even if it is a tourist trap, with all their yummy food and fresh flower stands, local artist booths, amazing restaurants, and hidden gem shops—a shop dedicated to old movie posters, a Chinese cantina, hand-knit mukluks from local Native Americans, the best magazine stand with every magazine from around the world, an umbrella store, a map store, a Mexican hot sauce and spices store.

Elsewhere in Washington, the entire town of Edison is about the length of half a New York City block! But there's a taco stand, a great café, a bread store, and a couple of shops including **HEDGEROW**, a mix of eclectic finds and housewares; **THE LUCKY DUMPSTER**, a collective of local artists who make and sell their fun ceramics and homemade art objects; and **SHOP CURATOR**, a gallery and shop in one. They make their own soap and incense sticks from fresh pine oil, which apparently is seasonal so stock up when you can.

FRYE ART MUSEUM SHOP, 704 Terry Ave., Seattle, WA 98104, +1-206-622-9250, store.fryemuseum.org.

PIKE PLACE MARKET, 1st Ave and Pike St., Seattle, WA 98101, pikeplacemarket.org.

HEDGEROW, 5787 Cains Ct., Edison, WA 98232, +1-206-605-8639, christy-erickson.squarespace.com.

THE LUCKY DUMPSTER, 14011 Mactaggart Ave., Bow, WA 98232, (360) 766-4049

SHOP CURATOR, 14010 Mactaggart Ave., Bow, WA 98232, +1-360-820-9912, shopcurator.blogspot.com.

TENDER LOVING EMPIRE

PORTLAND

OREGON

Backtalk

Right around the corner from the Ace Hotel, Katie Freedle spotlights clothing and accessories from emerging designers across the US, including her own RillRill jewelry line, as well as vintage and ceramics.

421 SW Tenth Ave., Portland, OR, 97205, +1-503-477-7144, backtalkpdx.com.

Canoe

Highly curated design store where every object leaves a distinct aesthetic impression, from a Portland-made oiled leather phone holder for your bike to a stainless-steel condom dispenser.

1233 SW Tenth Ave., Portland, OR 97205, +1-503-889-8545, www.canoe-online.net.

Cargo

A 20,000-square-foot warehouse full of Asian imports and knickknacks, such as paper lanterns, blue-and-white porcelain, Buddha statues, embroidered totes from India, indigo scarves, and pens made from old electrical wires.

81 SE Yamhill St., Portland, OR 97214, +1-503-209-8349, cargoinc.com.

Field Trip

Cheery, modern-hippie lifestyle shop and community space that brings together small-batch products—moccasins, maple wood hair combs, THE FUTURE IS FEMALE T-shirts, and more—from makers in Portland, Brooklyn, Santa Monica, and beyond.

3725 SE Division St., Portland, OR 97202, +1-971-703-4523, shop-fieldtrip.com.

Frances May

A top destination for men's and women's clothing from independent labels such as A.P.C., Ace & Jig, Whit, Rachel Comey, Acne, Industry of All Nations, and Raquel Allegra.

1003 SW Washington St., Portland, OR 97205, +1-503-227-3402, francesmay.com.

House of Vintage

Vintage wonderland with more than sixty-five vendors under one roof. Room after room of inexpensive finds, including a $12 shocking-pink crochet knit top and $25 cowboy boots.

3315 SE Hawthorne Blvd., Portland, OR 97214, +1-503-236-1991, houseofvintagenw.com.

Lizard Lounge

Upscale workwear for men and women from Levi's Made & Crafted, Raleigh Denim, Norman Russell, Red Wing, and more in a historic building in Portland's Pearl District.

1323 NW Irving St., Portland, OR 97209, +1-503-416-7476, lizardloungepdx.com.

Mario's

The most respected name in specialty retailing in Portland, Mario's was founded by Mario Bisio Sr. as a family clothing store in 1960. It was transformed into a menswear store by his son Mario Jr. in the 1970s, when he brought Italian luxury labels Canali, Ermenegildo Zegna, and Diesel to the US for the first time. The first women's store opened in the 1980s, introducing Prada, Loro Piana, and Brunello Cucinelli to the area. A Seattle location followed. The best of the best is represented here, including Valentino, Stella McCartney, Gucci, Hermès, Lanvin, Chloé, and Oscar de la Renta, plus contemporary offerings from Ulla Johnson, L'Agence, Vince, and more.

833 SW Broadway, Portland, OR 97205, +1-503-227-3477, marios.mitchellstores.com, and additional locations.

Monograph Bookwerks

"A small, very special art bookstore for new, used, and rare books on contemporary art, architecture, and design, plus ephemera, unique objects, and artworks," says Berkeley-based designer Erica Tanov. "Carefully curated and handpicked."

5005 NE 27th Ave., Portland, OR 97211, +1-503-284-5005, monographbookwerks.com.

Powell's City of Books

An independent bookstore that takes up a whole city block and caters to every esoteric interest. It stocks used books, too. Personal note: My favorite find? A fashion history book titled *Furs for Men.*

1005 W. Burnside St., Portland, OR 97209, +1-503-228-4651, powells.com, and additional locations.

Pendleton Home Store

The family-owned Pendleton Woolen Mills, known both for surfer- and grunge-rocker-approved plaid shirts and colorful wool blankets, was born in Oregon in 1889, and has been rediscovered in recent years by American heritage–loving hipsters. This is the brand's "experimental" store, and it does feel younger and hipper, mixing housewares and vintage Native American jewelry and belts with Pendleton shirts, pants, and skirts.

210 NW Broadway, Portland, OR 97209, +1-503-535-5444, pendleton-usa.com, and additional locations.

XTABAY VINTAGE

Tender Loving Empire

The dream of the '90s is alive at this indie store and record label (for real). This is the source for amusing local goods, including CATS AGAINST CATCALLS totes, PBR duct tape flasks, and MY DAD'S BEARD IS BETTER THAN YOUR DAD'S BEARD baby bibs. Is it any wonder Carrie Brownstein has called this her favorite shop in Portland?

3541 SE Hawthorne Blvd., Portland, OR 97214, +1-503-548-2927, tenderlovingempire.com, and additional locations.

Una

Modern romanticism is the name of the game at this top-notch boutique, which features pretty dresses by Gary Graham and A Détacher; high-waist pants by Rodebjer; dusters by Pas de Calais; and a drool-worthy selection of minimal, modern jewelry by Monica Castiglioni, Quarry, and others.

922 SE Ankeny St., Portland, OR 97214, +1-503-235-2326, unanegozio.com.

Xtabay Vintage

Girlie-girl heaven, this boudoir-like shop full of old hatboxes and gilded mirrors specializes in vintage cocktail frocks and gowns from the 1930s to the 1960s, and is Carrie Brownstein–approved. It's also a treasure trove of vintage wedding gowns.

2515 SE Clinton St., Portland, OR 97202, +1-503-230-2899, xtabayvintage.com.

SANTA FE

NEW MEXICO

Five & Dime General Store

Set in the historic Santa Fe Plaza, this general store is a reminder of the Santa Fe of yesteryear. "Whether you need a tote bag, postcards (usually vintage dead stock), or a pair of Foster Grant sunglasses, this institution has it all," says designer Claude Morais. "Don't forget to try the Frito Pie at the lunch counter, the best in New Mexico!"

58 E. San Francisco St., Santa Fe, NM 87501, +1-505-992-1800, fiveanddimegs.com.

Santa Fe Double Take

You can always find something amazing at this vintage Valhalla, whether it's the perfect black velvet broomstick skirt, a pair of broken-in-cowboy boots, or a Native American turquoise treasure. There are several different rooms to explore, including a vintage designer space, and Hacienda (for vintage Western furniture, quilts, and the like).

321 S. Guadalupe St., Santa Fe, NM 87501, +1-505-989-8886, santafedoubletake.com.

SANTA FE DRY GOODS

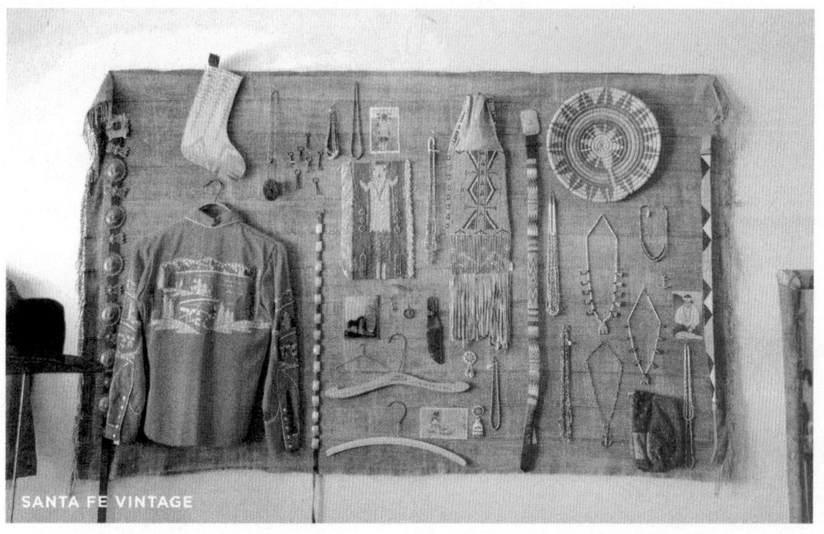
SANTA FE VINTAGE

Santa Fe Dry Goods

Located right on the plaza, SFDG has been a source for avant-garde design since 1979, when Santa Fe first arrived on the international art scene. Today, it's a favorite of LACMA Costume and Textiles department curator Sharon Takeda for browsing Rick Owens, Dries Van Noten, Issey Miyake, A.F. Vandevorst, and Monies.

53 Old Santa Fe Trail, Santa Fe, NM 87501, +1-505-992-8083, santafedrygoods.com.

Santa Fe Vintage

Santa Fe's best-kept fashion secret, this by-appointment spot is a destination for designers looking to source denim, cowboy boots, blankets, and antiques. "Every year I visit Scott Corey's vintage warehouse, Santa Fe Vintage, on the outskirts of Santa Fe, near the airport," says Sabah founder Mickey Ashmore. "It's full of so many gems, it's overwhelming. Scott is a prince of a person and a pleasure to spend time with."

7501 Avenger Way, Ste. B, Santa Fe, NM 87508, +1-505-690-1075, santafevintage.com

Shiprock Santa Fe

"The chicest turquoise jewelry," says fashion consultant Amanda Ross of this high-end source for Southwestern jewelry, textiles, and arts and crafts, as well as Visvim clothing. The gallery-like space is also filled with collectible modern furniture.

53 Old Santa Fe Trail, Santa Fe, NM 87501, +1-505-982-8478, shiprocksantafe.com.

ALLENS BOOTS

AUSTIN

TEXAS

Allens Boots

You can't miss the giant red boot above the entrance to this cowboy boot paradise with thousands of men's, women's, and children's styles, from old-school Luccheses that run in the $700 range to more-contemporary fringed booties in the $200 to $300 range, plus snap-front shirts, denim, prairie dresses, and accessories. After you shop, boot-scoot across the street to the Continental Club to listen to some live music.

1522 South Congress Ave., Austin, TX 78704, +1-512-447-1413, allensboots.com.

By George

The location on North Lamar Boulevard is the city's go-to for men's and women's high-end designers (Chloé, Jacquemus, Suno, Lanvin, Protagonist, Tome, Céline, Dries Van Noten, Novis), while the South Congress shop is fantastic for more-contemporary pieces from The Great, Maison Kitsuné, and Simon Miller.

524 N. Lamar Blvd., Austin, TX 78703, +1-512-472-5951, bygeorgeaustin.com, and an additional location on South Congress Ave.

Feathers

"A gold mine for quirky vintage finds," says Austin-based jewelry designer Kendra Scott. With its casual, boho vibe and edited collection, this store has offered such finds as a Koos van den Akker patchwork duster coat, gauzy floral-print Indian dresses, 1960s fringed jackets, and a vintage Michael Jackson *Thriller* T-shirt.

1700 S. Congress Ave., Austin, TX 78704, +1-512-912-9779, feathersboutiquevintage.com.

Friends & Neighbors

Located in an actual home, this place stocks vintage clothing, arty jewelry, planters, pipes, and other housewares, with beer, wine, Stumptown coffee, and snacks served in the backyard. Trust us, you'll want to stay awhile.

2614 E. Cesar Chavez St., Austin, TX 78702, friendsaustin.com.

JM Drygoods

Spot-on chic collection of Mexican- and Spanish-inspired clothing, Oaxacan ceramics, wax skull candles, bison wallets, Marfa Brands soap, and more goodies with a Texas vibe, opened by

BY GEORGE

former costume designer Michelle Teague.

215 S. Lamar Blvd., Ste. C, Austin, TX 78704, +1-512-579-0303, jmdrygoods.com.

Kendra Scott

The Austin-based jewelry designer started her company with $500 in 2002; today, she has boutiques nationwide. Her druzy drop earrings, colorful statement necklaces, and double rings make a perfect Austin souvenir. You can also design your own pieces at the store's Color Bar.

1400 S. Congress Ave., Ste. A-170, Austin, TX 78704, +1-512-354-4737, kendrascott.com, and additional locations.

Kick Pleat

Must-haves from modern minimalist labels including Sofie D'Hoore, Apiece Apart, Shaina Mote, Priory, and Creatures of Comfort. "A perfect edit of refined and cool fashion, from M. Martin to Lemaire to Isa Arfen," says accessories designer Lizzie Fortunato. "I never walk out empty-handed."

918 W. 12th St., Austin, TX 78703, +1-512-445-4500, kickpleat.com, and an additional location in Houston.

Olive

"Artful independent design with everyday dressing in mind," is how

KICK PLEAT

photographer and stylist Laura Uhlir describes her store, which stocks elevated basics, fun prints, easy day dresses, classic jeans, and cool jewelry. Designers include Ace & Jig, Dusen Dusen, Samantha Pleet, Whit, Wray, and Maryam Nassir Zadeh.

1200 E. 11th St., No. 101, Austin, TX 78702, +1-512-522-9462, oliveaustin.com.

Stag Provisions For Men

Hands down, one of the best menswear boutiques in the US, Stag stocks relaxed and rough-hewn Americana-inspired suiting and workwear by Alex Mill, General Assembly, Rogue Territory, RRL, and Levi's Made & Crafted alongside one-of-a-kind vintage furniture pieces, artwork, taxidermic animals, bags, belts, vintage books, classic vinyl albums, and more. This is the original location.

1423 S. Congress Ave., Austin, TX 78704, +1-512-373-7824, stagprovisions.com, and additional locations.

Tesoros Trading Company

Folk art, furniture, ethnic clothing, colorful beads, paper roses, Frida Kahlo postcards, oilcloth bags, multicolored button bags, and much more from Mexico, Guatemala, India, China, Nepal, and elsewhere.

1500 S. Congress Ave., Austin, TX 78704, +1-512-447-7500, tesoros.com.

Uncommon Objects

A gallery of antique oddities, from Lone Star belt buckles to dollhouses. "You can find anything from vintage indigo fabrics to antique anatomical pieces. It's incredible," says designer Mara Hoffman. "I could spend hours there," says designer Brandon Maxwell. "They have rooms and rooms of antiques and interesting little objects, cases and cases of vintage jewelry. Everything is so special and unique."

1512 S. Congress Ave., Austin, TX 78704, +1-512-442-4000, uncommonobjects.com.

FORTY FIVE TEN

DALLAS/FORT WORTH

TEXAS

Cabana and Canary

This pair of Highland Park stores owned by Merry Vose caters to students at neighboring Southern Methodist University. Cabana is beachy, with K. Jacques sandals, Mother denim, and Frank & Eileen shirts, while Canary stocks more sophisticated duds from Veronica Beard, Stella Jean, Preen, Sacai, Giada Forte, and Roksanda Ilincic.

4609 W. Lovers Lane and 4711 W. Lovers Lane, Dallas, TX 75209, +1-214-351-4400.

Dolly Python

When Jean Paul Gaultier came to Dallas for the opening of his retrospective at the Dallas Museum of Art in 2011, he discovered this vintage gem and tweeted about it. Since then, it's become a favorite of stylish shoppers, including Mary-Kate and Ashley Olsen and Florence Welch, who come for vintage clothes from the 1940s to the 1980s, old cowboy boots, vinyl records, and amazingly cool kitsch, such as velvet paintings, and taxidermic animals. "You can find everything from amber bugs, to those old hair dryers women used to sit under in hair salons in the 1960s," says style influencer Billy Fong. We're sold.

1914-1916 N. Haskell Ave., Dallas, TX 75204, +1-214-887-3434, dollypythonvintage.com.

Fort Worth Stockyards

"If you want a cool saddlebag, you don't have to go to Céline, come here," says Billy Fong, referring to the historic district—and former livestock market—just north of the central business district in Fort Worth. The Stockyards has several stores that capitalize on the city's cow town image, including bootmaker M.L. Leddy's and the Maverick Fine Western Wear, where shoppers can down a beer while they browse.

130 E. Exchange Ave., Fort Worth, TX 76164, +1-817-624-4741, fortworthstockyards.org.

Forty Five Ten

With clothes and housewares in an 8,000-square-foot historic building surrounding a lush courtyard with its own tearoom, Forty Five Ten is a legend in these parts. "The best game in town," says Billy Fong. There's something for everyone, from tried-and-true labels like The Row, Céline,

Chloé, and Dries Van Noten to edgy Vetements, Jeremy Scott, Maison Martin Margiela, and Sacai to up-and-comers Delpozo, Monse, Co, Brock Collection, and Rosie Assoulin. "Unlike many multi-brand stores, they still take risks on interesting, new designers," says designer Sally Perrin. "Great clothes, great food!" says fashion editor Karla Martinez de Salas. The store has attracted a clientele that includes Oprah Winfrey, Laura Bush, Gwyneth Paltrow, and Melissa Etheridge, and is a favorite of local celebrities Angie Harmon, Erykah Badu, and Jessica Simpson.

1615 Main St., Dallas, TX 75201, +1-214-559-4510, fortyfiveten.com, and additional locations.

Grange Hall

"A unique spot for gifts, including egg-shaped vases, Cire Trudon candles, Myriam Schaefer handbags, and Lydia Courteille chandelier earrings. There's also a florist. Every time I come, something ends up in my home!" says Cameron Silver. There's a wonderful restaurant, too, where "all the servers look like male models," says Billy Fong. "You have to get the Snob Sandwich, which has Petrossian smoked salmon, caviar, and crème fraîche."

4445 Travis St., Ste. 101, Dallas, TX 75205, +1-214-443-0600, ufgrangehall.com.

Gypsy Wagon

Cute, girlie clothing and accessories, plus home goods and gifts with a Texas/Western vibe. Come here for lacy florals and denim cutoffs.

2928 N. Henderson Ave., Dallas, TX 75206, +1-214-370-8010, the-gyspy-wagon.com.

Highland Park Village

The first self-contained shopping center in the US, this collection of shops opened in 1931 and became the model for the modern-day shopping mall. While planning the town-square-like design, original proprietors Edgar Flippen and Hugh Prather Sr. traveled to California, Mexico, and Spain to study architecture. Dior, Hermès, Chanel, Tom Ford, and the other usual luxury-brand suspects are all represented among the 100-plus stores. Both Gwyneth Paltrow's Goop and Reese Witherspoon's Draper James have hosted pop-ups here. And don't miss the great restaurants, including Mi Cocina, Bistro 31, and Café Pacific.

Mockingbird Lane at Preston Rd., Dallas, TX, 75205, hpvillage.com.

Neiman Marcus

This is the mother ship of the Dallas-based Neiman Marcus chain, located in the same spot since 1914. It's worth

STANLEY KORSHAK

stopping in for the nostalgic thrill of remembering all the innovation that the store has wrought, from establishing its own fashion awards, which brought the likes of Coco Chanel and Bonnie Cashin to Texas, to its over-the-top Christmas catalogs. Check out the vintage photos on the walls of the Zodiac restaurant, especially the ones of late store patriarch Stanley Marcus, and be sure to order the mandarin orange soufflé.

1618 Main St., Dallas, TX 75201, +1-214-741-6911, neimanmarcus.com, and additional locations.

Stanley Korshak

Another Texas institution. "They sell Prada next to cowboy boots. You can buy a Nancy Gonzalez alligator-skin bag with ostrich-skin boots to go with your Roberto Cavalli dress," says Billy Fong.

500 Crescent Court, Ste. 100, Dallas, TX 75201, +1-214-871-3600, stanleykorshak.com.

Vintage Martini

A vintage and consignment boutique that's full of 1970s-era Saint Laurent and also has a fabulous costume jewelry selection.

2923 N. Henderson Ave., Ste. A, Dallas, TX 75206, +1-469-334-0584, vintagemartini.com.

V.O.D.

The emphasis here is on cutting-edge indie labels—think Ryan Roche, Tsumori Chisato, Isabel Marant, Roseanna, and Lisa Marie Fernandez—and a relaxed aesthetic.

2418 Victory Park Lane, Dallas, TX 75219, +1-214-754-0644, vodboutique.com.

Ylang 23

Dallas's best boutique for designer fine jewelry stocks sparklers by Irene Neuwirth, Jennifer Meyer, Ileana Makri, Cathy Waterman, Sharon Khazzam, and Sydney Evan. The range includes colorful rings, edgy ear adornments, and personalized pendants, from $175 to $75,000 and up.

The Plaza at Preston Center, 8300 Preston Rd., Ste. 700, Dallas, TX 75225, +1-866-952-6423, ylang23.com.

À BIENTÔT

HOUSTON

TEXAS

À Bientôt

Betty Newton and Cristiana Anderson's two-story treasure trove has amazing jewelry from around the globe, including horn necklaces and shell and coral earrings, beaded clutch purses, and monogrammed totes, plus fun paper goods, cashmere wraps, and sandals.

2501 River Oaks Blvd., Houston, TX 77019, +1-713-523-3997, shopabientot.com.

Cheeky Vintage

This bungalow turned closet is a girlie destination for vintage clothing from the 1950s to the 1980s.

2134 Richmond Ave., Houston, TX 77098, +1-713-533-1121, cheeky-vintage.myshopify.com.

Elaine Turner

Houston is home base for the designer, whose colorful cork, raffia, and faux python accessories are available at department stores around the country and at her namesake boutiques. She started in 2000 with handbags and has since expanded to shoes, jewelry, and clothing, for an empire in the making.

2439 University Blvd., Houston, TX +1-713-255-0052, elaineturner.com.

Katia

This by-appointment-only, three-room boutique takes over half of a shopping center on Westheimer Road. Owner Denise Lucia and her daughter Katia are known for their edgy East-meets-West-Coast edit, stocking pieces by Anine Bing, Barbara Bui, Drome, Helmut Lang, Isabel Marant, and more.

5634 Westheimer Rd., Houston, TX 77056, +1-713-621-1817, katiaboutique.com.

Kuhl Linscomb

This lifestyle/home store spanning four storefronts is a one-stop-shop for gifts, including fragrances by Carthusia and LAFCO; plates by Tom Dixon and Astier de Villate; linens by K Studio, Missoni Home; and jewelry and accessories from Alexis Bittar, Me and Ro, Ten Thousand Things, and more.

2418 W. Alabama St., Houston, TX 77098, +1-713-526-6000, kuhl-linscomb.com.

Laboratoria

This hidden River Oaks boutique stocks clothing and accessories from edgy designers not often found between the East and West Coasts, such as Ellery, Rodebjer, Holly Fulton, Preen, and Simone

Rocha. A changing display of art by local artists is featured on the walls.
2803 Westheimer Rd., Houston, TX 77027, +1-832-407-2832, laboratoria-shop.com.

Little Bird

The place to find barely worn designer pieces consigned by Texas fashionistas. Hermès, Chanel, Céline, Gucci—it's all here.
1735 Post Oak Blvd., Houston, TX 77056, +1-832-767-4483, and an additional location in Aspen, littlebirdinc.com.

Myth and Symbol

Minimalist, cool clothing by Black Crane, Dusen Dusen, Apiece Apart, A.P.C., Samantha Pleet, and other arty brands, bags by Building Block, and delicate jewelry by Mociun.
2537 Times Blvd., Houston, TX 77005, +1-832-422-6984, mythandsymbol.com.

Pinto Ranch

Everything Texans need for that upscale-ranch lifestyle, including embroidered cowboy shirts, exotic leather boots, and trophy buckles. "I've gotten my fair share of cowboy boots here," says fashion tech entrepreneur Alexandra Wilkis Wilson. "I haven't figured out how to wear them yet in NYC, though. In Texas they look normal!"
1717 Post Oak Blvd., Houston, TX 77056, +1-713-333-7900, pintoranch.com.

Saint Cloud

Contemporary and globally sourced artisan-designed accessories and home goods from Clare Vivier, Creatures of Comfort, Lemlem, Gabriela Artigas, Brother Vellies, and Cold Picnic, plus embroidered Oaxacan pillows, Moroccan baskets, and more in a minimalist space.
5217 Kelvin Dr., Houston, TX, +1-713-522-0077, shopsaintcloud.com.

Sloan/Hall

Multi-category lifestyle store stocking avant-garde clothing and accessories by Christopher Kane, David Koma, Maison Martin Margiela, Sacai, Halleh, and Perrin Paris, alongside antiques, contemporary objects, fragrances, limited-edition books, and greeting cards.
2620 Westheimer Rd., Houston, TX 77098, +1-713-942-0202, sloanhall.com, and an additional location in San Antonio.

Tootsies

Houston's largest specialty store, Tootsies has 35,000 square feet of designer clothing by a lot of the majors, including Alexander McQueen, J. Mendel, Carolina Herrera, Rick Owens, Mugler, Moschino, and more, as well as contemporary offerings from Veronica Beard, Mara Hoffman, Mansur Gavriel, and others.
2601 Westheimer, Houston, TX 77098, +1-713-629-9990, tootsies.com.

CHARLOTTE

NORTH CAROLINA

Capitol and Poole

Laura Vinroot Poole created her trio of boutiques—Capitol for women's designer, Poole for women's contemporary, and Tabor for men—because she couldn't find any interesting retail options in her home state. And she brought it with her gorgeous courtyard space, punctuated by a two-story vertical garden by French landscape designer Patrick Blanc. She has an eye for what's new, as well as what works for Southern ladies, stocking Alexander McQueen, Barbara Tfank, Dolce & Gabbana, Dries Van Noten, Giambattista Valli, Rodarte, Altuzarra, Roksanda, fine jewelry, and fragrances in a space decorated with vintage furniture. "The most gorgeous dresses," says jewelry designer Irene Neuwirth. "Laura is one of my dearest friends and her shop is torture (in the best way)." "People must have thought she was completely crazy putting all that Giambattista Valli in a shopping center next to a Barnes & Noble," says Ann Mashburn. "But it is just the most fantastic space and assortment . . . and she has totally changed the way women in that city dress."

CAPITOL AND POOLE

4010 Sharon Rd., Charlotte, NC, 28211, +1-704-553-8868, capitolcharlotte.com.

Tabor

For men, Poole's converted bungalow offers Dries Van Noten, Mark McNairy, Rag & Bone, Steven Alan, and much more, plus on-site alteration, closet curation, and coffee!

421 Providence Rd., Charlotte, NC, 28207, +1-980-207-4860, capitolcharlotte.com.

ATLANTA

GEORGIA

Ann Mashburn

Pick up a pair of jeans or get measured for a custom suit, play ping-pong, listen to records, drink a Coke, and settle in for a while. Caran d'Ache pens and Musgo Real shaving creams are displayed below Sartorio suits and Isabel Marant jackets; Danish cattle horns and copies of *The Secret Garden* sit next to Laguiole knives and Mason Pearson hairbrushes; Levi's 501s and Saint James striped shirts hang alongside Sid and Ann Mashburn's preppy-with-a-global-punch clothing line.

1198 Howell Mill Rd., Atlanta, GA 30318, +1-404-350-7132, annmashburn.com, and additional locations.

Scott's Market

Monthly antiques show near the airport. "There is so much great stuff from dealers all over the South with a great mix of high and low . . . 100 percent worth making the trip," says boutique owner Ann Mashburn. "They also serve a great meat-and-three for lunch. The smartest dealers and designers go every month with a slew of new stuff."

3650 Jonesboro Rd. SE, Atlanta, GA 30354, +1-404-361-2000, scottantiquemarket.com.

ANN MASHBURN

PALM BEACH

FLORIDA

Tomas Maier

The designer, who is creative director of luxury powerhouse Bottega Veneta, also produces his own line, which has evolved from swimwear to a full lifestyle collection. He opened his first store in 2004, selling his clothing alongside art books and artisanal objects. "The best lifestyle brick-and-mortar I've ever been to," says author and filmmaker Liz Goldwyn.

38 Via Mizner, Palm Beach, FL 33480, +1-561-650-1221, tomasmaier.com, and additional locations.

VIA MIZNER, PALM BEACH

THE WEBSTER

MIAMI

FLORIDA

Alchemist

A jewel box in the sky, this arty concept shop on the ground and fifth floors of a parking garage was built by Swiss architecture firm Herzog and de Meuron. Stylist B. Åkerlund calls the Miami Design District stunner her favorite destination for "dark fashion" from Maison Martin Margiela, Junya Watanabe, Givenchy, Chrome Hearts, and more.

1111 Lincoln Rd., Miami Beach, FL 33139, +1-305-531-4815, shopalchemist.com.

Bal Harbour Shops

One of the most famous shopping malls in the world, this family-owned, open-air destination opened for business in 1965. Neiman Marcus and Saks Fifth Avenue are the anchor stores. "My Sunday ritual starts with brunch at the Zodiac Café, where they have the best popovers and strawberry butter," says fashion publicist Tara Solomon. There are more than 100 upscale stores here, including Balenciaga, Chanel, Gucci, Céline, Stella McCartney, Valentino, and Tom Ford.

9700 Collins Ave, Bal Harbour, FL 33154, +1-305-866-0311, balharbourshops.com.

Boho Hunter

Art District concept store that brings together designs from Mexico and South America including sexy cutout swimsuits by Suki Cohen, embroidered Pitusa beach bags, and Balkanica kimonos. "For unique gifts, great accessories, beach cover-ups, et cetera," says fashion editor Karla Martinez de Salas.

184 NW 27th St., Miami, FL 33127, +1-786-558-4486, bohohunter.com.

C Madeleine's

This 10,000-square-foot showroom located in North Miami Beach is a vintage lover's paradise with designer couture (Chanel, Versace) and other rare finds attracting the likes of Miley Cyrus and Lenny Kravitz. But don't let the prices scare you; there are things to be had for less than $100. "It's off the beaten path but well worth the visit, especially on rainy days," says designer Charlotte Ronson. "It's a huge space, but everything is very well organized into different eras and styled to inspire. Just the range and assortment make it overwhelming for all the right reasons."

13702 Biscayne Blvd., Miami, FL 33181, +1-305-945-7770, cmadeleines.com.

Chrome Hearts

The Los Angeles-based rock 'n' roll luxe lifestyle purveyor has stores around the world, but the 5,000-square-foot Miami flagship is the most impressive. The store features such delightfully decadent gifts as diamond-encrusted toilet plungers and 22K-gold toothpicks.

Miami Design District, 4025 NE 2nd Ave., Miami, FL 33137, +1-786-953-7384, chromehearts.com.

En Avance

Located in Miami's Design District, this multi-label boutique is always ahead of the curve in finding pieces from innovative young talent around the world, including ruffled silk dresses by Japan's Leur Logette and handwoven clutches by Turkey's ChuChuMai, Ellery, Sacai, Irene Neuwirth, Vilshenko, and Marques Almeida are also represented.

53 NE 40th St., Miami, FL 33137, +1-305-576-0056, enavance.co.

Fly Boutique

This consignment store is a must-visit for fab finds from Gucci, Jimmy Choo, Chloé, Chanel, and more, as well as funky rocker tees, ponchos, and kooky sunglasses in a Hollywood-worthy setting filled with chandeliers, vintage record players, love seats, and more.

7235 Biscayne Blvd, Miami, FL 33138, +1-305-604-8508, flyboutiquevintage.com.

Iniva Miami

Located in the trendy Arts District, Iniva is part art gallery, part concept store, featuring work by African artists, alongside African-made home furnishings, jewelry, and clothing. Look for fabric-covered glasses frames, clutch bags, shawls, and more.

Wynwood Block, Space 19-20, 2621 NW 2nd Avenue, Miami, FL 33127, +1-786-614-8380, inivaboutiques.com.

Malaquita

A showcase for contemporary Mexican designers making everything from cool knitwear to cowboy boots to woven mandalas and wicker coffee tables.

2613 NW Second Ave, Unit 13, Wynwood, Miami, FL 33127, +1-786-615-4917, malaquitadesign.com.

Miami Design District

Art, architecture, and fashion meet in a pedestrian-friendly retail neighborhood, located in what used to be Miami's furniture area. The district sprang up in the wake of the success of Art Basel Miami Beach, the American outpost of the famed Swiss art fair that draws a starry international crowd each December. The neighborhood is a who's who of luxury retailers, including Prada, Dior, Bulgari, Louis Vuitton, Maison Martin Margiela, Rick Owens, Hermès, Marni, and Van Cleef & Arpels; many stores have interesting architectural elements and their own cafés. Loewe has its only US store here. "It's outdoors, so you can see great art," says Laurie Lynn Stark, cofounder of Chrome Hearts, which has a stunning 5,000-square-foot boutique in the district with the largest living wall in the world, a gallery with rotating photo exhibitions, and a Ladurée café.

miamidesigndistrict.net.

Ramona La Rue

Hand-painted resort wear by Coconut Grove native Arianne Brown, whose one-of-a-kind silky bohemian blouses, pants, and dresses make a unique Miami souvenir.

3444 Main Highway, Miami FL 33133, +1-786-564-5286, ramonalarue.com, and additional locations.

The Rabbit Hole

No need to ask Alice, just jump in! The brick-and-mortar location of the beloved online vintage destination is now located in North Miami across the street from the Museum of Contemporary Art. You'll find everything from 1960s psychedelic floral house dresses to 1980s sunglasses.

791 NE 125th Street, North Miami, FL 33161, +1-305-892-0213, shoprabbithole.com.

The Webster

The boutique associated worldwide with Miami style, the 20,000-square-foot flagship (and first) location is in a historic art deco building designed in 1939 by famed architect Henry Hohauser. Founded by Laure Heriard Dubreuil in 2009, the store itself has become a brand, collaborating on capsule collections with Target in 2011 and Paris's Le Bon Marché in 2015. The store is an A-to-Z of fashion for men and women with an eye toward Miami's tropical vibes, from Alaïa to Yeezy, while not forgetting indie and up-and-coming names such as Vetements, Sofie D'Hoore, Creatures of the Wind, Mira Mikati, Hood by Air, and Thom Browne. "I love how they curate designers," says model-blogger Elizabeth Minett. "Awesome wallpaper and awesome clothes," says accessories designer Lizzie Fortunato. "The assortment is fantastic."

1220 Collins Ave., Miami Beach, FL 33139, +1-305-674-7899, thewebster.us, and additional locations.

NEW ORLEANS

LOUISIANA

Ashley Longshore Studio

A glittery, colorful gallery space bursting with energy, this is the home base for New Orleans local artist Ashley Longshore, whose bold, hilarious, pop artwork has made fans of celebrities like Blake Lively, Salma Hayek, and Penelope Cruz. It's the perfect place to pick up a (totally instagrammable) painting of a gorgeously bedazzled Frida Kahlo, Jesus holding a Louis Vuitton bag, or Anna Wintour surrounded by Care Bears.

4537 Magazine St., New Orleans, LA 70115, +1-504-333-6951, ashleylongshore.com.

Bambi Deville's Vintage Clothing

Swanky cocktail dresses, kimonos, Bakelite jewelry, and furs abound at this second-floor treasure trove of Blanche DuBois–worthy fashion finds embellished with plenty of beads and chiffon. Vintage Mardi Gras costumes and headdresses, too.

818 Royal St., New Orleans, LA 70116, +1-504-491-0824.

Bourbon French Parfums

This perfumery has been in the French Quarter for more than 170 years. They have their own Southern-inspired scents (Voodoo Love, Forever New Orleans, Magnolia) and also do custom blending. "One of our favorite olfactory haunts in the world," say designers Brian Wolk and Claude Morais. "We always look forward to getting lost in the dizzying array of intoxicating elixirs of love. For only $90—which includes a one-hour assessment of your likes and dislikes—the specialist will create an original essence for you, keep the formula on file, and mix and ship worldwide upon demand."

805 Royal St., New Orleans, LA 70116, +1-504-522-4480, store.neworleansperfume.com.

Clover

This newish Magazine Street boutique stocks sexy, minimalist-cool pieces by Anine Bing, Milly, Sir, L'Agence, Iro, and Frame Denim, plus slides by Avec Modération, scented candles by Maison La Bougie, and more.

2240 Magazine St. #101, New Orleans, LA 70130, +1-504-272-0792, boutiqueclover.com.

George Bass

After more than thirty years in the business, George Bass is an expert in the Southern gentleman's wardrobe. With a master tailor on the premises, alterations are available for everything from a new pair of jeans to a custom-tailored suit, and George will tell you how they're supposed to look, too. He stocks Isaia, Kiton, and Brunello Cucinelli clothing, Hamilton and Luciano Barbera shirts, Loro Piana knits, Alden shoes, and much more.

201 St Charles Ave. #103, New Orleans, LA 70170, +1-504-582-1180, georgebass.com.

Hazelnut

Old World meets modern at this fine gift and home accessories boutique owned by actor/decorator Bryan Batt (he played art director Salvatore Romano on HBO's *Mad Men*). In addition to ceramics, books, candles, New Orleans–inspired toile place mats and the like, Batt has several charming exclusives, including a brass lapel pin shaped like a king cake baby, and Laurel Wilder commemorative art-glass trays featuring New Orleans scenes.

5515 Magazine St., New Orleans, LA 70115, +1-504-891-2424, hazelnutneworleans.com.

Hove Parfumeur

Opened in 1931 by Mrs. Alvin Hovey-King, the daughter of a calvary officer and wife of a Navy commander. She spent much of her life traveling the world and expanding her love of making perfume, a craft learned from her French Creole mother. This 18th-century-style shop sells New Orleans–inspired blends (Carnaval, Creole Days, Kiss in the Dark), French milled soap (in Spanish moss and other scents), and handmade powder puffs, as well as gifts and antiques.

34 Chartres St., New Orleans, LA 70130, +1-504-525-7827, hoveparfumeur.com.

Lili Vintage

Located in a renovated Victorian house, this vintage haunt has elegant dresses, ball gowns, fur capelets, and more, with an eye toward the feminine. Great jewelry, too.

3329 Magazine St., New Orleans, LA 70115, +1-504-931-6848, lilivintage.com.

Meyer the Hatter

Venerable third-generation, family-run hat store, open since 1894. Some people consider it the best hat store in the South. Personal note: My hat-loving husband bought a straw boater, which was perfect for the heat.

120 St. Charles Ave., New Orleans, LA 70130, +1-504-525-1048.

Mignon Faget

One of New Orleans's beloved local jewelers, this is the place to go for a

MIGNON FAGET

special pair of fleur-de-lis earrings (the fleur-de-lis is the symbol of Louisiana). In fact, Faget has a whole Louisiana-themed collection (crawfish tie pin, anyone?). But don't overlook the more abstract pieces either, such as pearl-scarf lariat necklaces and honeycomb rings.

Mignon Faget, 3801 Magazine St., New Orleans LA 70118, +1-504-891-2005, mignonfaget.com.

Mimi

Housed in a 5,000-square-foot 1930s building, Mimi is the city's go-to boutique for high-end designer clothing, including Michael Kors, Derek Lam, Proenza Schouler, and Monique Lhuillier, plus shoes by Aquazzura, Tabitha Simmons, and Paul Andrew, jewelry by Aurélie Bidermann, and more. Alterations, manicures, and hairstyling services on-site.

5500 Magazine St., New Orleans, LA 70115, +1-504-269 6464, miminola.com.

Marion Cage

Handcrafted contemporary jewelry, from leather "O" ID bracelets to sculptural rosewood disc earrings, and tabletop items made in New Orleans by designer and architect Marion Cage McCollam. Worth a look.

3719 Magazine St., New Orleans, LA, 70115, +1-504-891-8848, marioncage.com.

Pied Nu

Chic Magazine Street lifestyle shop with breezy dresses by Dosa, Megan Park, Mes Demoiselles, and other indie labels, ceramics by Mud Australia and John Derian, gorgeous books, jewelry, handmade espadrilles from Spain, and more.

5521 Magazine St., New Orleans, LA 70115, +1-504-899-4118, piednunola.com.

Rendezvous Linen and Lace

Calling all Southern belles, this charming, old-world store on Jackson Square has delicate linens and lace, from napkins, handkerchiefs, and table runners to christening gowns, plus antique perfume bottles and tea sets.

Jackson Square, 522 St. Peters St., New Orleans, LA, 70116, +1-504-522-0225.

Trashy Diva

A must-shop in New Orleans. What started in 1996 as a vintage clothing store has grown into a full-fledged brand of vintage-inspired clothing nodding to the 1930s through the 1950s, designed by owner Candice Gwinn to fit modern bodies (sizes range from 0 to 24). Personal note: For less than $200, I picked up a 1940s-inspired dress in a Mardi Gras print that I treasure. Gwinn also sells pinup-worthy swimwear, lingerie, shoes, and accessories.

537 Royal St., New Orleans, LA 70117, +1-504-522-4233, trashydiva.com, and an additional location uptown.

Weinstein

What started as a family-owned men's store now caters to women with Rick Owens, Self-Portrait, Dries Van Noten, Co, Avant Toi, and other edgy labels.

4011 Magazine St., New Orleans, LA 70115, +1-504-895-6278, weinsteinsinc.com.

DRAPER JAMES

NASHVILLE

TENNESSEE

Draper James

Flagship for Reese Witherspoon's line of Southern-inspired clothing, accessories, and home accents. The white-and-Wedgwood-blue 3,000-square-foot space was designed by Los Angeles interior designer Mark D. Sikes, who also designed Witherspoon's home in Music City.

2608 Twelfth Ave. S., Nashville, TN 37204, +1-615-997-3601, draperjames.com.

Fond Object Records

Filled with new and used vinyl, vintage clothing, boots, and oddities curated by local fashion designers Poni Silver and Leslie Stevens, this funky place exemplifies Nashville's hipster scene.

1313 McGavock Pike, Nashville, TN 37216, +1-615-499-4498, fondobjectrecords.com.

Goodbuy Girls

Vintage cowboy boots, clothing, and turquoise jewelry, screen-print T-shirts, and other items by local designers.

1108 Woodland St., Nashville, TN 37206, +1-615-281-9447, goodbuygirlsnashville.com.

H. Audrey

Lily Aldridge, Gwyneth Paltrow, and Sheryl Crow are fans of this boutique, owned by singer-songwriter Holly Williams (her grandfather was OG country legend Hank Williams Sr.), which stocks everyday pieces from Anine Bing, Helmut Lang, Rag & Bone, Raquel Allegra, Veronica Beard, Ulla Johnson, and more.

4027 Hillsboro Pike, Nashville, TN 37215, +1-615-760-5701, haudrey.com.

Imogene and Willie

"Nashville is known for having a lot of small companies with singular retail spaces," says Nashville-based fashion publicist Libby Callaway, and this is one of them. The top shop for premium denim occupies a former 1920s gas station, and musicians like Brooks and Dunn, Matt Wertz, and Kings of Leon stop in for the brand's famously flattering cuts. Carrie and Matt Eddmenson opened the shop in 2009 with a belief in made-in-the-USA quality, and they have built a community around their Supper and Song event, which opens up the courtyard to live music in the warmer months.

2601 12th Ave. South, Nashville, TN, +1-615-292-5005, imogeneandwillie.com.

LIBBY CALLAWAY

FAVORITE NASHVILLE VINTAGE

After building a career in fashion journalism in New York City, Libby Callaway now calls East Nashville home. Former marketing director for Alabama fashion house Billy Reid and former media director for Nashville denim company Imogene and Willie, Callaway is the owner of a marketing consulting firm and makes frequent presentations on the subjects of style and the fashion industry.

Callaway is chair of the board of directors of the Nashville Fashion Alliance. A former wardrobe stylist and vintage clothing dealer, she is also a noted secondhand-shopping expert. Her personal style, and professional advice on the subject, has been featured in InStyle, Elle, Lucky, Us Weekly, Nylon, *and* Vogue, *and on Style.com, The Selby, and the Today show.*

Open since the late '90s, Trisha Brantley's East Side store **HIP ZIPPER** is the OG on the Nashville vintage scene. Her prices are incredibly reasonable and her selection unbelievably deep. The '60s and '70s are especially well represented.

Expensive, but Beverly Chowning from **SAVANT VINTAGE** has the best and deepest selection in town of highly collectible Americana and dressy wear from the mid- to late 20th century.

Proprietress of **HIGH CLASS HILLBILLY,** Nikki Lane is known in music circles as "the Queen of Outlaw Country"; in the world of vintage, she's got a reputation for excellent vintage Western wear and motorcycle gear.

Don't miss **PINK STAR VINTAGE.** You can find Lynda Herdelin's vintage collection at Fanny's House of Music in East Nashville and at Pre to Post Modern on Eighth Avenue. She's got everything from Victorian lace slips to '90s leather.

Carmen Jaudon has an excellent eye for goods from the 1930s through the mid-'70s, all housed in her Wedgewood Houston boutique **CLOSET CASE VINTAGE.** Lots of calico dresses and excellent collectible denim.

Every few months, Andrew Clancey and Laura Citron get a shipment of vintage dresses from Japan. Those, and pieces from model Karen Elson's personal collection, are some of the highlights to be found in their East Nashville store **ANY OLD IRON.**

I am passionate about **SOUTHERN THRIFT,** a Nashville chain of thrift stores. I've found vintage gems from Pucci, Gucci, YSL, Stephen Sprouse, Versace, and Bill Blass on the racks there, which is plenty to keep me coming back.

HIP ZIPPER, 1008 Forrest Ave., Nashville, TN 37206, +1-615-228-1942, hipzipper.com.

SAVANT VINTAGE, 2302 Twelfth Ave. S., Nashville, TN 37204, +1-615-385-0856, savantvintage.com.

HIGH CLASS HILLBILLY, 4604 Galatin Pike (back of building), Nashville, TN 37216, highclasshillbilly.com.

PINK STAR VINTAGE, 2110 Eighth Ave. S., Nashville, TN, 37204, +1-615-414-4881.

CLOSET CASE VINTAGE, 2407 Twelfth Ave. S., Nashville, TN 37210, +1-615-649-8410, closetcasevintage.com.

ANY OLD IRON, 1629 Shelby Ave., Nashville, TN 37206, +1-615-953-2502.

SOUTHERN THRIFT, 2710 Old Lebanon Pike, Nashville, TN 37214, +1-615-872-0499, and additional locations.

DRAPER JAMES

Jamie

Where the society set shops, this is the destination in Nashville for high-end designer duds by The Row, Brunello Cucinelli, Lela Rose, and Rosetta Getty. Owner Jamie Stream brought designer labels to Nashville before anyone else, and now her daughter and granddaughters are carrying on the tradition.

4317 Harding Pike, Nashville, TN 37205, +1-615-292-4188, Jamie-nashville.com.

Manuel's Custom Clothiers

Nashville's resident rhinestone expert has made custom clothing for all the music greats, including Bob Dylan, Elvis, Johnny Cash, Elton John, Dwight Yoakum, and Jack White. "I fell in love with Manuel Cuevas's embroidered blazers," says showroom owner Valery Demure of this shop, where you can also buy rhinestone-embellished T-shirts and scarves.

800 Broadway, Nashville, TN 37203, +1-615-321-5444, manuelcouture.com.

Old Made Good

Fun selection of vintage and locally made goods, artwork, and accessories, including Naughty Needlepoint hoops and custom necklaces.

3701B Gallatin Pike, Nashville, TN 37216, +1-615-432-2882, oldmadegoodnashville.com.

Peter Nappi

This leather accessory company (designed locally, made in Italy) situated in part of a Victorian-era meat pro cessing plant is one of fashion publicist Libby Callaway's Nashville faves for cool clogs and aged leather bags for women, and work boots and belts for men. The large, industrial-chic space serves as the brand's studio, store, and events space, and is filled with vintage decor.

1308 Adams St., Nashville, TN 37208, +1-615-248-3310, peternappi.com.

Two Old Hippies

Guitars, boho apparel, and gifts, plus live music five nights a week? What's not to love about this eclectic boutique in Nashville's trendy Gulch neighborhood? You'll find premium guitars, music memorabilia, western rock 'n' roll-inspired clothing, and gifts.

401 Twelfth Ave. S., Nashville, TN 37203, +1-615-254-7999, twooldhippies.com.

Two Son

This *Vogue*-approved East Nashville store is minimalist and bright, with an in-house design studio turning out denim, clothing, and accessories to augment collections by Ace & Jig, Norse Projects, Freenote Cloth, and other indie brands, and a photo booth for customers.

918 Main St., Nashville, TN 37206, +1-615-678-4953, twoson.com.

White's Mercantile

Owned by H. Audrey's Holly Williams, this general store stocks Williams's favorite cookbooks, candles, pillows, locally made bread mixes, Turkish towels, and other homey items, plus baby gifts and custom dog collars.

2908 Twelfth Ave S., Nashville, TN 37204, +1-615-750-5379, whitesmercantile.com.

Wilder

This design shop and arts space opened by a couple of New York transplants sells gifts and objects from near and far, including alpaca scarves by New York–based label A Peace Treaty, brooches by Azumi Sakata, jewelry by local artists, and more.

1212 Fourth Ave. N., Nashville, TN 37208, +1-615-679-0008, wilderlife.com.

Since the late 1990s, fashion rabble-rouser Jeremy Scott has dressed nearly every celebrity in the pop culture pantheon (Miley! Kanye! Katy!) in cheeky designs from his namesake label, as well as in tracksuits and teddy-bear sneakers from his collection for Adidas Originals. In 2013, he was appointed creative director of Italian fashion house Moschino, where he has brought his witty commentary to the runway. His collections reflect on the Barbie beauty ideal and how fast food meets fast fashion. Before Scott began jet-setting around Milan, Los Angeles, and the rest of the world, he grew up in Kansas City, Missouri. As a teenager, he spent afternoons in thrift stores, digging through military uniforms and prom dresses to assemble outfits for his friends. Even now, he hasn't forgotten where he came from and visits home often.

Kansas City has one of the best spots for iconic furniture design at Rod Parks's **RETRO INFERNO**. You will find things that are out of books, things that you have never seen in real life before, and pieces that you won't know how you lived without until having discovered them at his amazing store.

When in Kansas City, stop by **PEGGY NOLAND'S** fun fashion boutique. She changes the displays and themes a few times a year; her passion and bravado make the boutique a real experience and something completely unique.

PANACHE CHOCOLATIER on the Country Club Plaza has my favorite guilty pleasure—Choco Poppo. It's chocolate-covered popcorn (I prefer the milk chocolate version). Their chocolate chip cookies with chunks of chocolate the size of half-dollars and their hot chocolate, made with real chocolate, are must-haves for those with a sweet tooth.

RETRO INFERNO, 1500 Grand Blvd., Kansas City, MO 64108, +1-816-842-4004, retroinferno.com.

PEGGY NOLAND, 124 W. 18th St., Kansas City, MO 64108, +1-816-221-7652, peggynoland.com.

PANACHE CHOCOLATIER, 418 Nichols Rd., Kansas City, MO 64112

CHICAGO

ILLINOIS

Azeeza

Chicago-based designer Azeeza Khan has made fans of the Blonde Salad's Chiara Ferragni, Sarah Jessica Parker, Sophia Bush, Gabrielle Union and Erica Pelosini with her voluminous, off-the-shoulder babydoll dresses, satin slips and wrap gowns in silk crepe de chine and velvet, her embellished chokers, and clutch bags.

900 N. Michigan Ave., Level 5, Chicago, IL 60611, +1-312-649-9373, azeeza.us.

Blake

This minimalist mainstay stocks everything from The Row to Rick Owens, in a pared-down space that used to be a post office. You'll also find Dries Van Noten, Saint Laurent, Balenciaga, Pierre Hardy, and more at this Chicago institution.

212 W. Chicago Ave., Chicago, IL 60654, +1-312-202-0047.

Ikram

"High fashion's ambassador from the Midwest," is how the *New York Times* described Chicago's powerful retailer Ikram Goldman. A longtime advocate for young designers, Goldman was among the first supporters of American labels Thakoon, Proenza Schouler, and Prabal Gurung, and counts Michelle Obama and Mellody Hobson among her well-heeled clients. Her 16,000-square-foot boutique features a mix of American, European, and Japanese labels, including the most over-the-top-gorgeous runway pieces from Comme des Garçons, Dolce & Gabbana, Givenchy, Junya Watanabe, Simone Rocha, Moschino, Sacai, Rodarte, and Monse, along with newer names you may not have heard of yet but will be happy to discover. "Ikram's singular eye never disappoints," says Karen Erickson, jewelry designer and cofounder of Erickson Beamon. The store also has a restaurant featuring farm-to-table cooking, and an art gallery, "so you can really make a day of it," Erickson says.

15 E. Huron St., Chicago, IL 60611, +1-312-587-1000, ikram.com.

Luxury Garage Sale

"I found them on eBay originally, and then discovered their brick-and-mortar store was in Chicago when I was getting ready to head out there for *Empire*," says Paolo Nieddu, the show's costume designer. "They are a designer consignment store that has a huge selection of

MADISON HALL

clothing, shoes, bags, and accessories by the best designers, from seasons back to very current stuff. I have gotten amazing pieces for all of my ladies here."

1658 N. Wells St., Chicago, IL 60614, +1-312-291-9126, luxurygaragesale.com.

Madison Hall at Chicago Athletic Association Hotel

Occupying two storefronts along the hotel's Madison Street entrance, Madison Hall takes visitors for a trip in time with apothecary items and men's accessories that hark back to the old-school drugstores of the 1930s. There's also a women's lounge with accessories and a florist. "Somewhere great that I found without really looking for it," Tere Artigas says of the store, conceived by celebrated Chicago independent retailers Lance Lawson and Jim Wetzel, who also own Space 519.

71 E. Madison St., Chicago, IL 60602, +1-312-683-9586, madisonhallchicago.com.

Robin Richman

Robin Richman opened her namesake store in 1997, in Bucktown, laying the foundation for what would become an enclave of indie boutiques. She stocks an inspiring collection of under-the-radar, avant-garde fashion and home accessories brands from around the world, including Eckhaus

SPACE 519

Latta, Uma Wang, and Parts of Four.
2108 N. Damen Ave., Chicago, IL 60647, +1-773-278-6150, robinrichman.com.

Space 519

Lance Lawson and Jim Wetzel scour the globe for fab finds for this concept store, including Atea Oceanie dresses, Trademark basket-weave bucket bags, French cookbooks, handmade botanical prints, and more.
900 N. Michigan Ave., level five, Chicago, IL 60611, +1-312-751-1519, space519.com.

Store B

"I love to rework vintage pieces for my actors," says Paolo Nieddu. "It's fun and keeps things interesting and inspiring. I've found great long dresses here that I cut into minis, cool jewelry and bags, too. They have clothing organized by designer, which is really helpful when shopping vintage."
1472 N. Milwaukee Ave., Chicago, IL 60654, +1-773-772 4296, storebvintage.com.

DETROIT

MICHIGAN

Linda Dresner

"Her store curation rivals any around the globe," says Karen Erickson of Detroit's landmark boutique, which stocks an avant-garde modern/streetwear mix, including Balenciaga, Hood by Air, Comme des Garçons, Vetements, and Zaid Affas. Brooke Taylor Corcia, owner of TheDreslyn.com, says, "She has a great curatorial eye and understanding of her customers, which explains her longevity in the space."

299 W. Maple Rd., Birmingham, MI 48009, +1-248-642-4999, lindadresner.com.

Pewabic Pottery

"Timeless handmade tiles, vases, bowls, et cetera," says fashion writer Robin Givhan. "It dates back to the Arts and Crafts Movement, and the tiles are featured in some of the grand, architecturally significant buildings and houses around the country." Visit the studio and take a self-guided tour of this nonprofit studio.

10125 E. Jefferson Ave., Detroit, MI 48214, +1-313-626-2100, pewabic.org.

TENDER BIRMINGHAM

Shinola

This is the flagship for the made-in-Detroit retro watch, leather accessory, and bicycle brand that has been a hometown success story, bringing jobs and hipster cachet back to Motor City. The store, which now spans 10,000 square feet, is outfitted with American white oak cabinetry, chairs, sofas, and tables, a lounge area, a reference library, and a café that serves fare from local purveyors. It's just a few doors down from Jack White's Third Man Records. "It also sparked a lot of retail in the area," says Robin Givhan. "Oh, and there's an adjacent Shinola dog park!"

441 W. Canfield St., Detroit, MI 48201, +1-313-285-2390, shinola.com, and additional locations.

Tender Birmingham

The more feminine and sweet yin to Linda Dresner's yang, this boutique, owned by sisters Karen and Cheryl Daskas, carries Marni, Isabel Marant, Simone Rocha, Thakoon, Marques' Almeida, and Peter Pilotto.

271 W. Maple Rd., Birmingham, MI 48009, +1-248-258-0212, tenderbirmingham.com.

LOST & FOUND

TORONTO

CANADA

Chosen Vintage

One of the city's best-kept secrets, this store has clothing and accessories that aren't just chosen, they're "handpicked," according to the sign. "An amazing collection of cheap and chic vintage," says model-turned-blogger Elizabeth Minett.

1599 Dundas St. W., Toronto, ON M6K 1T9, +1-647-346-1993, chosen-vintage.com.

DAVIDS

"A must for shoes," says stylist Jessica de Ruiter of this 50-plus-year-old, family-owned Toronto institution. You'll find the hottest styles from Chloé, Christian Louboutin, Valentino, Sophia Webster, Charlotte Olympia, and more.

66 Bloor St. W, Toronto, ON M5S 1L9, +1-416-920-1000, davidsfootwear.com, and additional locations.

Ewanika

Designer Trish Ewanika is the mastermind of this überchic boutique, which sells her streamlined modern classics alongside items by local and international designers such as MM6 Maison Margiela, Samuji, and Hope Stockholm, plus Sophie Buhai jewelry and shoes by the Palatines and Martiniano.

1083 Bathurst St., Toronto, ON M5R 3G8, +1-416-927-9699, ewanika.ca.

Frank and Oak

Founded in 2012, this trailblazing millennial men's lifestyle brand continues to focus on tech-enabled service. It has an app with chat bots and stylists to make recommendations based on your personal preferences, and offers two-hour delivery in select cities. The Toronto flagship combines clothing with a barbershop, café, and community space. Customer accounts are synced online and in the brick-and-mortar stores for ease of shopping.

735 Queen St. W., Toronto, ON M61 1J1, +1-647-930-8711, frankandoak.com, and additional locations.

Holt Renfrew

Holt Renfrew started out in 1837 as a modest hat shop, and eventually expanded to become Canada's premier destination for luxury retail. In 1947, it hosted Christian Dior when he launched his New Look. The department store carries Tom Ford, Dior, Chloé, Gucci, Alexander McQueen, and Manolo Blahnik, as well as emerging Canadian luxury labels Greta Constantine and Sid Neigum. The flagship is in Toronto, and there are several other stores across Canada.

50 Bloor St. W., Toronto, ON, M4W 1A1, +1-416-922-2333, holtrenfrew.com, and additional locations.

Klaxon Howl

"Super hidden gem of an outpost in Toronto, where I grew up," says Citizens of Humanity women's creative director Catherine Ryu. "Cool vintage collectibles, specializing in military gear. They also produce their own line of Canadian-made men's workwear and military-inspired clothing. The entrance is located in the back alley of an old coach house."

694 B Queen St. W. (back alley entrance off Manning), Toronto, ON M6J 1E7, +1-647-436-6628, KlaxonHowl.com.

Lost & Found

Menswear and coffee shop that curates classic heritage brands including Alden, Champion, Dickies, Shinola, Steven Alan, Patagonia, and Levi's.

44 Ossington Ave., Toronto, ON, M6J 2Y7, +1-647-348-2810 shoplostfound.com.

Nomad

When Justin Bieber's *Purpose* tour rolled into Toronto, this is where he popped up with his tour merch, created by Fear of God designer Jerry Lorenzo. It's no surprise, then, that Nomad is the place to find cool international men's brands like Off-White by Virgil Abloh, Engineered Garments, and Gosha Rubchinskiy alongside Canada's own Wings and Horns, Naked & Famous Denim, and Reigning Champ.

819 Queen St. W., Toronto, ON M6J 1G1, +1-416-202-8777, nomadshop.net.

Nordstrom at the Toronto Eaton Centre

The US department store chain is slowly making inroads in Canada, and the new Eaton Centre store is worth checking out for the cocktail bar and in-store Madewell boutique (Canada's first) alone.

260 Yonge St., Toronto, ON M5B 2L9, +1-416-552-2900.

OVO

Canadian rapper Drake's flagship for his owl-festooned OVO streetwear line, much of which is made in Canada, including his collaboration with Canada Goose.

899 Dundas St. W., ON M6J 1W1, +1-416-276-0568, octobersveryown.com.

Pink Tartan

The flagship for Kimberley Newport-Mimran's Toronto-based label, known for elegant sportswear in understated, super-luxe fabrics, also carries a curated selection of clothing by other

SUSIE SHEFFMAN
TORONTO

Toronto-based Susie Sheffman has spent thirty years creating award-winning fashion editorials for Canada's leading magazines, as well as shaping the vision for Canadian brands and retailers, including Holt Renfrew, Joe Fresh, Roots, and Hudson's Bay. Her career started at age five, when she forced friends to play "store" in her bedroom. (No one left without a tissue-wrapped package and a receipt!) She's collaborated with international fashion icons, including Linda Evangelista, Jessica Stam, and Coco Rocha, and styled numerous celebrities (Rihanna, Britney Spears, Taylor Swift, and Ashley Olsen, to name just a few).

Since **JONATHAN + OLIVIA** rolled into town, I've found my shopping mecca, and built a wardrobe of all-time personal favorites along the way. Owner-buyer Jackie O'Brien is a retail risk-taker and pioneer who stocks her hip Ossington Avenue boutique with the kind of cult closet classics that cool girls (and guys) dream about. With a confident eye and wicked taste, she was the first to launch Topshop in Canada, and she carried cult favorites like Vetements and Jacquemus long before they were even whispered about abroad. Alexander Wang, Acne Studios, A.P.C., Isabel Marant, Étoile, and local designers like Horses round out the selection of clothing, shoes, bags, and jewelry that manages to hit everything on your list. If it's not there, you probably don't want it. Plus killer coats—this is Canada, after all.

The jam-packed shoe store **GRAVITYPOPE** (half a block from Jonathan + Olivia) hits all the right shoe notes, everything from Church's and Marni to Converse and Vans for men, women, and kids, plus a great private-label line. The second floor is full of clothing from Marni, Rachel Comey, Isabel Marant, Jil Sander Navy, and other killer lines whose labels you may not recognize and won't find elsewhere. Check out the all-white sneaker collection, the jewelry and leather goods plus fragrance and body care. The store originated in Calgary, and there's also an outpost in Vancouver. **GRAVITYPOPE** and **JONATHAN + OLIVIA** are the main retail anchors in this West End neighborhood that is rapidly gentrifying with a solid mix of restaurants, bars,

OVER THE RAINBOW

In terms of local midtown hits (small independents within a block of each other), **GEE BEAUTY** is a one-stop beauty bar/day spa run by former makeup artist/beauty editor Miriam Gee and her three gorgeous and stylish daughters. (You can find them at their Bal Harbour outpost as well.) Entering **6 BY GEE BEAUTY**, their teeny-tiny gift emporium, feels like you're stepping into a beach vacation. Grab Le Labo candles and fragrance, beachy caftans, books, sunglasses, and personal jewelry.

ADVICE FROM A CATERPILLAR has baby and kids' clothes—nothing cloying or cutesy, just the most perfect bite-size bits that you'll wish you could squeeze into yourself! Plus tepees, baby moccasins, vintage toys, and other delights in an übercool, airy space. ("My favorite kids' store of all time," says stylist Jessica de Ruiter.)

In the Bloor Yorkville area, which is like Toronto's Fifth Avenue, you'll find all the designer mono-brand boutiques. **SPECCHIO** has a roster of Marni, Dries Van Noten, Stella McCartney, and Fiorentini and Baker, so it's hard to go wrong—this small shoebox of a shop gets it right every season. Handsome owner Albert Moryoussef handpicks a highly personalized collection of lust-worthy, hard-to-resist shoes and boots that ramp up my heart rate before I've even walked in. (He's also known to offer hard-to-find small sizes!) Gotta love a shoe store that stocks killer over-the-knee suede boots as a basic.

At **119 CORBO,** pieces from Dries Van Noten, Céline, Haider Ackermann, Stella McCartney, Sacai, and other lusted-after labels keep company with equally drool-worthy shoes and bags in this beautifully sophisticated Yorkville shop.

Family-run denim destination **OVER THE RAINBOW** has been going strong for forty years thanks to Dr. Denim himself, Joel Carman, who understands just how important it is to get your jeans right. With an enormous selection and a genuine, friendly spirit, Carman boasts all the best denim brands and still gets down on his hands and knees to check the fit. Need an inch here, a maternity panel there? Done! On-the-spot alterations and service with a smile are the key to his longevity and success. Plus, no charge for hugs!

A couple of randoms: **HER MAJESTY'S PLEASURE** downtown is a beauty emporium that goes way beyond the blowout! You can hang out for hours in this potent, pampering space that's also part cocktail lounge and part coffee/dessert bar, and elevate your mani to the next level!

For more than fifty years, trusted North Toronto family shoe store **CIRCLE SHOES** has been serving up the kind of unironic normcore footwear that fashion people freak for. All the major shoe trends are covered, from Birkenstocks and Sorels to Minnetonka moccasins. Look closely and you might find original versions of the stacked-heel loafers and crossover sandals that have inspired designers everywhere of late. The good old-fashioned service here not only encourages special orders but also writes them in an actual notebook with a pen.

JONATHAN + OLIVIA, 49 Ossington Ave., Toronto, ON M6J 2Y9, +1-416-849-5956, and also in Vancouver, jonathanandolivia.com.

GRAVITYPOPE, 1010 Queen St. W., Toronto, ON M6J 1H6, +1-647-748-5155, gravitypope.com.

GEE BEAUTY, 2 Roxborough St. W., Toronto, ON M5R 1T8, +1-416-486-0080, geebeauty.com, and an additional location in Miami.

ADVICE FROM A CATERPILLAR, 8 Price St., Toronto, ON M4W 1Z4, +1-416-960-2223, advicefromacaterpillar.ca.

SPECCHIO BOUTIQUE, 1240 Bay St., Toronto, ON M5R 2A7, +1-416-961-7989, specchioshoes.com.

119 CORBO, 119 Yorkville Ave., Toronto, ON M5R 1C4, +1-416-928-0954, 119corbo.com.

OVER THE RAINBOW, 101 Yorkville Ave., Toronto, ON M5R 1C1, +1-416-967-7448, rainbowjeans.com.

HER MAJESTY'S PLEASURE, 556 King St. W, Toronto, ON M5V 1M3, +1-416-546-4991, hermajestyspleasure.ca.

CIRCLE SHOES, 2597 Yonge St., Toronto, ON M4P 2J1, +1-416-489-4379, circleshoes.ca.

labels such as Mira Mikati, Rochas, Narciso Rodriguez, and Tome, and accessories and gifts by Tabitha Simmons, No. 21, Castañer, Want Les Essentials, and Mark Cross.

77 Yorkville Ave., Toronto, ON M5R 1C1, +1-416-967-7700, pinktartan.com.

The Drake General Store

A traditional hotel gift shop, general store, flea market stand, and museum gift shop rolled into one is how fans describe this Toronto staple, which has since expanded to a few more stores around the city. You'll find the best of locally designed Canadian goods, including classic toque hats, "Canada creatures" kids' tees, a Canadian log-print "lumber" pillow, and more.

1151 Queen St West, Toronto, ON M6J 1J4 +1-647-346-0742, drakegeneralstore.ca, and additional locations.

The Narwhal

"A great little boutique for contemporary women's fashion," says stylist Jessica de Ruiter of this spot where Edie Parker acrylic clutches sit next to Golden Goose sneakers, and Rachel Comey linen blazers hang alongside Apiece Apart and Ulla Johnson skirts.

8 Price St., Toronto, ON M4W 1Z4, +1-647-351-5011, narwhalboutique.com.

TNT

Arguably the toniest fashion destination in town. Founders Arie Assaraf and Carrie Richmond have three locations in Toronto and one in Montréal offering men's and women's streetwear-inspired labels such as Yeezy, D. Gnak, and Vancouver-based Wings and Horns, alongside luxe mainstays Balmain, Brunello Cucinelli, and The Row.

87 Avenue Rd., Toronto, ON M5R 3R9 +1-416-975-1810, tntfashion.ca, and additional locations.

The Room at the Bay

This is Hudson's Bay Company department store's high-end section, with top-of-the-line ready-to-wear and accessories from Giambattista Valli, Balmain, Alaïa, Sonia Rykiel, and Canadian designer Marie Saint Pierre (a favorite of Sophie Grégoire Trudeau, wife of the Canadian prime minister) among others.

176 Yonge St., The Bay Queen Street, Toronto, ON M5C 2L7, +1-416-861-6251, www2.thebay.com/theroom.

VSP Consignment

Stylist and blogger favorite for designer consignment fashion finds.

1410 Dundas St West, Toronto, ON M6J 1Y5 +1-416-588-9821, vspconsignment.com.

MONTRÉAL

CANADA

Cahier d'Exercices

Sleek, industrial space with an eclectic array of women's clothing from Céline, Stella McCartney, Dries Van Noten, Junya Watanabe, and other well-known designers, as well as lesser-known names.

369 Rue Saint-Paul O., Montréal, QC H2Y 2A7, +1-514-439-5169, cahierdexercises.com.

Éditions de Robes

At the flagship for Julie Pesant's chic Montréal-based brand, you'll be hard-pressed not to find the perfect dress for work or cocktails—dresses are the sole focus. You'll find cape-back ones, trapeze silhouettes, floral lace designs, and more, and while they don't always come cheap, they are made to last.

178 Rue Saint Viateur O. Montréal, QC H2T 2L3, +1-514-271-7676, editionsderobes.com.

Espace Pepin

One-stop shop in Old Montréal for down-to-earth clothing, accessories, and rustic home design objects and furniture with an emphasis on Canadian artists and makers. There's also a lunch counter, Le Comptoir Végétarien, in the back of the store.

350 Rue Saint-Paul O., Montréal, QC H2Y 2A3, +1-514-844-0114, thepepinshop.com.

Eva B

This bistrò, boutique, and fabulously cluttered used clothing store tucked inside a graffiti-covered building is unique, that's for sure. It's a junk-lover's paradise—you just can't be afraid to get your hands dirty.

2015 Boul. Saint-Laurent, Montréal, QC H2X 2T3, +1-514-849-8246, eva-b.ca.

General 54

Originally conceived as a gallery/general store (hence the name), General 54 evolved into a boutique selling women's clothing, accessories, and jewelry with a playful twist. More than sixty Canadian labels, including Birds of North America and Heidi Martens, are represented. Located in the highly shoppable, indie Mile End area (some call it the Brooklyn of Montréal!).

5145 Boul. Saint-Laurent, Montréal, QC H2T 1R9, +1-514-271-2129, general54.ca.

Harricana

Workshop and boutique for the

CAHIER D'EXERCICES

Montréal-based brand that uses recycled fur to create cool scarves, mittens, hats, ski jackets, and even fringe necklaces and mules.

416 Rue McGill, Montréal, QC H2Y 261 +1-514-287-6517, harricana.qc.ca.

Henri Henri

One of the most renowned hatmakers in Canada, this old-school shop was founded as a family business in 1932. According to store lore, Henri Henri introduced the expression "hat trick" into hockey in the 1950s, by rewarding players who scored three goals or more in a single game with a custom-made hat.

189 Rue Sainte-Catherine E., Montréal, QC H2X 273, +1-514-288-0109, henrihenri.ca.

La Maison Simons

The Quebec City–based department store chain has locations throughout Canada, including two in Montréal. The downtown store carries international labels both well known (Philosophy, Acne, Dries Van Noten, McQ, Faith Connexion) and new (Paskal) alongside the best of Canadian designers, including Denis Gagnon, Smythe, and UNTTLD.

977 Rue Sainte-Catherine O., Montréal, QC H3B 4W3, +1-514-282-1840, simons.ca, and additional locations.

Les Etoffes

One of the city's most carefully curated boutiques, Les Etoffes has a fashion-forward point of view, stocking Samuji, Apiece Apart, Rodebjer, and other labels.

5253 Boul. Saint-Laurent, Montréal, QC H2T 154 +1-514-544-5500, lesetoffes.com.

Ssense

The brick-and-mortar outpost of the online luxury purveyor has an encyclopedic offering, with everything from Altuzarra and Dolce & Gabbana to Giuseppe Zanotti and Yang Li.

90 Rue Saint-Paul O., Montréal, QC H2Y 3S5, +1-514-289-1906, ssense.com.

WANT APOTHECARY

Want Apothecary

Launched in Montréal in 2006 by twin brothers Byron and Dexter Peart, Want Les Essentials is known for its architectural-looking bags for men and women (Sophie Grégoire Trudeau, wife of the Canadian prime minister, carries one). This store also features clothing by like-minded labels such as Tomorrowland, Acne Studios, and Maison Kitsuné, plus apothecary items by Byredo and others.

4960 Sherbrooke St. W., Westmount, QC, H3Z 1H3, +1-514-484-3555, wantapothecary.com, and additional locations.

Unicorn

Also in the Mile End neighborhood, Unicorn is dedicated to showcasing casual clothing, most of it by local designers such as Betina Lou and Melissa Nepton.

5135 Boul. Saint-Laurent, Montréal, QC H2T 1R9, +1-514-544-2828, boutiqueunicorn.com.

SECRET LOCATION

VANCOUVER

CANADA

A'hoy Goods

Launched by Jamie and Lyndon Cormack, founders of the popular Vancouver-based bag label Herschel Supply, this store features a nautical-themed apparel line inspired by the Deep Cove neighborhood and sporting such slogans as LOCALS ONLY and A'HOY OR HIGH WATER. The shop also carries classic threads and accessories by Levi's, Vans, Patagonia, Stussy, Hunter, and, of course, Herschel Supply.

4391 Gallant Ave., North Vancouver, BC V7G 1L2, +1-604-770-3100, ahoygoods.com.

Lululemon Lab

Opened in 2009 by the Vancouver athleisure giant, this concept store is an incubator for the brand's newest styles, such as bomber jackets, tunics, and onesies, designed to extend Lululemon's appeal from the gym to the street.

50 Powell St., Vancouver, BC V6A 1E7, +1-604-708-1126, lululemonlab.com, and additional locations.

Oak + Fort

Since its inception in 2010, the Vancouver-based Oak + Fort has curated collections of uncomplicated, thoughtfully designed clothing. You'll find androgynous pieces in languid silhouettes that hark back to the 1990s.

355 Water St., Vancouver, BC V6B 1B8, +1-604-566-9199, oakandfort.com, and other locations.

Secret Location

Located in the city's trendy Gastown neighborhood, this gallerylike concept store is one part retail, selling cutting-edge fashion and objets by David Koma, Ileana Makri, Osman, No. 21, Thierry Lasry, and Yazbukey, and one part modern café, where you can enjoy a six-course tasting menu.

1 Water St., Vancouver, BC, V6B 2H9, +1-604-685-0090, secretlocation.ca.

Roden Gray

Top-notch menswear store stocking everything from Thom Browne and Givenchy to Buscemi and John Elliott, from Carhartt to Engineered Garments.

8 Water St., Vancouver, BC V6B 2K8, +1-604-689-7302, rodengray.com.

Wings + Horns

Inspired by trips between Tokyo and Vancouver, this contemporary menswear label is one of Canada's best, integrating innovative fabrics with a meticulous approach to detail. Look for knit bombers, washed-linen blazers, and awesome collaborations, like deconstructed Wings and Horns x New Balance sneakers. This is the flagship.

133 West Fifth Ave., Vancouver, BC V5Y 1H9 +1-604-568-0140, wingsandhorns.com.

JENNIFER MORRISON
VANCOUVER

American actor/model/producer Jennifer Morrison calls Vancouver her "home away from home." She's been living on and off in the city often referred to as "the Hollywood of the North," since the 1990s, when she filmed the pilot of House, *the medical drama in which Morrison played Dr. Allison Cameron alongside star Hugh Laurie. She's back in Vancouver again for her current role as Emma Swan on the fantasy-adventure series* Once Upon a Time.

My favorite boutique is **MISCH** on Granville. The buyers are very consistent and always select good stuff (Isabel Marant, Forte Forte, Vanessa Bruno, Co, Protagonist).

There's a boutique called **BLUEBIRD** on Alberni that I also like a lot. They have a great jeans selection. (Plus contemporary labels like A.L.C., Derek Lam 10 Crosby, Mackage, Jonathan Simkhai, etc.)

NORDSTROM just opened in downtown Vancouver, and people are very excited about it. Nearby is the flagship of Vancouver-based **ARITZIA**. The vibe and feel of the brand is a great reflection of Vancouver style. The focus is on quality fabrics that last and affordable prices. I've taken a tour of their offices and warehouse, and find them a very impressive quality-driven and forward-thinking company.

For secondhand shops, **COMMERCIAL DRIVE** is the place to go. Store after store with vintage finds.

There are also a few great more-specialty boutiques in Gastown. I like **THE BLOCK** on Cordova Street. Consistently good finds and cool shoes and bags by A Détacher, No. 6, A.P.C., Wendy Nichol, etc.

MISCH, 2960 Granville St., Vancouver, BC V6H 3J7, +1-604-731-1017, misch.ca.

BLUEBIRD, 1055 Alberni St., Vancouver, BC V6E 1A1, +1-604-257-0700, also in Oakridge Centre, bluebird.ca.

NORDSTROM, Pacific Centre, 799 Robson St., Vancouver, BC V7Y 0A2, +1-604-699-2100.

ARITZIA, 1110 Robson St., Vancouver, BC V6E 1B2, +1-604-684-3251, aritzia.com, and additional locations.

THE BLOCK, 350 West Cordova St., Vancouver, BC, V6B 1E8 +1-604-685-8885, theblock.ca.

SO MANY SHOES
SO LITTLE TIME

MEXICO & SOUTH AMERICA

MEXICO

BRAZIL

ARGENTINA

PERU

MEXICO CITY

MEXICO

180°

This streetwear-oriented shop features locally designed T-shirts, art magazines, sunglasses, and bicycles. You can't miss the eye-catching black-and-white awning outside. Inside, make sure to take a look at the front counter made out of old VHS tapes.

Calle Colima 180, Roma Norte, 06700 Ciudad de México, D.F., +52-55-5525-5626, 180grados.mx..

Anatole 13

Fashion, food, tea, and design objets in a minimalist, gallerylike environment. Carries a variety of clothing from Mexico, the US, and Europe, and has an organic café.

Anatole France 13, Polanco III Secc, 11550 Ciudad de México, D.F., +52-55-5280-5267, anatole13.net.

Caballería

A stylish, multilevel men's marketplace (*caballería* translates to "chivalry") with an assortment of clothing and accessories, a barbershop, a tattoo parlor, and a pizza-and-beer restaurant.

Calle Havre 64, Col. Juárez, 06600 Ciudad de México, D.F., caballeria.com.

Cañamiel

This store is dedicated to showcasing styles from independent Latin American designers, including shoes by Minhk, bags by Oriana Rodriguez, jewelry by Paula Mendoza, and clothing by Julia y Renata, and more.

Zedec Santa Fe, Av. Javier Barros Sierra 540, Col. Lomas de Santa Fé, 01219 Ciudad de México, D.F., +52-55-5292-3869, canamielmx.com.

Carla Fernández

Fernández launched her namesake fashion label in 2000, with the goal of working with indigenous communities in Mexico to preserve handweaving and dyeing, felting, and embroidery techniques. Her collection, priced from $50 to $600 or more for special orders, has a look that is more avant-garde than arts and crafts. "Worth a stop for her signature wrap-this-way-and-that-way Cobra dresses alone," says fashion journalist/retailer Rose Apodaca.

Isabel La Catolica 30, First Floor, Mexico City 06000 Ciudad de México, D.F., +52-55-5510-9624, carlafernandez.com, and additional locations.

Carmen Rion

Another fashion designer who often works with indigenous communities, Rion's blouses and wraps have a graphic sensibility. Her store also carries flat leather sandals and modern silver jewelry.

Av. México 135 A, Hipódromo, 06140 Ciudad de México, D.F., +52-55-5564-1666, carmenrion.com.

Chic by Accident

French expat Emmanuel Picault's gallery, workshop, and design studio juxtaposes traditional Mexican folk objects with midcentury antiques. The gallery was established in 2000; in 2010, a design studio was added. Picault has worked on commercial and residential projects in Mexico City and Paris.

Lago Texcoco 112, Anáhuac I Secc, 11320 Ciudad de México, D.F., +52-55-5511-1312, chicbyaccident.com.

Common People

This concept shop in a 1940s colonial-style mansion in Mexico City's high-end Polanco district has been called Mexico City's answer to Paris's colette. It has three floors of clothing, shoes, and decor items at all price points from well-established international and up-and-coming local brands, including Vivienne Westwood, Maison Martin Margiela, THVM, Opening Ceremony, Avocet, and Pays. On the second floor, recharge with a Hungarian coffee at Café Budapest.

Emilio Castelar 149, Polanco III Secc, 11560 Ciudad de México, D.F., +52-55-5281-0800, commonpeople.com.mx.

El Bazaar Sabádo

Open on Saturdays from 9 a.m. to 6 p.m., this pop-up flea market showcases a selection of handmade traditional and contemporary jewelry, ceramics, decorative items, artwork, and textiles by local artisans, many of whom also sell in local boutiques and galleries. Top contemporary Mexican fashion designer Carla Fernández has a stall, and our stylish shoppers also recommend Androna Textiles "for the best Mexican traditional clothes—the quality of the product is incredible," says jewelry designer Daniela Villegas.

San Jacinto 11, San Ángel, 01000 Ciudad de México, D.F, +52-55-5616-0082, elbazaarsabado.com/mx.

El Palacio de Hierro - Moliere

Mexico's biggest department store chain with more than a dozen locations (this is the granddaddy) has a wide selection of international and local designers. "Great shop-in-shops from Tiffany & Co. to Louis Vuitton," says fashion editor Karla Martinez de Salas. Don't miss the 20,000-square-foot food hall,

THE ARTIGAS SISTERS

MEXICO CITY FAVORITES

In 2003, while studying fabric design in her hometown of Mexico City, Gabriela Artigas fashioned her first cuff bracelet out of a supermarket toothbrush, minus the bristles. Now based in Los Angeles, she has a full-fledged label, Gabriela Artigas, designed and handcrafted in L.A., which counts Carey Mulligan, Emma Roberts, and Tyra Banks among its fans. Her sister, Tere Artigas, handles sales and press for the minimalist-yet-edgy brand, which is known for its signature gold tusks and shooting stars.

In Mexico City, there is an organic restaurant and grocery store called **OJO DE AGUA**. It reminds me of a traditional fruit-and-vegetable market stall. You can buy amazing avocados or pressed juices, pastries or marmalades and preserves. For hot chocolate and tortas after a long day shopping, **ABARROTES DELIRIO** is another great find. It has a beautiful wine and mescal selection—perfect for gifts! **ONORA** sells traditional crafts and textiles in nontraditional colors that you won't find anywhere else. You can buy ceramics made out of traditional materials but designed in a contemporary way. **CASA BOSQUES** is another gem, and I don't want to forget **AVERY**, which sells super-minimal-style clothes in black, gray, or white. It's one of my favorite stores in Mexico City.

If you want to experience something truly local, **LA LAGUNILLA MARKET** is a must-visit. It's a traditional Mexican market selling antiques, furniture, art, clothes—everything you could possibly imagine! A friend of mine once found a Knoll dining room table and chairs in brand-new condition. Go on a Sunday morning, order a *michelada* (*cerveza* with lime juice and assorted sauces, and spices on the rim of the glass), and take the time to hunt for treasures.

OJO DE AGUA, Calle Citlaltépetl 23C, Hipódromo, 06100 Ciudad de México, D.F., +52-55-6395-8000, grupoojodeagua.com.mx.

ABARROTES DELIRIO, Colima 114, Cuauhtemoc, Roma Norte, 06700 Ciudad de México, D.F., +52-55-5264-1468, abarrotes.delirio.mx.

ONORA, Lope de Vega 330, Polanco V Secc, 11560 Ciudad de México, D.F., +52-55-5203-0938, onoracasa.com.

CASA BOSQUES, Calle Córdoba 25, Roma Norte., 06700 Ciudad de México, D.F., +52-55-6378-2976, casabosques.net.

AVERY, Córdoba 25, Roma Norte, 06700 Ciudad de México, D.F., +52-55-6378-2976 Ext. 105, averyshop.com.

LA LAGUNILLA MARKET, La Lagunilla, 06020 Ciudad de México, D.F.

a terrific spot for hot chocolate and churros, and pretty much everything else you'd ever want to eat.

Av. Moliere 222, Polanco III Secc, 11570 Ciudad de México, D.F., +52-55-5283-7200, elpalaciodehierro.com.

Fábrica Social

This organization with a fair-trade philosophy helps train Mexican women who are already skilled in traditional textile work become more proficient in fashion design, so that they can produce more commercial pieces. Price tags include the artisan's name and the number of hours it took for her to make the garment.

Calle Isabel la Catolica 30, Centro Histórico, 06000 Ciudad de México, D.F., +52-55-5512-0730, fabricasocial.org.

Goodbye Folk

One of Mexico City's most beloved fashion haunts, this vintage store and hair salon is known for its handmade brogues, some of which incorporate serape blanket remnants or floral-print fabric. "Handmade shoes and redone vintage at great prices," says fashion editor Karla Martinez de Salas.

Calle Colima 198, Cuauhtémoc, 06700 Ciudad de México, D.F., +52-55-5525-4109, goodbyefolk.com.

Lago DF

This arty boutique by local designers Regina Barrios, of the jewelry brand Ishi, and Alessandro Cerutti, of Boca MMXII, features their favorites from Mexico and the rest of the world.

Calle Emilio Castelar 209, Polanco V Secc, 11560 Ciudad de México, D.F., +52-55-655-2059, lagodf.com.

Lemon Chic

Right next door to many of the city's luxury-brand stores on Masaryk, Lemon Chic has a great assortment of party dresses, rompers, and must-have denim by contemporary brands such as Alice and Olivia, Iro, Frame Denim, and Rebecca Taylor.

Masaryk 311, Third Floor N. 4 , Polanco, IV Secc, 11550 Ciudad de D. F., +52-55-9155-5318, lemonchic.com.

Onora

One of Mexico City's coolest design stores, Onora strikes a balance between traditional and contemporary in their shop, which stocks modern-looking black clay candleholders from Oaxaca, table runners from Chiapas, serving dishes from Puebla, and more.

Lope de Vega 330, Polanco V Secc, 11560 Ciudad de México, D.F., +52-55-5203-0938, onoracasa.com.

Pineda Covalin

This Mexico City–based brand has gone global with its Hermès-style silk ties, scarves, clothing, bags, and small accessories in colorful, artisan-designed prints inspired by Latin American culture, with sophisticated takes on sugar skulls, dream catchers, huipil embroidery, and more. This is the headquarters; there are also boutiques across Mexico and around the world.

Sinaloa 237, Roma Norte, 06700 Ciudad de México, D.F., +52-55-5256-3606, pinedacovalin.com.

Raquel Orozco

Caters to sophisticated Mexican ladies with sexy, cape-back Halston-esque cocktail dresses, jumpsuits, and sleek coats, plus bold, modern accessories, all at prices that won't break the bank.

Calle Emilio Castelar 2271-B, Polanco IV Secc, 11550 Ciudad de México, D.F., +52-55-5280-5081, raquelorozco.mx.

Roma Quince

Housed in a century-old mansion, this concept store features individual fashion boutiques (including the Mexico City–based Les Filles du Nord brand of cute resortwear and tote bags), antique furniture, luxury linens, a café, and a gelato stand.

Medellín 67, Roma Norte, Ciudad de México, D.F., +52-55-5207-8682.

Sandra Weil

One of Mexico City's most talented young designers, Weil founded her line in 2008 with a vision of creating contemporary, feminine clothing and gowns with subtle nods to her South American roots. Think colorful tweed bustiers, navy zigzag-stripe organza blouses, and lace maxi dresses with appliquéd sequins.

Calle Emilio Castelar 185, Polanco III Secc, 11560 Ciudad de México, D.F., +52-55-5280-7597, sandraweil.com.

Sangre di mi Sangre

Designer Mariana Villarreal creates edgy contemporary jewelry with skull, pyramid, and snake motifs.

Edificio Balmori L-F, Orizaba 101, Roma Norte, 06700 Ciudad de México, D.F., +52-55-551-8599, sdemis.com.

Silver Deer

This superb menswear store stocks a contemporary luxe mix of clothing, shoes, books, grooming products, accessories, and home furnishings, including Thom Browne, Isaia, Drakes, and exclusive collabs such as Alden for Silver Deer.

Av. Javier Barros Sierra 540, Zedec Sta Fé, 01219 Ciudad de México, D.F., +52-55-5292-9587, thesilverdeer.com.

YAKAMPOT

Tane

Since the 1940s, this Mexico City–based luxury brand has been the go-to for sleek silver jewelry inspired by pre-Hispanic design and crafts. It continues to thrive today, thanks to collaborations with contemporary designers and style-setters such as Iris Apfel. You'll find chunky silver chains, silver-and-wood cuffs, and silver minaudières, as well as gold pieces, silk and leather accessories, and candles.

Av. Presidente Masaryk 430, Polanco III Secc, 11560 Ciudad de México, D.F., +52-55-5282-6200, tane.com.mx, and additional locations.

Taxonomía

Located on the first floor of Hotel Carlota, this shop curates the best of contemporary Mexican fashion, jewelry, and home design, including shirts by 1/8 Takamura, leather goods by Robin Archives, and mescal cups by Lagos del Mundo.

Hotel Carlota, Calle Río Amazonas 73, 06500 Ciudad de México, D.F, +52-55-116300, taxonomia.mx.

Yakampot

Francisco Cancino's line of feminine blouses, tunic dresses, and ponchos is a big hit among Mexico's stylish set, including fashion editor Karla Martinez de Salas. Cancino sources fabrics in Mexico or from specialty mills in Europe and collaborates with indigenous artisans. The first Yakampot shop in Polanco, designed by Emiliano Godoy and Tuux, was built with the same sustainable practices. Check out Yakampot's sister brand, Arroz con Leche, for adorable kids' clothes.

Calle Emilio Castelar 215B, Polanco III Secc, 11550 Ciudad de México, D.F., +52-55-6721-3324, yakampot.com.

Void

This high-end vintage store, owned by former model and current Mexico City "It" girl Olympia de la Macorra, features everything from collectible Chanel to rocker T-shirts.

Calle Juan Escutia 89, Col. Condesa, 06140 Ciudad de México, D.F., +52-55-5211-7213, voidmx.com.

MIXTA

SAN MIGUEL DE ALLENDE

MEXICO

Abrazos

Shirts, napkins, aprons, baby bibs, tote bags, and more in Day of the Dead, lucha libre, cactus, and other colorful cotton prints that capture the spirit of Mexico.

Zacateros 24, Centro, 37700 San Miguel de Allende, GTO., +52-415-154-8580, sanmigueldesigns.com.

Artisan Alley

Three blocks of small stores and tented stalls selling embroidered pillowcases, tablecloths, purses, sugar skulls, jewelry, tin lamps, Catrina dolls, and more.

Lucas Balderas S/N, Centro, 37700 San Miguel de Allende, GTO.

Camino Silvestre

Gorgeous collection of hummingbird feeders, birdhouses, ceramics, glassware, and gifts in an enchanting setting.

Zacateros 46, Centro, 37700 San Miguel de Allende, GTO., +52-415-121-3359, caminosilvestre.com.

Casa Kiri

Hand-embroidered blouses, dresses, shawls, table runners, pillowcases, and more, all with a traditional-meets-boho modern vibe. One of the best spots in town to find something truly unique.

Calle Diez de Sollano 27, Centro, 37700 San Miguel de Allende, GTO., +52-415-152-3758, kiri.com.mx.

Ceramica Lopez

Colorful, hand-painted ceramics, including bowls, vases, dinnerware, and mugs, with a traditional-meets-contemporary feel.

Recreo 10, Centro, 37700 San Miguel de Allende, GTO., +52-415-154-4009.

Mixta

This beautiful 1700s courtyard building has several rooms full of eclectic clothing, housewares, accessories, furniture, and art, mostly by contemporary Mexican designers.

Pila Seca 3, Centro, 37700 San Miguel de Allende, GTO., +52-415-152-7343, mixtasanmiguel.com.

TULUM

MEXICO

Caravana

Jacopo Janniello Ravagnan's collection of artisan-made leather bags, choker necklaces, fringed shawls, ponchos, and more, with an earthy Mayan vibe and all housed in a giant tent.

5 miles along the main beach road in Tulum—Carretera Tulum Ruinas Boca Paila km 7.5, 77780 Tulum, Q.R., +52-985-856-0665, caravan.land.

Josa

Cute caftans, kimonos, maxi dresses, and jumpsuits to take you from the beach to the dance floor, by New York transplant and photographer-turned-designer Joanne Salt and co-founder Ana Cabello.

5 miles along the main beach road in Tulum—Carretera Tulum Boca Paila km 7.5, 77780 Tulum, Q.R., +52-984-115-8441, josatulum.com.

KM33

Handmade luxury accessories produced in Mexico and South America, including colorful exotic leather

CARAVANA

SHOPPING FOR THE FRIDA KAHLO LOOK IN MEXICO

Susana Martínez Vidal literally wrote the book on Frida Kahlo style. Based in Mexico City and Madrid, Vidal is a fashion and lifestyle journalist with more than twenty-five years of experience. Frida Kahlo inspired the first fashion editorial she produced as director of Elle Spain. *Since then, she has passionately followed the artist's influence on fashion, music, and culture. After seeing the first-ever exhibition of Frida's clothing at La Casa Azul in 2012, Vidal was inspired to write* Frida Kahlo: Fashion as the Art of Being. *If you're looking for a more authentic take on Frida's look, one beyond the T-shirts, tote bags, and tchotchkes you can find on every corner in Mexico, these are Vidal's favorite places.*

There are wonderful shawls in the store at the **MUSEO DE ARTE POPULAR (MAP)**, at the **CIUDADELA MARKET**, and at the well-stocked **EL BAZAAR SÁBADO** in San Ángel.

Frida's jewelry, which was made from silver filigree and semiprecious stones, inspires the jewelry line **SANGRE DE MI SANGRE**, which has a store in Colonia Roma, and also ships all over the world.

There's an Argentine chain store, **RAPSODIA**, with several branches in Mexico and across South America that sometimes has Frida-inspired looks with embroidery and an ethnic air.

MUSEO DE ARTE POPULAR, Calle Revillagigedo 11, Centro, 06050 Ciudad de México, D.F., +52-55-5510-2201, map.cdmx.gob.mx .

LA CIUDADELA: MERCADO DE ARTESANÍAS, Av. Balderas Centro, 06040 Ciudad de México, D.F., +52-55-5510-1828, laciudadela.com.

EL BAZAAR SÁBADO, San Jacinto 11, San Ángel, 01000 Ciudad de México, D.F, +52-55-5616-0082, elbazaarsabado.com/mx.

SANGRE DE MI SANGRE, Edificio Balmori L-F, Orizaba 101, Roma Norte, 06700 Ciudad de México, D.F., +52-55-551-8599, sdemis.com.

RAPSODIA, Av. Tamaulipas 88, Condesa, Ciudad de México, D.F., +52-55-5211-6372, rapsodia.com, and additional locations.

ONLINE SHOPPING TIP

CooperativaShop.com is a terrific website founded by Araceli Graham, that brings top Latin American designers together (Carla Fernandez, Johanna Ortiz, Mercedes Salazar, Yakampot, and more) under one shoppable site that ships internationally.

Susana Martínez Vidal recommends **Jalinedesign.com** for "exquisite designs produced artisinally in southern Mexico." She also likes **olgaprieto.es** for "wonderful jewelry that illuminates any look, made by hand." And **shoprarely.com** is worth a look for "quality ready-to-wear sweatshirts and T-shirts."

For discovering new designers all over the world, Designer Carla Fernandez looks to **NotJustALabel.com**, a global e-commerce platform and organizer of a trade show called The Future Of Fashion, dedicated to sustainable design. Another site she likes is **Yoox.com**. "They showcase funky fashion that has folk spirit."

backpacks, fringed clutches, chunky gold jewelry, straw hats, and more.

5 miles along the main beach road in Tulum—Carretera Tulum Boca Paila km 8.5, 77780 Tulum, Q.R., +52-55-4592-3594, km33tulum.com.

La Troupe

Breezy bohemian clothing, accessories, and home goods made locally by Mayan women, with lots of hand embroidery but also a contemporary look, thanks to soft, neutral colors.

5 miles along the main beach road in Tulum—Carretera Tulum Boca Paila km 7.5, 77780 Tulum, Q.R., +52-984-147-1178, latroupe.com.mx.

Mixik

Day of the Dead figurines, glassware, ceramics, scarves, and folk art abound at this gem for Mexican souvenirs. There is no street address, but the store is a block away from the bank in town, next to Charlie's restaurant.

Ave. Tulum, Centro, 77780 Tulum, Q.R.

Mr. Blackbird

Quartz necklaces, fringed and knotted leather jewelry, crochet bags, and sandals can be found at this tiny, sandy-floored boutique.

5 miles along the main beach road in Tulum—Carretera Tulum, Boca Paila km. 7.5, 77780 Tulum, Q.R., +52-948-114-3796

CARLA FERNANDEZ

SHOPPING FOR TRADITIONAL MEXICAN CLOTHING

Susana Carla Fernández is one of Mexico's best-known, and best-loved, fashion designers. Inspired by the architecture and textile traditions of her homeland, she launched her namesake fashion label in 2000, with the goal of working with indigenous communities around Mexico to preserve handweaving, dyeing, felting, and embroidery techniques.

For amazing folk clothes I like Oaxaca, a big city in the south of Mexico that is full of clothes woven or embroidered by hand and dyed with the most exquisite natural dyes. My favorite store in Oaxaca is **TIENDA Q**, where you can find new Mexican designs mixed with accessories from Toledo or traditional blouses dyed with indigo. Another store I love is **LOS BAÚLES DE JUANA CATA**, which is owned by Remigio Mestas Revilla, an advocate for the local textile industry.

I love traditional garments. I love to go to old bookstores and buy traditional garment patterns of the country I am visiting. If you are in downtown Mexico City, visit **DONCELES STREET** and you will see the kinds of bookstores I am talking about. I also like to go to local markets in little towns in Mexico. When you arrive in a new town, ask when the local market day is and don't miss it.

I love San Miguel de Allende, which is three hours from Mexico City. It has amazing Mexican design and delicious food. A new concept shopping center, **DOCE18,** recently opened in a historic San Miguel building. It has six restaurants and several little design boutiques. Another must is **THE RESTAURANT,** *the* place to eat in San Miguel.

TIENDA Q, Manuel Bravo 109, Centro, 68000 Oaxaca, OAX., +52-951-514-8855.

LOS BAÚLES JUANA CATA, Macedonio Alcala 403, Lazaro Cardenas 1ra Secc, 68140 Oaxaca, OAX., Mexico.

DÔCE 18, Calle Relox 18, Centro, 37700 San Miguel De Allende, GTO., +52-415-152-0215, doce-18.com.

THE RESTAURANT, Calle Sollano 16, Centro, 37700 San Miguel de Allende, GTO., +52-415-154-7877, therestaurantsanmiguel.com.

RIO DE JANEIRO

BRAZIL

Andrea Marques

Up-and-coming designer distinguished by her striking use of color and prints, and her classic yet sensual silhouettes, including printed bodysuits and midi skirts reminiscent of Diane von Furstenberg classics.

Rua Garcia d'Avil, 149, Sobreloja 201, Ipanema, Rio de Janeiro-RJ, 22421-010, +55-21-3202-2700.

Animale

One of the largest brands in Brazil, with more than eighty freestanding boutiques, the Rio-based Animale caters to professional women, with sexy, draped dresses, blouses, and pants that show off Brazilian bods, plus biker jackets, velvet slip dresses, and edgy accessories.

Av. Rio Branco 128, Loja B, Centro, Rio de Janeiro-RJ, 20040-002, +55-21-2224-4387, animale.com.br, and additional locations.

Antonio Bernardo

Rio-based fine jeweler whose designs are organic, sculptural, and glam (his gold folded-fan-shaped Scandal earrings are perfect for the disco). His flagship has a gallery next door that features contemporary art.

Rua Garcia d'Avila 121, Ipanema, Rio de Janeiro-RJ, 22421-010, +55-21-2512-7204, antoniobernardo.com.br, and additional locations.

Blue Man

This iconic Brazilian swimwear company has been in business since the 1970s, first becoming famous for its denim bikini, and later, for running afoul of the Roman Catholic Church when it produced a bikini with an image of Jesus on the seat. Today, it remains a fashion favorite, selling a range of colorful, itty-bitty women's styles as well as one-pieces, men's *sungas* (the Brazilian mankini), kids' bathing suits, and resort and workout wear.

Rua Visconde de Pirajá 351, Ipanema, Rio de Janeiro-RJ, 22410-003, +52-21-2247-4905, blueman.com.br, and additional locations.

Dona Coisa

This concept store (Brazil's colette) serves up the best of Brazilian and international designers, as well as beauty and lifestyle items. A must-stop for serious fashion fans.

Rua Lopes Quintas 153, Jardim Botânico, Rio de Janeiro-RJ, 22460-020, +55-21-2249-2336, donacoisa.com.br.

HELENA BORDON MAKES A CASE FOR THE MALL

Who says malls are dead? Not Helena Bordon, the popular Brazilian entrepreneur, model, and fashion blogger based in São Paulo. Bordon began her fashion training earlier than most thanks to her mother, Donata Meirellescurrent style director of Vogue Brazil. *When Bordon was seven, she started accompanying her mom on trips to Europe, attending Chanel shows and meeting designers like Valentino. Bordon spent her formative years learning buying tips and engaging with fashion teams and retailers. She cofounded Brazilian fast fashion chain 284 with childhood friends. An avid follower of fashion, Bordon regularly updates her website (helenabordon.com) with style, travel, and beauty tips. You can see her in ad campaigns for Cîroc Vodka, L'Oréal Professionnel, Tod's, and Salvatore Ferragamo.*

In Brazil we tend to shop more in malls than in street shops. My two favorites are **SHOPPING IGUATEMI** and **SHOPPING CIDADE JARDIM**. They both carry all the international brands and the local must-have ones. The Cidade Jardim is very beautiful and open with lots of trees. It's very nice to go there just to walk around and have lunch.

At the Iguatemi, they recently opened **MANI**, which is my favorite restaurant in São Paulo. The food and the caipirinha (Brazil's traditional drink) are amazing. Ask for the Mani caipirinha—a *must*. Both of the malls have hair salons and a gym, so you can basically spend the entire day there.

SHOPPING IGUETEMI SAN PAOLO, Av. Brigadeiro Faria Lima 2232, Jardim Paulistano, São Paulo-SP, 01489-900, +55-11-3048-7344, iguatemi.com.br.

SHOPPING CIDADE JARDIM, Av. Magalhães de Castro 12000, Cidade Jardim, São Paulo-SP, 05502-001, +55-11-3552-3560, shoppingcidadejardim.com.

Farm

Dressing the fashionable girls of Rio since the late 1990s, Farm started as a stall at a flea market and has since grown into a lifestyle brand with festive, tropical prints as its signature.

Rua Visconde de Pirajá 365, Ipanema, Rio de Janeiro-RJ, 22410-003, +52-21-99834-4486, farmrio.com.br.

Fiera do Rio Antigo

Famous for its antiques, this market is "a local gem," says swimwear designer Lenny Niemeyer. There is also a selection of arts and crafts stalls. Open the first Saturday of the month, from 10 a.m. to 7 p.m.

Rua do Lavradio, Lapa, Rio de Janeiro-RJ, 20230-014.

Francesca Romana Diana

Colorful and chic costume jewelry featuring quartz, amethysts, citrines, and other stones, inspired by Rio's *bossa* lifestyle.

Rua Visconde de Pirajá 547, Ipanema, Rio de Janeiro-RJ, 22410-003, +55-21-2274-8511, francescaromanadiana.com.br.

H.Stern

Founded in 1945, Rio's very own luxury jewelry brand captures the spirit of Brazilian modernism in fine metals and stones. It's stayed relevant by collaborating on collections with international style-setters, including Diane von Furstenberg and architect Oscar Niemeyer. There are more than 160 H. Stern stores worldwide, but the flagship is in Ipanema, where you can take a self-guided workshop tour.

Rua Garcia d'Avila 113, Primeiro andar, Ipanema, Rio de Janeiro-RJ, 22410-002, +55-21-3204-1334, hstern.net, and additional locations.

Isabela Capeto

One of Brazil's buzziest contemporary fashion designers, Capeto is known for her hand-dyed, embroidered, boho dresses and skirts (think Isabel Marant, Brazilian-style), as well as kids' clothes and home accessories.

Rua Alberto Ribeiro 17, Horto, Rio de Janeiro-RJ, 22460-250, +55-21-2537-3331, isabelacapeto.com.br, and an additional location in São Paulo.

Lenny Niemeyer

With flattering cuts, sensual draping, and bold, nature-inspired prints, Niemeyer's swimwear and beachwear reflect her past experience as a landscape architect. (She's the niece of architect Oscar Niemeyer.)

Rua Garcia d'Avila 149, Loja A, Ipanema, Rio de Janeiro-RJ, 22421-010, +55-21-2227-5527, lennyniemeyer.com, and additional locations.

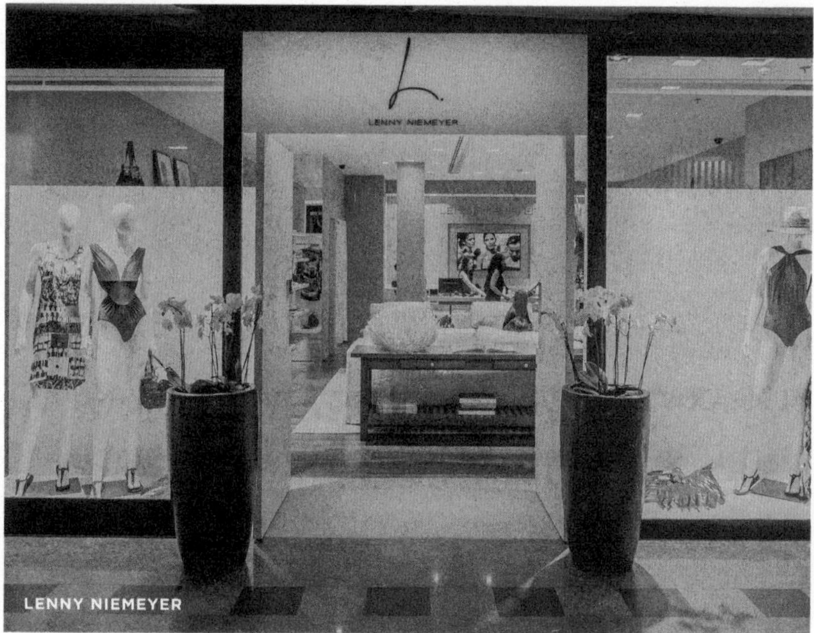

LENNY NIEMEYER

Rosa Chá

Another Brazilian brand elevating swimwear to high fashion is Rosa Chá. "I love seeing all the swimwear designs in Rio," says fashion tech entrepreneur Alexandra Wilkis Wilson. "I also love that the women there are confident no matter their shape."

Av. das Américas 7777, Barra da Tijuca, Rio de Janeiro-RJ, 22793-081, +55-21-4062-7953, rosacha.com.br.

Sobral

Carlos Sobral started his business in Rio in the 1960s, after coming across the material resin at the Hippie Fair in Ipanema. His Brazilian-made resin jewelry, including chunky necklaces and rings, makes colorful souvenirs.

Fórum de Ipanema, Rua Viscconde de Pirajá 351, Ipanema, Rio de Janeiro-RJ, 22410-003, +55-21-2267-0009, sobraldesign.com.b.

SÃO PAULO

BRAZIL

Adriana Degreas

With couture-like construction, luxury fabrics, and cheeky designs (such as a bikini bottom with trompe l'oeil lips), Degreas's swimwear and beachwear is stylish enough to wear to the club. No wonder that Alessandra Ambrosio, Poppy Delevingne, and Erica Pelosini are fans.

Shopping Iguatemi, Av. Brigadeiro Faria Lima 2232, Jardim Paulistano, São Paulo-SP, 01489-900, +55-11-3045-5646, adrianadegreas.com.br.

Herchcovitch Alexandre

One of Brazil's first designers to become internationally known in the 1990s, Herchcovitch has shown his pretty-punk collections in New York and Paris as well as Brazil.

Rua Melo Alves 561, Jardim Paulista, São Paulo-SP, 01417-010, +55-11-3063-2888, loja.herchcovitch.com.br.

Amir Slama

A history professor-turned-swimwear designer who was the designer/owner of beach brand Rosa Chá before launching under his own name, Slama now counts Naomi Campbell and many other stylish girls as devotees. "I can only buy my swimsuits from him now—and I also bring them back as gifts," says L.A. retailer Desiree Kohan. "He executes the perfect string bikini for all shapes and sizes as well as bodysuits that rival Wolford. I have a collection of minimal architectural suits as well as non-structured string bikinis. I'm really into great fabrics, especially for swimsuits and he does it best."

Rua Oscar Freire 977, Jardim Paulista, São Paulo-SP, 01426-001, Brasil, amirslama.br.

Cartel 011

"One of the coolest stores in the city," says stylist/designer Maryam Malakpour. "Right in the entrance there is an art gallery, in the back you will find a great restaurant, and they have a good selection of modern clothing in the store. A great mix of art, design, fashion, and gastronomy."

Rua Artur de Azevedo, 517 - Pinheiros, São Paulo-SP, 05404-001, +55-11-3081-4171, www.cartel011.com.br.

Casa Juisi

"Located in an old mansion in São Paulo's historical downtown that was

UXUACASA

converted into a boutique vintage retailer with an offering that is carefully curated by its eagle-eyed creators," says Helena Bordon of this off-the-beaten--path place, where she scored her best find ever, a vintage Lanvin coat.

Rua Roberto Símonsen, 108 - Sé, São Paulo-SP, 01017-020, +55-11-3063-5766.

Fernanda Yamamoto

This Brazilian-born fashion designer draws on the local landscape and her Japanese ancestry to create conceptual, multitextured pieces in minimalist, architectural silhouettes. A bit Comme des Garçons–like.

Rua Aspicuelta 441, Pinheiros, São Paulo-SP, 05433-011, +55-11-3032-7979, fernandayamamoto.com.br.

Gig Couture

Founded in 2002 by Gina Guerra and Patricia Schettino, Gig Couture has risen to success on its vividly patterned knitwear, created with jacquards and special yarns in Belo Horizonte. Beyoncé gave the label her stamp of approval when she chose a Gig Couture look from the spring/summer 2016 collection for her film *Lemonade*.

Rua Peixoto Gomide 1789, Jardim Paulista, São Paulo-SP, 01409-003, +55-11-2386-1500, gigcouture.com.

Havaianas

Situated on the high-end Rua Oscar Freire is the flagship for Brazil's native shoe. Behind the minimalist facade is an impressive space with greenery to

THE BEST OF BOSSA DESIGN

Ana Kozak is so enthusiastic about Brazilian design, she brought it to Los Angeles when she relocated from São Paulo, opening Le Magazyn in Venice Beach in 2016. When she returns to Brazil twice a year to scout new designers and artisans for her store, these are the places she does not miss.

For swimsuits and cool bikinis, I go to **LENNY NIEMEYER.** Lenny is a "Carioca" brand, which means, "born in Rio." She has several stores in many Brazilian cities. In São Paulo, **ADRIANA DEGREAS** has the best swimsuits and the coolest lounge outfits. For amazing sandals you can't go wrong with **PAULA FERBER**. They are exquisite sandals and original creations; I'm very proud to exclusively represent her in the US at Le Magazyn.

For casual clothing with Brazilian DNA, I would recommend **A. NIEMEYER** in São Paulo. **ADRIANA BARRA** has the best colorful print long dresses in exotic patterns with tropical flowers and birds and I love Rio label **OSKLEN** for fashionable sneakers. Also in Rio is **DONA COISA,** a store that mixes fashion and home decor, and has a cafe inside the store. It is located in the Jardim Botanico neighborhood—a destination worth taking some time to explore.

A nice lifestyle store in São Paulo is **AMOREIRA,** where you can have a coffee and a piece of cake while shopping. I usually spend my Sunday mornings in São Paulo at the **MUSEU BRASILEIRO DA ESCULTURA** where they have a market. While mostly focused on antiques, you can also find some vintage clothing. Once there, take the opportunity to have lunch at **CHEZ MIS** restaurant, which is one block away from MuBE.

C&A is an international Dutch retail (like Topshop and H&M) that cannot be classified as chic but is definitely cheap and cool! In Brazil they often collaborate with local designers like Alexandre Herchcovitch, Lenny Niemeyer and others. The collaborations are really good and things fly from

One of my favorite vacation spots in Brazil is Trancoso, in Bahia; my family meets there once a year and I really try to not skip a single spring (the best season). Trancoso is a small little village full of charm and a great vibe. I love the woodwork of **MARCENARIA TRANCOSO** (I carry at Le Magazyn) and I always visit **UXUACASA HOME**. They are both located in the "quadrado" (central square).

TRANCOSO

LENNY NIEMEYER, Av. Ataulfo de Paiva, 270, 2F, Leblon, Rio de Janeiro - RJ, 22440-033, +55-21-3114-8887, lennyniemeyer.com, and additional locations.

ADRIANA DEGREAS, Rua Haddock Lobo, 1151, Cerqueira César, São Paulo - SP, 01414-002, +55-11-3331 1113, adrianadegreas.com.br, and additional locations.

PAULA FERBER, Shopping Iguatemi São Paulo, Av. Brigadeiro Faria Lima, 2232, Jardim Paulistano, São Paulo - SP, 01451-000, +55-11-3811 9810, paulaferber.com.

A. NIEMEYER, Shopping Iguatemi, Av. Brg. Faria Lima, 2232, Jardim Europa, São Paulo - SP, 01489-900, +55-11-3034-4411, aniemeyer.com.br, and additional locations.

ADRIANA BARRA, Alameda Franca, 1243, Jardim Paulista, São Paulo - SP, 01422-001, +55-11-2925-2300, adrianabarra.com.br, and an additional location in Leblon.

OSKLEN, Rua Maria Quitéria, 85, Ipanema, Rio de Janeiro - RJ, 22410-040, +55-21-2227-2911 osklen.com, and additional locations.

AMOREIRA, Rua dos Macunis, 510, Vila Madalena, São Paulo - SP, 05444-001, +55-11-3032-5346, amoreira.com.

DONA COISA, Rua Lopes Quintas, 153, Jardim Botânico, Rio De Janeiro-RJ, 22460-020, +55-21-2246-2336.

MUBE MUSEUM, Rua Alemanha, 221 - Jardim Europa, São Paulo - SP, 01448-010, +55-11-2594-2601, mube.com.br).

CHEZ MIS, Av. Europa, 158, Jardim Europa, São Paulo - SP, 01449-000, +55-11-3467-3441, chezmis.com.br.

C&A, for locations and online store see c-and-a.com.

MARCENARIA TRANCOSO, Square St. John, 12, Trancoso, Porto Seguro - BA, 45818-000, +55-73-3668-1179, mtrancoso.com, and additional locations.

UXUACASA, Porto Seguro - BA, 45810-000, Brazil, +55-73-3668-2277, uxua.com

FERNANDA YAMAMOTO

accent the shoes, plus rotating art installations. You can also have your own designs made.

Rua Oscar Freire 1116, Cerqueira César, São Paulo-SP, 01426-000, +55-11-3079-3415, havaianas.com.br, and additional locations.

Lilly Sarti

Cool boho pieces with a sophisticated-city-girl twist. Think airy silk chiffon dresses, blouses, and asymmetrical skirts, and relaxed cotton jumpsuits, all in neutral tones.

Rua Peixoto Gomide 1749, Jardins, São Paulo-SP, 01409-003, +55-11-3083-4509, lillysarti.com.br.

Lolitta

Up-and-coming talent Lolita Zurita Hannud is making a mark with her sexy, intricately knit designs reminiscent of Herve Leger and Missoni.

Shopping Iguatemi, Av. Brigadeiro Faria Lima 2232, Piso Superior, São Paulo, 55-11-3034-0610, lolitta.com.br.

Melissa

This is the impressive flagship for Brazil's stylish plastic and rubber footwear brand, which has collaborated with a host of designers on exclusive designs, including Vivienne Westwood, Jason Wu, and Jeremy Scott. The store also features a series of rotating installations by local artists.

Rua Oscar Freire 827, Cerqueira César, São Paulo-SP, 01426-003, +55-11-3083-3612, melissa.com.br, and additional locations.

NK Store

Founded by Natalie Klein in 1997 in São Paulo, this concept store boasts a well-curated selection of designers. "One-stop shop for a great selection of brands including Isabel Marant, Stella McCartney, Balmain, and their own brand," says Brazilian style blogger Helena Bordon. Klein has two in-house labels: the NK collection and the diffusion line TalieNK.

Rua Sarandi 34, Jardim America, São Paulo-SP, 01414-010, +55-11-3897-2600, nkstore.com.br.

Osklen

Designer, environmental activist, and United Nations Goodwill Ambassador Oskar Metsavaht balances sustainability and luxury in his stylish collection, one of Brazilian fashion's biggest success stories with more than 50 stores worldwide. His designs are graphic and earthy with a slight edge, often using raffia and raw linen contrasted with colorful tropical prints.

Rua Oscar Freire 645, Cerqueira César, São Paulo-SP, 01412-100, +55-11-3083-7977, osklen.com, and additional locations.

Riachuelo

Owned by Brazil's largest fashion group, Riachuelo is the Brazilian H&M, with more than 200 stores. The fast-fashion giant has collaborated on collections with well-known Brazilian designers such as Oskar Metsavaht and Pedro Lourenço, as well as international names Versace and Karl Lagerfeld. This is the brand's concept store.

Rua Oscar Freire 777, Jardim Paulista, São Paulo-SP, 01426-003, +55-11-2739-1960, riachuelo.com.br, and additional locations.

Schutz

Designer Alexandre Birman's affordable Brazilian footwear chain has gone global with its sexy, boho sandals, wedges, and boots that feature fringe, woven accents, pom-poms, and beads.

Rua Oscar Freire 944, Jardim Paulista, São Paulo-SP, 01426-000, +55-11-4508-1409, schutz.com.br, and additional locations.

BUENOS AIRES

ARGENTINA

Arandú

This three-story town house brands itself as a *talabartería*, or equestrian store, but in addition to beautiful burnished-leather riding boots and saddles, it also sells fabulous leather goods, silver jewelry, needlepoint belts, and home accessories, as well as *alpargatas*, a traditional Argentine shoe, in every color and pattern. "Best selection for a weekend in an Argentine *estancia*," says model/blogger Sofia Sanchez de Betak. "Great hats and handwoven leather accessories," says Ulla Johnson.

Ayacucho 1924, C1112111J Buenos Aires, +54-11-4800-1575, arandu.com.ar.

Ayres

Trendy chain with eclectic prints and casual pieces (bomber jackets, moto zip jeans, sharp-tailored jackets), most priced for less than $300. Look for the store in the Alto Palermo mall, along with other interesting Argentine brands such as Maria Cher and A.Y. Not Dead.

Alto Palermo Shopping Center, Primero piso, Av. Santa Fe 3253, C1425BGH Buenos Aires, +54-11-5777-8228, ayres.com.ar.

Benito Fernandez

Crazy colors and prints and unusual combinations of textures characterize the whimsical looks of local designer Benito Fernandez. You'll find geometric-print blazers, fringed sweaters, patchwork-print button-down shirts, and even fun socks.

El Salvador 4666, C1414BPJ Buenos Aires, +54-11-4833-0303, benitofernandez.com.ar.

Casa Fagliano

In this little shop in Hurlingham, right outside of Buenos Aires, the Fagliano family handcrafts the best riding boots in the world. Among their exclusive clientele are top polo players, the king of Spain, Prince Charles, and the sultan of Brunei. A bespoke pair of boots starts at $2,600. The workshop opened in 1892 and is still family-run.

Tambo Nuevo 1449, B1686EOU Hurlingham, Buenos Aires, +54-11-4665-0128, fagliano.com.ar.

Celedonio

Local designer Celedonio Lohidoy's nature-inspired jewelry makes a statement, particularly his massive necklaces constructed of giant amethyst floral bouquets, or faux pearls, crystal and glass beads, and butterflies.

Av. del Libertador 1774, C1425AAQ Buenos Aires, +54-11-4803-7598, celedonio.com.ar.

Comme Il Faut

This is the place to go for a pair of handmade tango shoes stylish enough for a night on the town or on the dance floor. Styles come in lizard, suede, or lace, with heart embellishments or sequin fringe on the heels. The store, tucked away in a courtyard, also carries slingbacks and pumps.

Arenales 1239, Cdad. Autónoma de Buenos Aires, +54-11-4815-5690, commeilfautshoes.com.

EDITOR Market

Buenos Aires's hip, new lifestyle hub, created by Gabriel Brener, the man behind Maria Cher and A.Y. Not Dead. The eight-floor building, inspired by New York City's Dover Street Market and Paris's merci, features a carefully curated selection of Argentine design, including lighting by Federico Churba, Monochrome bicycles, Fueguia perfumes and candles, fashion, jewelry, and accessories. There's also a café with fresh juices and artfully decorated lattes.

Av. Corrientes 503, C1043AAF Buenos Aires, +54-11-5356-2575, editormarket.com.ar.

El Ateneo Grand Splendid

One of the oldest bookstores in Argentina, the building—a converted theater—is as much an attraction as the thousands of volumes inside.

Av. Santa Fe 1860, C1123AAA Buenos Aires, +54-11-4813-6052.

Elementos Argentinos

Design your own rug or choose from hundreds of colorful designs at this local gem, which specializes in handloomed llama wool rugs, sofa throws, table runners, colorful cushions, stools, and more.

Gurruchaga 1881, C1414DIK Buenos Aires, +54-11-4832-6899, also in Recoleto, elementosargentinos.com.ar.

Gil Antigüedades

High-end vintage clothing institution. The beaded dresses and jeweled minaudières will take you back to pre-revolution Argentina.

Humberto Primero 412, C1103ACJ Buenos Aires, +54-11-4361-5019, gilantiguedades.com.ar.

Jessica Kessel

This young designer's innovative color-block mules, ankle booties, and slingbacks are a real find.

Defensa 1009, C1065AAS Buenos Aires, +54-11-4362-2144, jkshoes.com.ar.

VASALISSA
TRAMANDO
DE MARIA
AVENIDA LEANDRO N. ALEM
COMME IL FAUT
A FE
AVENIDA LEANDRO N. ALEM
RDOBA
EDITOR MARKET
RRIENTES
AVEN

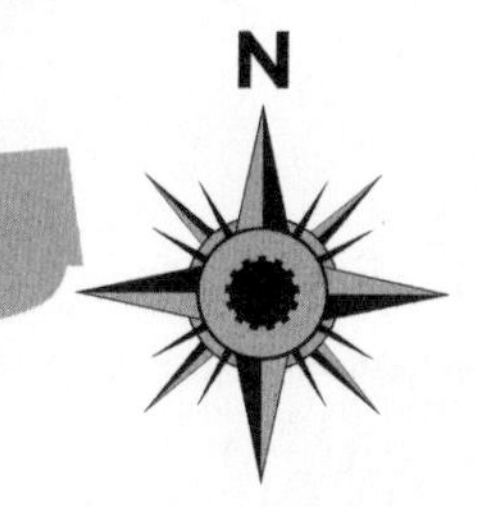

BUENOS AIRES

LAGUNA DE LA
GAVIOTAS

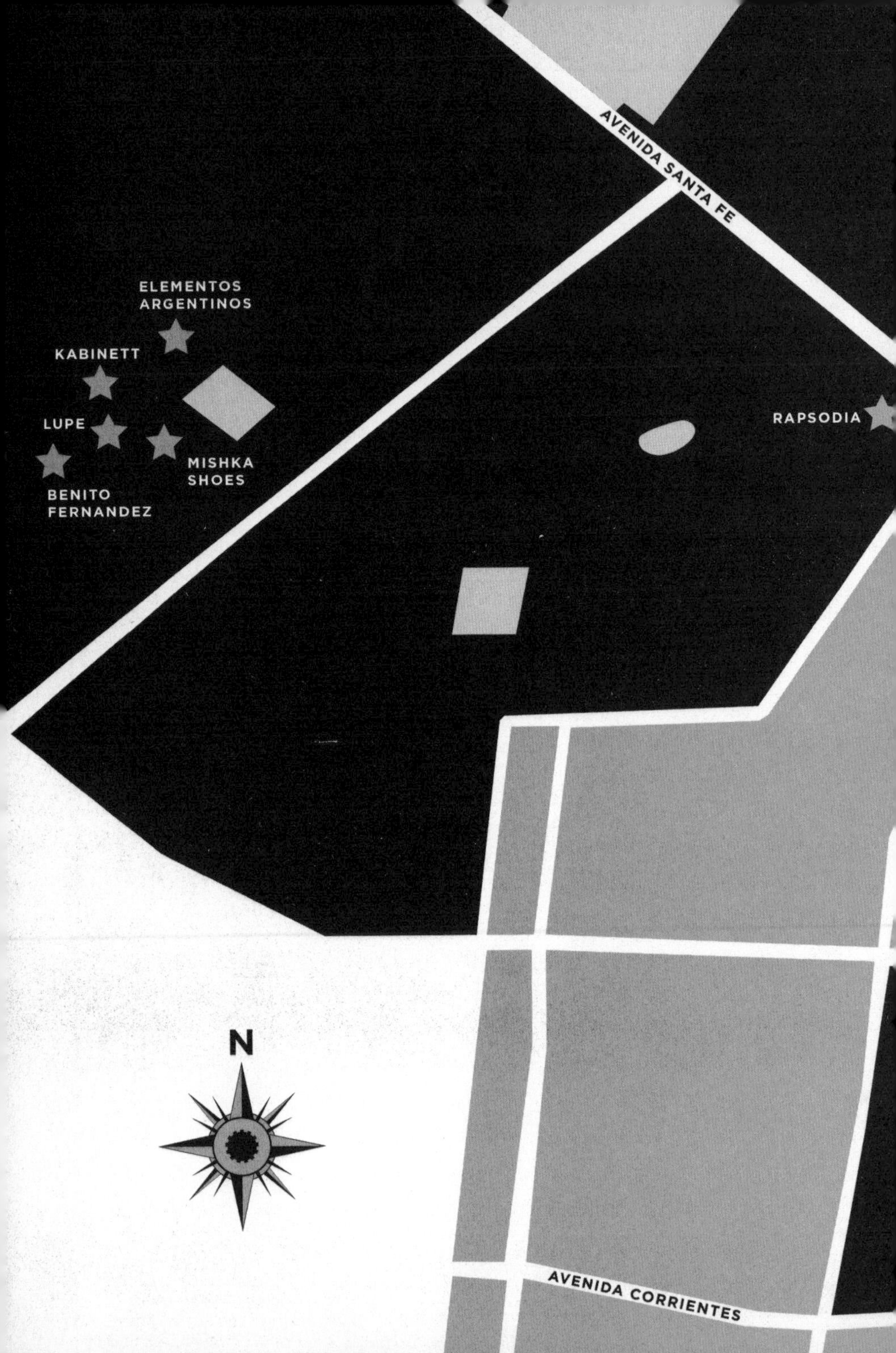
AVENIDA SANTA FE
ELEMENTOS ARGENTINOS
KABINETT
LUPE
MISHKA SHOES
BENITO FERNANDEZ
RAPSODIA
N
AVENIDA CORRIENTES

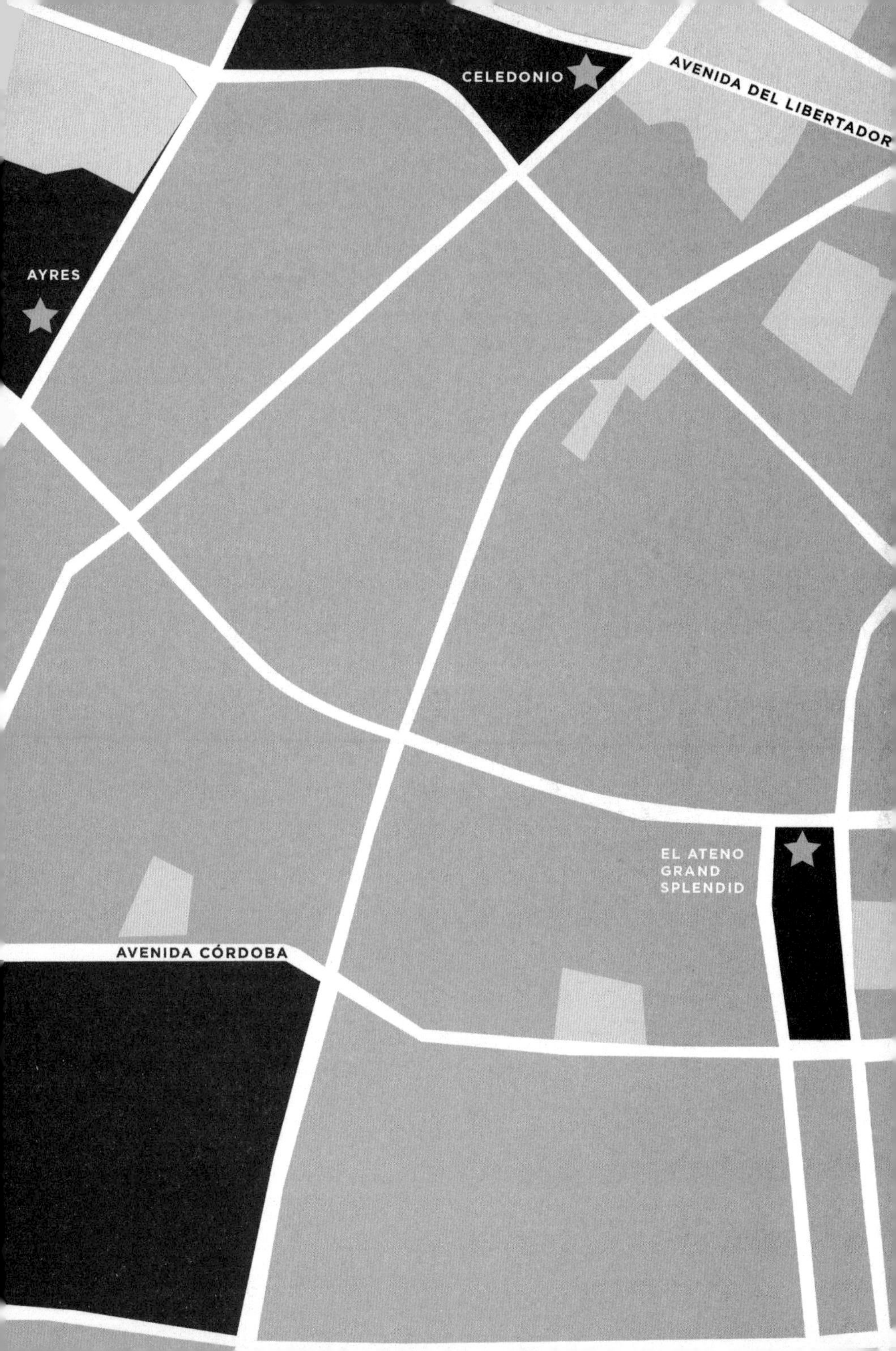
CELEDONIO
AVENIDA DEL LIBERTADOR
AYRES
EL ATENO
GRAND
SPLENDID
AVENIDA CÓRDOBA

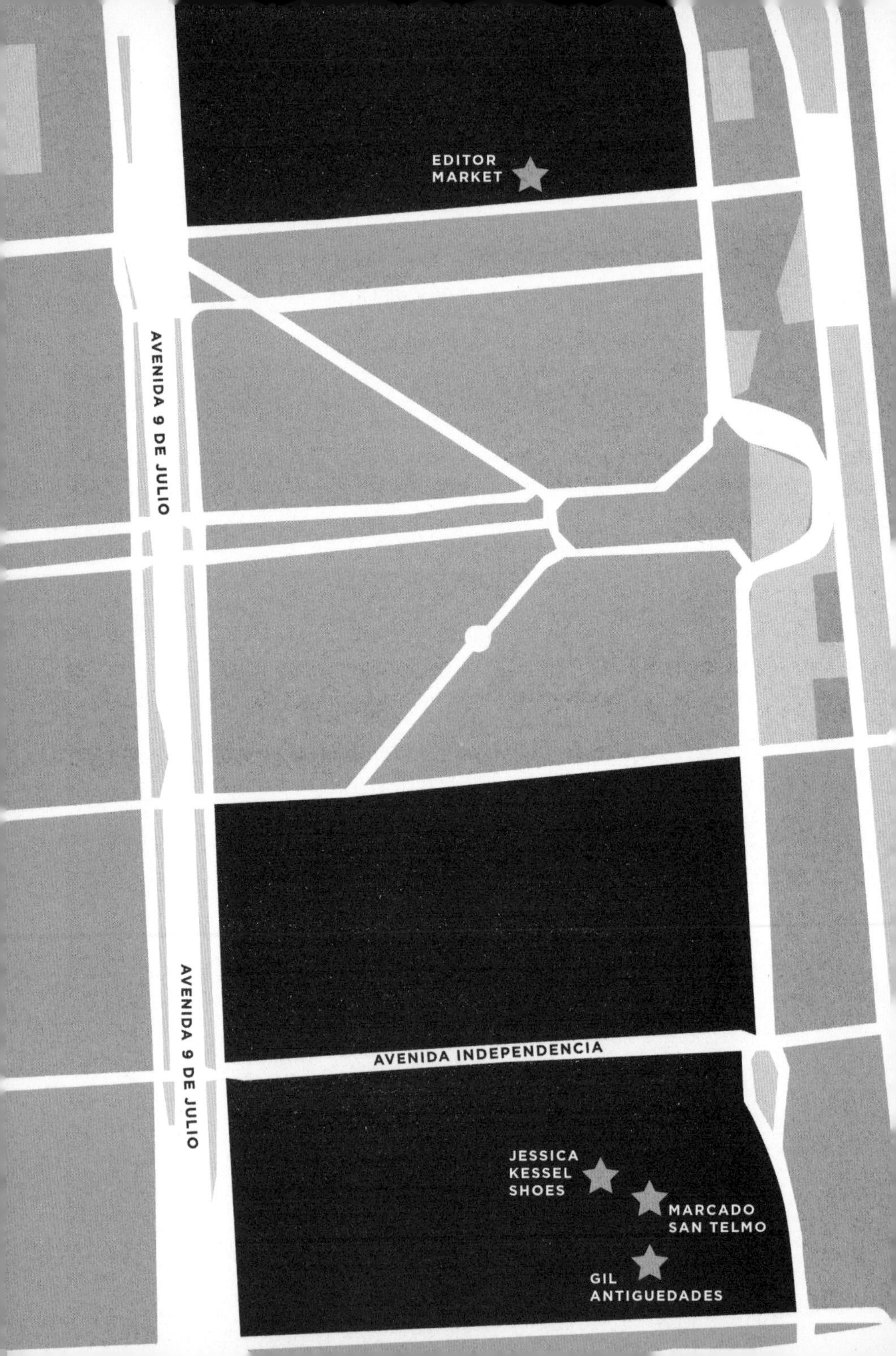

EDITOR
MARKET

AVENIDA 9 DE JULIO

AVENIDA 9 DE JULIO

AVENIDA INDEPENDENCIA

JESSICA
KESSEL
SHOES

MARCADO
SAN TELMO

GIL
ANTIGUEDADES

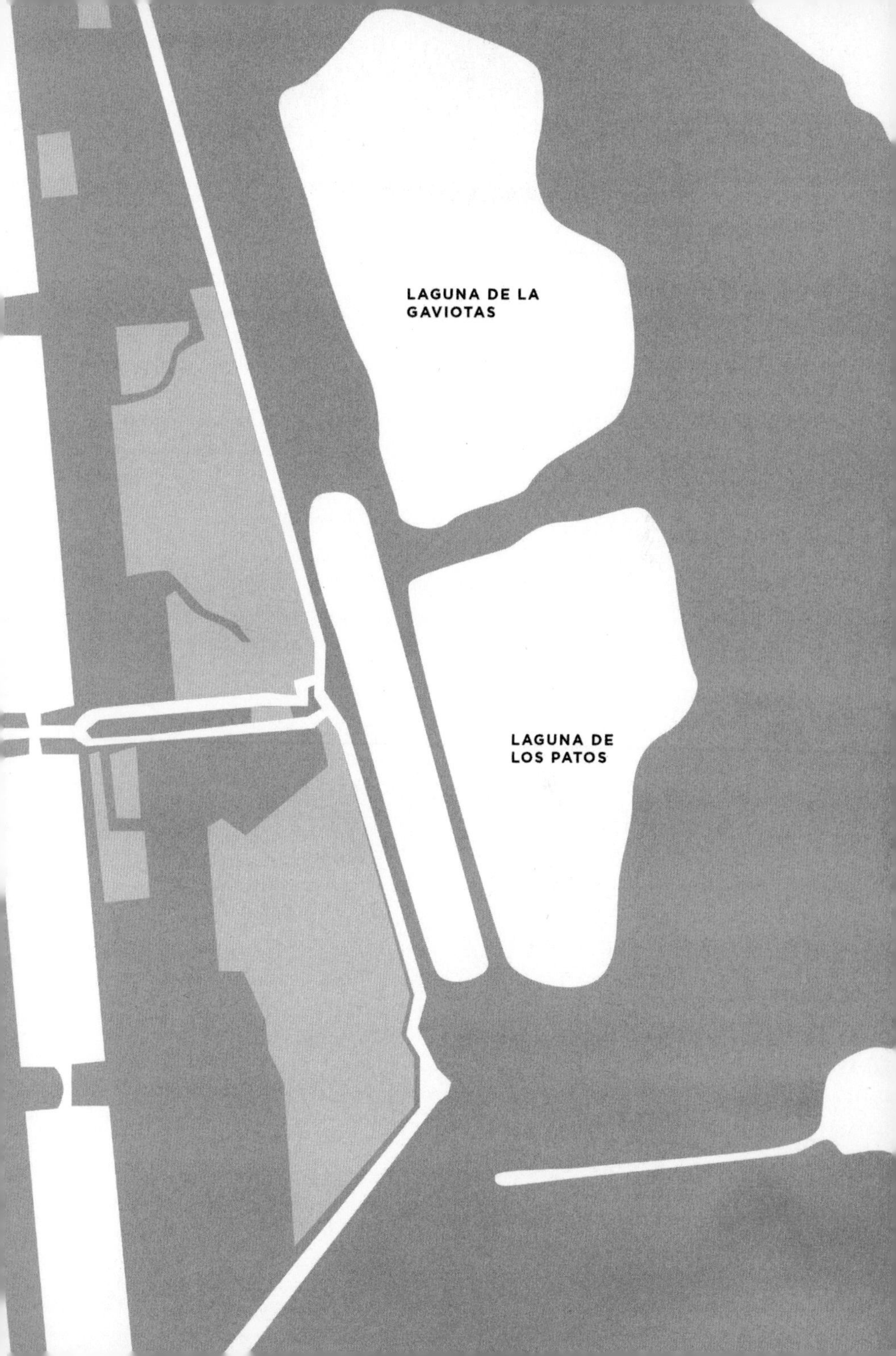
LAGUNA DE LA
GAVIOTAS
LAGUNA DE
LOS PATOS

Kabinett

Expect collaborations with leading local and international designers and artists in this ever-changing concept boutique. You'll find colorful woven cuff bracelets, clutch bags, wooden sunglasses, hats, and whimsical home accessories.

Gurruchaga 1744, C1414DIJ Buenos Aires, +54-11-4833-7447, kabinett.us.

Lupe

Local designer Guadalupe Villar's selection in this Palermo shop is charming and feminine—think a cross between A.P.C. and rock 'n' roll. Melissa Magsaysay snagged her favorite fashion find of all time here: "Probably the most comfortable brown leather loafers ever. I wear them nonstop."

El Salvador 4666, C1414BPJ Buenos Aires, +54-11-4832-6743.

Mishka

This trendy shoe store chain has supercool platform loafers and chunky-heel ballet pumps, plus a rotating selection of clothing and denim, all at similar prices to fast fashion chain COS.

El Salvador 4673, C1414BPI Buenos Aires, +54-11-4833-6566, mishka.com.ar, and additional locations.

Feria de San Pedro San Telmo

Don't miss the Sunday antiques market in the oldest neighborhood in Buenos Aires, with hundreds of stalls of knickknacks and souvenirs, street performers, tango dancers, and more. Sofia Sanchez de Betak makes it a regular stop when she's in town.

Defensa 1098, C1103AAA Buenos Aires, +55-11-3181-5188, feriadesantelmo.com.

Rapsodia

This Argentine chain is boho paradise. You'll think you've entered bohemian babe Alessandra Ambrosio's closet when you see all the fab patchwork maxi skirts, embroidered velvet jackets, and fringed booties, at prices that won't break the bank.

Alto Palermo, Av. Santa Fe 3251, C1425 CABA, Buenos Aires, +54-11-5777-81111 rapsodia.com, and additional locations.

Tokonoma

Gallery owner Oli Martinez has curated a selection of handmade pottery, jewelry, glass, and tableware by local designers at this minimalist spot accessed by a metal bridge.

José Antonio Cabrera 5037, C1414BGQ Buenos Aires, +54-11-4831-8365.

COMME IL FAUT

Tramando

This luxury label, founded in Buenos Aires by textile designer and former photographer Martín Churba, is known for its experimental weaving, futuristic prints, and avant-garde silhouettes.

Rodríguez Peña 1973, C1021ABO Buenos Aires, +54-11-4811-0465, tramando.com.

Vasalissa

"The best chocolates and the chicest wrapping," says fashion consultant Amanda Ross. The red-and-white toile boxes are indeed gorgeous, and the tango-shoe-shaped confections a must.

Av. Callao 1940, C1024AAS Buenos Aires, +54-11-4806-4158, vasalissa.com.

Zapatos de Maria

Sophisticated handmade shoes in rich colors, including mesh ballet flats, loafers, ribbon-tie oxfords, and ankle-strap pumps.

Libertad 1655, C1016ABG Buenos Aires, +54-11-4815-5001, zapatosdemaria.com.

LIMA

PERU

Alessandra Petersen

The Peruvian designer, and local fashion industry advocate, is known for her beautifully edgy crochet work, including sweaters, dresses, and neckpieces. Her clothing has been featured in *Vogue*.

Calle Atahualpa 479, Miraflores 15074, Lima, Peru, +51-1-242-5378, alessandrapetersen.com.

Andrea Llosa

Drawing inspiration from her time living abroad in Spain and London and from her Peruvian heritage, this buzzy young designer creates cool contemporary clothing and silhouettes. Visit her showroom or look for her designs at Hanger.

Av. Mariscal La Mar 352 350 348, Miraflores 15074, Lima, Peru, +51-1-4400711, andreallosa.com.

Artesanías Las Pallas

"For incredible crafts," says designer Ulla Johnson of this Lima gem, which promotes the traditional art of the coast, highlands, and jungle by working directly with artisans and paying fair prices. It offers high-quality alpaca clothing, jewelry, retablos, carved gourds, masks, ceramics, and more. Owner Mari Solari displays it all in several rooms of her fine Barranco house.

Cajamarca 212, Barranco 15063, Lima, Peru, +51-1-477-4629.

Dédalo Arte

A contemporary art gallery and café in a restored colonial home that is also a store featuring gifts, accessories, and jewelry (check out the pieces by Hiro Yoshimoto) by local designers. If you don't make it to Barranco, there's another store in the Larcomar shopping mall.

Paseo Saenz Peña 265, Barranco 15063, Lima, Peru, +51-1-652-5400.

Galería Indigo

Great selection of high-end Peruvian art, pottery, and one-of-a-kind jewelry.

Av. El Bosque 260, San Isidro 15073, Lima, Peru, +51-1-441-2232, galeriaindigo.com.pe.

Jallpa Nina

Amazing pottery, from dinner sets to lamps, from all over Peru with a look more modern than traditional. Artisans here also make ceramics for Jonathan Adler.

Federico Villareal 290, Miraflores 15074, Lima, Peru, +51-1-430-1435, jallpaninaperu.com.

Kuna

Inspired by Incan textile heritage, this high-end alpaca and vicuña clothing brand has multiple stores in Lima and throughout Peru.

Av. Larco 671, Miraflores 15074, Lima, Peru, +51-1-447-1623, kuna.com.pe, and additional locations.

Museo Larco

This privately owned museum of pre-Columbian art has a beautiful garden-facing café and a boutique featuring Peruvian-designed clothing and gifts.

Av. Simón Bolivar 1515, Pueblo Libre 15084, Lima, Peru, +51-1-461-1312, museolarco.org.

Meche Correa

One of Peru's best-known designers uses native fabrics and techniques to create gorgeous embroidered shawls, chunky gilt necklaces, plastic handbags with see-through pockets full of religious charms and offerings, and horn jewelry. Visit her atelier by appointment, or look for her collection at Dedalo and Gallery Indigo.

Av. Aurelio Miroquesada 136, San Isidro 15073, Lima, Peru, +51-1-441-1441, mechecorrea.com.

The Hanger

Great selection of Instagram-worthy styles by young Peruvian designers, including colorful Capittana swimsuits, Karen Mitre fringe clutches, feminine striped dresses by Carolina Tola, streetwear-inspired denim and knits from Camote Soup, cool handmade wood platform shoes by Quimera, and more.

Calle Miguel Dasso 110, San Isidro 15073, Lima, Peru, +51-1-421-6462.

Verné

Hip art gallery, restaurant, and clothing store selling local designers.

Av. 269, Barranco 15063, Lima, Peru, +51-1-586-8677.

CUSCO

PERU

Mercado Central de San Pedro

"This large open-air market in Cusco is a great place to find all types of local Peruvian craftwork," says jewelry designer Monique Péan.

Cascaparo, Cusco 84.

PRADA
PRADA
PRADA

EUROPE

UNITED KINGDOM

IRELAND

FRANCE

ITALY

SPAIN

GERMANY

SWEDEN

ROKSANDA

LONDON

UNITED KINGDOM

THE MAJORS

Harrods

"Probably my favorite big-city store," jewelry designer Kara Ross says of this institution whose branded tote bags and teddy bears are beloved souvenirs. "It has everything you can imagine. People come from all over the world and it really has something for everyone, from very expensive luxury items to more affordable things. It is such a chic store, but very approachable—and don't get me started on the food court." Don't miss the fish-and-chips at Bentley's Sea Grill on the ground floor, some of the best in the city; the Georgian Restaurant is great for tea. The shoe department is pretty epic, as are the pet and toy departments.

87-135 Brompton Rd., London SW1X 7XL, +44 (0)20 3626-7020, harrods.com.

Harvey Nichols

"I love a spin through Harvey Nichols," says costume designer Jenn Rogien of this Barneys-like department store with a fifth-floor market (don't miss the Harvey Nichols–brand stem ginger biscuits), a champagne bar, a rooftop café, and a Yo! Sushi conveyer-belt sushi spot. "I bought a fantastic dress there when I was nominated for a Costume Designers Guild award a few years ago. Even on sale it involved some creative financing," Rogien says. "A friend and I kicked off that shopping day with tea and scones upstairs. When in London, right?"

109-125 Knightsbridge, London SW1X 7RJ, +44 (0)20 7235-5000, harveynichols.com.

Liberty London

This Regent Street department store, housed in several buildings (including an incredible Tudor Revival constructed from the timber of two ships), harks back to Britain's imperial past in the best possible way. Liberty opened in 1875 selling ornaments, fabric, and *objets d'art* from the East. Today, it features an eclectic selection of top designer fashion and accessories, plus furniture, home accessories, fabrics and trims. The store played a key role in shaping British style in the 1890s, by helping to popularize art nouveau and Arts and Crafts styles. These are still celebrated in the store brand's iconic Liberty silk scarves, button-down shirts, and notebooks, as well as in collaborative collections with Manolo Blahnik, Nike, Barbour,

ONLINE SHOPPING TIP

"Hoodlondon.com presents the work of independent milliners from California to Colombia. I love even just 'window' shopping and imagining myself in all those incredible flights of crowning fancy," says fashion journalist/retailer Rose Apodaca.

and Vans. "The haberdashery department is amazing," says Olympia Le-Tan. "I can also spend hours looking at their fabrics." "When I worked at *Harper's Bazaar* UK, the office was right around the corner from Liberty, perfect for lunch meetings—Cafe Liberty, on the second floor, is gorgeous!" says fashion editor Alison Edmond. "I loved that there was such a mix of clients, and I still aspire to grow into one of the store's signature chic older ladies, shopping in my '90s, still wearing black, still into fashion, with Chanel Rouge Noir lipstick and white hair."

Regent St., London W1B 5AH, +44 (0)20 7734-1234, libertylondon.com.

Marks & Spencer

It may not be as fancy as Harrods or Selfridges, but it's beloved nonetheless for its no-frills fashion and food. (The underwear is a staple for most Brits, because it is so longwearing.) The clothing is basic and well priced, and now ships to the States!

458 Oxford St, London W1C 1AP, +44 (0)20 7935-7954, marksandspencer.com, and additional locations.

Selfridges

"There's not a lot you can't find within those walls," says shoe designer Sophia Webster. "My husband and I go there every Christmas Eve and do our holiday shopping in one big sweep." "I love a good stationery shop. The one inside Selfridges is pretty great and it's next to their chocolate selection, which is also dreamy," says tastemaker Liz Goldwyn. "Not only does the store proper have everything—*everything* —anyone could ever need, but the luxurious personal-shopping suites are divine," says designer Karen Erickson. "I can spend hours at the ground floor beauty workshop, which is essentially a playground of the newest trend brands and products," says fashion expert Tania Mohan. "

400 Oxford St., London W1A 1AB, United Kingdom, +44 0(11) 3369-8040, selfridges.com, and additional locations.

MAYFAIR/SOHO/COVENT GARDEN/PICCADILLY

Accessorize

A high-street mainstay since 1984, this tons-of-fun accessories chain owned by fashion retailer Monsoon has gone international with its irresistible mix of statement jewelry, hats, beach bags, embellished sandals, swimwear, iPhone covers, and more. Most items are less than $50.

55-59 Oxford St., London, W1C 2PX +44 (0)20 7287-0531, accessorize.com, and additional locations.

Alex Eagle

Located in a town house, this retail experience showcases "a great combo" of high-end fashion, accessories, art, design, houseware, beauty, and photography from around the globe, says accessories designer Lee Savage. Fashion industry vet Alex Eagle not only champions timeless pieces by Rosetta Getty, Blazé Milano, Lemaire, Vilshenko, Pallas, and Vita Kin but also produces an in-house line of luxury staples, as well as collaborations with specialists such as tailor New & Lingwood; customized Rolex and Cartier watches by MAD; jewelry by Fernando Jorge and Sophie Buhai; and hand-selected antique pieces by Catherine Noll, Hervé Van Der Straten, and Gucci.

6-10 Lexington St., London W1R OLB, +44 (0)20 7589-0588, alexeagle.co.uk

Alexander McQueen

As a provocateur, McQueen helped elevate British fashion to the international stage with his unconventional and sometimes macabre designs. He died in 2010, but his brand lives on under the direction of Sarah Burton, who has left her own indelible stamp on the style world, from designing Kate Middleton's royal wedding gown, to dressing former First Lady Michelle Obama. There are several McQueen stores in London, including the women's flagship on Bond Street, the men's store on Savile Row (McQueen the man got his start as an apprentice for a Savile Row tailor), and McQ, the less expensive contemporary collection.

4-5 Old Bond Street, London W1S PD, +44 (0)20 7355-0088, mcqueen.com, and additional locations.

Browns Fashion

Retail icon and Browns founder Joan Burstein is known for her early discovery of British designers John Galliano, Alexander McQueen, and Christopher Kane and for introducing labels such as Calvin Klein, Missoni, and Sonia Rykiel to the UK market. Open since the 1970s, the store is still a fashion mainstay in London for men's, women's, and bridal apparel, even though Burstein has since retired.

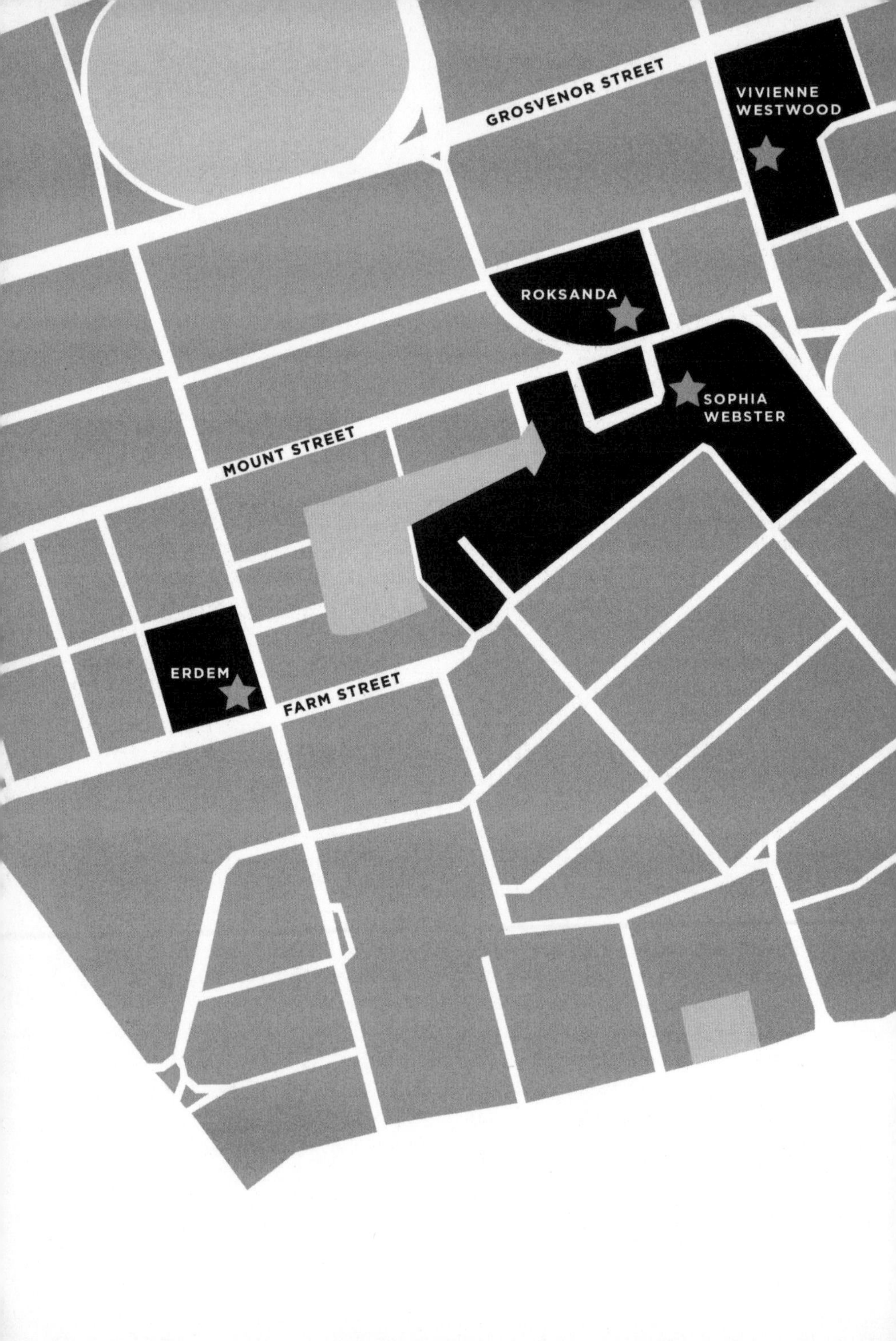
GROSVENOR STREET
VIVIENNE WESTWOOD
ROKSANDA
SOPHIA WEBSTER
MOUNT STREET
ERDEM
FARM STREET

STELLA McCARTNEY

MILLER HARRIS

BRUTON STREET

BURL-INGTON ARCADE

VICTORIA BECKHAM

OLD BOND STREET

DOVER STREET

N

LONDON

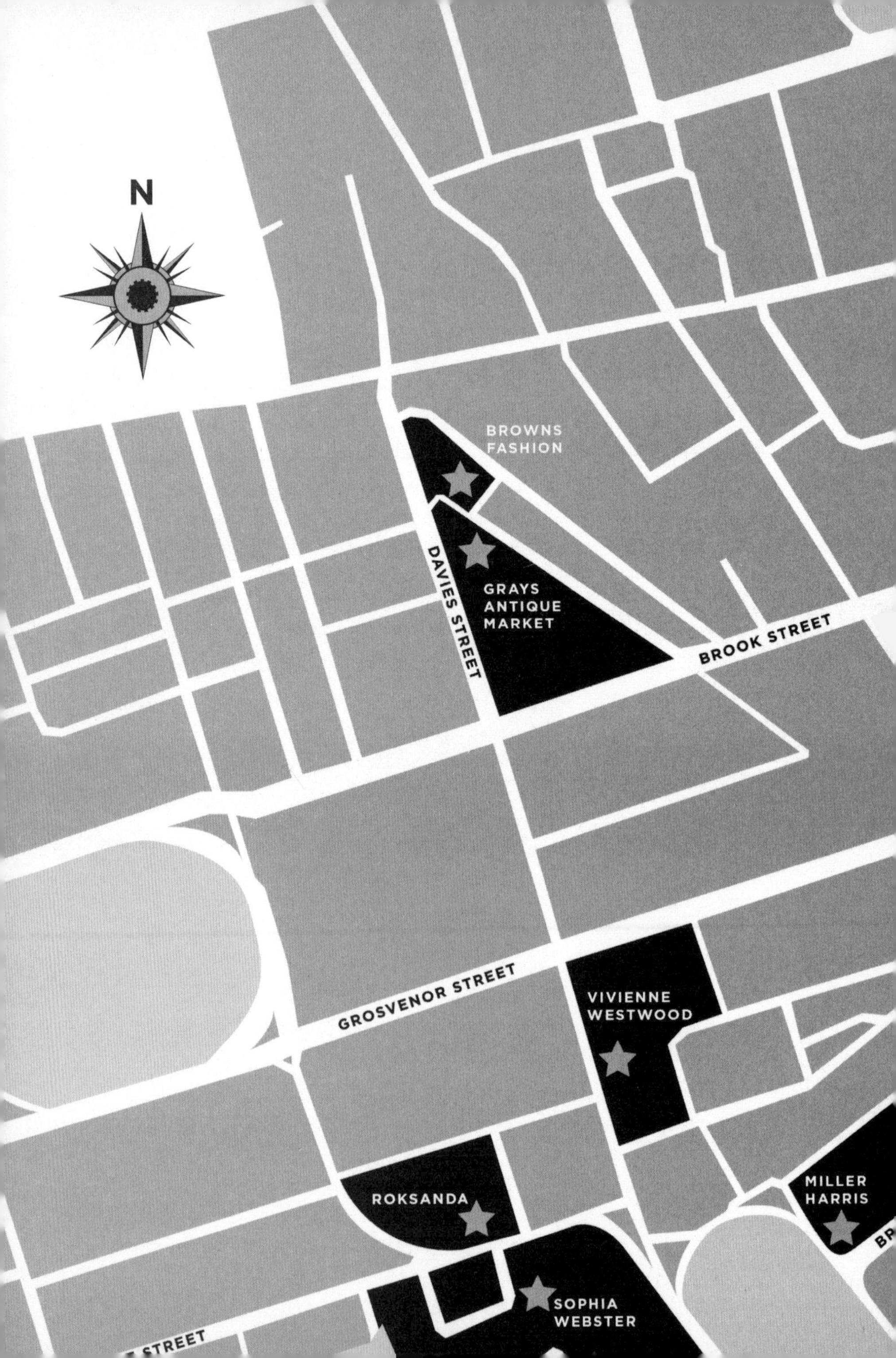
N
BROWNS FASHION
GRAYS ANTIQUE MARKET
DAVIES STREET
BROOK STREET
GROSVENOR STREET
VIVIENNE WESTWOOD
ROKSANDA
MILLER HARRIS
SOPHIA WEBSTER
STREET

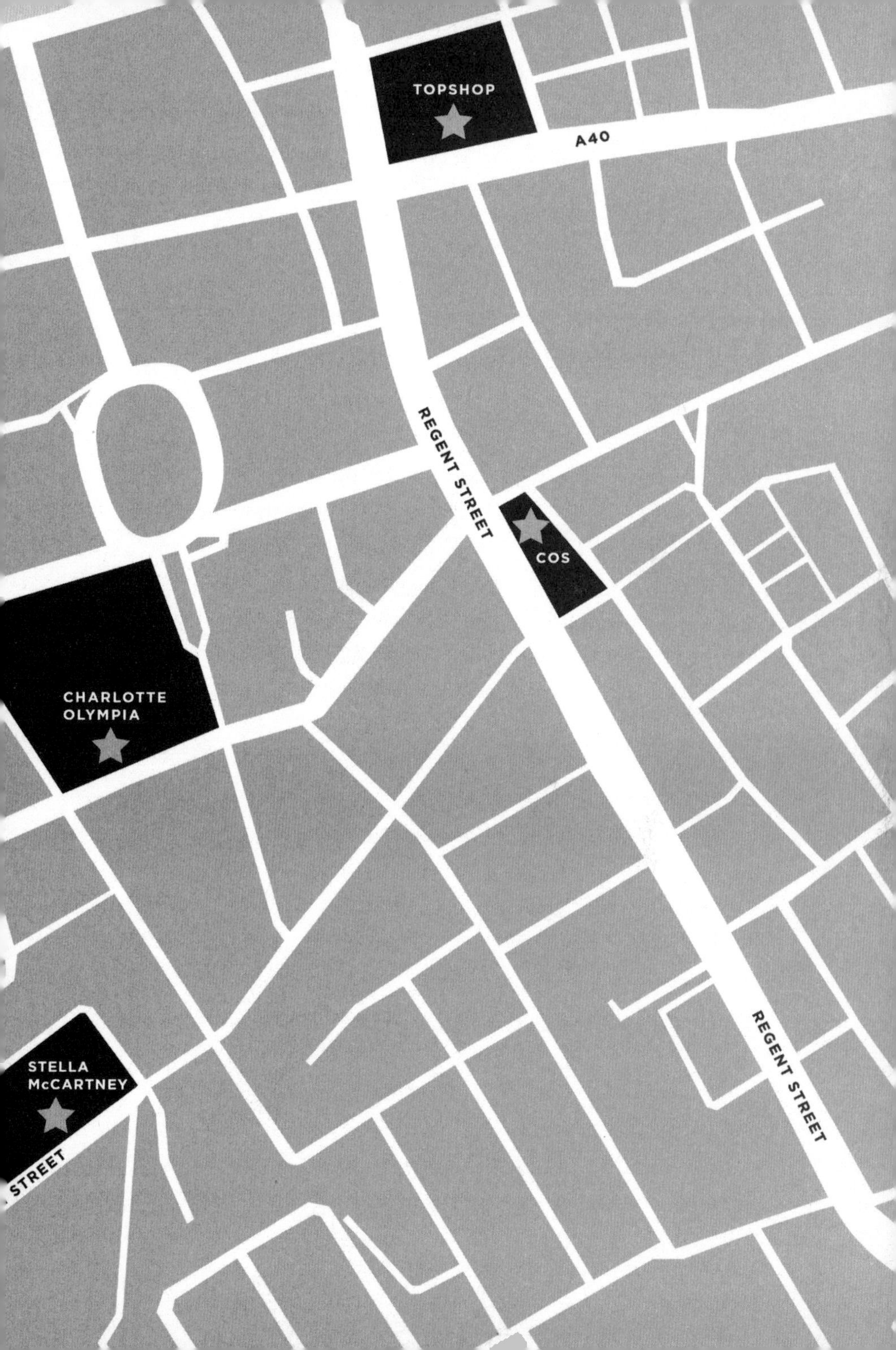
TOPSHOP
A40
REGENT STREET
COS
CHARLOTTE
OLYMPIA
STELLA
McCARTNEY
STREET
REGENT STREET

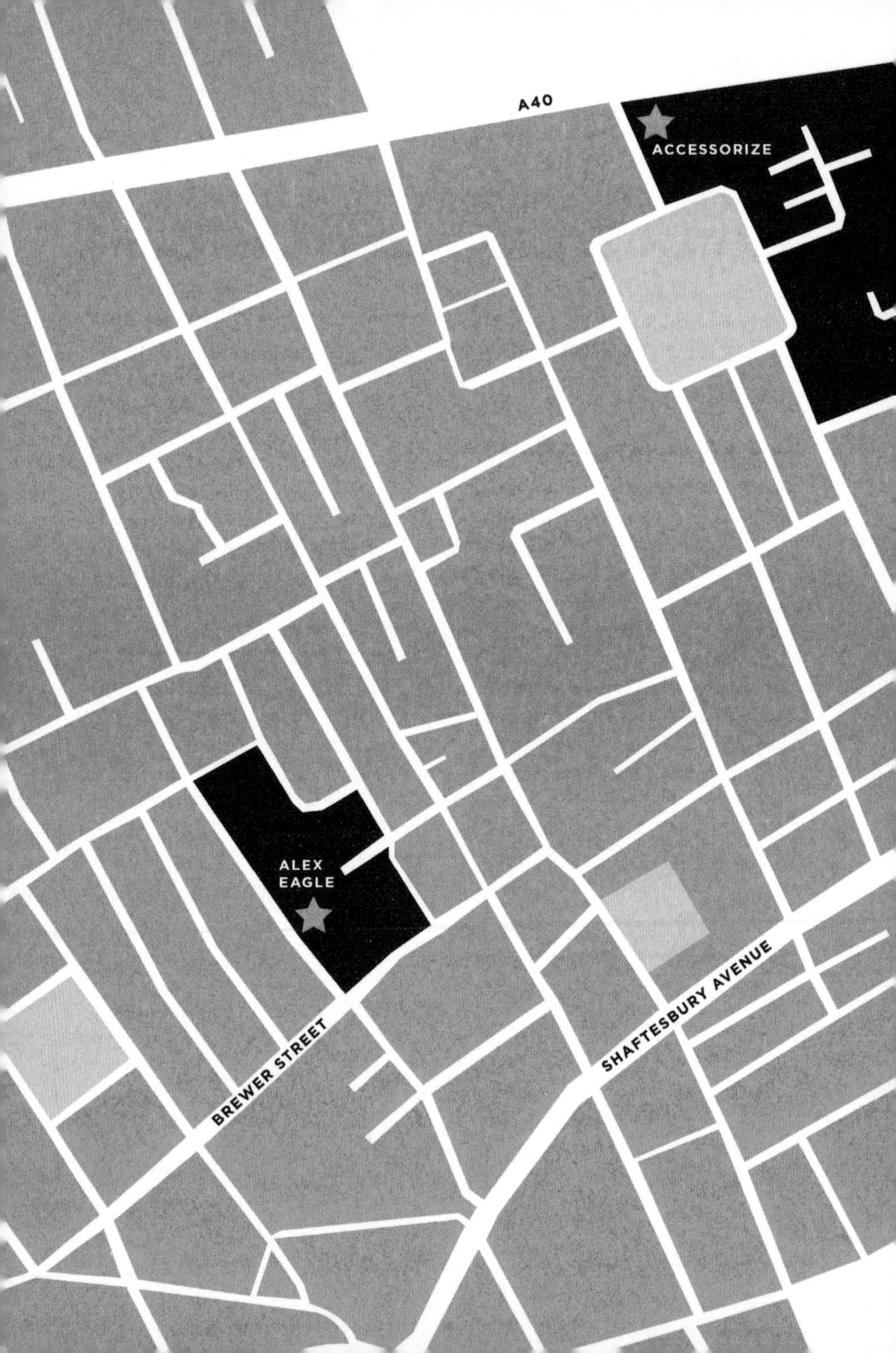
A40
ACCESSORIZE
ALEX
EAGLE
BREWER STREET
SHAFTESBURY AVENUE

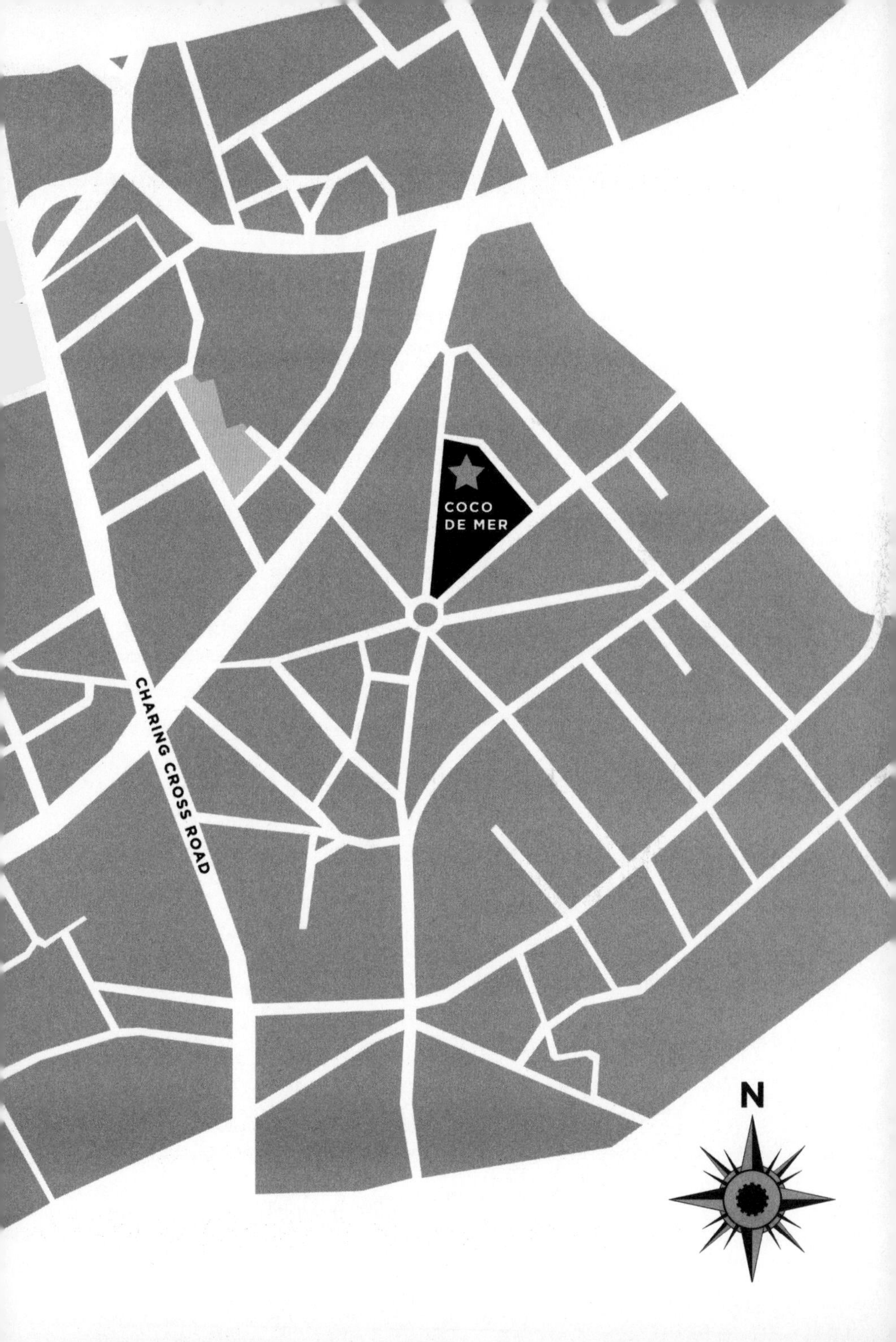
COCO DE MER
CHARING CROSS ROAD
N

24-27 South Molton St., London. W1K 5RD, +44 (0)20 7514-0016, and an additional location on Sloane St., brownsfashion.com.

Burlington Arcade

Open since 1819, this beautiful covered shopping arcade that runs behind Bond Street, from Piccadilly to Burlington Gardens, is a true London experience, and one of the precursors to the modern shopping center. Tenants include N. Peal Cashmere, Penhaligon's, Manolo Blahnik, Church's, and Ladurée, the French patisserie.

51 Piccadilly, London W1J 0QJ, +44 (0)20 7493-1764, burlingtonarcade.com.

Charlotte Olympia

London-based shoe and bag designer Charlotte Dellal is known for such cheeky, feminine classics as her Kitty smoking slippers, Pandora clear plastic box clutches with fabric pouch inserts, and the iconic Dolly pumps in a rainbow of colors, with island-shaped exterior platforms.

56 Maddox St., London W1S 1AY, +44 (0)20 7499 0145, charlotteolympia.com, and additional locations.

Christopher Kane

Designed by British architect John Pawson, the London designer's first boutique is split over two floors, with womenswear on the ground floor and men's in the basement. The gallerylike space is sparsely furnished, allowing Kane's colorful clothing to shine on floating bars, and the handbags on floating shelves.

6 Mount St., London W1K 3EH, +44 20 7493 3111, christopherkane.com.

Coco de Mer

This tasteful erotica shop sells beautiful sex toys and apothecary items, and lingerie by Stella McCartney, Mimi Holliday, and more (including some risqué latex items from the in-house brand).

23 Monmouth St., London WC2H 9DD, +44 (0)20 7836-8882, cocodemer.com.

COS

The H&M-owned, minimalist-chic chain's first store is on Regent Street. A must for stylish shoppers, COS offers modern clothing with clean lines and utilitarian details. It's akin to Marni and Céline, but with most pieces priced at less than $300.

222 Regent St., London W1B 5BD, +44 (0)20 3139-2440, cosstores.com, and additional locations.

Erdem

Known for exquisite fabrics and laces and moody floral prints, London designer Erdem Moralioglu established his collection in 2005 and quickly made

ONLINE SHOPPING TIPS FROM DESIGNER/PERSONAL SHOPPER RAVEN KAUFFMAN:

I really love the modaoperandi.com edit. I feel like I am introduced to a new designer every time I visit the site and I love getting first access with their trunk shows.

Gal Stern tights at etsy.com/shop/SternTights out of Tel Aviv: I own a few of her tights with metallic details and they are fabulous for dancing away the night at Giorgios. They look like something McQueen might do.

French consignment boutique valoisvintage-paris.com has an amazing Hermes selection. Like raiding your French best friend's closet. The British version of theoutnet.com is the best secret spot for Alaïa shoes at an amazing discount. I'm an Alaïa junky and I stalk this site for amazing shoes in my size. I've been able to amass quite a collection.

fans of Keira Knightley, Michelle Dockery, and Emma Stone. His flagship sells the brand's luxury, ready-to-wear, and accessories collections, including exclusive scarves and leather pouches.

70 S Audley St., London W1K 2RA, United Kingdom, +44 (0)20 3653-0360, erdem.com.

Fortnum & Mason

"I carve out extra room in my luggage for a tin or two of tea from Fortnum and Mason," says costume designer Jenn Rogien. "I visited the store because a chef friend mentioned that it is the Queen's grocery store and I couldn't resist. Only on my first visit to all the floors did I find that it's also a fantastic department store complete with a millinery boutique."

181 Piccadilly, London, W1A 1ER, +44 (0)20 7734-8040, fortnumandmason.com.

Grenson

This British purveyor of traditional shoes for men and women has been at it since 1866, and now stocks classic styles, along with trendier wedge sole tassel loafers and derby boots and platform brogues.

40 Lamb's Conduit St., London WC1N 3LB, +44 (0)20 3689-2970, grenson.com.

Gray's Antiques

This labyrinthine Mayfair antiques center, which has more than 200 stalls, is a fave of Liz Goldwyn's for vintage costume jewelry and accessories. Interesting factoid: there's a lost tributary of the Tyburn river running underneath the Mews section of the building, which has been channeled into a water feature stocked with fish.

58 Davies St., London W1K 5AB, +44 (0)20 7629-7034, graysantiques.com.

Hussein Chalayan

One of fashion's biggest thinkers, Chalayan has designed remote-controlled dresses, collapsible coffee table skirts, and dresses covered in rows of fake fingernails. The designer's low-key, black-and-white flagship, designed by his long-term collaborator, architect Zoe Smith, is a blank canvas for all that. It features a tiled floor resembling a backgammon board, and a center table evocative of the hull of a boat.

2 Bourdon St., London W1K 3PA, +44 (0)20 7493-8157, chalayan.com.

Jimmy Choo

Designed by David Collins Studio, the 3-story flagship for this Brit brand of It shoes oozes luxury, from the raw crystal chandeliers to the bridal salon with fully stocked bar. The store showcases the brand's range, from glitter fabric pumps to sunglasses and fragrance.

27 New Bond Street, London, W1S2RH, +44 (0)20 07493-5858, jimmychoo.com, and additional locations.

Miller Harris

Lyn Harris launched her brand in 2000, which uses globally sourced ingredients, from Florentine iris to Tunisian orange flower. The result? Fragrances such as Rose en Noir (my favorite), Coeur d'Ete, and Feuilles de Tabac inspired by "Parisian elegance" and "London's eclectic style-driven streets," according to the brand. Harris has since moved on to create a new project, Perfumer H, but this brand remains a beloved classic.

21 Bruton St., London W1J 6QD, +44 (0)20 7629-7750, millerharris.com, and additional locations.

Mulberry

The British heritage leather goods brand was recently turned over to designer Johnny Coca, formerly of Céline, who has given the bags and ready-to-wear a newly streamlined, dare we say, French touch.

50 New Bond St., London W1S 1BJ, +44 (0)20 7491-3900, mulberry.com, and additional locations.

Nicholas Kirkwood

The award-winning shoe designer's London flagship features his architec-

BRONWYN COSGRAVE

NEXT GEN DESIGNERS

The director of Cosgrave Global Media, a London-based firm that focuses on luxury brand communications strategy, Bronwyn's fashion CV includes serving as features editor of British Vogue, *and penning six fashion history books.*

I love Mount Street in London. A generation of designers whom I got to know when they were all just starting out have established boutiques in and around this luxury thoroughfare. **MARC JACOBS** was the first designer to open on Mount Street. Then came **BALENCIAGA, CHRISTIAN LOUBOUTIN,** and **CÉLINE**. But the very special aspect of this street is the boutiques that young British designers established. **CHRISTOPHER KANE** and **ROKSANDA ILLINCIC** commissioned the architects John Pawson and David Adjaye, respectively, to design retail spaces that are more like galleries than shops. Nearby on South Audley Street, **ERDEM** designed his own boutique with his partner, Philip Joseph.

MARC JACOBS, 24-25 Mount St., London W1K 2RR, +44 (0)20 7399-1690, marcjacobs.com.

BALENCIAGA, 12 Mount St., London W1K 2RD, +44 (0)20 7317-4400, balenciaga.com.

CHRISTIAN LOUBOUTIN, 17 Mount St., London W1K 2RD, +44 (0)20 843-227 4322, us.christianlouboutin.com.

CÉLINE, 103 Mount St., London W1K 2AP, +44 (0)20 7491-8200, celine.com.

CHRISTOPHER KANE, 6 Mount St., London W1K 3EH, +44 (0)20 7493-3111, christopherkane.com.

ROKSANDA ILLINCIC, 9 Mount St., London W1K 3NG, +44 (0)20 7613-6499, roksanda.com.

ERDEM, 70 S Audley St., London W1K 2RA, +44 (0)20 3653-0360, erdem.com.

tural styles with dynamic, boomerang-shaped straps, mirrored triangular heels and pearl embellishments.

5 Mount St., London W1K 3NE, +44 20 7290 1404, nicholaskirkwood.com, and additional locations.

Roksanda

Designer Roksanda Ilincic launched her collection at London Fashion Week in 2005, and has gained fame for her boldly colored, feminine, draped silhouettes that often feature cutouts and have been worn by the Duchess of Cambridge, Cate Blanchett, Daisy Ridley, Gwyneth Paltrow, and Keira Knightley. Ilincic's first store opened in 2014, in a space with a marble herringbone floor, rose gold rails, and concrete walls conceived by architect David Adjaye. "I never miss a chance to pop in to her exquisite boutique," says Refinery29's Christene Barberich. "It's a full sensory experience, for sure!"

9 Mount St., London W1K 3NG, +44 (0)20 7613-6499, roksanda.com.

Simone Rocha

Since her London Fashion Week debut in September 2010, the designer's star has risen quickly, thanks to her rebellious-yet-romantic take on femininity and fresh, craftsy approach to using fabrics and textures. In 2015, she opened her first store, on London's Mount Street, showcasing her ready-to-wear, bags, shoes, knitwear, and jewelry, next to artworks, including a glazed ceramic chandelier by Los Angeles artist Pae White and a set of three original lithographs by Francis Bacon from 1984.

93 Mount St., London W1K 2SY, +44 (0)20 7729-7004, simonerocha.com.

Sophia Webster

A former assistant to shoe designer Nicholas Kirkwood, Sophia Webster now has her own fabulous footwear line characterized by candylike colorways, graphic detailing, and whimsical embellishments. Her Mount Street store features the full upbeat collection of shoes and bags, plush lavender velvet seating, and a place for shoppers to take butterfly-wing selfies.

124 Mount St., London W1K 3NR, +44 (0)20 7729-70004, sophiawebster com.

Stella McCartney

The daughter of Sir Paul McCartney, and a lifelong vegetarian, Stella McCartney has built a luxury brand from the ground up based on the principles of sustainability and "no leathers, feathers, or fur." A recent ad campaign, featuring that slogan graphically superimposed over photos of her collection in collaboration with the American artist Ed Ruscha. McCa-

ONLINE SHOPPING TIP

Most big name London-based designers (Mulberry, Alexander McQueen, Mary Katrantzou, etc.) have their own international e-commerce businesses. If you want to discover more up-and-coming names, check out UK-based Netaporter.com, Matchesfashion.com, and Avenue32.com, all of which do a good job of introducing new talent, and which ship globally. Another good UK-based global e-comm site is WolfandBadger.com, for indie labels from London and beyond.

rtney is a resource for sporty tailored pieces, printed T-shirts, Falaballa bags and those platform brogues that bloggers can't get enough of. She has stores around the world.

30 Bruton St., London W1J6QR,+44 (0)20 7518-3100, stellamccartney.com, and additional locations.

Topshop

This British retailer may be a fast-fashion juggernaut, with hundreds of stores around the globe and a collaboration with Beyoncé on her activewear collection, Ivy Park, but the Oxford Street store was the original. The 65,000-square-foot retail mecca has its own radio station and manicure bar, and receives multiple daily deliveries of on-trend merchandise to satisfy the throngs who come through the doors. "So much fun," says British TV presenter, blogger and model Louise Roe. "I make a beeline for it whenever I'm back in London. There's a DJ, a blowout bar, a candy bar, a café, and an unreal shoe section." "Can also be overwhelming just by its sheer size," says Charlotte Ronson. "Luckily there is a sweet shop inside to give you that much needed sugar rush." Topshop was early on to the fast-fashion–designer collaboration game, sponsoring London Fashion Week and partnering with emerging British designers as far back as the mid-1990s.

Oxford Circus, 214 Oxford St., London W1W 8LG, +44 (8)44 848-7487, topshop.com, and additional locations worldwide.

Victoria Beckham

Designed by female architect Farshid Moussavi, who also worked on the London 2012 Olympic Park, the conceptual space features the entire VB universe, including her sexy, sophisticated runway collection and the less expensive Victoria Victoria Beckham collection. And occasionally, the former Spice Girl has been known to drop by!

36 Dover St., London W1S 4NH, +44 (0)20 7042-0700, victoriabeckham.com.

VICTORIA BECKHAM

Vivienne Westwood

The one, the only, Dame Vivienne Westwood, queen of the punk past and present, who has dressed everyone from Naomi Campbell (remember when she tottered on the runway in those famously tall shoes?) to Pharrell Williams, whose Mountain hat caused a sensation a few years back. In the 1970s, Westwood and her then-husband Malcolm McLaren played a major role in the punk movement in London, believing they could wage a social revolution through fashion and rock 'n' roll from their Kings Road shop, which was alternatively named "Let It Rock" and "Too Fast to Live, Too Young to Die." In 1974 they changed the store's name to Sex to give a symbolic middle finger to the establishment that prosecuted them under British obscenity laws for making shirts with pornographic images. And the rest is history. She has stores all over the world, but shopping for her twisted tartans and T-shirts in London feels right. **44 Conduit St., London W1S 2YL, +44 (0)20 7439-1109, viviennewestwood.com, and additional locations.**

Wolf and Badger

If you're interested in discovering something beyond London's well-known fashion brands, this is the place to find indie fashion, jewelry, and home accessories design from around the world, and at reasonable prices. Launched in 2009, the company has two brick-and-mortar stores, in Mayfair and Notting Hill, and an e-commerce site. It carries more than 600 independent labels, including Rixo, Lautem, and Latelita London. More than 75 percent of each purchase goes back to the designer, and the owners also nurture the brands they stock with business advice and product development. There's also a juice bar by Raw Press.

32 Dover St., London W1S 4NE, +44 (0)20 3627-3191, wolfandbadger.com, and an additional location in Notting Hill.

MARYLEBONE

Alfie's Antique Market

One of the largest indoor antiques markets in the country (35,000 square feet over five floors), this spot is a must for interior decorators and fashion enthusiasts. Liz Goldwyn shops Alfie's for costume accessories and jewelry. There's also a rooftop restaurant.

13-25 Church St., London NW8 8DT, +44 (0)20 7723-6066, alfiesantiques.com.

Mouki Mou

"Feels like you've stepped back in time—in a good way—with their old-world service and curated offering of clothes, jewelry, and beauty," says Tere Artigas of this store, which features indigo clothing by 45rpm, sundresses by Rachel Comey, sandals by Ancient Greek Sandals, jewelry by Pippa Small, and more.

29 Chiltern St., London W1U 7PL, +44 (0)20 7224-4010, moukimou.com.

Perfumer H

Lyn Harris, founder of Miller Harris, launched this fragrance concept space in late 2015, offering bespoke and seasonal fragrances. You can create a custom fragrance with her from scratch (a collaborative process that can take up to six months), buy a one-of-a-kind Laboratory Edition (after the customer takes the bottle, the formula is reserved as exclusively his or hers), or choose one of her ready-to-wear seasonal fragrances. The midcentury spot offers a warm welcome—and serves tea.

106a Crawford St., London W1H 2HZ, +44 (0)20 7258-7859, perfumerh.com.

William Vintage Shop

"One of my favorite, most unforgettable shopping experiences was when I met William Banks-Blaney and visited his extraordinary store," says Rachel Zoe. "This was my first time really 'shopping' in over a year—my longest time without a purchase since my son, Skyler, was born. I ended up spending six hours in the store—Skyler got comfortable and took a nap! I found some unbelievable Christian Dior haute couture pieces and a Jean Patou vintage gown that I wore on the cover of my second book, *Living in Style*. It was hands down the best shopping day I have ever had."

2 Marylebone St., London W1G 8JQ, +44 (0)20 7487-4322, williamvintage.com.

KNIGHTSBRIDGE/SLOANE STREET/BELGRAVIA

Anya Hindmarch

Handbag designer darling Anya Hindmarch founded her business in London in 1987 at age nineteen. Over the years, her hits have included beaded evening bags designed to look like British candy packets, and clutches modeled after Walkers potato chip bags. In 2001, Hindmarch launched the "Be a Bag" concept, which allowed shoppers to turn a favorite photograph into a bag. In 2007 her $15 canvas I AM NOT A PLASTIC BAG totes raised awareness about plastic bag waste and caused a worldwide frenzy. In recent years, in addition to bags, her sticker business has been booming.

157-158 Sloane St., London SW1X 9AB, +44 (0)20 7730-0961, anyahindmarch.com, and additional locations.

egg

Hidden in a mews house on a noncommercial street, egg sells luxurious, casual basics. "I live for their supersoft cashmere, which I can never get enough of," says fashion industry consultant Fern Mallis.

36 Kinnerton St., London SW1X 8ES, +44 (0)20 7235-9315, eggtrading.com.

Emilia Wickstead

A favorite of the Duchess of Cambridge, the British designer is known for her classy, feminine, wearable pieces in pretty pastels and florals that make high-profile dressing a breeze. Spanning two floors and 2,000 square feet, her Sloane Street store offers the complete ready-to-wear collection, while maintaining the services that launched her career: made-to-order, made-to-measure, and bespoke options.

162A Sloane St., London SW1X 9BS, +44 (0)20 7235-1104, emiliawickstead.com.

Feathers

An icon of Swinging '60s London, Feathers was founded in 1968 by Jean and Willie Burstein, brother of Sidney Burstein, who founded

SOPHIA WEBSTER

EAST LONDON AND CAMDEN TOWN GEMS

Sophia Webster debuted her quirky, fun shoe collection for spring 2013 after working as design assistant to Nicholas Kirkwood. In just a few years, she's built a following that includes Katy Perry, Rita Ora, and Elizabeth Banks. Spring 2014 saw the launch of her iconic Butterfly collection, which included the signature Chiara sandals. Her collections have expanded to include a wide range of styles, from flats to espadrilles, and the classic Coco pump showcasing the flamingo detail at the back of the heel, an image now synonymous with the brand. She opened her first London store in 2016.

As a glasses wearer I am always on the lookout for unique frames, and in London there is no place better than **GENERAL EYEWEAR** in Stables Market, Camden. They have an incredible selection of one-of-a-kind vintage frames; they handle your prescription as well, so it's all really good value for something so individual. I love buying art from **PRINT CLUB LONDON** in Dalston, East London. They have affordable contemporary prints in limited runs. I have lots of their prints in my house, ranging from pink pineapples to huge toucans to my favorite: a multicolored Beyoncé print, by illustrator Hattie Stewart.

BOROUGH MARKET in South East London is amazing for fresh, good-quality food, and **BROADWAY MARKET** in Hackney, East London, has so many cute cafés and shops selling original clothing and arts and crafts as well as food stalls offering authentic street food.

GENERAL EYEWEAR, The Stables Market, Arch 67, Chalk Farm Rd., London NW1 8AH, +44 (0)20 7428-0123, generaleyewear.com.

PRINT CLUB LONDON, 10-28 Millers Av., Unit 3, London E8 2DS, +44 (0)20 7254-9028, printclublondon.com.

BOROUGH MARKET, 8 Southwark St., London SE1 1TL, +44 (0)20 7407-10002, boroughmarket.org.uk.

BROADWAY MARKET, Broadway Market—pedestrian route between London Fields Park and Regent's Canal, London E8 4QJ, broadwaymarket.co.uk.

luxury boutique Browns a year later with his wife, Joan. The Knightsbridge store, where Manolo Blahnik worked as a young lad, is still going strong with more than ninety designer collections, including Moschino, Junya Watanabe, Sacai, and Etro. "Supercool boutique right across the street from Harrods," says the Gem Palace's Shalini Kasliwal.

42 Hans Crescent, London SW1X 0LZ, +44 (0)20 7589-5802, feathersfashion.com.

Philip Treacy

Irish hat designer Philip Treacy has elevated millinery to an art form. Championed from a young age by the late fashion editor Isabella Blow, Treacy opened his shop on Elizabeth Street in 1994, next door to Blow's old house, where Treacy's business first began in the basement. His famously iconic pieces worn by the likes of Kate Middleton and Grace Jones include hats fashioned into boats and lobsters. There are handmade couture items, and more affordable floral headbands, too.

69 Elizabeth St., London SW1 W9PJ, +44 (0)20 7730-3992, philiptreacy.co.uk.

Victoria & Albert Museum store

The V&A might be the best museum bookstore in the world, with must-have fashion, art, and design books, killer jewelry, scarves, and other accessories, plus cool cards, wrapping paper, and more. Give yourself plenty of time. Costume designer Arianne Phillips counts it among her favorites, and so do I.

Cromwell Rd., London SW7 2RL, +44 (0)20 7942-2000, vam.ac.uk.

KINGS ROAD

L.K. Bennett

Founded in London in 1990, the brand rose to international fame in 2011, when it was revealed to be Kate Middleton's go-to source for sensible kitten heels. Known for classic, feminine shoes, $300-to-$500, and a range of clothing to match, L.K. Bennett has stores across Europe, the US, and in the Middle East.

164-166 Kings Rd., London SW3 4UR, +44 (0)20 7351-9659, lkbennett.com, and additional locations.

Manolo Blahnik

With a career spanning forty years, Blahnik was a luxury shoe designer before it was a thing. His designs have been worn by every celebrity under the sun (and earned him the honor of having his shoes referred to simply as Manolos), and he even collaborated with Rihanna on a recent capsule collection. Born in the Canary Islands, Blahnik designed sets before shoes, and was "discovered" by

RICCARDO TORTATO

BESPOKE LONDON AND BEYOND

Riccardo Tortato was born in Venice and lives in New York, but he takes an airplane every ten days to discover the best fashion trends around the world. Men Fashion Director and Online Fashion Director at Tsum Moscow, he is a style expert and best friend and business partner of Anna Dello Russo. He is also famous for his long gray beard and hardly ever wearing socks . . . even during the winter in Moscow.

For cashmere sweaters I go to **TURNBALL AND ASSER,** one of the most historic English bespoke shirtmakers—it serves Prince Charles and the British Royal family. **GEO TRUMPER** is one of the oldest barber salons in London, and it's where I buy all my grooming products, except perfume, which I buy at **FLORIS,** the best perfume store in London. I order velvet slippers from **FOSTER AND SON,** customized with my intials.

TELERIE SPADARI in Milan is a great place to order custom-made pajamas and tablecloths. **LARUSMIANI** in Milan is a wonderful Italian gentleman's clothing store in the center of Milan fashion district. I used to go to **CAMICERIA SAN MARCO** in Venice when I was child to have my shirts custom made. The Duke of Windsor and Hemingway are also former clients. They can make ladies blouses and dresses, too.

MERCURY in Moscow is the best place to buy watches from Patek Philippe, because the store stocks the best collections. I visit **CHARVET** in Paris for pocket squares and silk scarves and **AGLITITALY** online for unique sneaker laces.

TURNBULL ASSER, 71-72 Jermyn St., London SW1Y 6PF, +44 (0)20 7808 3000, turnballandasser.com, and additional locations.

GEO TRUMPER, 9 Curzon St., London W1J 5HQ, +44 (0)20 7499-1850, trumpers.com, and an additional location in St. James.

FLORIS, 89 Jermyn St., London SW1Y 6JH, +44 (0)20 7747 3612, florislondon.com, and an additional location in Belgravia.

FOSTER AND SON, 83 Jermyn St., London SW1Y 6JD, +44 20 7930 5385, foster.co.uk.

TELERIE SPADARI, Via Spadari, 13, 20123 Milano +39 02 8646 0908.

CAMICERIA SAN MARCO, Sant'Angelo, Venice, 3627, 30124 VE, +39 041 522 1432.

MERCURY, Tretskayov Passage 1, Moscow, and additional locations, mercury.ru.

LARUSMIANI, Via Monte Napoleone, 7, 20121 Milano, +39 02 7600 6957, larusimiani.it.

CHARVET, 28 Place Vendôme, 75001 Paris, +33 1 42 60 30 70, charvet.com.

AGLITITALY, aglititaly.com/shop.

LIBERTY LONDON

iconic *Vogue* editor Diane Vreeland in 1970. He moved to London and his breakthrough came in 1971, when he was asked by the flamboyant British fashion designer Ossie Clark to create shoes for his runway show. Blahnik made a high-heeled sandal that entwined the ankles with straps of ivy and cherries, and he hasn't stopped creating since.

49-51 Old Church St., London SW3 5BS, +44 (0)20 7351-5822, manoloblahnik.com, and additional locations.

The Shop at Bluebird

A cabinet of curiosities located in a stunning art deco building that used to be a car showroom, this concept store specializes in laid-back luxe lifestyle. Open since 2006, Bluebird stocks a great mix of Brit and international brands for men and women (Mary Katrantzou, Emilia Wickstead, Chloé, Preen, Isa Arfen, Missoni, Junya Watanabe, Gant). There's a real emphasis on new talent, too, with the shop hosting events and pop-up shops featuring exclusives from around the world. On-site cozy café and spa.

350 Kings Rd., London SW3 5UU, +44 (0)20 7351-3873.

Whistles

When Kate Middleton was dubbed "princess of the High Street," before she married Prince William, Whistles was one of her favorite brands. More sweet than sexy, the brand made the scalloped-edge ivory blouse Middleton wore in some of her engagement photos. Personal note: The Kings Road store is my favorite.

31 Kings Rd., London SW3 4RP, +44 (0)20 7730-2006, whistles.com, and additional locations.

NOTTING HILL

Couverture & The Grabstore

"A cool mix of housewares, kids' clothes, and jewelry you can't find anywhere else," says M.i.h Jeans' Chloe Lonsdale. There's an emphasis on indie designers like Rachel Comey, A Détacher, Apiece Apart, Martiniano, and Clare V.

188 Kennsington Park Rd., London W11 2ES, +44 (0)20 7229-2178, couvertureandthegrabstore.com.

NOTTING HILL

Matches Fashion

Husband-and-wife duo Tom and Ruth Chapman opened their first boutique in Wimbledon Village in 1987 and were the first retailers in the UK to stock Prada. Over the past three decades, their business has grown to include four stores, all in London, selling Alexander McQueen, Mary Katrantzou, Isabel Marant, Delpozo, and other top brands, as well as an international online luxury site that reaches more than 100 countries. "The shop in Notting Hill looks like a showroom," says interior designer Brigette Romanek. "The clothes are displayed hanging at eye level, which makes it easy to shop. And the white walls as background makes everything pop. I have to control myself when I walk in that place."

60-64 Ledbury Rd., London W11 2AJ, +44 (0)20 7221-0255, matchesfashion .com, and additional locations.

Soler

"Where my friend Alex al-Badr makes the most charming and lovely dresses, blouses, fur vests, and leather skirts," says jewelry designer Liseanne Frank.

88 Bevington Rd, London W10 5TW, +44(0)20 8968-4694, soler.co.uk.

East London

Goodhood Store

This 2,000-square-foot boutique for men and women specializes in elevated minimalist clothing and streetwear with a fun grab'n'go items mixed in (T-shirts, sneakers, buttons, and stickers). The space is filled with wooden fixtures, and there's even a log cabin. "If you journey downstairs, they have amazing housewares and a café," says Tere Artigas.

151 Curtain Rd., London EC2A 3QE, +44 (0)20 7729-3600, goodhoodstore.com.

Hostem

Hostem, located in East London, is Harry Styles's go-to for high-end runway and street labels Junya Watanabe, Raf Simons, and Visvim. The brainchild of menswear visionary James Brown, the store expanded to include womenswear in 2013, with a focus on up-and-coming designers.

28 Old Nichol St., London E2 7HR, +44 (0)20 7739-9733, hostem.co.uk.

House of Hackney

House of Hackney was founded in 2011 around a kitchen table by husband-and-wife team Javvy M Royle and Frieda Gormley. Sharing a passion for interiors and a background in fashion and product design, they decided to create a new brand in the great tradition of British print houses, to champion print, color, and texture, taking inspiration from the past and the present. The 2,000-square-foot town house that is home to the brand is a print paradise of home design (wallpaper, lampshades, porcelain, towels, bedding fabric), plus fashion and accessories.

131 Shoreditch High St., London E1 6JE, +44 (0)20 7613-5559, houseofhackney.com.

J.W. Anderson Workshops

Not a store, but rather an exhibition space that occasionally sells things . . . Got that? The young British designer took inspiration from the Bloomsbury Group's Omega Workshops to create the space next to the Ace Hotel, which hosts rotating events, some lasting weeks, others just a few days. Anderson collaborates with different artists (photographer Ian David Baker was one, A$AP Rocky was another) on the installations, with spin-off merchandise for sale.

100 Shoreditch High St., London E1 6JQ, +44 (0)20 3441-7030, j-w-anderson.com.

LNCC

Edgy concept store in Dalston,

LNCC (short for Late Night Chameleon Café) features top designer names and young talent (Acne, Gucci, Proenza Schouler, J.W. Anderson), plus interesting eco-conscious brands (Blackyoto, Eckhaus Latta) in a groovy spot designed by Gary Card with a bar and club space. You'll also discover hard-to-find vinyl and first edition books.

18-24 Shacklewell Ln., basement level, London E8 2EZ, +44 (0)20 3174-0744, ln-cc.com.

YMC

You Must Create is ground zero for London's modern minimalists, with canvas culottes, workwear jackets and boilersuits galore, inviting shoppers to create their own style, plus nifty things like a collab with groundbreaking 1980s designer Katherine Hamnett, queen of the slogan tee.

23 Hanbury St., London E1 6QR, +44 (0)20 3432 3010, youmustcreate.com.

PADDINGTON/ST. GEORGE'S FIELD

Merchant Archive

Sophie Merchant's original vintage shop served as a source of inspiration for designers, but has now developed into a full-fledged store and her own label. "She has vintage clothing and new clothing, in addition to beautiful old dishware, books, and paintings by local artists," says Brigette Romanek. "She brings in lots of interesting odds and ends and has a very keen eye for bohemia chic."

19 Kensington Park Rd., London W11 2EU, +44 (0)20 7229-9006, merchantarchive.com.

Pebble London

"For amazing jewelry," says designer Stephanie von Watzdorf of this appointment-only treasure chest where founder, designer, and curator Peter Adler makes his own jewelry using metals, stones, wood, glass, coral, and amber sourced from India, China, Africa, Thailand, and South America, as well as stocking traditional pieces from tribal groups in Africa, the Pacific, China, Afghanistan, Nepal, and India. Over the years, Adler has worked with or sold to many fashion designers, including Alexander McQueen, John Galliano, Roberto Cavalli, Issey Miyake, Matthew Williamson, Emilio Pucci, Allegra Hicks, and Donna Karan.

191 Sussex Gardens, London W2 2RH, +44 (0)20 7262-1775, pebblelondon.com.

PORTOBELLO ROAD MARKET

Viola Boutique

Sara Lauchlan opened Viola after a career spent buying for London boutiques and moonlighting as a personal stylist. Tucked away on leafy Connaught Street since opening its doors in 2009, the store has acquired a loyal following of women who appreciate Lauchlan's laid-back approach to London style. The range of womenswear and jewelry designers includes Tsumori Chisato, Forte Forte, Roseanna, Stouls, Pedro Garcia and Raquel Allegra.

25 Connaught St., London W22AY, +44 (20) 7262-2722, violalondon.com.

BERMONDSEY

Kerry Taylor Auctions

"At this auction house for fabulous vintage, I bought an insanely beautiful custom dress by the first female couturier, Jeanne Paquin," says jewelry designer Kara Ross. "I actually bought it sight unseen. It's the most beautiful dress; I'm hoping that one of my daughters will wear it as a wedding dress."

249-253 Long Lane, London SE1 4PR, +44 (0)20 3137-0112, kerrytaylorauctions.com.

PORTOBELLO

Portobello Road Market

This world-famous antiques market features hundreds of vendors on any given day, but Fridays are when you might see Kate Moss or Sienna Miller wandering the stalls looking at vintage clothes, military jackets, cashmere sweaters, and belts. "Fridays at Portobello Market still hold unearthed treasures, and on any given day you will be able to spot a handful of key stylists and designers," says M.i.h Jeans's designer Chloe Lonsdale. "I always source the best vintage there even though I travel all over the world for research."

Portobello Rd., London W11 1LA, +44 (0)20 7727-7684, portobelloroad.co.uk.

Rellik

Opened in 1999 by three partners, Rellik has high-end vintage from the 1930s onward by Vivienne Westwood, Comme des Garçons, Bill Gibb, Azzedine Alaïa, and many more. "The most amazing vintage shop," says jewelry designer Jordan Askill. "The owners—Fiona, Claire, and Steven—are all dear friends. I used to work there when I was about nineteen and living in London for the first time. Each owner keeps their own selection, and each has a specialty, but the store operates as one unit."

8 Golborne Rd., London W10 5NW, +44 (0)20 8962-0089, rellikondon.co.uk.

IRISH DESIGN SHOP

DUBLIN

IRELAND

Arnotts

The oldest department store in Dublin, Arnotts was founded in 1843, and acquired by Selfridges in 2015. In addition to top fashion and housewares brands, it also carries Irish craft brands, including glassware, pottery, textiles, and home accessories.

12 Henry St., Dublin 1, +353-1-805-0400, arnotts.ie.

Brown Thomas

The most prestigious department store in the city, Brown Thomas stocks exclusive brands, as well as collections by top Irish designers such as Paul Costelloe, Lainey Keogh, and Louise Kennedy. Part of the same retail family that includes Selfridges in the UK and Holt Renfrew in Canada. The Grafton Street flagship opened in 1849.

88-95 Grafton St., Dublin 2, +353-1-605-6666, brownthomas.com, and additional locations.

Cleo

High-end, family-run source for incredible knitwear handmade throughout Ireland (Donegal, Kerry, the Aran Islands, etc.). Features gorgeous sweaters and shawls, linen shirts, and tweed jackets.

18 Kildare St., Dublin, +353-1-676-1421.

Costume

Launched in 1997 by three sisters, Costume is a Dublin fashion institution, with designs from Isabel Marant, Roland Mouret, Cédric Charlier, MSGM, Jérôme Dreyfuss, and more, plus top-notch customer service.

10 Castle Market, Dublin Southside, Dublin, +353-1-679-4188, costumedublin.ie.

Folkster

Owned by Irish stylist Blanaid Hennessy, this successful independent retail store specializes in the boho-romantic look with a mix of vintage and contemporary clothing and accessories, as well as bridal and housewares.

9 Eustace St. Temple Bar, Dublin 2, +353-1-679-4188, folkster.com

Havana

Destination for high-end, avant-garde fashion by Irish labels Simone Rocha, Sphere One, and Sian Jacobs, alongside international names like Rick Owens, Stella Jean, and Junya

FOLKSTER

Watanabe. Nearly all of owner Nikki Creedon's designer stock is exclusive to her in Ireland.

2 Anglesea House, Donnybrook Road, Donnybrook, Dublin 4, +353-1-260-2707 havanaboutique.ie.

Harlequin

You'll want to play dress-up for hours in this chicly cluttered shop, with fabulous vintage finds from the 1920s onward, including evening gloves, top hats, and beaded choker necklaces.

13 Castle Market, Dublin 2, Ireland, +353-1-671-0202.

Indigo & Cloth

One of Ireland's top menswear boutiques, Indigo & Cloth opened in 2007. It features leading menswear labels, both international and Irish, alongside a ground-floor Clement & Pekoe café.

9 Essex St. E, Temple Bar, Dublin 2, Ireland, +353-1-670-6403, indigoandcloth.com.

Irish Design Shop

Established in 2008 by jewelry designers Clare Grennan and Laura Caffrey, this place promotes the work of

ONLINE SHOPPING TIP

There are lots of places online to buy Irish knitwear and crafts, but I like the fashion-forward eye of AranSweaterMarket.com and TheIrishWorshop.com which ship worldwide.

Ireland's contemporary makers, including crockery, candles, knit hats, and modern-looking jewelry.

41 Drury St., Dublin 2, +353-1-679-8871, irishdesignshop.com.

Jenny Vander

Considered by many to be Ireland's best vintage store, Jenny Vander has been open since the 1970s, and carries an eclectic mix of clothing, accessories, flamboyant hats, and jewelry that dates back to the 1800s.

50 Drury St., Dublin, Ireland, +353-1-677-4006.

Om Diva

What started as a stall on Georges Street Arcade in 1999 has since become a five-floor boutique in the creative quarter of Dublin. Owner Ruth Ni Loinsigh is a champion of Irish design and fashion who mixes clothing by cutting-edge talents with carefully curated vintage from the 1950s to the 1980s, plus jewelry and accessories. A truly funky shopping experience.

27 Drury St., Dublin 2, Ireland, +353-1-679-1211, omdivaboutique.com.

Penneys/Primark

The international fast-fashion giant (it's known as Penneys in Ireland and Primark in the rest of the world) is the biggest retail success story to come out of the country, and this is the mother ship. Open since 1969, the store now occupies nearly 100,000 square feet, filled with trendy casual wear for men, women, and kids. "We watch how real people are wearing clothes; we watch celebrities, bloggers, and freestylers," a Primark buyer told the *Irish Times*.

47 Mary St., Dublin 1, Ireland, +353-1-888-0500, primark.com, and additional locations.

DEYROLLE

PARIS

FRANCE

THE MAJORS

colette

There's only one colette in the world, which is by owner Sarah Andelman's design. In other words, you have to visit Paris to experience the 7,500-square-foot temple of cool. Established in 1997, you'll find everything from Valentino party dresses to Vans sneakers, plus plenty of limited-edition art and fashion collabs (a Gary Baseman x Doc Martens pair of boots, *oui),* a great selection of music, magazines, and knickknacks, and a restaurant that serves more than 100 kinds of water. "I may actually love their displays even more than the shopping," says fashion editor/TV personality Joe Zee. "Everything is perfectly curated and merchandised and styled. Sometimes, I'm not even sure if I can buy it, but it does look meticulous." "A pop culture museum," adds designer Karen Erickson. "I love having lunch at the Water Bar," Olympia Le-Tan remarks. "I stole a lighter once!" admits Rodarte designer Laura Mulleavy. "We had an opening party there and [the photographer] Nan Goldin came, and she needed a lighter for her cigarette. They wouldn't sell it to her because the store was closed, so we took it. I have it in a shrine in our office!"

213 rue Saint-Honoré, 75001 Paris, +33 (01)-55-35-33-90, colette.fr.

Le Bon Marché

Founded in 1852, Le Bon Marché was the first modern department store, but that's just one reason to visit this remarkable place, now owned by luxury conglomerate LVMH. The fashion edit is top-notch, with all the best European and Japanese designers represented, a terrific contemporary mix (Mira Mikati, Tibi), an *épicerie* (grocery store), top-floor shoe heaven, inspirational home furnishings, themed pop-up shops, and more. "They often have special items created just for the season by a particular designer," says fashion editor Robin Givhan. "They did a special Vanessa Bruno Le Cabas in gray boiled wool and silver sequins for winter 2015 that became my regular work/gym bag. I also love the housewares and the helpful sales clerks who can translate the sizes from centimeters into inches or what have you." "By far the most elegant, beautiful department store," says stylist and designer Maryam Malakpour. "You can find everything you need in one stop. I particularly love their displays." When in Paris, accessories designer Sally Perrin likes to say, "If I go missing, you'll find me at the Bon Marché!" "Aside from clothing, shoes, and accessories, there are several charming cafés, a bookstore, an amazing perfume and cosmetics section, a gourmet grocery store, and, of course, a fantastic hat department. The salesgirls still know me by name—this is where I began collecting hats more than a decade ago."

24 rue de Sèvres, 75007 Paris,
+33 (01)-44-39-80-00, lebonmarche.com.

L'Eclaireur

Since 1980, when founders Martine and Armand Hadida opened their first space in an art gallery on the Champs-Élysées, L'Eclaireur has been a visionary retailer of fashion and design. Today, there are multiple stores, selling avant-garde styles by Fendi, Sacai, Saint Laurent, Rick Owens, Margiela, Marni, Giambattista Valli, and names that you probably haven't heard of—yet. (The Hadidas are the ones who introduced the Antwerp Six to Paris. They also own the Paris trade show Tranoï.) "A wide and eclectic mix of merchandise in a very cool atmosphere," says fashion editor Robin Givhan. "I've bought everything from a ski cap with a strip of Swarovski crystals down the front—it was practically glued to my head last winter—to the softest cashmere scarf ever to a Dries Van Noten jacket with a tulle front." All the locations are different; the Boissy is close to shopping on rue de Faubourg Saint-Honoré. "They have the largest collection of Fornasetti objects in the world," famed dandy Patrick McDonald says of this location. "I adore the men's area upstairs, and they always have a fabulous chapeau for me."

10 rue Boissy d'Anglas, 75008 Paris,
+33 (01)-53-43-03-70, leclaireur.com, and additional locations.

MONOPRIX

This clothing, housewares, and grocery store chain (think Target, but chicer) is a fashion week insider go-to for cute cotton underwear, socks and sleepwear, kids' clothes, and such everyday necessities as notebooks, bottled water, warm croissants, and snacks. "My friends joke that my favorite place to shop in Paris is Monoprix on the Champs-Élysées," says Alina Cho. "They're not wrong. I stock up on Nuxe hand cream, La Roche-Posay skin-care products, and small umbrellas, which are sturdier than the $5 versions you buy on the street in New York." "I wear their black or white denim almost exclusively," says fashion journalist Christina Binkley. "I must have eight pairs. Also, their socks are the best. And it's worth checking out their seasonal fashions as sometimes they can be quite good in design and fabrication (though they can also be quite boring—I don't quite understand their fashion strategy). Monoprix has stores all over, but I favor the one just off boulevard Saint-Germain in the Sixth Arrondissement." "Beautiful kids' clothing at a steal," adds blogger/model Elizabeth Minett.

52 rue de Rennes, 75006 Paris, +33 (01)-45-48-18-08, monoprix.fr, and additional locations.

ST. GERMAIN DES PRES/LATIN QUARTER/7th ARR.

Alexandra Sojfer

An entire store dedicated to handmade umbrellas? Only in Paris, *mes amis*. Textile designer Olya Thompson calls out this place as "a hidden gem." The family has been in the business since the 1930s, and also handcrafts walking sticks. Materials are super-luxe. Think ebony, ostrich skin, organza, and silk satin. Almost too good for the rain.

218 bvld. Saint-Germain, 75007 Paris, +33 (01) 42-22-17-02, alexandrasojfer.com.

A.P.C.

Founded in 1987 by Jean Touitou in Paris, A.P.C. stands for Atelier de Production et de Création. The brand's vision of minimalist cool, in slim cuts, (selvedge jeans, military-inspired jackets, streamlined basics, simple boots) has gone global, but this is the flagship—and the headquarters.

35 (men) & 38 (women) rue Madame, 75006 Paris, France, +33 (01) 42-22-12-77, apc.fr, and additional locations.

Aurélie Bidermann

A mix of casual and glam is what has made Paris-based jewelry designer Aurélie Bidermann a fashion-world favorite. She's created modern-day heirlooms out of one-of-a-kind pieces of vintage cotton lace, dipping them in 18-karat gold and molding them into cuffs with a weathered patina. She's also elevated the humble friendship bracelet to must-have status, using gold hardware to anchor the braided threads and give the pieces strength and permanence. She is influenced by pre-Columbian art, Brazilian handicrafts, Santa Fe style, and the architecture of Miami Beach. Beyoncé, Naomi Watts, and Keira Knightley are fans. This jewel box of a shop features her casual (most pieces less than $2,000) and fine collections.

55 bis rue des Saints-Pères, 75006 Paris, +33 (01)-45-48-43-14, aureliebidermann.com, and additional locations.

L/UNIFORM
BULY 1803
DRIES VAN NOTEN
QUAI
RUE DE L'UNIVERSITÉ
RUE BONAPARTE
RUE DE SEINE
SIMRANE
BELLEROSE
JÉRÔME DREYFUSS
SONIA RYKIEL
MES DEMOI-SELLES
MONOPRIX
LEFRANC-FERRANT
BOULEVARD SAINT-GERMAIN
ON
THIERRY LASRY
TARA JARMON
LEON & HARPER
UE DE SÈVRES
LES TROIS MARCHES DE CATHERINE B
SAINT JAMES
SANDRA SERRAF
DES PETITS HAUTS
SAINT LAURENT
TABIO
IE
VANESSA BRUNO
RUE DE SEINE
A.P.C.

SAINT-GERMAIN

PARIS

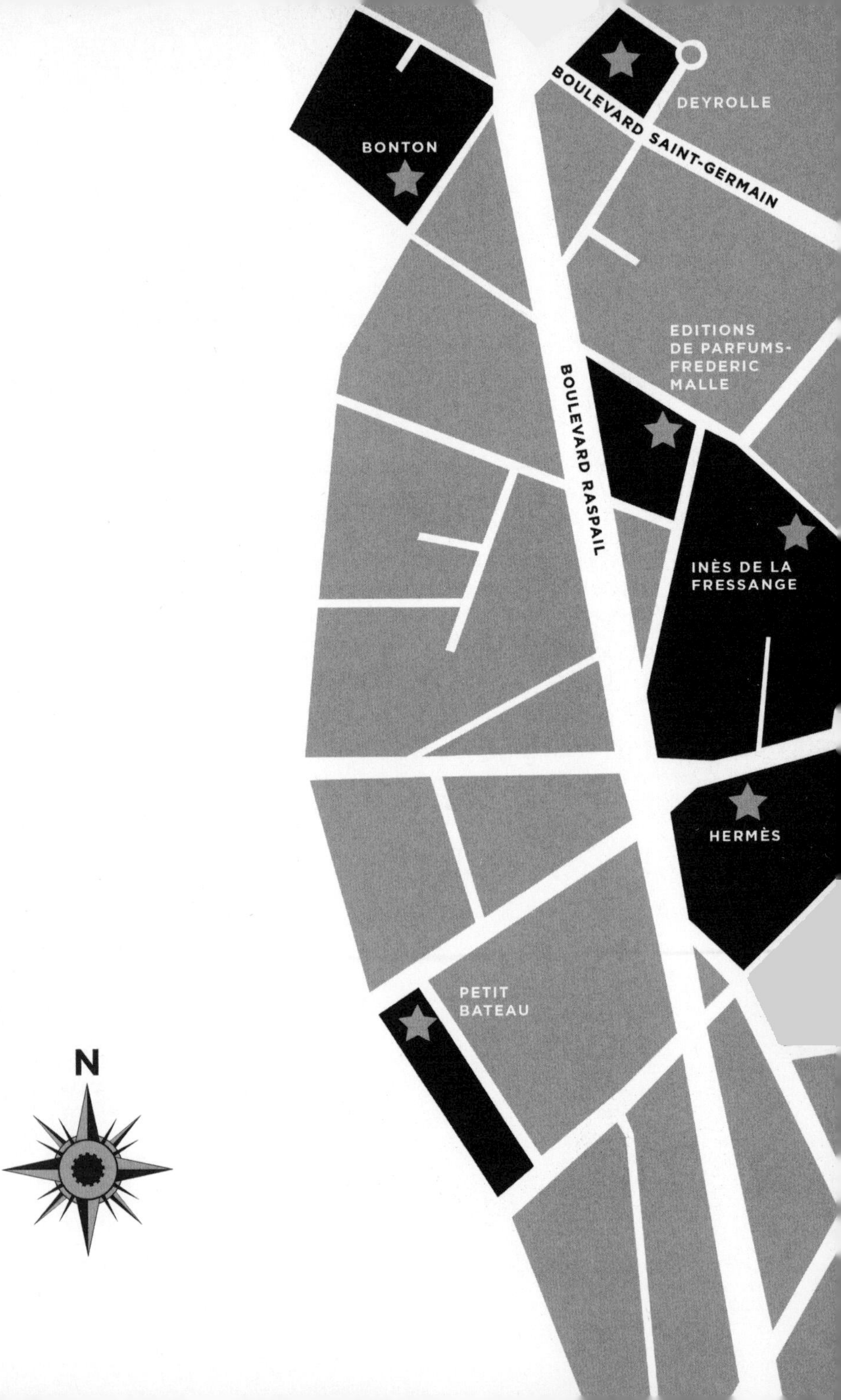

BONTON

BOULEVARD SAINT-GERMAIN

DEYROLLE

EDITIONS
DE PARFUMS-
FREDERIC
MALLE

BOULEVARD RASPAIL

INÈS DE LA
FRESSANGE

HERMÈS

PETIT
BATEAU

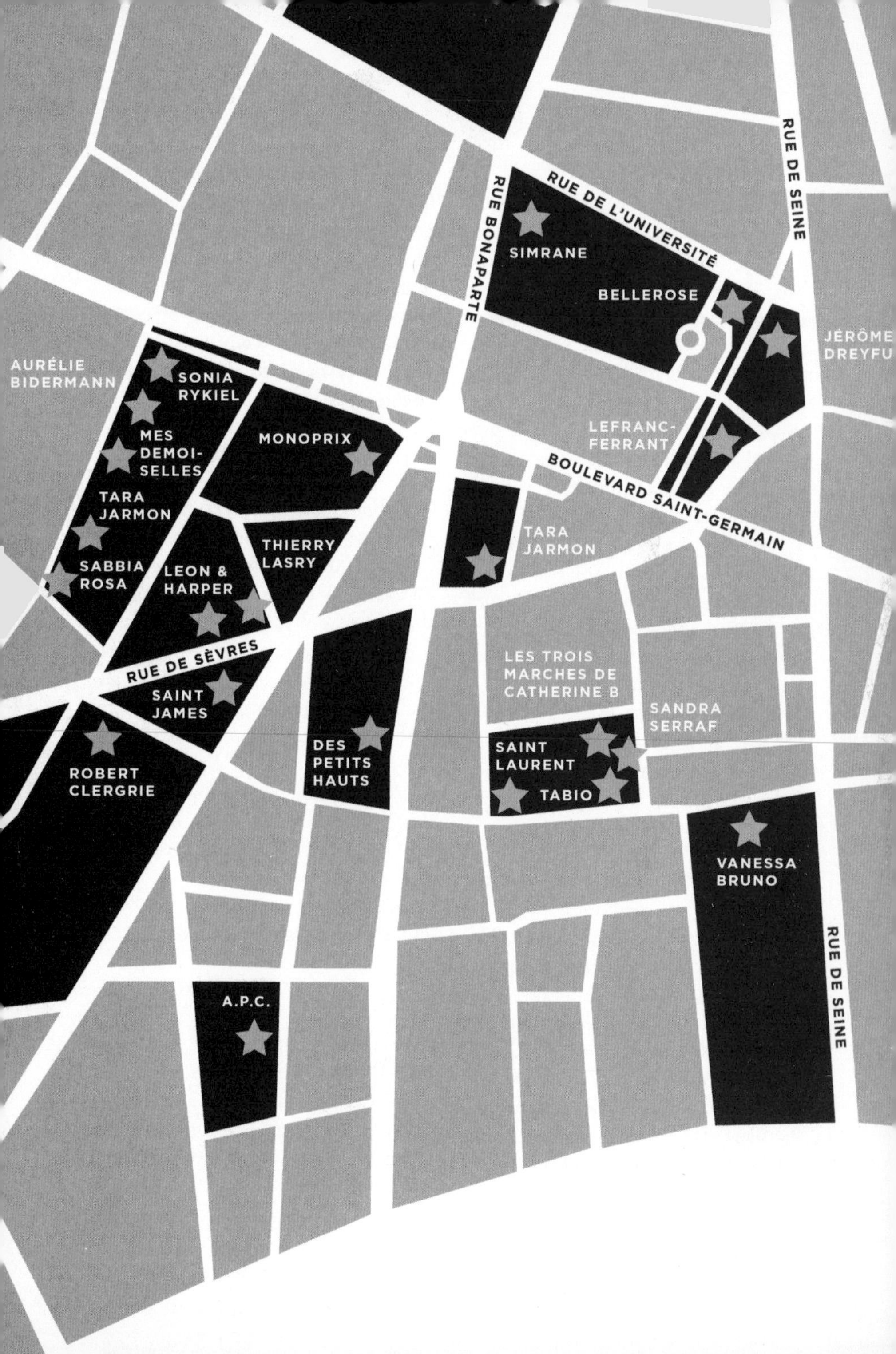
RUE DE L'UNIVERSITÉ
RUE BONAPARTE
RUE DE SEINE
SIMRANE
BELLEROSE
JÉRÔME
DREYFU
AURÉLIE
BIDERMANN
SONIA
RYKIEL
MES
DEMOI-
SELLES
MONOPRIX
LEFRANC-
FERRANT
BOULEVARD SAINT-GERMAIN
TARA
JARMON
THIERRY
LASRY
TARA
JARMON
SABBIA
ROSA
LEON &
HARPER
RUE DE SÈVRES
SAINT
JAMES
LES TROIS
MARCHES DE
CATHERINE B
SANDRA
SERRAF
ROBERT
CLERGRIE
DES
PETITS
HAUTS
SAINT
LAURENT
TABIO
VANESSA
BRUNO
RUE DE SEINE
A.P.C.

Bellerose

A chain store that doesn't feel like one. Bellerose started in Belgium in 1990 and has since expanded to France. The stores are homey, like walking into a close friend's apartment, with wood floors and calm music. On the rails you'll find the kind of understated chic clothing you'll want to wear every day, but that still feels special and fashionable, for example a great silk pajama blouse, a reversible Chinese patterned bomber jacket, a metallic rose gold sweatshirt and slouchy khaki pants. You'll also find select pieces from other brands, such as Golden Goose sneakers, Birkenstock sandals and more. Most pieces are less than $300.

3 rue Jacob, 75006 Paris,
+33 (01)- 43-54-77-90, bellerose.be, and additional locations.

Bonton

Where else but in Paris would you find a concept store dedicated to young people? Created in 2001 by Thomas Cohen (his parents created the popular children's brand Bonpoint), Bonton is casual, timeless, and fun. The brand quickly went international, selling clothing, furniture, toiletries, and gifts, and has done collaborations with the likes of A.P.C. and *Peanuts*. Some stores have hairdressers and host workshops and cooking classes. "It's a kids' store, but it's the best," says stylist Kate Young. "I love the bed linens, the party favors, the kids' toys and clothes. It's got the most fun stuff ever." Other fans include Victoria Beckham, Sofia Coppola, Kate Winslet, Stella McCartney, and Charlotte Gainsbourg.

82 rue de Grenelle, 75007 Paris,
+33 (01)-44-39-09-20, bonton.fr, and additional locations.

Buly 1803

"The brand has been around for something like 200 years and makes beautiful soaps and lotions," says *Washington Post* fashion editor Robin Givhan of this old school apothecary where they have a calligrapher on hand to write gift messages. "I'm in love with their candles. They're in marble containers; my favorite is one that smells of cypress, like a Japanese temple." You'll also find facial oil, hand cream, fragrances and more in packaging so beautiful, you'll want to display it on your vanity long after the product is gone.

6 rue Bonaparte, 75006 Paris,
+33 (01)-43-29-02-50, buly1805.com.

Des Petits Hauts

This French contemporary clothing brand, started by two sisters, is a terrific source for sweet lace-inset silk blouses, angora boyfriend cardigans, shiny Lurex jumpsuits, star-print miniskirts, suede ankle booties, and other cool-girl staples with that certain Parisian *je ne sais quoi.* Nothing is more than $400.

70 rue Bonaparte, 75006 Paris, +33 (01)-75-44-05-82, despetitshauts.com, and additional locations.

Deyrolle

"If you can't find a gift here for your crazy aunt, you can't find one anywhere," fashion journalist Christina Binkley says of this taxidermy place, which isn't a just a cabinet of curiosities, it's a whole store full. "From books to taxidermic bugs, it's totally exotic. Vanessa Friedman of the *New York Times* first took me to Deyrolle years ago, and now I go all the time with my daughter."

46 rue du Bac, 75007 Paris, +33 (01)-42-22-30-07, deyrolle.com.

Dries Van Noten

The Belgian designer's jewel box of a boutique in Saint Germain is a must-stop for the fashion flock looking for his artful coats and dresses, versatile knitwear, and fun shoes, especially since his collection is distributed through only a few international retailers. "I go to Dries because he's a personal favorite and there's usually something from the previous season's show that has stuck in my memory that I'm keen to try on," says fashion editor Robin Givhan. "I have done serious Amex damage." "Probably my favorite place to shop in the world," says accessories designer Lizzie Fortunato, while accessories designer Sally Perrin loves "the surge of colors and textures." "I love the prints," says jewelry designer Aurélie Bidermann. "Moreover, the interior design of this store is really amazing." There are men's and women's boutiques, both on the Quai Malaquais.

7 and 9 Quai Malaquais, 75006 Paris, +33 (01)-44-27-00-40, driesvannoten.be, and additional locations.

Editions de Parfums by Frédéric Malle

Paris-based fragrance nose Frédéric Malle grew up in the perfume industry; his grandfather founded Parfums Christian Dior. After working as a consultant in the industry, Malle founded Editions de Parfums Frédéric Malle in 2000 to support more-artisanal perfume creation as an alternative to marketing-driven perfume companies. Since then, he's had a number of hits, including Carnal Flowers and Portrait of a Lady. The fragrances' packaging is simple, and the labels bear the signature of the perfume creator just as a painting would bear the signature of an artist. Malle's original store feels like a fragrance lab inside a Parisian apartment.

37 rue de Grenelle, 75007 Paris, +33 (01)-42-22-76-40, fredericamalle.com.

EDITIONS DE PARFUMS

Hermès

Founded as a saddlery in 1880, the original store at 24 rue Faubourg de Saint-Honoré may be better known than the Left Bank boutique, which opened in 2010. But the Left Bank shop surpasses the original with its cool concept. French architecture firm RDAI transformed the 1930s art deco building and swimming pool into a modern marvel with other-worldly braided wood pods defining the accessories, fashion, tableware, and furniture departments. There's an in-house florist, a bookshop, and a café that serves tea and light lunch. Scattered throughout are items from the Petit H collection made entirely of production remnants, including bracelets fashioned from pieces of silk scarves, and a lamp made of coffee cup. "It's such an inspiration to see a luxury brand not take themselves so seriously," says Olivia Kim. "Best known for their leather craftsmanship, I love how they take that and create objects that wouldn't be expected—pinwheels, standing animals, rocking horses, even bird-houses."

17 rue de Sèvres, 75006 Paris,
+33 (01)-42-22-80-83, hermes.com.

WHERE TO SHOP ON SUNDAYS IN PARIS

You're in the capital of couture on a Sunday and everything is closed (and we mean everything, even Monoprix), due to state regulations rooted in religious tradition. What's a shopaholic to do?

Three vintage stores in the Marais:

VINTAGE DÉSIR might try to fool you with the name Coiffure on the sign outside, but inside, it's a vintage bonanza—and not too expensive.

FREE'P'STAR has some vintage and some secondhand, meaning you're just as likely to find a sweater from Zara as an old pair of Levi's.

KILO SHOP sells clothing by the pound, er, kilo.

The Marais branch of **L'ECLAIREUR,** on Rue de Sévigné, is a work of art in and of itself, designed in collaboration with Belgian artist Arne Quinze and featuring two tons of wooden planks and 147 video screens. Menswear and womenswear collections, including Yohji Yamamoto, 08 Sircus, Haider Ackermann, and Boris Bidjan Saberi, are alternately concealed and revealed by moving walls.

With more than 150,000 objects, the **MUSÉE DES ARTS DÉCORATIFS** is dedicated to the French art of living, including the art of dressing. Not only is this a fabulous place to catch a fashion exhibition (past shows have been dedicated to everyone from Dries Van Noten to Barbie), the shop is top-notch. "An exceptional selection of exclusive objects, mostly related to current and past exhibitions," says Tatiana Sorokko. "You can find things like melamine René Magritte motif plates and a 5-inch square Jean Paul Gaultier microfiber navy stripe fabric swatch."

In 2009, stores in France's 569 existing tourist zones, including the Champs-Élysées, were allowed to be open on Sundays. (Before then, only stores having to do with sports, culture, or tourism were allowed.) So you can shop the headquarters of **LOUIS VUITTON** every day of the week. The store includes an art gallery accessible from a separate entrance. Also on the Champs-Élysées and open on Sundays are Tiffany & Co., Swarovski, Sephora, Montblanc, Longchamp, and the Publicis Drugstore (which is more like a high-end department store, food emporium, and restaurant than a drugstore).

Paris's largest flea market, **MARCHÉ AUX PUCES DE SAINT-OUEN** is actually fifteen markets in one. Stylist Cristina Ehrlich likes Marché Dauphine for "antiques, amazing vintage pieces, old photos, and postcards all housed under this amazing greenhouse-like space." Accessories designer Sally Perrin's favorite is Marché Paul Bert Serpette, where she has found beautiful vintage kimonos in the back alley. Shoe designer Isa Tapia prefers to wander around for "the best 1940s, '50s, and '60s exotic handbag selections. Also good for cosmetic packaging and old graphic rubber stamps and furniture." "You will find so many great little shops at Les Puces selling everything from antiques to junk to vintage clothes," says designer Marie France Van Damme. "I have found everything from drums to cacti to medieval jousting armor," says stylist Tara Swennen. "I found a beautiful vintage leather doctor's bag that I vowed would be an integral part of my collection should I start a handbag company. And it has been!" adds accessories designer Fiona Kotur Marin.

VINTAGE DÉSIR, 32 rue des Rosiers, 75004, Open every day 11:30 a.m.–9:00 p.m.

FREE'P'STAR, 8 rue Sainte-croix de la Bretonnerie, 75004, Mon–Fri: 11:00 a.m.–9:00 p.m.; Sat–Sun: 12:00 p.m.–2:30 p.m., freepstar.fr.

KILO SHOP, 69-71 rue de la Verrerie, 75004, Mon & Sun: 2:00 p.m.–7:45 p.m.; Tue–Sat: 11:00 a.m.–7:45 p.m., kilo-shop.fr.

L'ECLAIREUR, 40 rue de Sévigné 75003 Paris, +33 (01)-48-87-1022, open Mon-Sat: 11 a.m.–7 p.m.; Sun: 3 p.m.–7 p.m.

MUSÉE DES ARTS DÉCORATIFS, 107 rue de Rivoli, 75001, open Tue-Sun: 11 a.m.–6 p.m., Thurs: 11a.m.–9 p.m.

LOUIS VUITTON FLAGSHIP ON THE CHAMPS-ÉLYSÉES, 101 Ave. des Champs-Élysées, 75008 Paris, +33 (01)-53-57-52-00, louisvuitton.com.

MARCHÉ AUX PUCES DE SAINT-OUEN, Located at the Porte de Cligman Court metro, 75018 Paris, marcheauxpuces-saintouen.com. open Sat-Mon: 10a.m.–1p.m. and 2p.m.–5:30p.m.

Ines de la Fressange

Model/designer/author Fressange has added retailer to her considerable list of talents, with a new lifestyle boutique on the Left Bank showcasing her own clothing and accessories made in the atelier in back (think silk pajamas, logo T-shirts, suede miniskirts, vintage silk dresses, and ballet flats), alongside fun housewares, notebooks, iPhone cases, tea, and trinkets.

24 rue de Grenelle, 75007 Paris, +33 (01)-45-48-19-06, inesdelafressange.fr.

Jérôme Dreyfuss

Paris-based Dreyfuss shares his laid-back, bohemian design sensibility, and his home, with designer Isabel Marant. Dreyfuss's under-the-radar bags are logo-less and, in keeping with their tomboyish look, have boys' names. They also have clever design details, such as multiple straps to allow carrying by hand or over the shoulder, removable wallets, attached key rings, and mini-flashlights. Dreyfuss also designs cool shoes and boots. He launched his accessory collection in 2002 with the goal of creating practical, light, soft bags that feel as good next to your body as a teddy bear. Prices range from $115 for a small pouch to $2,515 for an oversized hobo. Dreyfuss's shoe store is across the street.

1 rue Jacob, 75006 Paris, +33 (01)-43-54-70-93, jerome-dreyfuss.com, and additional locations.

LES 3 MARCHES DE CATHERINE B

Karry O

Fashion journalist and blogger Divia Harilela recommends this as a source for vintage jewelry by Chopard, Van Cleef & Arpels, Dior, and more, plus original pieces designed by owner Karine Berrebi.

41 rue de Saint-Honoré, 750008 Paris, +33 (01)-45-48-94-67, karryo.com.

Les 3 Marches de Catherine B

Vintage expert Catherine B opened her first store in 1994, selling timeless, pristine-quality bags, belts, and scarves by Hermès and Chanel. Next to the original store is a newer one dedicated to shoes, clothing, and travel bags. Some pieces are so rare, they are not for sale, including a Chanel bicycle featuring two sidesaddle "handbags" and a seat with signature Chanel quilting. Catherine B also owns an original Birkin bag with the initials JB, for Jane Birkin. "An amazing vintage selection of Chanel and Hermès," says jewelry designer Aurélie Bidermann. "I always find something."

1 rue Guisarde, 75006 Paris, +33 (01)-43-54-74-18, les3marchesdescatherineb.com.

Lefranc-Ferrant

"The proprietress and designer, Béatrice Ferrant, used to show her collections at Paris Haute Couture Week, but she has downsized and now sells her modern, architectural designs from her shop," says fashion journalist Christina Binkley. "She will do custom looks and sizes in addition to her ready-to-wear. On any given day, you're likely to find her in her shop serving clients."

22 rue de l'Echaudé, 76006 Paris,
+33 (01)-40-21-03-29, lefranc-ferrant.fr.

Leon and Harper

After twenty-five years at Et Vous, Philippe Corbin launched Leon and Harper in 2011. The casual-boho chain sells distressed army jackets, embroidered tunics, frilly blouses, high-waist jeans, fringed moccasins, clog sandals, and more fun stuff.

46 rue du Four, 75006 Paris,
+33 (01)-45-44-17-27, leonandharper .com, and additional locations.

L/Uniform

Why buy a designer bag when you can create your own? That's the concept behind Jeanne Signoles's preppy-utilitarian brand L/Uniform, launched in 2014. A veteran of luxury leather goods brand Goyard (which is owned by her father-in-law), Singoles opened her first L/Uniform store in 2015 with a sleek interior designed by Masamichi Katayama. Choose your bag shape (backpack, messenger, tote, pencil case, and more) and the color of canvas and trim; you can have it monogrammed, too. Most styles are less than $500.

21 quai Malaquais, 75006 Paris,
+33 (01)-42-61-76-27, luniform.com.

Maison Kitsune

All the classicism of A.P.C., but with more whimsy and color, this contemporary French label, launched in 2002 by Gildas Loaëc and Masaya Kuroki, channels preppy Paris-meets-Tokyo style. You'll find intarsia fox head sweaters, French slogan tees, flannel sweatpants, and shrunken blazers. Maison Kitsune also has its own music label, and a couple of cafes, including one at the Palais Royale.

38 rue Madame, 75006 Paris,
+33 (01)- 53-71-76-62, maisonkitsune .com, and additional locations.

Mes Desmoiselles

This vintage-boho French contemporary brand's boutiques are Aladdin's caves of maxi dresses and chunky knits, Lurex stripe caftans, silk bed jackets, and embroidered slippers. The collection is carried in a ton of multilabel stores around the world, but going to the source is a different feel altogether.

57 rue des Saints-Pères, 75006 Paris, +33 (01)-43-35-12-52, mesdesmoiselles.com, and additional locations.

Petit Bateau

"I love the utilitarian chic of the small but ubiquitous Petit Bateau shops in Paris," says textile designer Olya Thompson of this French chain store, which has been around for more than 100 years. "The best-cut kids' footies with snaps that actually work, great pj's and underwear, and T-shirts with a great price-quality ratio."

53 bis rue de Sèvres, 75006 Paris, +33 (01)-45-49-48-38, petit-bateau.fr, and additional locations.

Robert Clergerie

Sturdy, comfortable, untrendy, and 1990s-nostalgic, Robert Clergerie shoes have been embraced by a bevy of celebs, including Shailene Woodley, Scarlett Johansson, and Rihanna. The company has been around since 1895, when founder Joseph Fenestrier took over a small men's shoe manufacturing company. It chugged along through the 20th century, producing 1,200 shoes a day in 1926, and opening stores in France. Then, in 1978, Robert Clergerie purchased the company. He continued to produce men's styles until he hit on the idea, in 1981, of making women's shoes built on a men's last. His first collection of oxfords was an instant success. In 1987, his legacy was sealed when he was named designer of the year by *Footwear News*. He went on to win the award twice more. Today, the brand has more than two dozen boutiques worldwide. In 2011 French designer Roland Mouret, known for his formfitting dresses, was appointed creative director, and he has introduced sexier stiletto styles. Still, at Clergerie, simplicity will always be the guiding principle. These are shoes made for walking; key styles include mules and lace-ups. This is the flagship.

5 rue du Cherche-Midi, Paris 75006, +33 (01)-42-84-03-14, robertclergerie.com, and additional locations.

Sabbia Rosa

"For feminine, exquisite silk lingerie, and available in *sooo* many colors," says designer Marie France Van Damme of this upscale lingerie shop, opened in 1976 by owner/designer Monette Moati. Legend has it that one month after the opening, French singer Serge

VANESSA SEWARD'S ADDRESS BOOK

Paris-based designer Vanessa Seward founded her namesake brand in 2014, after two years of creating capsule collections for French denim and casual wear label A.P.C., and nearly a decade designing for the high-end house of Azzaro before that. Her personal style is influenced by Ali MacGraw (preppy chic to perfection), a teenage Brooke Shields, and Caroline de Monaco.

I love **LE BON MARCHÉ** for its very chic selection of clothes and its beauty floor where there's lots of exclusive international brands to discover. I would cross Paris to do my grocery shopping at their food parlor the **GRANDE ÉPICERIE**, but luckily it's just across the street! I also like **SPREE**, a multi-label boutique located in Montmartre. I've been friends with the owner Roberta for years and I've always admired her impeccable taste. Bruno Hadjadj her husband is an artist and they also host art and design exhibitions.

For vintage, **THE DRESSING FACTORY** is small, but I could buy half the shop each time I go and they are very well priced.

GANTS MURIEL, this little glove shop is great, they propose the chicest glove selection in the most exquisite leathers and colors, all made in France. Very good for presents.

The French chain store **PRINCESSE TAM TAM** is very good for lingerie and home wear.

In Paris, they have great garage sales in summer and the best one was one on the very chic Rue Trochet. I bought a Burberry trench (which I wear practically every day), a '70s Céline blue suede trench and a few gorgeous YSL print scarves for around 200€.

LE BON MARCHÉ, 24 rue de Sèvres, 75007, +33 (01)-44-39-80-00, lebonmarche.com.

LE GRANDE ÉPICERIE, 38 rue de Sèvres, 75007, +33 (01)-44-39-81-00, lebgrandeepicerie.com.

SPREE, 16 rue La Vieuville, 75018, +33 (01)-42-23-41-40, spree.fr.

THE DRESSING FACTORY, 18 rue Saint Simon, Paris 75007, dressing-factory.com.

GANTS MURIEL, 4 Rue des Saussaies, Paris 75008, +33 (01)-42-65-95-34.

PRINCESSE TAM TAM, 109 Ave. Victor Hugo, 75116 Paris, +33 (01)-47-27-77-53 princesstamtam.eu, and additional locations.

Gainsbourg stopped by to purchase a gift for his then-partner Jane Birkin, and the experience inspired his song "Les Dessous Chics." Whether or not the story is true, it helped secure Sabbia Rosa's enduring popularity.

73 rue des Saints-Pères, 75006 Paris, +33 (01)45-48-88-37.

Saint James

Saint James is the maker of the nautical Breton shirts in combed cotton jersey that have been part of the official French naval uniform since 1858. According to lore, each of the 21 stripes corresponds to a naval victory of Napoleon's fleet against the British. The brand has expanded to a full range of casual wear for men, women, and children and is sold around the world.

66 rue de Rennes, 75006 Paris, +33 (01)-53-63-09-82, saintjamesboutique.com, and additional locations.

Saint Laurent

In 1966, Yves Saint Laurent opened a ready-to-wear boutique in Paris called Saint Laurent Rive Gauche, the first time a couturier successfully launched a ready-to-wear line in France. (You could call it the original cheap chic.) Located in a former antiques store in the student-dominated Left Bank, the store was a complete 180 from the gilded interior of Saint Laurent's haute couture salon. Rive Gauche was such a success, some customers waited up to three hours to purchase items, and the store became a hub of youth culture. Although there are several Saint Laurent boutiques in Paris (and more around the world), the *rive gauche* spirit is particularly potent at this location, near Saint-Sulpice, inside a 17th-century building.

6 place Saint-Sulpice, 75006 Paris, +33 (01)-43-29-43-00, ysl.com, and additional locations.

Sandra Serraf

I always find something at this low-key multi-brand boutique. The look is Parisian boho, with offerings from Isabel Marant Étoile, Forte Forte, Masscob, Humanoid and Jacquie Aiche.

18 rue Mabillon, 75006 Paris, +33 (01)-43-25-21-24, sandraserraf.fr.

Simrane

"I buy something here every time I'm in Paris," says fashion journalist Christina Binkley. "It carries all sorts of clothing and household goods from India, and the quality is higher than you typically find in bargain boutiques. I have a half-dozen blouses with such beautiful prints from here, and a couple of dresses." Also carries beautiful napkins, scarves, pillows, robes, and doorknobs.

23 and 25 rue Bonaparte, 75006 Paris, +33 (01)-43-54-90-73, simrane.com.

SONIA RYKIEL

Sonia Rykiel

In her heyday in the 1960s and '70s, Sonia Rykiel was synonymous with French chic, from the shrunken "poor boy" sweater that landed on the cover of *Elle* magazine and launched her career in 1968 to endless interpretations of her iconic striped sailor sweater, to the safety pin brooch that was a favorite fashionable Paris souvenir. The Rykiel store in the bohemian Saint Germain-des-Prés neighborhood, across the street from the Café de Flore, is the brand's spiritual home, filled with thousands and thousands of paperback books nestled into bookcases, with whimsical lip-printed carpeting on the floor. Julie de Libran took over as artistic director in 2014, and is earning rave reviews and fans in Miranda Kerr, Suki Waterhouse, Leighton Meester, and Selena Gomez.
175 blvd. Saint-Germain, 75006 Paris, +33 (01)-49-54-60-60, soniarykiel.com, and additional locations.

Tabio

This made-in-Japan hosiery brand's Paris store is "a must-stop for sparkly socks," says accessories designer Lizzie Fortunato. "They will monogram them for an extra three euros in 15 minutes" "I try to visit whenever I'm in Paris, because who doesn't love fun socks?" says stylist Cristina Ehrlich.
32 rue Saint-Sulpice, 75006 Paris, +33 (01)-43-26-28-12, tabio.com.fr, and additional locations.

Tara Jarmon

"I discovered this brand in Paris," says author Aliza Licht of Canadian-born, Paris-based Jarmon's feminine label of metallic pleated skirts, printed minidresses, and lacy blouses. "It's my favorite place to shop when I'm there. The store is filled with clothing that I haven't seen before. The prices are reasonable, and the quality is amazing."
18 rue du Four, 75006 Paris, +33 (01)-46-33-26-60, tarajarmon.com, and additional locations.

Thierry Lasry

The French eyewear designer favorite of Rihanna and Gigi Hadid opened his first flagship in Paris in 2016 as a showcase for his colorful frames, including vintage acetate styles. Designed by artistic multi-hyphenate Vincnt Darré, the storefront beckons passersby to gaze at themselves through a reflective pupil and blue iris surrounded by rows of shelves. Stocked inside, the full collection of Thierry Lasry sunglasses, plus Harry Lary's frames, his other optical label, and his eyewear collaborations with Fendi and tattoo artist Brian Woo (aka Dr. Woo).

40 rue du Four, 75006 Paris, +33 (01)-43-27-44-65, thierrylasry.com.

Vanessa Bruno

Bruno started her namesake brand in 1996, to create a modern everyday wardrobe. She opened her first store on the Left Bank in 1998, the same year she launched the Cabas tote bag. With some sequins on cotton canvas, she created a new classic, and it became an international best-seller. The contemporary brand is a great source for sweet blouses, pointelle knits, laid-back culottes, and print dresses.

25 rue Saint Sulpice, 75006 Paris, +33 (01)-43-54-41-04, vanessabruno.fr, and additional locations.

BASTILLE

Come on Eileen

"A thrift store that features super-high-end vintage," says Gabriela Artigas. "My sister, Tere, bought two Céline coats there at an amazing price. One of them is a floor-length, mustard-yellow suede coat with leather buttons that she still wears to this day. We love this store because they always remember us; they make us feel like part of their family, which is so important and keeps us going back time and again."

16/18 rue des Taillandiers, 75011 Paris, +33 (01)-43-38-12-11.

Isabel Marant

Marant is the master of Paris-meets-L.A. boho chic (greatest hits include the hidden platform sneaker, the Dicker Western-style boot, and the Kady washed-leather biker jacket). Even though the designer has stores around the world, it feels right shopping her collection in Paris. This store, her first, opened in 1998.

16 rue de Charonne, 75011 Paris, +33 (01)-49-29-71-55, isabelmarant.fr, and additional locations.

Sessún

Started in 1996 after owner Emma

François took a trip to South America, this French brand's vision of boho clothing features contemporary basics (drapey trench coats, poet blouses, loose-fit trousers) in natural fabrics with the occasional handicraft-inspired tassel or fringe.

34 rue de Charonne, 75011 Paris, +33 (01)-48-06-55-66; sessun.com, and additional locations.

MARAIS

Azzedine Alaïa Outlet

Easily missed, because it's difficult to spot, the outlet is accessed around the corner from the rue de Moussy boutique, on a side street under an archway. Inside, you'll find previous seasons' clothing, shoes, and accessories discounted at least 50 percent.

18 rue de la Verrerie, 75004, Paris, +33 (01)-42-72-19-19, alaia.com.

The Broken Arm

Paris's latest concept store, the Broken Arm was opened in 2013 by the team behind De Jeunes Gens Modernes. The shop stocks avant-garde and streetwear brands for men and women, including Vetements, Jacquemus, Lemaire, Nike, Gosha Rubchinskiy, Raf Simons, and Our Legacy, and also has a café with its own blend of coffee. "An incredible modern concept store," says costume designer Janie Bryant. "There's a great café attached," says Malone Souliers' co-designer Ma Malone. There's even a Broken Arm fragrance designed to evoke the materials used to construct the store.

12 Rue Perrée, 75003 Paris, +33 (01)-44-61-53-60, the-broken-arm.com.

Hod

"The girls who run this store travel all over the world and bring fine jewelry treasures back to their beautiful little boutique," says stylist Cristina Ehrlich. "It exudes a chic, young approach to jewelry that is distinctly French while showcasing jewels that reflect the far corners of the world."

104 rue Vieille du Temple, 75003 Paris, +33 (09)-53-15-83-34, hod-boutique.com.

Merci

Occupying a former wallpaper factory, Merci is the laid-back, boho alternative to colette, a concept store with designer furniture and vintage items, tableware, men's, women's, and kids' clothing, and more. There's a restaurant in the basement ("Just the right place to sip tea," says handbag designer Clare Vivier), and a bookstore, and some of the profits go to charity. "I love the all-encompassing experience with the home stuff and

MERCI

the restaurant," says designer Rebecca Minkoff. "The way they merchandise makes me want to buy things I don't even need. During fashion week, I fell in love with all these African textiles."

111 blvd. Beaumarchais, 75003 Paris, +33 (01)-42-77-00-33, merci-merci.com.

Tom Greyhound

"Hipster haven," designer Bridget Romanek says of the Korean multi-brand store, which also has this branch in Paris. "Curated with items you haven't seen before. They carry some collections you know, but they pick the pieces that other stores don't. It's fun in there." Behind a wall of rotating wood slats, you'll find sections dedicated to young, independent labels.

19 Rue de Saintonge, 75003 Paris, +33 (01)-44-61-36-59, tomgreyhound.fr.

Vanessa Seward

Seward founded her namesake brand in 2014 and her vision of comfortable Parisian glamour is gaining steam on both sides of the Atlantic. French stars such as actor Marion Cotillard and actor-model Farida Khelfa have been wearing her retro print dresses, while model Karlie Kloss likes Seward's French-phrase tee (UNE FEMME FRANÇAISE). Seward makes great denim, too, and you can personalize the back pocket with your name. Prices range from about $150 to $2,100.

7 blvd. des Filles du Calvaire, 75003 Paris, +33 (01)-70-36-06-11, vanessaseward.com.

Odetta

"One of my favorite consignment stores," says jewelry designer Gabriela Artigas. "It's not super cheap but they have every designer you can imagine: Azzaro, Leonard, Yves Saint Laurent, Lanvin. Nearby is a great little coffee shop called Fragments, which is a must-visit."

76 rue des Tournelles, 75003 Paris, +33 (01)-48-87-08-61, odettavintage.com.

RUE DE FAUBOURG SAINT-HONORÉ/OPERA/ PLACE VENDÔME

Anouschka

"By appointment only, but such divine frocks and accessories," says designer and personal shopper Raven Kauffman of this insiders' spot, owned by a former model. "I love the secret feel of the space—it's like you are rifling through the private closets of one of the most chic women in the world."

6 ave. du Coq, 75009 Paris, +33 (01)-48-74-37-00.

Astier de Villatte

Known around the world since 1996 for handmade black terra-cotta ceramics and tableware finished in white paint, city-inspired incense, and candles. The ceramics are made in the Bastille, and deliberate surface imperfections add to their charm. "Everything they make is gorgeous," says stylist Kate Young. Personal note: My favorite piece is the Antoinette incense burner, a cheeky ode to Marie Antoinette's end that features her head on a plate.

173 rue Saint-Honoré, 75001 Paris, +33 (01)-42-60-74-13, astierdevillate.com, and an additional location on the Left Bank.

Chanel

Coco Chanel's first independent boutique, Chanel Modes, opened in 1910 on this spot and sold hats, which were her specialty at the time. In 1913, she expanded to the resort towns of Deauville and Biarritz selling casual sports clothes that appealed to women's increasingly active lifestyles. By 1919, Chanel had established her couture house (also on this site), near her home at the Ritz Hotel. The rest is fashion history. Chief designer Karl Lagerfeld has not only kept the Chanel flame burning since 1983 but also fueled incredible growth, bringing the house codes (the suit, the pearls, the chain-handled bag) into the 21st century with over-the-top shows. There are many Chanel stores around the world (and around Paris), but this is the one that started it all.

31 rue Cambon, 75001 Paris, +33 (01)-44-50-66-00, chanel.com, and additional locations.

Chantal Thomass

"Important to any [lingerie] aficionado," says filmmaker and author Liz Goldwyn of this designer shop, where lingerie is treated as fashion. The modern boudoir carries Thomass's collections of bras, merry widows, garter belts, thongs, bloomers, bikinis, bustiers, and stockings.

211 rue Saint-Honoré, 75001 Paris, +33 (01)-42-60-40-56, chantalthomass.com.

Charvet

High-end purveyor of bespoke and ready-to-wear men's shirts, neckties, pajamas, and suits, founded in 1838 by the son of the "wardrobe curator" to Napoléon Bonaparte, Charvet has outfitted kings, princes, heads of state, and creatives such as Charles Baudelaire, George Sand, Jean Cocteau, the Duke of Windsor, Yves Saint Laurent, Charles de Gaulle, Winston Churchill, Henry Kissinger, and John F. Kennedy. A great place to pick up a linen pocket square or a pair of passementerie-knot cuff links (which were invented by Charvet) for a gift.

28 place Vendôme, 75001 Paris, +33 (01)-42-60-30-70, charvet.com.

Goyard

The understated yin to Louis Vuitton's yang, Goyard has been making its signature chevron-patterned canvas trunks and bags since 1853, and is older than LV by one year. The brand is known for eschewing advertising and e-commerce, and limiting distribution, which has protected the allure. Pablo Picasso, Jacques Cartier, the Agnellis and the Rockefellers, the Romanovs and the Grimaldis, Estée Lauder and Barbara Hutton, Coco Chanel and Jeanne Lanvin, Edith Piaf and Karl Lagerfeld have all been customers, and chef Alain Ducasse had a Goyard culinary trunk custom made at this historic store. In 2008 Le Chic du Chien (Canine Chic) boutique dedicated entirely to pet accessories opened at 352 rue Saint-Honoré, right across the street.

233 rue Saint-Honoré, 75001 Paris, +33 (01)-42-60-57-04, goyard.com.

Hervé Chapelier

The French fashion company is known for its made-for-travel tote bags that come in a range of sizes and materials, including cotton and nylon, with braided handles made from seat belts. A great souvenir or solution for carting extra purchases home. Made in France.

390 rue Saint-Honoré, 75001 Paris, +33 (01)-42-96-38-04, hervechapelier.com, and an additional location on the Left Bank.

Opéra National de Paris Gift Shop

"I recently came across this shop and I was blown away by its great selection, from kids' storybooks to ballet flats, that I have never seen before!" says stylist and designer Maryam Malkapour.

La Galerie de l'Opéra de Paris, Palais Garnier, 8 rue Scribe, 75009 Paris, +33 (01)-53-43-03-97, boutique.operadeparis.fr.

Longchamp

Founded in 1948 as a pipe company (leather-covered pipes, natch), Longchamp expanded into accessories in the 1950s, and grew into a global brand on the success of its foldable Pliage nylon tote, first designed in 1993. More than 30 million Le Pliage bags have been sold worldwide, and it takes more than 100 steps to make each one. The brand has enlisted several designers to collaborate on designs, including Jeremy Scott, and it also has a modest ready-to-wear collection to accessorize the bags and small leather goods.

404 rue Saint-Honoré, 75001 Paris, +33 (01)-43-16-00-16, Longchamp.com, and additional locations.

Olympia Le-Tan

"A tiny little shop near Palais Royale with the most charming clothing and accessories by the designer herself," says jewelry designer Sonia Boyajian. Best known for clutch bags designed to look like books with fanciful artwork, Olympia Le-Tan's boutique also features her girlish print dresses and accessories.

Passage des Deux-Pavillons, 5 rue Des Petites Champs, Paris 75001, +33 (01)-42-36-42-92, olympialetan.com.

Perrin

Founded in 1893 in central France, Rigaudy-Perrin began a century-long tradition of glove making. In 2006, the family resurrected the brand and added luxury handbags, many of which nod to the brand's origins with their unusual grips (glove-like handles on clutch bags, for example). Other bags attach to the wrist with fur cuff bracelets, and others look to architecture for inspiration, such as the basketweave Ball bag. The Paris flagship was designed by Chahan Minassian, with shelves displaying the items if they were rare specimens.

3 rue D'Alger, 75001 Paris, +33 (01)-42-53-54, perrinparis.com, and additional locations.

Repetto

Rose Repetto founded the French ballet shoe company in 1947, after her son, choreographer Roland Petit, came home from class complaining of sore feet. The company gained international attention for creating the Cendrillon ballet flat for Brigitte Bardot's 1956 film *And God Created Woman*. In 1959 Repetto opened the store at 22 rue de la Paix near the Paris Opera, and it remains open today. The brand has since gone global, with boutiques around the world selling professional dancewear, plus the Cendrillon flat, oxfords, Mary Janes, loafers, and bootie-style shoes that work as well on the street as on the stage.

22 rue de la Paix, 75002 Paris, +33 (01)-44-71-83-12, Repetto.com, and additional locations.

Roger Vivier

French designer Roger Vivier was the most famous shoemaker in the world in the 1950s. He invented the stiletto (depending on whom you ask), created the curved "comma" heel, was the first to use plastic in footwear, and designed the Belle Vivier chrome buckle-front pump that Catherine Deneuve wore in the 1967 film *Belle de Jour*. Since 2004, designer Bruno Frisoni has been at the helm of the brand, making exquisite creations, including red-carpet-worthy shoes and handbags, as well as the everyday Gommette flats.

29 rue du Faubourg Saint-Honoré, 75008 Paris, +33 (01)-53-43-00-85, rogervivier.com, and additional locations.

AVENUE MONTAIGNE/AVENUE GEORGE V

Azzedine Alaïa

The revered designer has been going his own way his whole career, eschewing fashion week and trends in favor of his own timeline. After thirty years in business, he opened this maison in 2013. The renovated three-story 18th-century town house contains his showroom, offices, a workshop, and a boutique featuring an amazing chandelier as well as ready-to-wear and accessories. "The display, the clothes, and the accessories are always exquisite," says designer Zainab Sumu.

5 rue de Marignan, Paris 75008, +33 (01)-76-72-91-11, alaia.fr.

Balenciaga

Demna Gvasalia, the product of war-torn Georgia in the former Soviet Union, has redefined fashion at the vaunted house of Balenciaga with an off-kilter sense of cool that expresses itself in lopsided folksy floral dresses, trench coats designed to sit back on the shoulders, asymmetrical sweaters, and "broken heel" boots. Two side-by-side stores in the bottom of the iconic maison sell the clothing and accessories.

10 ave. George V, 75008 Paris, +33 (01)-47-20-21-11, Balenciaga.com, and additional locations.

Céline

Danish artist FOS created custom furnishings for the brand's divine, light-filled Avenue Montaigne flagship, including modern lamps, seating, and chandeliers that mimic the clean lines and raw materials that characterize the clothing and must-have shoes and handbags. Between the palm plants and pink marble tables, you'll get as much interiors inspiration here as fashion inspiration.

53 ave. Montaigne, 75008 Paris, +33 (01)-40-70-07-03, celine.com, and additional locations.

Dior

This maison is where Monsieur Dior himself used to fit his clients, including Marlene Dietrich, Ava Gardner, and Eva Perón, and where the haute couture creations are still made on the top floor. Dior presented his legendary New Look collection within these walls in 1947, and Carrie Bradshaw fell on the store's marble floor during the final episode of *Sex and the City*. The flagship offers the full collection of men's, women's, and children's clothing (the first Baby Dior store was established here), along with accessories, makeup, and perfume.

30 ave. Montaigne, Paris 75008, +33 (01)-40-73-73-73, dior.com, and additional locations.

Les Suites

Combining couture and ready-to-wear, the salon-like store is the brainchild of Ukrainian-born Eka Iukuridze, who was exposed to couture at an early age thanks to her parents. Pieces from Giambattista Valli, Haider Ackermann, and Rochas, as well as lesser-known designers from around the world, sit alongside made-to-order eveningwear from Copenhagen's Trash Couture, furs from Terzakou, and tailoring from Tailleur Premium Paris. "I work in interiors, so I'm entranced from the moment I walk in," says Brigette Romanek. "It's as if I'm walking into a palace and borrowing some of the queen's clothes. The dressing rooms, or 'suites,' are the most beautiful; the brands are elegant and sophisticated, like the store itself."

47 rue Pierre Charron, 75008 Paris, +33 (01)-56-59-11-11, boutiquelessuites.com.

Montaigne Market

"Always has all of my favorite pieces from every current designer," Rachel Zoe says of this multi-label boutique with more than 100 international brands, from haute to street, resortwear to denim, including Chloé, Altuzarra, Off-White, Victoria Beckham, Vetements, Frame Denim, Pitusa, Rochas, Rosetta Getty, and more. "The best-curated selection of must-have and up-and-coming designers," adds Shea Marie of Peace Love Shea. "It's also right by one of my favorite lunch spots, L'Avenue. I love sitting on the patio and people/fashion-watching. You can spot the chicest women (and men) in the world."

57 ave. Montaigne, 75008 Paris, +33 (01)-42-56-58-58, Montaignemarket.com.

PALAIS ROYAL/LES HALLES

agnès b.

Synonymous with French chic since 1975, agnès b. sells the look defined by such icons as Jean Seberg and Françoise Hardy—subtle, everyday cool. There are more than 300 agnès b. stores worldwide selling simple tailored suits, long-sleeved striped T-shirts, and snap-front fleece sweatshirt cardigans. Founder Agnès Andrée Marguerite Troublé is an interesting character who has plenty of pursuits outside of fashion: She opened a gallery to exhibit graffiti artists in the 1980s, has dabbled in photography, and made a feature film in 2012, *My Name Is Hmmm*. It wasn't that much of a leap; an early agnès b. T-shirt read J'AIME LE CINEMA (the style is still available today), and it was an iconic agnès b white button-down shirt that Uma Thurman's character Mia Wallace wears in the 1994 film *Pulp Fiction*. Fans include Yoko Ono, Helena Bonham Carter, Natalie Portman, Philippe Starck, and Gérard Depardieu. She manufactures almost entirely in France. This is her original boutique.

6 rue du Jour, 75001 Paris, France, +33 (01)-42-33-04-13, agnesb.com, and additional locations.

Christian Louboutin

The Parisian shoemaker struck gold when he introduced his signature red soles, which have been worn by the most stylish ladies in the world. If there were a capital of Loubou-

ONLINE SHOPPING TIP

Famed Paris boutique Merci offers a nice selection of clothing, accessories, and home items that ship internationally at merci-merci.com. Another fun thing to do online is design your own Longchamp nylon Pliage tote at Longchamp.com. The French brand allows you to customize your own color, trim, and monogram, and ship it any place in the world. Jewelry designer Liseanne Frankfurt also recommends Poilane.fr, where you can order the best bread and have it sent from Paris. "Not the best for your carbon footprint, but really a treat once in a while and amazing to send to friends," she says.

tin World, it would be here, in the storied retail arcade, Passage Véro-Dodat, where he opened his first store in 1991. The spot has such sentimental value, Louboutin designed the Passage bag with arch-shaped metal handles in honor of it. There is a men's store nearby.

19 rue Jean-Jacques Rousseau, 75001 Paris, +33 (08)-00-94-58-04, christianlouboutin.com, and additional locations.

Didier Ludot

The destination for museum-quality vintage clothing in Paris. This is where Reese Witherspoon's stylist and Haney designer Mary Alice Haney found the 1950 Christian Dior gown with rose garland embellishment, which Witherspoon wore to accept the Best Actress Oscar in 2006. "A regular haunt for my design team," says designer Tory Burch. "Like stepping back into a time of elegance and haute couture," says famous street style dandy Patrick McDonald.

Jardin du Palais Royal, 24 Galerie Montpensier, 75001 Paris, +33 (01)-42-96-56, didierludot.fr.

Pierre Hardy

The accessories designer, who founded his brand in 1999, is known for his quirky, architectural styles, including sneakers and messenger bags. He has also been responsible for Hermès's shoe design since 1990, and its fine jewelry design since 2001. In 2016, Hermès took a minority stake in Hardy's business.

Jardin du Palais Royal, 156 Galerie de Valois, 75001 Paris, +33 (01)-42-60-59-75, pierrehardy.com, and other locations.

MONTMARTRE

Spree

Roberta Oprandi's version of the Paris concept store includes clothing and accessories by Acne, Marc by Marc Jacobs, Carven, Helmut Lang, and MM6 Maison Margiela casually draped on pieces of classic '50s designer furniture by Eames, Pierre Paulin, and others (the furniture is also for sale). Rotating artwork is featured on the walls. Across the street, you'll find more vintage furniture and art exhibitions in the gallery run by Roberta's husband, artist-designer Bruno Hadjadj, in an old DIY shop still marked Papiers Peints.

16 rue La Vieuville, Paris 75018, +33 (01)-42-23-41-40, spree.fr.

REPUBLIQUE

Centre Commercial

Industrial space featuring artisan-minded clothing and accessories for men, women, and kids, plus lifestyle items. Brands include A Peace Treaty, Atlanta Mocassin, Birkenstock, Bodkin, Etudes, Filson, Norse Projects, Patagonia, and more.

2 rue de Marseille, 75010 Paris, +33 (01)-42-02-26-08, centrecommercial.cc.

Thanx God I'm A VIP

"Hands down the best vintage store in Paris," says Christene Barberich, editor in chief and cofounder of Refinery29.com of this spot, featuring racks of clothes arranged by color. It was launched in 1994 by Sylvie Chateigner, who is also a player in the Parisian nightlife scene, hosting regular house music parties at different locations around the city where the worlds of fashion, music, and media meet.

12 rue de lancry 75010 Paris, +33 (01)-42-03-02-09, thanxgod.com.

TROCODERO

Reciproque

"Over the years, I accumulated a lot of amazing ball gowns and special finds from this secondhand store," says fashion tech entrepreneur Alexandra Wilkis Wilson of the Paris institution, which is actually six boutiques in a row selling tens of thousands of items from every brand in the fashion universe, from Alaïa to Yohji Yamamoto and everything in between.

89-101 rue de la Pompe, 75116 Paris, +33 (01)-47-04-30-28, reciproque.fr.

MILAN

ITALY

THE MAJORS

10 Corso Como

Many consider this to be the first concept store in the world, founded in 1990 by former magazine editor Carla Sozzani (the sister of *Vogue* Italia editor in chief Franca Sozzani). "One of the first stores to do a cultural mix in the same space," says designer and stylist Maryam Malakpour. "It unites shopping (great brands, from Converse to Azzedine Alaïa), with a gallery, café, and bookshop." "I could spend hours, and I have, wandering through," adds retailer Emily Holt. Over the years, Sozzani has boosted the careers of everyone from Alaïa to Rei Kawakubo. The store's fragrance collection is top-notch, as is the accessories selection, and you'll always find interesting exclusives and collaborations, with everyone from Balmain to Swatch. In 2002, a 10 Corso Como branch opened in Tokyo, followed by Seoul, Shanghai, and Beijing. The brand's recognizable black-and-white logo, designed by American artist Kris Ruhs, as well as other artist-created graphics, has been splashed on fragrances, T-shirts, sneakers, and tote bags, making great souvenirs.

Corso Como, 10, 20124 Milano, +39 02 2900 2674, 10corsocomo.com.

Galleria Vittorio Emanuele II

One of the world's oldest shopping malls, this marble arcade with a stunning iron and vaulted glass roof dates back to the 19th century. Known as Milan's living room, it's the perfect place for an afternoon stroll, with plenty of cafés (have an apertivo at Bar Zucca, which Verdi and Toscanini favored) and, of course, shopping (Prada, Louis Vuitton, Tod's, Gucci, and more).

Piazza del Duomo, 20123 Milano, +39 02 8845 5555.

la Rinascente

The department store where Giorgio Armani got his start as a photographer and a buyer, this is the place to rub elbows with in-the-know Italians. Shop here for upscale clothing and accessories, plus sneakers, stockings (always better in Europe), and lingerie (who doesn't need a leopard-print Dolce & Gabbana undershirt?). The home section is full of colorful ceramics, tablecloths, and napkins, and the food hall on the top floor is a great resource for made-in-Italy delicacies. "A multi-brand department store with a view," says stylist Susie Sheffman. "Don't miss a post-shopping glass of prosecco at the rooftop bar, where you

10 CORSO COMO

can practically reach out and touch Milan's magnificent Duomo." "I love it because they have such a beautiful and varied lingerie and hosiery department," adds costume designer Janie Bryant.

Piazza del Duomo, 20121 Milano, +39 02 88521, rinascente.it, and additional locations.

Prada at Galleria Vittorio Emanuele II

A mecca for fashion pilgrims, it has an old-world feel, with built-in wood shelves, a black-and-white checkerboard floor, and even the original cashier's desk and sign. The upstairs is packed with handbags; down the marble staircase in the basement is a treasure trove of shoes and clothing for men and women, as well as the brand's signature nylon totes and cosmetic bags displayed in antique steamer trunks—a nod to Prada's origins in the luggage business.

Galleria Vittorio Emanuele II, 63-65, 20121 Milano, Italy, +39 02 876979, prada.com, and additional locations.

Golden Quadrangle

Italy's biggest names are all represented on the cobblestone streets of the city's luxury shopping district—Versace, Valentino, Etro, Fendi, Tod's, Marni, Moncler, La Perla, Moschino, Miu Miu, Missoni, Emilio Pucci, Brunello Cucinelli, Roberto Cavalli, Borsalino, Tod's, and Gianvito Rossi—along with most international brands. "It's like the biggest mall in the world, only outdoors," says street-style star Anna Dello Russo. "You can go from one shop to the other one easily, and you can have fresh clothes right away."

Bordered by Via Manzoni (NW), Via della Spiga (NE), Corso Venezia (SE), and Via Montenapoleone (SW), 20123, Milano.

Golden Quadrangle

Alan Journo

"Has a great selection of hats," says Anna Dello Russo, of this whimsical, high-end accessories boutique, where she picked up both her legendary cherry headpiece and her Peruvian doll headpiece, among many others. "For me, there's no vintage and no online. I like to spend time in the shops, talking to people."

Via della Spiga, 36, 20121 Milano, +39 02 7600 1309.

Aspesi

Understated sportswear and outerwear (including down-filled shirts) beloved by the Milanese. "I always stock up on their cashmere-and-silk scarves, which are amazing quality but won't break the bank," says fashion consultant Amanda Ross.

Via Monte Napoleone, 13, 20121 Milano, +39 02 7602 2478, aspesi.com.

GALLERIA VITTORIO EMANUELE II

Armani

Giorgio Armani's lifestyle emporium occupies an entire block on Via Manzoni. This minimalist palace features the designer's main line of suits and red-carpet gowns, as well as Emporio Armani, Armani Jeans, Armani Dolci (the best chocolates!), a florist, and a bookshop, as well as Milan's very own Nobu restaurant.

Via Alessandro Manzoni, 31, 20121 Milano, +39 02 7231 8600, armani.com.

Bottega Veneta

The first of the Italian luxury brand's "maison" concept stores is a massive residential-style space across two floors of an 18th-century building, with a curved staircase and windows opening onto a lush green courtyard. Creative director Tomas Maier designed the space, and the furniture inside. Featured is the entire product range of understated luxe ready-to-wear, accessories, and jewelry.

Via Sant'Andrea, 15, 20121 Milano, +39 02 7787 8116, bottegaveneta.com, and additional locations.

Brunello Cucinelli

Cashmere king Brunello Cucinelli's brand of casual super-luxe has made fans of Leonardo DiCaprio, Bradley Cooper, Jennifer Garner, and *Girls* Allison Williams, as well as one-percenters the world over. He has his headquarters in the medieval hilltop village of Solomeo in Umbria, Italy, but Milan is where his showroom is. His collections are well-represented in his boutique on Via della Spiga, which features made-to-measure suiting, plush cashmere sweaters and shawls, relaxed tailored separates, and the label's distinctive chain mesh embellished shoes and accessories.

Via della Spiga, 5, 20121 Milano, +39 02 7601 4448, brunellocucinelli.com, and additional locations.

DMAG Outlet

Nestled right in the high-end heart of Milan is this gem of an outlet (there are three locations), in which you can find overstock and past-season items from all the top brands, including Lanvin, Proenza Schouler, Tory Burch, and more.

Via Bigli, 4, 20121 Milano, +39 02 3664 3888, dmag.eu.

Dolce & Gabbana, Boutique Sartoria and Bar Martini

Housed in the 16th-century palazzo that has been home to the men's collections for years, Dolce & Gabbana Sartoria shares space with the men's shoe boutique, plus its Barbiere barbershop, Beauty Farm spa, and Martini Bar and Bistrot (in partnership with the Italian spirits brand Martini).

The store opens onto a courtyard garden of citrus trees, palms, prickly pears, and other plants common to Sicily, the birthplace of Domenico Dolce. The women's boutique is just steps away at 2 Via Spiga.

Boutique Sartoria Man, Corso Venezia, 13, 20121 Milano +39 02 799135.

Fausto Puglisi

For Puglisi, who has dressed Katy Perry and Madonna on their tours, there was no question that Milan would be the location for his first store. Although he's known for a sexy, rock'n'roll aesthetic, the store also stocks tailored jackets and pleated skirts. The space is designed to resemble a Roman domus, complete with a geometric marble mosaic at the entrance that represents Puglisi's signature symbol, the sun.

Via della Spiga, 1, 20121 Milano, +39 02 7634 0454, faustopuglisi.com.

Gaimbattista Valli

Located in the courtyard of one of the historic buildings of Via Sant'Andrea, the Italian designer's Milan flagship showcases his entire frothy, flowery, elegant universe, including ready-to-wear and accessories, bags, shoes, jewels, and furs—even his signature sweet-smelling candle.

Via Sant'Andrea, 12, 20121 Milano, +39 02 780 218.

Gio Moretti

"Located on the famous Via della Spiga, it reminds me of Intermix in New York. I never leave without a pair of shoes. They have a great selection!" says tastemaker Shalini Kasliwal.

Via Della Spiga, 4, Milano, +39 02 7600 3186, giomoretti.com.

Gucci

The Montenapoleone flagship store is ground zero for the new, maximalist Gucci, as envisioned by creative director Alessandro Michele. Rihanna even stopped by to browse the Florentine brand's colorful handbags and clothes. This store sets the tone for others around the world and was the first to introduce the Gucci DIY service, with bags, denim jackets, silk bombers, tailored jackets, and more that can be customized in-store with patterns, patches, embroideries, and monograms. Head downstairs to the basement for the latest women's shoes and clothes.

Via Monte Napoleone, 5/7, 20121 Milano, +39 02 771271, Gucci.com, and additional locations.

La Sermoneta

The Rome-based glove maker has been in operation as a family-run business since 1960, offering gloves in every color and fabric imaginable.

Via della Spiga, 46, 20121 Milano, +39 02 7631 8303, sermonetagloves .com, and additional locations.

Madina Milano

This makeup store is a fashion insider favorite for must-have products like its Crystal Bronzing Powder and the Chic & Shine Highlighter Stick. It's great stuff and the prices are drug store–cheap.

Corso Venezia, 23, 20100 Milano, +39 02 7601 1692, madina.it.

Moschino

The Italian brand's biggest flagship in Italy, this boutique is a supersized showcase for creative director Jeremy Scott's wonderfully wacky vision. Feast your eyes on a giant mannequin that stretches across the entire store window, an XL-size leather-jacket-shaped handbag that serves as a display counter, a pair of huge high-heel pumps that act as shelves for actual shoes, and a gigantic teddy bear in the children's area.

Via Sant'Andrea, 12, 20121 Milano, +39 02 7600 0832, Moschino.com, and additional locations.

Ottod'ame

This Italian casual chic line with a girlie touch has fun frilly blouses, Lurex pleated skirts, faux fur coats, velvet sandals, and more, all at a contemporary price point.

Via Alessandro Manzoni, 39, 20121 Milano, +39 02 6556 0409, ottodame.it.

DUOMO/CORSO VITTORIO EMMANUEL

Dixie

This Italian fast fashion chain is somewhere between H&M and & Other Stories, both in price point and aesthetic. In addition to trendy jogger pants and slip dresses, there are some surprisingly elegant pieces in the shops, including an oversized cable-knit sweater with pearl detail that was reminiscent of Dries Van Noten, Lurex pleated skirts in a range of colors, and retro-print pussy bow blouses. It's worth a look.

Via San Maurillo, 2, 20100 Milano, +39 02 7209 4475, shop.dixie.it, and additional locations.

Excelsior Milano

This luxury department store, designed by Jean Nouvel and Vincenzo de Cotiis, occupies a former Milanese cinema. The store spans 4,000 square

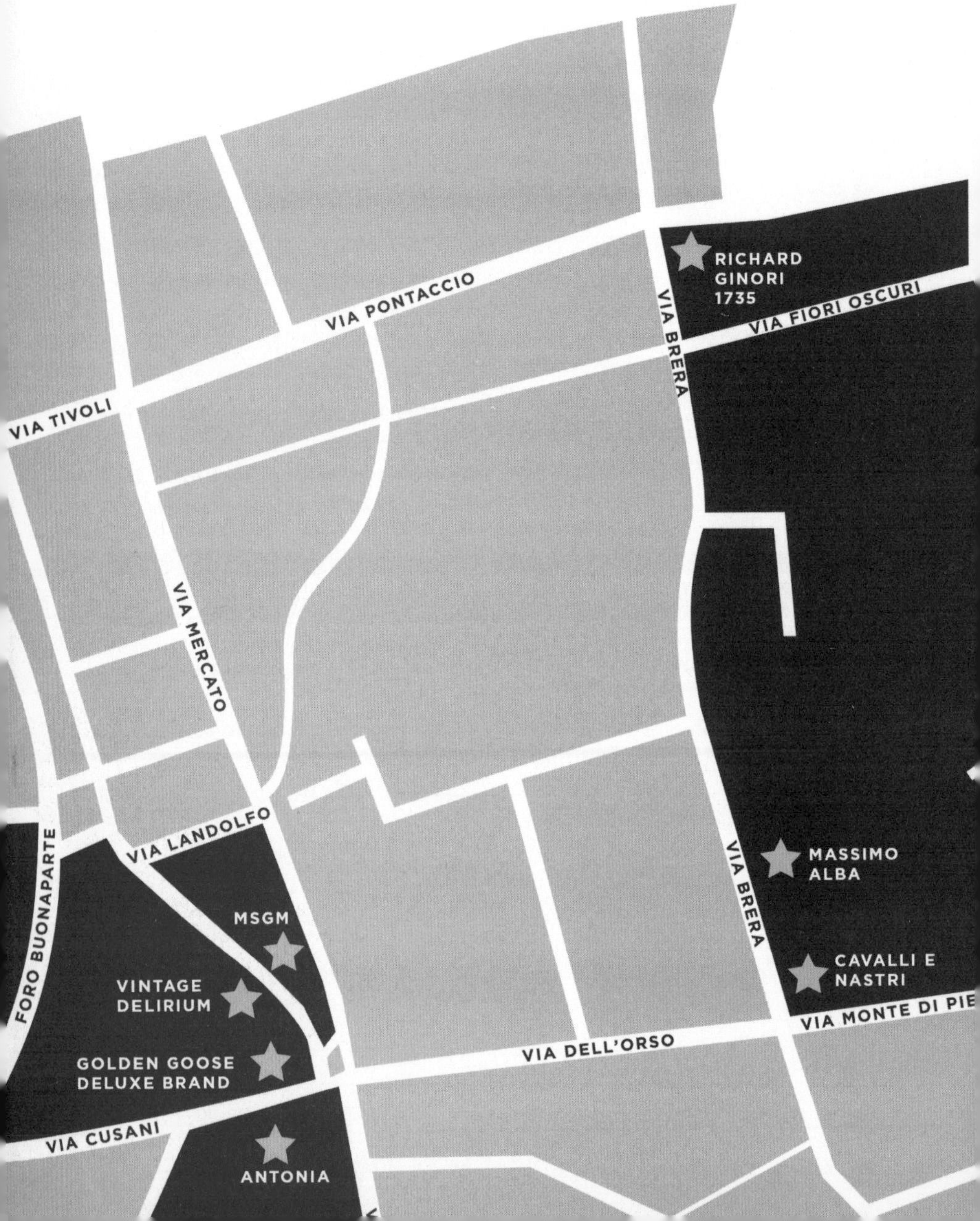

RICHARD GINORI 1735
VIA PONTACCIO
VIA FIORI OSCURI
VIA BRERA
VIA TIVOLI
VIA MERCATO
VIA LANDOLFO
FORO BUONAPARTE
MSGM
VINTAGE DELIRIUM
GOLDEN GOOSE DELUXE BRAND
MASSIMO ALBA
CAVALLI E NASTRI
VIA MONTE DI PIE
VIA DELL'ORSO
VIA CUSANI
ANTONIA

BRERA

MILAN

VIA SANTO SPIRITO
Nº21
VIA GESU
VIA ALESSANDRO MANZONI
VIA MONTE NAPOLEONE

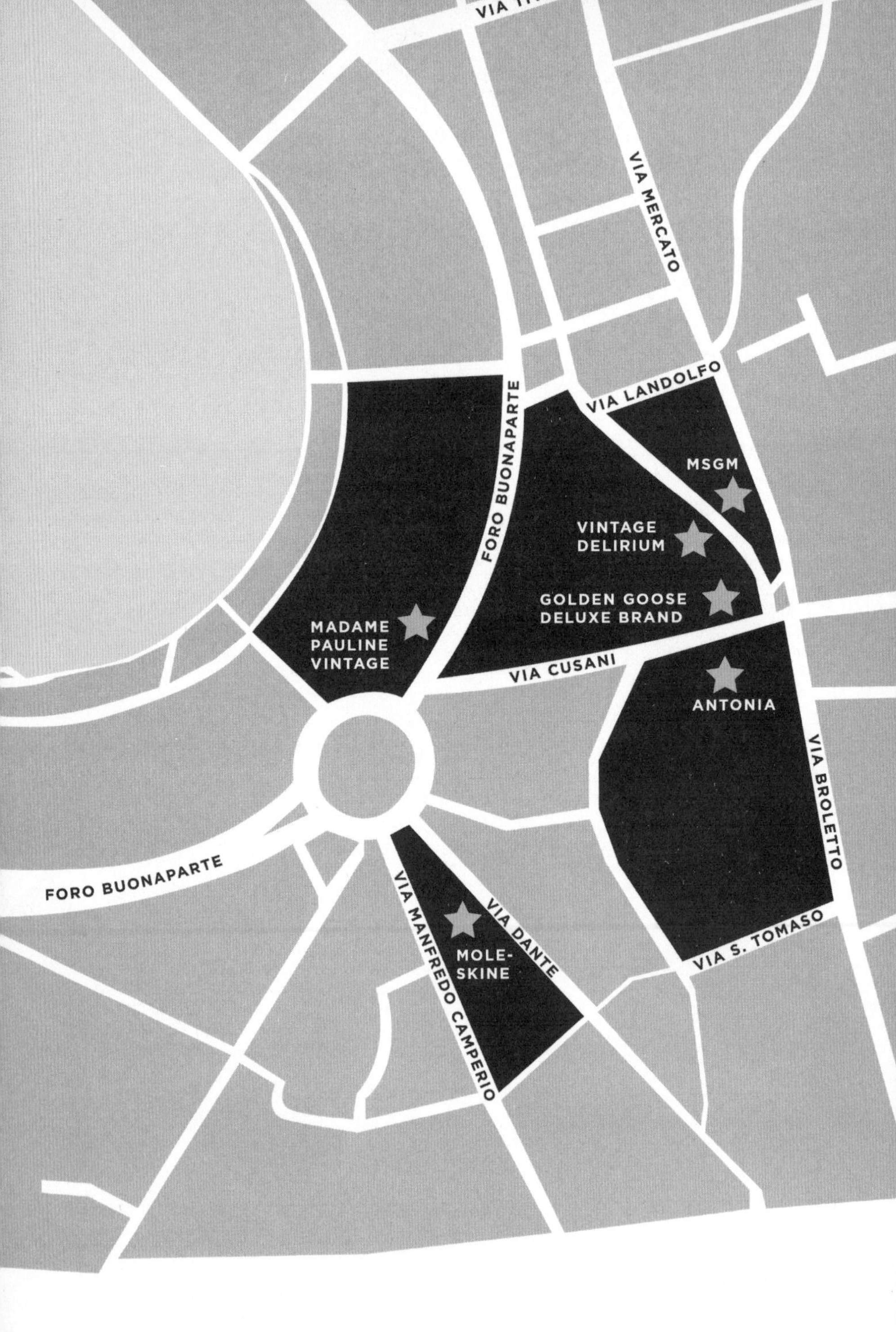
VIA TIVO
VIA MERCATO
VIA LANDOLFO
FORO BUONAPARTE
MSGM
VINTAGE DELIRIUM
GOLDEN GOOSE DELUXE BRAND
MADAME PAULINE VINTAGE
VIA CUSANI
ANTONIA
VIA BROLETTO
FORO BUONAPARTE
VIA MANFREDO CAMPERIO
VIA DANTE
MOLE-SKINE
VIA S. TOMASO

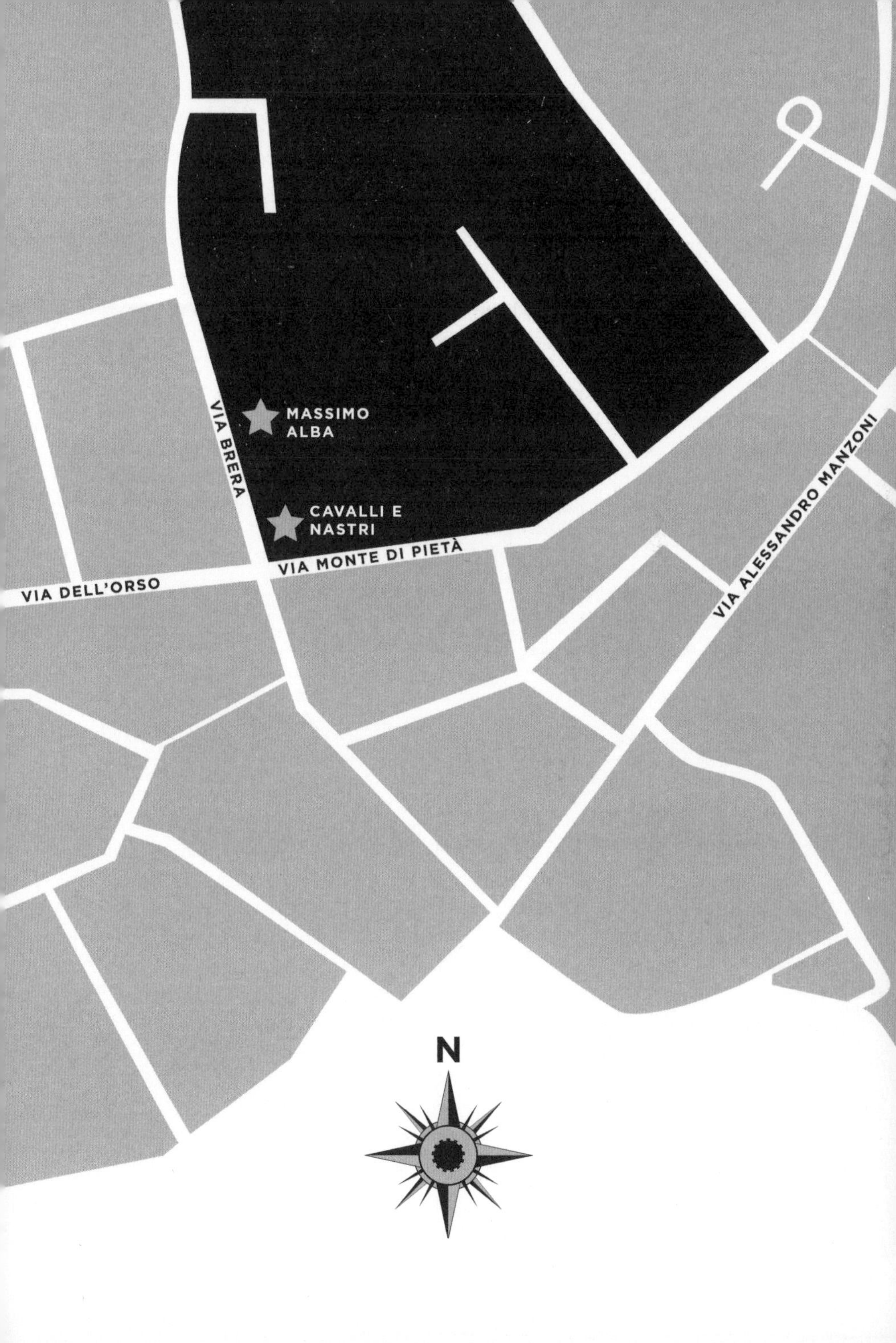
MASSIMO ALBA
CAVALLI E NASTRI
VIA BRERA
VIA MONTE DI PIETÀ
VIA DELL'ORSO
VIA ALESSANDRO MANZONI
N

feet and seven floors, with a perfume gallery, a Tiffany & Co. shop-in-shop, and clothing for men and women with denim and high-end streetwear (Enfants Riches Déprimés, K-Way, Yeezy, Visvim), ready-to-wear (Cédric Charlier, Chloé, Stella Jean, Versace, Facetasm), plus must-have accessories from Sophia Webster, Sara Battaglia, Aquazzura, Manolo Blahnik, and more. "I love the food hall downstairs," says fashion journalist Divia Harilela of the underground gourmet grocery, which boasts what was the most beautiful selection of fresh tomatoes I've ever seen. Only in Italy!

Galleria del Corso, 4, 20122 Milano, +39 02 7630 7301, excelsiormilano.com.

Funky Table

This fun home décor store across the street from Wait and See carries mismatched dishes, lace-like baskets, furry totes and more fun stuff.

Via Santa Marta, 19, 20123 Milano, +39 02 3674 8619, funkytable.it.

Wait and See

"Carries lots of great under-the-radar labels, often from Belgium and Holland," says Christina Binkley. "I buy clothes there, and sometimes other things, like a bunch of silver spoons engraved with YOU ARE LOVED that I gave my kids, husband, and mom."

Via Santa Marta, 14, 20123 Milano, +39 02 7208 0195, waitandsee.com.

NAVIGLIA/PORTE TICINESE

Antonioli

Dark and edgy men's and women's boutique housed in a 1920s silent-movie theater, Antonioli stocks Rick Owens, Rodarte, Givenchy, Vetements, and more.

Via Pasquale Paoli, 1, 20143 Milano, +39 02 3656 6494, antonioli.eu.

Biffi

A cornerstone of the Milan boutique scene since the 1960s, when the Biffi sisters, Rosy and Adele, opened two stores in Milan. They've stocked such international designer labels as Kenzo and Yohji Yamamoto since the beginning. You'll also find Marni, Stella McCartney, MSGM, Stella Jean, Sacai, Tod's, Alexander McQueen, and Thom Browne, both men's and women's. The sister store, Banner, is in the Golden Quadrangle at Via Sant'Andrea 8.

Corso Genova, 6, 20123 Milano, +39 02 8311 1601, biffiboutiques.com.

LADoubleJ

Fashion journalist, consultant, street style favorite, and L.A.-to-Italy transplant JJ Martin opened this gorgeous showroom for her überchic collection of clothing (boy shirts, ball skirts, swing dresses, scarves, and more) and furniture made from reissued vintage prints from Italian textile company Mantero. Designed by architect Luca Cipoletti, the space features a white exhibition grid, called Wunderwall, which displays clothing, vintage jewelry that once belonged to legendary Italian fashion editor Anna Piaggi, design objects, and ceramics. Email for an appointment. And be sure to check out Martin's website for all things chic in Milan (and a killer selection of vintage clothing and jewelry that ships worldwide).

Piazza Arcole 4, 20143 Milano, ladoublej.com.

Navigli Antiques Market

Held on the last Sunday of the month, this market hosts 400 antiques dealers along the canals. "I always find great vintage finds and new treasures here," says shoe designer Brian Atwood. "Italy isn't big on vintage, but in this area you can find some interesting shops and cafés."

Alzaia Naviglio Grande, starting at the Via Valenza bridge on Viale Gorzia, 20144, Milano.

Pupi Solari

A Milan institution, the silver-haired Solari started with a children's shop in 1969, expanding her store over the years to include women's clothing and accessories (there's also a men's store, Host, next door). She is the arbiter of the classic, non-flashy Italian look, with understated clothing and accessories from Dusan, Emma Hope, Mantu, Sofie D'Hoore, Tomas Meier, George Esquivel, Massimo Alba, Massimo Piombo, Alberto Biani, and Aspesi.

Piazza Tommaseo, Via Lorenzo Mascheroni, 20123 Milano, +34 02 463 325, pupisolari.com.

PORTO VENEZIA

Imarika

This small boutique packs a big punch with elegant, but sparkly frocks from Rochas, Simone Rocha, shoes by Elena Iachi, and more. It also has its own private label.

Via Giovanni Morelli, 1, 20129 Milano, +39 02 7600 5268, imarika.it.

PORTO ROMANA

Etro Outlet

One of the few true outlet experiences left, meaning you'll still experience the thrill of the hunt in this small shop, where you can dig through bins of paisley scarves, a basement full of racks of last season's patchwork blazers and silk patterned dresses, and shelves of fringed leather goods from the Italian luxury stalwart. Its recent boho turn has found fans with Florence Welch, Rosie Huntington-Whiteley, and other stars. If you're a fan of the label, it's worth a stop.

Via Spartaco, 6, Milano, +39 02 5502 0218, etro.com, and other locations.

Rose's Roses Shoes

"Rosa Aiuto sells her designs—the brand is Rose's Roses—mainly in Italy," says fashion journalist Christina Binkley. "She used to design shoes for Marni and for Vera Wang. Her own style is more modern-classic, and she's always way ahead of the pack. I bought oxfords from her two years before they became a 'thing.' She recently launched online sales, but I go to her studio in Milan's Porta Romana neighborhood. "

Corso Lodi, 5, 20135 Milano, +39 02 5412 1998, rosesroses.it.

BRERA/CASTELLO/CORSO COMO

Antonia

The multi-brand boutique began with accessories in 1999, followed by a menswear location. In 2013 the two stores were combined in a renovated 17th-century palazzo. The menswear is street-casual (think Riccardo Tisci for Nike, Hood by Air, Balmain, Saint Laurent, Sacai), while the women's combines streetwear and denim (Fenty x Rihanna, Frame Denim, Isabel Marant) with haute labels (Gucci, Fendi, Anthony Vaccarello). Whenever she's in Milan, Amanda Ross hits this spot to shop the "design collaborations and exclusives" she can't get anywhere else.

Via Cusani, 5, 20121 Milano, +39 02 8699 8340, antonia.it.

Cavalli e Nastri

Italian designers head to these cheery vintage boutiques, which feature a masterful mix of high and low from Kenzo, Moschino, Gucci, and more. Each location has a different twist: At Via Brera, 2, you'll find dresses and accessories from 1940 to today as well as pieces by young new designers; on Via Gian Giacamo Mora, 12, you can pick up more unique pieces; while Via Gian Giacomo Mora, 3, stocks vintage menswear, as well as interior and housewares.

Via Brera and Via Gian Giacomo Moro, 20121 Milano, +39 02 7200 0449, cavallienastri.com.

Corso Como Outlet

If your wallet is on the light side, this outlet offers past-season merch from the big store, in addition to the odd pair of Prada or Manolo Blahnik shoes.

In the courtyard at Via Tazzoli, 3, 20154 Milano, +39 02 2901 5130.

Elena Iachi

This made-in-Italy shoe brand founded in 2011 is known for embellished cowboy booties and clogs, but what's kept us coming back lately is the elegant slip-on sneakers in floral velvet or sequined fabric, with crystal or fur embellishment.

Piazza Venticinque Aprile, 9, 20154 Milano, +39 02 6556 0413, elenaiachi.it.

ERAL 55

"I always appreciate a very singular point of view, and Ermanno Lazzarin really pulls it off," says Ann Mashburn of this menswear destination where you'll find everything from Japanese and American workwear to Italian tailoring, from ascots to cowboy boots. "He is not following trends, but driving trends himself."

Piazza Venticinque Aprile, 14, 20124 Milano, +39 02 659 8829, eral55.com.

Golden Goose Deluxe Brand

Founded in 2000, this Italian brand, which is responsible for lived-in luxury sneakers that have become a fashion cult classic, opened its first boutique in Milan in 2013. The store also features the leather jackets, classic shirts, and distressed boots that round out the collection.

Via Ponte Vetero, 1, 20121 Milano, +39 02 8901 1921, goldengoosedeluxebrand.com, and additional locations.

Madame Pauline Vintage

"I found this place by accident," Christene Barberich, editor in chief and cofounder of Refinery29, says of this vintage store. "I was running from lunch to a show and spotted all the bright colors and textiles out of the corner of my eye. Even though I was running late, I did a crazy speed round, and returned the next day when I had more time. I found a gorgeous lipstick-red topcoat that people always ask me about. The tailoring is next level."

Foro Buonaparte, 74, 20121 Milano, +39 02 4943 1201, madamepaulinevintage.it.

Massimo Alba

Based in Milan, Alba creates luxury T-shirts, chinos, and linen jackets that exemplify the new Italian elegance. Cashmere is a speciality.

Via Brera, 8, 20121 Milano, +39 02 7209 3420, massimoalba.com.

Moleskine Flagship and Cafe

The Milan-based brand of notebooks and planners opened this hybrid café–art gallery in 2016 in the heart of the Brera Design District. Milanese coffee roaster Sevengrams serves single-origin brew, notebooks are for sale, and hanging out is encouraged. Breakfast learning sessions and exhibitions are part of the concept.

Corso Garibaldi, 65, 20121 Milano, +39 02 7200 0608, moleskine.com.

Momoni

What started in 2009 as a lingerie brand has grown into a full line of casual, colorful ready-to-wear, including dreamy garden-floral silk blouses, Lurex knits, softly tailored jackets, and boyfriend jeans with silver embroidered details.

Corso Como, 3, 20154 Milano, +39 02 6379 3466, momoni.it, and additional locations.

MSGM

Launched by former DJ Massimo Giorgetti in 2009, this Italian contemporary brand specializes in bright hues, digital prints, and fun, Insta-friendly shapes.

Via Ponte Vetero, 9, 20121 Milano, +39 02 36595680, msgm.it.

No° 21

After parting ways with his namesake brand in 2009, Italian designer Alessandro Dell'Acqua founded No° 21—named after his birthdate and lucky number. His Milan flagship features sumptuous marble floors and an accessories room with walls and floor made of the same stones used to build the Duomo. You'll find clothes and accessories with lots of romantic folds and flourishes that still manage to be sporty. Dell'Acqua also designs for the French house of Rochas.

Via Santo Spirito, 14, 20121 Milano, numeroventuno.com.

Piazza Gae Aulenti

Milan's newest business hub boasts the highest skyscraper in Italy (the Unicredit Tower) and is surrounded by arcades with numerous upmarket boutiques, including funky Italian design brand Toiletpaper. Opened in 2012 adjacent to Milan's main train station, the futuristic-looking square has become a tourist attraction with its vast reflecting pool, colosseum-style outdoor seating and pedestrian walks.

Piazza Gae Aulenti, 20154 Milano.

Richard Ginori 1735

For more than two centuries, this Florentine porcelainmaker has created tableware in cheery colors with Italian flair. "The most beautiful porcelain . . . it and the shop feels like a sanctuary," says retailer Ann Mashburn. "I love the little painted insects."

Piazza San Marco, 3, Milano, +39 02 8901 1646, richardginori1735.com.

Vintage Delirium

One of the world's best vintage stores, Vintage Delirium has museum-quality pieces by Thierry Mugler, Versace, Pucci, Pierre Cardin, and Callot Soeurs.

Via Giuseppe Sacchi, 3, 20121 Milano, +39 02 8646 2076, vintagedeliriumfj.com.

SEMPIONE

Riedizioni

Milan-born textile designer Cevese's charming collection of bags, pouches, and clutches made out of feathers, fabric scraps, and industrial waste pressed in plastic is available by appointment at her showroom and store.

Via Pallavicino, 22, 20145 Milano, by appointment only, +39 02 3982 6647, riedizioni.com.

ORTICA

Outlet Marni

Tucked away on a residential street, this fashion insider favorite is worth the trip. "Knowing editors and buyers discreetly slip behind the iron gate that swings open and shuts with a jarring clang. If you've come this far, rejoice! Once inside, count your blessings and gawk at heaps of whimsical, marked-down Marni print dresses, coats, jewelry, furs, leathers, bags, and shoes, and at the squealing editors paying respects to the church of Marni," says stylist Susie Sheffman. You'll find an array of outerwear, fur, dresses, sweaters, bags, jewelry, and sunglasses for men, women, and children starting at 50 percent off.

Via Giancarlo Sismondi, 65, 20133 Milano, +39 02 7104 0332, marni.com.

ROME

ITALY

Battistoni

The classic Rome tailor has made bespoke pieces for everyone from Marlon Brando to Sophia Loren. "A real treat to visit," says retailer Ann Mashburn. "The chicest men's shop, and amazing art on every wall."

Via dei Condotti, 61A, 00187 Roma, +39 06 697 6111, battistoni.com.

Eleuteri

Dates back to 1897, when it opened as a café, just off the Spanish Steps. Owner Pietro Eleuteri's son, Carlo, moved from the restaurant business into collecting antiques, specializing in vintage jewels. Fast-forward to today, and Eleuteri is one of Italy's premier vintage and antique jewelry destinations, attracting an international jet set that browses pieces by Bulgari, Cartier, and Van Cleef & Arpels alongside 18th-century Southern Italian coral items and rare silverware. There is also a branch of the store in New York.

Via dei Condotti, 69, 00187 Roma, +39 06 678 1078, eleuteri.nyc.

Fendi

After becoming the benefactor of the Trevi Fountain's restoration and resurrecting the Palazzo della Civiltà, an abandoned Fascist gem that is now

ONLINE SHOPPING TIP

For Italian style, **Luisaviaroma.com** can't be beat. The site (which also has bricks-and-mortar spaces in Florence) features the best of the best of Italian (and European, Asian, and American) designers, including their most over-the-top pieces, as well as showcasing new talents, and it also ships internationally. Another must-shop site is **LaDoubleJ.com**, which has an expertly curated selection of vintage fashion and accessories come to life within the worlds of high style and interior design in Milan, plus the latest information about the city's creative talent, hidden shops, tantalizing food, and best-kept secrets. For made-in-Capri sandals online, delivered to your doorstep, try **Canfora.com**.

the Rome-based luxury brand's headquarters, Fendi opened its largest flagship in the world right by the Spanish Steps. The Palazzo Fendi includes two floors of retail space designed by architect Gwenael Nicolas, a boutique hotel, a VIP apartment, a restaurant, and a rooftop bar. Most of the furniture is by Fendi Casa, and the Fendi family's art collection is on display. Inside the store, you'll find everything from fashion's most over-the-top furs to fur bag charms.

Via della Fontanella di Borghese, 48, 00187 Roma, +39 06 33 4501, fendi.com, and additional locations.

Saddlers Union

Launched in 1957, Rome's heritage leather-goods-maker gained a cult following, including Jackie Kennedy, who sported the shop's saddlebag. You can find all kinds of leather bags here, from bucket shapes to briefcases.

Via Margutta 11, 00186 Roma, 00187, +39 06 3212 0237, saddlersunion.com.

Valentino

It's fitting that the Roman fashion house's biggest flagship would be here, neighboring the 16th-century Palazzo Mignanelli, where the brand is headquartered. Opened in 2015, it was designed by architect David Chipperfield and houses the men's and women's collections, as well as accessories and made-to-measure denim for men.

Piazza di Spagna, 35/38, 00187 Roma, +39 06 9451 5710, valentino.com, and additional locations.

JJ MARTIN

ITALIAN INSIDER'S GUIDE

One of Milan's most stylish women, JJ Martin's ladoublej.com is dedicated to the best of Italian style, talent, and fashion.

My favorite big-city shop in Milan is **PRADA** in Montenapoleone. It sounds banal, but I associate the brand so closely with the Milanese aesthetic that it comforts me to go in there and just breathe in the style of the city that I admire. I also know most of the staff, which, for me, counts more than anything—I walk in and we chat, we play, they bring out a bunch of shoes no one else likes that they know I will appreciate. It's a very personal, homey environment, one that feels more and more essential to where I go and how I spend my time. (Be sure to stop by the Prada-owned **HISTORIC PASTICCERIA MARCHESI** next door for a snack.)

I love the upstairs emporium of **ROSSANA ORLANDI'S** design gallery in Milan. She's got an amazing selection of colorful plates, plastic glasses, and tabletop items you never knew you needed. When you go in the springtime you feel like you've entered an enchanted garden. I never miss going to the vintage furniture shop owned by **RAIMONDO GARAU**. He picks pieces no one else would ever consider and they look incredible together—plus, I love sitting and discussing decorating ideas with him. I also make sure to browse the colorful combination of unusual and not-that-expensive fashion at Uberta Zambeletti's well-edited shop **WAIT AND SEE**. These are creative Italian people who embody the qualities that I admire.

On the weekends we often travel to my husband's hometown of Pesaro, a small town on the Adriatic coast that no one cool ever visits and is not on any tourist hit list. This seaside town is a quintessential example of the Italian provinces. What was amazing to me was discovering two important shops here. One is an impressive multi-brand store called **RATTI**, which has been around for 100 years, and has an Hermès shop-in-shop in addition to edgy clothes from Christopher Kane and Erdem and an amazing selection of Valentino. I love finding these shrines dedicated to beauty in the middle of nowhere, where women come out like ants after the rain and you're like, "Where do all of these people live?" The other shop in Pesaro is **ZUCCA**, which has a very small but perfectly edited collection of vintage jewelry and furniture. No one in Pesaro shops there, so I'm not sure how it stays in business. I met the owners years ago and they have impeccable taste—whenever I go, we sit for hours, have an *aperitivo*, and recount vintage stories.

PRADA, Via Monte Napoleone, 6, 20121 Milano, +39 02 7602 0273, prada.com.

HISTORIC PASTICCERIA MARCHESI, Via Monte Napoleone, 6, 20121 Milano, +39 02 76008238, pasticceriamarchesi.it.

ROSSANA ORLANDI, Via Matteo Bandello, 14/16, 20123 Milano, +39 02 467 4471, rossanaorlandi.com.

RIAMONDO GARAU, Viale Francesco Crispi, 5b, 20121 Milano, Italy, +39 02 659 9913, riamondogarau.com.

WAIT N' SEE, Via Santa Marta, 14, 20123 Milano, +39 02 7208 0195, waitandsee.it.

RATTI, Via Gioacchino Rossini, 71/74, Pesaro, +39 07 213 1031, rattiboutique.com.

ZUCCA, Via Sabbatini, 12, Pesaro, +39 33 5597 5176, zuccadesign.it.

FLORENCE

ITALY

Elio Ferraro

Ferraro is known as Italy's maestro of vintage, and is a legendary figure on the fashion scene who has worked as a consultant and curated luxury vintage shops around the world. McQueen, Missoni, Mugler, and more, he's got the most important pieces, plus vintage furnishings. "Fabulous vintage emporium," says designer/personal shopper Raven Kauffman. "From vintage Pucci to rare Fornasetti housewares, there is always something wonderful to bring home."

Via Pavione, 47/R, 50123 Firenze, +39 055 290 425, ElioFerraro.com.

Gucci Museo and Icon Store

When Guccio Gucci opened his leather goods store in Florence in 1921, he couldn't have dreamed that his name would go global, and the brand grow big enough to warrant this three-story museum, full of archival clothing, accessories, and one-offs, such as a Cadillac upholstered in GGs. To round out the Gucci experience, there's a café, bookstore, gift shop, and Icon store dedicated to limited-edition products available only here.

Piazza della Signoria 10; +39-055-7592-3302, guccimuseo.com.

Lorenzo Villoresi

"Bypass his more available scents that you might see in boutiques and go directly to his atelier," says Raven Kauffman. "It's like entering a medieval alchemist's workshop. He takes only a few appointments each week, and it's a totally divine indulgence."

Via de'Bardi, 12, 50125 Firenze, +39 055 234 1187, lorenzovilloresi.it.

Loretta Caponi

"For the most beautiful nightgowns and custom linens," says Raven Kauffman. "Their embroidery is exquisite and you can work with the amazing artisans to create your own patterns. The lingerie is frothy and delicate, and their cotton pajamas are the best."

Piazza degli Antinori, 4/red, 50123 Firenze, +39 055 211 074, lorettacaponi.com.

Luisaviaroma

The three-floor, eighty-year-old Florentine fashion institution was early to the e-commerce game, launching its site in 1999, and building a loyal community of online shoppers with an edgy edit of more than 600 designers. The brick-and-mortar flagship

LUISAVIAROMA

doesn't disappoint, with all the top designers represented, from Alexander McQueen to Zuhair Murad, and a special emphasis on the Italians. "I could spend all day there," says tastemaker Shalini Kasliwal.

Via Roma, 19-21r; +39 055 906 4116, luisaviaroma.com.

Luisaviaroma Contemporary

This outlet store sells clothing and accessories from previous seasons starting at 30 percent off. Canadian model-blogger Elizabeth Minett found her best score of all time here, a YSL clutch.

Via Silvio Pellico, 9, 50121 Firenze, +39 05 521 782, luisaviaroma.com.

Playground

This two-story men's and women's boutique is young and fun all right, with wear-it-out-the-door pieces by tons of modern contemporary brands, including Masscob, No. 21, Derek Lam 10 Crosby, Seafarer, and Iro, plus Golden Goose and Common Projects sneakers, Herschel Supply bags, and more.

Viale Don Giovanni Minzoni, 31/A, 50129 Firenze, +39 055 575 654, playgroundshop.com.

Salvatore Ferragamo Museo and Flagship

This 700-year-old Palazzo Spini Feroni, purchased by the shoemaker to the stars in 1938, is the spiritual home of the brand, with a fresco ceiling, arched entrances, many archival photographs, and shoes made from 1927 to 1960, the year Ferragamo died.

Flagship: Via dei Tornabuoni, 4r-14r, +39 055 292123. Museum: entrance on Palazzo Spini Feroni, Piazza Santa Trinita, 5r, 50123 Firenze, +39 055 3360 456/455, ferragamo.com.

ERICA PELOSINI
FLORENCE & CAPRI

A stylist, art director, and magazine contributor, Leeman is a jet-setting street-style star with a look that's equal parts rock-and-roll and la dolce vita. She hails from Florence and is married to Dutch shoe designer Louis Leeman. The couple make their home in Los Angeles, though they return to Italy as often as possible.

I love to shop at **LUISAVIAROMA** in Florence, maybe because it is in the city where I grew up and I remember going with my mum when I was little! It feels like home to me, with the best clothes ever.

Everything in Florence is within walking distance, and while shopping, I love to get a cappuccino at **GIACOSA,** the historic bar in the **ROBERTO CAVALLI** boutique, or a prosecco and a truffle sandwich at a classic winery on via Tornabuoni.

What is magical about Florence? Well, besides walking around some of the world's most incredible monuments, you can find yourself in hidden shops or restaurants inside some majestic Renaissance palazzo filled with *affresco* walls and precious chandeliers. It's art meets fashion, in the best way.

CAFFÉ GIACOSA

A secret local gem is **IL RICCIO** in Capri. It's an adorable beach club hidden on a top of a hill in Capri. Not easy to reach! The best way to get there is with a little old *gozzo*, the typical wooden Capri boat. Once you arrive you will be enchanted by all the blue-and-white décor and the most delicious cuisine you've ever had. It's no wonder I chose them to cater my wedding (even though it was on the opposite part of the island). To finish you can visit their "Temptation Room," a place filled with beautiful desserts, and even get your new beach outfit at their little boutique located in a rock on the cliffside.

One of my favorite things about vacationing in Capri in the summer is my shopping routine. There is a little sunglasses store called **CAPRI PEOPLE,** which makes the cutest sunglasses. You can even choose your lenses to go with them. **LA BOTTEGA CAPRESE**, a few steps away, is where you can make your own Capri sandals. By the time you are finished with your ice cream, your sunglasses and sandals will be ready! Of course, after all these years spent in Capri, I have a huge collection—but I just can't resist!

LUISA VIA ROMA, Via Roma, 19/21, 50123 Firenze, +39 055 217 826, luisaviaroma.com.

CAFFÈ GIACOSA, Via della Spada 10/r 50123 Firenze, +39 055 277 6328, caffegiacosa.com.

ROBERTO CAVALLI, ia dè Tornabuoni, 83/r, 50123 Firenze, +39 055 239 6226, robertocavalli.com.

ILL RICCIO, Via Gradola, 4, Anacapri, +39 081 837 1380, capripalace.com.

CAPRI PEOPLE, Via Le Botteghe, 27, Anacapri, +39 081 837 8664, capripeople.it.

LA BOTTEGA CAPRESE, Via G. Orlandi, 26, Anacapri.

VENICE

ITALY

Attilio Codognato

"When I first came across this extraordinary jewelry store, I stood mesmerized in front of the shop window—the jewelry pieces were like nothing I had ever seen before," says model-muse Tatiana Sorokko. "Enormous snake bracelets in gold and diamonds, stunning memento mori scull rings and necklaces, intricate blackamoor brooches, all exquisite works of art, and elaborately crafted. I knew instantly that I was hooked. I learned later that the Codognato jewelry house was Venice's best-kept secret. It was founded in 1866 by the great-grandfather of the present owner, Attilio Codognato. It soon became a go-to for European royalty as well as such tastemakers as Coco Chanel, Barbara Hutton, Maria Callas, and Elizabeth Taylor. Attilio has become my good friend, and I visit with him in Venice at least once a year; each time I come to his store, I am struck by the unique and inimitable elegance and beauty of his creations." Designer and personal shopper Raven Kauffman is also a devotee. "It's for the decadent Victorian Goth that lurks inside me," she says. "One of his snake cuffs and delicate cameo rings is on my manifestation board for 'One day you will be mine.'"

VENICE

San Marco, 1295, 30124 Venezia,
+39 041 522 5042, attiliocodognato.com.

Dittura Giani

For velvet furlane shoes like the gondoliers wear, Venice's version of the espadrille, this is the place.

San Vio, 871, 30123 Venezia,
+39 041 522 3502.

HOW TO HOLIDAY IN CAPRI LIKE MARY ALICE HANEY

A twenty-year veteran of the fashion industry in L.A., Haney worked as an editor at Allure, Marie Claire, *and* GQ, *a stylist for A-listers such as Blake Lively and Sarah Jessica Parker, and a TV host before launching her collection of luxury eveningwear in 2013. Since then, she's dressed Taylor Swift, Reese Witherspoon, Kate Hudson, and many more. The Chatanooga, Tennessee, native travels to Capri almost every summer, and was even married there.*

The tiny **SUD CAPRI** swim shop, squeezed into the island's main luxury drag, has a sexy assortment of clothes that are not just swimsuits. You have to dig and the store gets super hot in the summer, but I love it.

LA PARISIENNE is the store where Jackie Kennedy first bought her capri pants. The same family has owned it since it opened, and it's still the best place to get the original Jackie O look. A made-to-measure pair of capris takes only one day to make. The boutique also sells flamboyant designs by Roberto Cavalli and the latest Fendi bags.

My favorite sandal store is **DA COSTANZO**. Founded by Costanzo Ruocco in the 1960s, the small workshop is now run by Costanzo's son Antonio, who can whip up a new set of sandals in a matter of hours (or the next day for unusual requests). Prices start around $95.

SUD CAPRI, Via Camerelle 61, 80076 Capri, +39 08 1838 9445.

LA PARISIENNE, Piazza Umberto I/7, 80076 Capri, +39 08 1837 0283, laparisiennecapri.it.

DA COSTANZO, Via Roma 49, 80076 Capri, +39 06 697 6111.

MADRID

SPAIN

Adolfo Domínguez

The Galician designer's beautifully cut suits, asymmetrical dresses, and quirky footwear are mainstays in Spain, where he is known for a certain urban sophistication. He recently launched an eco-chic line of clothing made of sustainable materials. There's also a coffee shop that serves organic food and smoothies.

Calle de Serrano, 5, 28001 Madrid, +34 914 36 26 00, adolfodominguez.com.

Agatha Ruiz de la Prada

One of Spain's most colorful designers (think, a Spanish Betsey Johnson), the Madrid-born Ruiz specializes in fun, fearless designs for men, women, children, and the home, with lots of rainbows and hearts.

Calle de Serrano, 27, 28001 Madrid, +34 913 19 05 01, agatharuizdelaprada.com.

Beni Room

A cute, contemporary boutique founded by fashion industry vet Beatriz Nicolás, who has an eye for spotting new international brands.

Calle de Claudio Coello, 14, 28006 Madrid, +34 917 37 37 80, beniroom.com.

Bimba y Lola

Established in 2005 by two nieces of designer Adolfo Domínguez, the Vigo-based Bimba y Lola has nearly 200 stores across the world. The emphasis is on jackets, blouses, dresses, and pants in playful, fashion-forward shapes and cool prints. Great statement jewelry, too.

Calle de Serrano, 22, 28001 Madrid, +34 915 76 11 03, bimbaylola.com, and additional locations.

Capas Seseña

Founded in 1901, this famous, capes-only store has sold capes to Picasso, Michael Jackson, and Hillary Clinton. The velvet-lined style that designer Carolina Herrera gave to fashion editor André Leon Talley? It came from this Spanish treasure, which has styles from the traditional (an elegant cloak with frog closures, for example) to the contemporary (bomber capes) for men and women.

Calle de la Cruz, 23, 28012 Madrid, +34 915 31 68 40, sesena.com.

GRAN VÍA, MADRID

Casa Hernanz

There are countless stores selling rope-soled espadrilles in Spain (including Casa Crespo), but only one Casa Hernanz, which dates back more than 150 years, when Toribio Hernanz, the great-grandfather of the current owners, opened it in 1840. You'll find dozens of colors, seasonal prints, and styles, in cotton, canvas, and silk, at prices that encourage buying multiple pairs.

Calle de Toledo, 18, 28005 Madrid, +34 913 66 54 50, alpargatashernanz.com.

Antigua Casa Crespo

This rival espadrille shop has also been around for a century and a half, is family owned, and is packed ceiling to floor with *alpargatas*, as they are known in Spain, in every silhouette imaginable. Among the many customers is Queen Sofia of Spain.

Calle del Divino Pastor, 29, 28004 Madrid, +34 915 21 56 54, alpargateriacrespo.com.

Delitto E Castigo

Ranked by *Vogue* as one of the world's top twenty-five stores, with an exquisite selection of labels for men and women, including Emilio Pucci, Dolce & Gabbana, Balmain, Comme des Garçons, Givenchy, and many others.

Calle de Claudio Coello, 26, 28001 Madrid, +34 915 77 77 29, delittoecastigo.com.

Delpozo

Jesús del Pozo founded his Madrid fashion house in 1974. Since his death, Delpozo has found new life under the direction of Josep Font. The architect-turned-designer's dresses and tops with playful volumes and couture-level embroideries are a hit with the social set and with young Hollywood celebs, including Kiernan Shipka. Font opened this flagship in 2013.

Calle de Lagasca, 19, 28001 Madrid, +34 912 19 40 38, delpozo.com

El Corte Inglés

Spain's most prominent department store carries everything from auto parts to groceries, lingerie to designer fashion. Madrid's largest branch is on the corner of Calle Raimundo Fernández

Villaverde and Castellana. "You can literally get your teeth cleaned, your hair done, insure your car, buy a Carolina Herrera gown, and a Chanel lipstick," says jewelry designer Liseanne Frankfurt. "If they don't have it, it doesn't exist!" The store's Gourmet Experience offers food products from all over Spain and features the creative cuisines of notable Spanish and international chefs, including Michelin-star chefs David Muñoz, Jordi Roca, and Roberto Ruiz. "I like to eat at StreetXO," says author and journalist Susana Martínez Vidal. "It's the less expensive offshoot of the three-star DiverXO. David Muñoz delights with exquisite plates, prepared quickly and at incredibly low prices."

Calle de Raimundo Fernández Villaverde, 79, 28003 Madrid, +34 914 18 88 00, elcorteingles.eu, additional locations.

Ekseption

"The most important multi-brand store in Madrid," says Susana Martínez Vidal. This gallerylike space stocks top designers, including Alaïa, Balenciaga, Prada, Givenchy, and Marc Jacobs. Next door, Eks targets the younger crowd with Alexander Wang, Acne, and the like.

Calle de Velázquez, 28, 28001 Madrid, +34 915 77 43 53, ekseption.es.

Felipe Varela

Hailing from Madrid, Varela is Queen Letizia's go-to for understated, anti-flash fashion. Before she helped put his name on the international stage, other members of the Spanish monarchy tapped him for special-occasion wear. Varela founded his namesake brand in 1996, opening his first store two years later.

Calle de José Ortega y Gasset, 30, 28006 Madrid, +34 915 77 92 20, felipevarela.com, and additional locations.

Intropia

This Madrid-born contemporary brand was started in 1994 by a team of female designers managed by Paloma Vázquez de Castro, former costume designer for the National Ballet of Spain. The clothing—embroidered maxi dresses, beaded blouses, silk jumpsuits—has a Mediterranean glam that has carried it to stores overseas and to websites such as Revolve.com.

Calle de Serrano, 18, 28001 Madrid, +34 917 81 06 12, intropia.com, and additional locations.

Loewe

What started in Madrid in 1846 as a small, artisan-run leather goods shop has turned into an international luxury fashion brand, owned by LVMH Möet Hennessy Louis Vuitton and under the creative direction of British designer Jonathan Anderson. The Madrid flagship remains a must-stop for colorful Amazonia bags, wallets, shoes,

SUSANA MARTÍNEZ VIDAL
SECRET MADRID SPOTS

The fashion journalist and author lives in Mexico City and Madrid.

JOYERÍA MARQUISE has the most fabulous vintage jewelry. Each piece is a discovery. **DO DESIGN** mixes the latest trends with the more rustic and traditional, the organic and artisanal. Everything appears to be an object found during a long journey around the world. It's a place not only for shopping but also inspiration. **GALIPÓ VINTAGE** on Velarde Street specializes in customizing Levi's 501s. Ask for what you want and they will make it happen.

JOYERÍA MARQUISE, Calle Ayala, 10, 28001 Madrid, +34 914 35 79 06.
DO DESIGN, Calle Fernando VI, 13, 28004 Madrid, +34 913 10 62 17, dodesign.es.
GALIPÓ VINTAGE, Calle Velarde, 28004 Madrid.

CAPAS SESEÑA

and ready-to-wear. The Gran Via shop has pop-up art installations.

Calle de Serrano, 26, 28001 Madrid, +34 915 77 60 56, and Calle Gran Vía 8, 28013 Madrid, +34 91 522 6815, loewe.com, and additional locations.

Malababa

Designer Ana Carrasco produces her simple, chic bags and shoes in Spain, using local artisans for every step of the process, from tanning the leather to sewing the bags. You'll find chunky-soled espadrille sandals, leather collars decorated with geodes, and weathered, woven leather tote bags, most for less than $500.

Calle Lagasca, 68, 28001 Madrid, +34 912 03 59 90, malibaba.com, and additional locations.

Masscob

Spanish designers—and life partners—Marga Massanet and Jacobo Cobián take inspiration from their seaside hometown of La Coruña to create the kind of sophisticated, beachy boho tunics, frilly blouses, kimono jackets, and loose dresses you'll want to live in all year long.

Calle Puigcerdà, 2, 28001 Madrid, +34 914 35 85 96, and an additional location in La Coruña, masscob.com.

Mercado Central de Diseno

Held the first weekend of every month, this market showcases emerging Spanish designers and artists selling everything from wood sunglasses to cool ceramic jewelry to modern-looking chairs.

Centro Cultural Matadero, Paseo de la Chopera, 14, 28045 Madrid, +34 918 05 05 76, mercadodediseno.es.

Pedro del Hierro

In business since 1974, this Madrid designer creates simple, wearable women's pieces that suggest a bit of Spanish flair; think off-the-shoulder, ruffled maxi dresses, bow-tie lace-paneled blouses, and scallop-hem shorts, all at moderate prices.

Calle de Serrano, 29, 28001 Madrid, +34 914 35 22 10, pedrodelhierro.com.

Pez

Opened in 2004 in a former pharmacy, Pez is a concept store that sells the best of European and Spanish designs (Humanoid, Forte Forte, Golden Goose, Masscob), along with home goods, Danish, and industrial furniture, and more. "Where you find trends before they arrive elsewhere," Susana Martínez Vidal says. Next door, Pez Chico carries menswear.

Calle de Regueros, 15, 28004 Madrid, +34 913 10 66 77, pez-pez.es.

Sita Murt

Bohemian-chic tunics, shorts, and skirts à la Isabel Marant Étoile are the specialty of this Catalan designer, whose flagship is a whitewashed wood oasis of cool.

Calle Claudio Coello, 88, 28006 Madrid, +34 915 77 50 38, sitamurt.com.

Zara

The fast-fashion giant was born in the north of Spain, and succeeds on its low prices and its ability to turn around runway trends in a matter of weeks. The Gran Via store is the largest in Madrid; the Calle de Serrano store, which opened in 2014, is spread over six floors and houses the brand's showroom on top. "They nail it with making affordable fashion look very expensive," says model/TV presenter Louise Roe. "From simple tanks to more ornate coats and dresses, I always buy a few pieces from Zara every season." Adds costume designer Janie Bryant, "Zara is inexpensive but if you buy smart, it doesn't have to be throw-away fashion. I've had pieces from there that I've had for many years and still wear." Zara "covers the basic closet builders without breaking the bank and always has a fun selection of classic yet fun pieces," says stylist Tara Swennen.

Calle Gran Vía, 34, 28013 Madrid, +34 915 21 12 83, zara.com, and additional locations.

LA COMERCIAL

BARCELONA

SPAIN

Ailanto

Created by brothers Iñaki and Aitor Muñoz, Ailanto is one of Spain's big designer success stories in recent years. Known for their prints and patterns inspired by art and artists (recent collections have been inspired by artist David Hockney and Canadian painter Lawren Harris), Iñaki and Aitor are a regular presence on the runways in Madrid. They've collaborated with Campari, Lladró, Nespresso, Chupa Chups, W Hotels, and L'Oréal; in 2013, they designed the new uniform for the staff of the Guggenheim Museum Bilbao.

Carrer Enrique Granados, 46, 08008 Barcelona, +34 934 51 31 06, ailanto.com, and additional locations.

Beatriz Furest

Located just steps from the Basílica de Santa Maria del Mar, as well as lots of other must-see boutiques in the trendy El Born district, designer Beatriz Furest's store features her entire range of contemporary classic bags, sandals, woven bracelets, and belts, all of which make perfectly chic Barcelona souvenirs.

Carrer de l'Esparteria, 1, 08003 Barcelona, +34 932 68 37 96, beatrizfurest.com, and additional locations.

Boo

Named after *To Kill a Mockingbird*'s Boo Radley, this store with a Silver Lake vibe features a mix of lovable labels from near (Barcelona-based geometric-jewelry-makers Après Ski and resortwear-focused Med Winds) and far (Saint James and Petit Bateau) along with plenty of exclusives, and a warm, inviting interior that includes a telephone booth repurposed as a dressing room.

Bonavista, 2, 08012 Barcelona, +34 933 68 14 58, boocn.com.

Colmado

The clothing and accessories at this El Born boutique have a candylike quality. It specializes in locally produced wares as well as ones from London, Milan, and beyond with a modern, arty edge, including geometric jewelry and handbags and fuzzy loafers.

Brosoli 5 (corner of Mirallers), 08003 Barcelona, +34 931 722 966, colmadoshop.tumblr.com.

Colmillo de Morsa

Designer Isabel Vallecillo and Javier Blanco have turned Colmillo de Morsa into a minimalist-chic cult brand reminiscent of New York's Creatures of Comfort. The duo shows their collection at Madrid Fashion Week and have opened outlets in Taipei and Moscow. Their showroom/store features not only their collection but also those of young designers with similar aesthetic.

Carrer de Vic, 15, 08006 Barcelona, +34 645 20 63 65, colmilliodemorsa.com, and additional locations.

Coquette

"The multi-brand store of reference in Barcelona," author/journalist Susana Martínez Vidal says of this trio of boutiques that stocks feminine frocks, blouses, and shoes by Mes Demoiselles, Masscob, Isabel Marant, Swildens, and more in an industrial-yet-warm space. The Calle Rec location is the original.

Calle Rec, 65, 08003 Barcelona, +34 93 319 29 76, coquettebcn.com, and additional locations.

Castañer

Perhaps the most internationally famous espadrille brand to come out of Spain, Castañer has Yves Saint Laurent to thank for its success. When the designer was walking the stalls at a Paris trade show in the early 1970s looking for someone to make espadrille wedges for his collection, the shoemaking family scion Lorenzo Castañer was happy to oblige. Since then, Castañer has been the high-fashion answer to Spain's less expensive espadrille shops. In addition to manufacturing shoes for brands such as Hermès, Louis Vuitton, and Christian Louboutin, Castañer has its own label, which is sold around the world and in its Barcelona flagship. (The brand is headquartered about 60 miles away, in Girona.) Prices are in the $100 to $300 range.

Carrer del Rosselló, 230, 08008 Barcelona, +34 934 14 24 28, castaner.com, and additional locations.

QK BCN

"A concept store with items from all over the world, including furniture, perfumes, and music," says author/journalist Susana Martínez Vidal. "An experience for all five senses." Look for boho-chic scarves and dresses by M Missoni, Antik Batik, Schutz, and more.

Cavrer de Calvet 29, 080021 Barcelona, +34 932 09 55 18, qkbcn.com.

Iriarte Iriarte

Carolina Iriarte's handmade leather designs resemble schoolgirl satchels and briefcases in the best possible way. Her showroom/studio is on the picturesque Plaza Real; the second location is on Cotoners.

Cabrer de Cotoners, 12, 08003 Barcelona, +34 933 19 81 75, iriateiriate.com.

L'Arca

A treasure trove of antique linens, vintage dresses by international designers (Dior, Chanel, Yves Saint Laurent) and Spanish ones (Balenciaga, Pertegaz), wedding gowns, and period turbans, lace gloves, and Spanish fans. They don't come cheap, though.

Banys Nous 20, 08002 Barcelona, +39 93 302 15 98, larca.es.

La Comercial

Located on Carrer de Rec in El Born, the wildly successful La Comercial is actually six stores in close proximity, each one featuring a different focus on international labels for men and women, for example, accessories, fragrances, home furnishings, and objects. Some of the brands you'll find along the shopping stretch are Aesop, Astier de Villatte, Jonathan Adler, Kenzo, Paul Smith, Carven, and Surface to Air, but you'll also find cheap and cheerful tchotchkes. The W Hotel in Barcelona recently tapped La Comercial to create its hotel shop.

MAN, Rec 73, +34 93 319 24 35.
and Rec 75, +34 93 310 49 68.
WOMAN, Rec 52, +34 93 319 34 63.
CONCEPT STORE, Paul Smith Shoe, Rec 77 +34 93 319 86 01.
SELECTION, Paolo Pecora, Bonaire 7, +34 93 160 01 14.
HOME, Bonaire 4, +34 93 295 46 30 08003 Barcelona, LaComercial.com.

La Manual Alpargatera

Yet another espadrille store, this one claiming to cater to Penelope Cruz, Catherine Zeta-Jones, Jack Nicholson, and others. Like Antigua Casa Crespo in Madrid, La Manual features inexpensive handmade slip-ons, slides, lace-ups, and wedges.

Carrer Avinyó, 7, 08002 Barcelona, +34 933 01 01 72, lamanualalpargatera.com.

Le Swing

This well-curated vintage store with a funky 1960s vibe has "unique pieces," says Susana Martínez Vidal, including clothing in whimsical prints, chunky jewelry, and colorful handbags galore.

Rec, 16, 08003 Barcelona +34 933 101 449, leswingvintage.com. Sister store Blow: Carrer Bonaire, 6, 08003 Barcelona, +34 93 302 36 98.

Lupo

Barcelona's heritage leather brand since 1920, Lupo is known around the world for its architecturally inspired bags. Many of them echo Gaudí designs, including the fan-shaped Abanico, with pleated leather details. In 2015 the brand launched its first ready-to-wear collection.

Carrer de Mallorca, 257, 08008 Barcelona, +34 934 87 80 50, lupo.es, and additional locations.

LA COMERCIAL

Majoral

Enric Majoral's beautiful, organic-form jewelry is inspired by the island of Formentera, the Mediterranean Sea, popular culture, and nature.

Carrer del Consell de Cent, 308, 08007 Barcelona, +34 934 67 72 09, majoral.com.

MANGO

This Barcelona-based fashion chain is another one of the major players in the fast-fashion game. Over the years, the brand has tapped Kate Moss, Penélope Cruz, and her sister Mónica Cruz to design special collections. The Gràcia flagship showcases all the brand's lines (women's, men's, kids', sport, intimates, and accessories) in a spacious interior.

Passeig de Gràcia, 36, 08008 Barcelona, +34 901 15 05 43, mango.com, and additional locations.

Med Winds

A budding Mediterranean-inspired lifestyle collection of men's and women's resort-ready pieces, Med Winds began in Barcelona in 2011. It's distinguished by watercolor-like prints, seaside-inspired jewelry, chic sandals, and curated home accessories and gifts. Most items are less than $250, and most everything is made in Spain or Italy.

Elisabets 7, 08001 Barcelona, +34 935 210 056, medwinds.com.

Mushi Mushi

A Parisian-style boutique in the trendy Gràcia district, where there are lots of cute shops to browse (including Boo, Pinc, and the Outpost), Mushi Mushi features casual-cool T-shirts by Sessùn, feminine blouses by Des Petits Hauts, Saltwater sandals, jewelry by Barcelona-based Mimi Scholer, and more.

Carrer de Bonavista, 12, 08012 Barcelona, +34 932 92 29 74, mushimushicollection .com.

Pinc

The studio/store of Ana Tichy, a Barcelona-based designer who creates wonderfully whimsical prints and casual pieces with a quirky twist.

Encarnació, 39, 08024 Barcelona, +34 93 200 97 71, anatichy.com.

Santa Eulalia

Founded in 1843, Santa Eulalia is the city's oldest design house and also the grande dame of multi-label luxury shopping in Barcelona, featuring Tom Ford, Dior, Maison Martin Margiela, Proenza Schouler, Céline, Etro, and Saint Laurent, alongside its own line of ready-to-wear for women and tailoring and shirts for men. The William Sofield–designed store sits near the designer flagship stores on Passeig de Gràcia. To keep things interesting, Santa Eulalia has a rotating pop-up space and a lovely outdoor terrace bistro and champagne bar.

Passeig de Gràcia, 93, 08008 Barcelona, +34 932 15 06 74, santaeulalia.com.

Stradivarius

Founded in 1994 in Barcelona, Stradivarius is part of Inditex, which also owns Zara. The fast-fashion brand, which has a slightly younger, more casual point of view than Zara (lots of graphic tees, cutoff shorts, and varsity jackets), has expanded to hundreds of stores worldwide.

Avinguida Portal del Ángel, 24, 08002 Barcelona, +34 934 15 42 67, stradivarius.com, and additional locations.

Studiostore

This El Born concept shop and events space is the brainchild of Federica

ONLINE SHOPPING TIP

One of my favorite Spanish brands, Masscob (think, Isabel Marant but not everywhere), ships to some countries from Masscob.com. Select pieces are also carried at Barneys.com and Matches.com.

Sandretti (aka Lafede), an architect who started her career in window design for print-heavy fashion brand Custo Barcelona. Sandretti works on retail, furniture, lighting, and graphic design projects, and runs Studiostore, a Fiorucci-like showcase for whimsical furniture, pillows, tabletop accessories, objets, sunglasses, and gifts by designers from Barcelona and beyond. Many items are accessibly priced.

Calle Comerç, 17, 08003 Barcelona, +34 93 222 50 75, studiostore.es.

The Outpost

Wood-paneled destination for haute men's shoes and accessories from top labels such as Want Les Essentiels, Marsèll, Mark McNairy, Thom Browne, Tomas Maier, and more, lovingly chosen by the stylish owner, Pep Esteva.

Rosselló 281 bis, 08037 Barcelona, +34 93 457 71 37, theoutpostbcn.com.

The Perfumery

"The most magical perfume shop," says costume designer Janie Bryant. "It's located in the heart of the Jewish quarter, the Gothic section of the city. I stumbled across it when I was traveling around Spain a couple of years ago. There are fragrances there that were worn by kings and queens. My favorite being Rance 1795, Eau Superbe. Worn by Napoleon himself."

Baixada de Santa Eulàlia, 3, 08002 Barcelona, +34 930 08 37 51, theperfumery.es.

BERLIN

GERMANY

KaDeWe

The Kaufhaus des Westens ("Department Store of the West"), usually abbreviated to KaDeWe, is the best department store in Berlin, with a food hall and a rooftop buffet that have to be seen to be believed (lobster tails, champagne, schnitzel, it's all here). Marlene Dietrich used to buy her lingerie in the store, and you can find everything from the top fashion labels to German magazines and tobacco. The food hall has concessions from all over the world, too. The US selection is a hoot (who knew there was an appetite in Germany for Marshmallow Fluff?).

Tauentzienstraße 21-24, 10789 Berlin, +49 30 21210, kadewe.de.

Bikini Berlin

Berlin's concept mall runs alongside the city zoo, so you can sit and watch the monkey enclosure through a big picture window, or from above, at 25hours Hotel's Monkey Bar. Inside the concrete-and-steel mall, which gets its name from the design of the two-building structure with exposed midsection, you won't find many chain stores, apart from a few sneaker and streetwear outposts. Instead, you'll find wood packing crates housing a rotating selection of designer pop-ups, plus spaces such as LNFA, a public relations firm/store featuring the work of many young Berlin designers who show at Berlin Fashion Week.

Budapester Straße 38-50, 10787 Berlin, +49 30 55496454, bikiniberlin.de.

Andreas Merkudis

Perhaps the best known boutique in Berlin, this concept store was founded in 2003, and recently moved north of Potsdamer Platz to an industrial space in the former *Tagesspiegel* newspaper building. It's out of the way, but an interesting stop as a reference point for Berlin's fashion scene. Designers featured include Dries Van Noten, Céline, Marni, The Row, and Aspesi for women; Kolor, Martin Margiela, and Sunspel. Founder Andreas Murkudis comes from the art scene, and his curation has a similar focus, with objects and furnishings rounding out the vast space. "Understated, simple, chic," says designer Zainab Sumu.

Potsdamer Straße 81e, 10785 Berlin, +49 30 6807 98306, andreasmerkudis.com.

Annette Görtz

Flagship for the German designer, whose understated, sophisticated clothes are a mix of Rick Owens and Donna Karan. Wearable and utilitarian but with an edge.

Markgrafenstraße 42, 10117 Berlin, +49 30 2007 4613, Annettegoertz.com.

Frau Tonis Parfum

The Berlin-based perfumer's signature scents make the perfect souvenir (there's even one named Berlin Summer that captures the essence of the city, with lime and lemon balm, peppermint, and orange).

Zimmerstraßee 13, 10969 Berlin,+49 30 20215310, frau-tonis-parfum.com.

Kauf Dich Glücklich

This chainlet of indie concept boutiques started as a waffle bar/vintage shop. The stores (visualize a cross between Aritzia and Urban Outfitters) have a calm, cool vibe, and stock the men's and women's KDG collections (drapey coats, tunic dresses, etc.) as well as pieces by Cheap Monday, Levi's, Sessùn, Jeffrey Campbell, Adidas, and more. Also shop for books, music, and accessories. This is the flagship.

Rosenthaler Straße 17, 10119 Berlin, +49 30 2887 8817, kaufdichgluecklich-shop .de, and additional locations.

Konk

Founded by Ettina Berrios-Negrón, this Mitte boutique features a spot-on, elevated edit of up-and-coming Berlin designers making all kinds of things, from sophisticated knits to 3-D printed jewelry to handmade hats. Look out for designer Tata Christiane's collagey pop art–inspired clothing.

Kleine Hamburger Straße, 15 10117 Berlin, +49 30 2809 7839, konk-berlin.de.

Lala Berlin

Designer Leyla Piedayesh's knitwear and print–based designs with a glam-rock twist have managed to win the hearts of celebrities including Heidi Klum, Claudia Schiffer, and Mischa Barton. Don't miss her signature cashmere triangle scarves.

Alte Schönhauser Straße 3, 10119 Berlin,+49 30 2009 5363, lalaberlin.com.

Mauerpark Flea Market

This Sunday flea market near the Berlin Wall Memorial is a must-see to experience local culture, from skateboarding kids to the crowd-pleasing karaoke sing-alongs that spring up. You'll find everything from vintage leather jackets to Trabant-shaped plastic earrings and other curiosities.

Bernauer Straße 63-64, 13355 Berlin, +49 30 2977 2486, flohmarktimmauerpark.de.

TOP BERLIN TIPS FROM STEFANIE HANSSEN

CREATIVE DIRECTOR OF FRAU TONIS PARFUM

Shop at **BIKINI BERLIN.** Not only can you buy Frau Tonis perfumes there but you can also have lunch with an incredible view of the city at the Asian-fusion restaurant **NENI**. You'll find exciting concept stores like **LNFA** (which features lots of Berlin designers), **SUPER** (a restaurant and home accessories concept space), and, on the top floor, **ANDREAS MURKUDIS**. Next to the concept mall is one of Berlin's most stylish movie theaters: **THE ZOO PALAST**.

I love to visit the **WINTERFELDTMARKT** on Saturdays, Berlin´s biggest and best-known farmers' market. Don't miss the incredible mix of edible flowers, locally made grilled sausages, escargot soup, and organic bread! The space is packed with more than 250 stalls. Sometimes, if you're lucky, you may run into Academy Award–winner Christoph Waltz there! Stroll around Berlin's flea markets. I often find beautiful vintage clothes on Sundays at Fehrbelliner Platz or at Rathnas Schöneberg. It's a paradise for those who love cashmere knitwear and silk dresses!

LNFA, Neni Super and Andreas Murkudis at Bikini Berlin, Budapester Straße 38-50, 10787 Berlin, +49 30 5549 6454, lnfa.de, neniberlin.de, super-space.de, andreasmurkdis.com.

NENI, Budapester Str. 40, 10787 Berlin, +49 30 1202 21200, neniberlin.de.

WINTERFELDTSTRASSE, 10777 Berlin, +49 17 5437 4303.

FLEA MARKET AT FEHRBELLINER SATURDAYS AND SUNDAYS, Platz 1, 10707 Berlin.

FLEA MARKET AT RATHAUS SCHONBERG SATURDAYS AND SUNDAYS, John F. Kennedy Platz 1, 10825 Berlin.

FRAU TONIS PARFUM

MDC

Opened by Melanie Dal Canton, former manager of the concept store Andreas Murkudis, this cosmetics store carries products by Australia-based Aesop, Italy's Santa Maria Novella, and other coveted brands. "A lovely, small perfume and cosmetic store in Prenzlauer Berg, they stock little-known perfume brands and also offer great beauty treatments," says Valery Demure.

Knaackstrasse 26, 10405 Berlin, +49 30 40056339, mdc-cosmetics.de.

Rianna and Nina

Amazing collection of caftans, pillows, lamps, and kimonos, all made from vibrant vintage scarf fabrics, Rianna and Nina was created by two friends, former high-end-vintage dealer Rianna Kounou and former fashion publicist Nina Kuhn. Each piece is unique and ever so chic.

Steinstraße 4, 10119 Berlin, +49 30 28879122, riannaandnina.com.

Ritter Sport

You can make your own version of Germany's favorite chocolate bar here in thirty minutes or less. Choose from ingredients such as coconut, Pop Rocks, and pink peppercorn.

Französische Straße 24, 10117 Berlin, +49 30 2009 50810, ritter-sport.de.

Sabrina Dehoff

This Berlin-based jewelry designer makes superchic treasures, including modernist

ONLINE SHOPPING TIP

Frau Tonis can deliver the scent of Berlin to your doorstep. Check out frau-tonis-parfum.com. If you're looking to discover new Berlin design talent, the Konk boutique website is a good place to start, konk-berlin.de. Another good curation of talent (many of whom show at Berlin Fashion Week) can be seen at LNFA-shop.de, the online site for the store/PR agency, though unfortunately neither site ships internationally.

abstract cocktail rings and chokers, tiny bar earrings, and bold, Bauhaus-looking cuffs. Dehoff has boutiques around the world, but the flagship is in Mitte.

Torstraße 175, 10115 Berlin,
+49 30 9362 4680, sabrinadehoff.com, and additional locations.

The Store

"A really nice, curated shopping space," says designer Rosetta Getty of this high-end boutique and industrial-yet-warm hangout at Soho House Berlin that is curated by retailer Alex Eagle. "Everything is for sale and they have a great café with pressed juices and a bookstore." Designers represented include Balenciaga, The Row, Jil Sander, Christophe Lemaire, Proenza Schouler, Issey Miyake, and Junya Watanabe.

Torstraße 1, 10119 Berlin,
+49 30 4050 44550, thestores.com.

The Corner

Luxury lifestyle boutique selling the best from established labels, including Céline, Givenchy, Isabel Marant, Valentino, Nike, and Apple Watch, and up-and-comers such as Stella Jean, MSGM, and Sara Battaglia. There is also a branch in West Berlin, as well as a men's store.

Französische Straße 40, 10117 Berlin,
+49 30 2067 0940, thecornerberlin.de.

Voo

Off-the-beaten shopping path in Berlin's Kreuzberg district, Voo is the city's edgy streetwear-meets-runway purveyor. It carries Henrik Vibskov, Surface to Air, Acne, 3.1 Phillip Lim, Raf Simons, J.W. Anderson, Nike x Kim Jones, and more, plus indie magazines, cosmetics, and coffee.

Oranienstraße 24, 10999 Berlin,
+49 30 6957 972710, vooberlin.com.

& OTHER STORIES

STOCKHOLM

SWEDEN

& Other Stories

Swedish fast-fashion giant H&M's premium lifestyle brand of fun, funky clothing, accessories, and beauty products is built on the concept of personal style, and designed to appeal to all ages. (The Stockholm-based label launched in 2013 with an ad campaign that included, among others, nonagenarian Iris Apfel.) "I frequent & Other Stories for trousers, T-shirts, and knitwear because it is young, funky, and inexpensive," says author/fashion editor Bronwyn Cosgrave. Managing director Samuel Fernström, who studied at the Stockholm School of Economics before starting at H&M's buying office, created the concept. & Other Stories has collaborated with several designer brands and tastemakers, including Rodarte, Clare V., and Garance Doré. H&M also owns the Cheap Monday, Monki, and Cos brands.

Biblioteksgatan 11, 111 46 Stockholm, +46 8 440 5290, stories.com, and additional locations.

Acne Studios

This quintessentially Swedish, high-end fashion and denim brand for men and women is headquartered in the bank building where the infamous "Stockholm syndrome" heist took place. Check out the Acne Archive store for past-season merchandise at discounted prices.

Norrmalmstorg 2, 111 46 Stockholm, +46 8 611 64 11, and Acne Archive, Torsgatan 53, 113 37 Stockholm, +46 8 30 2723, acnestudios.com.

Aplace

A local retail chainlet and magazine founded in 2007, Aplace is a gem that aims to help shoppers discover the best fashion from Scandinavia and beyond, including Wood Wood, Back, BLK DNM, Dagmar, Henrik Vibskov, and Sandqvist.

Norrlandsgatan 11, 111 43 Stockholm, +46 8 643 3230, aplace.com, and additional locations.

Army of Me

Samuel Fernström, managing director of & Other Stories, advises checking out this local brand of menswear, which has an edgy, cyberpunk vibe. "Go down to their basement to try on the latest long-lasting pieces," he says.

Bergsgatan 49, 112 31 Stockholm, armyofmedesign.com.

Byredo

Former pro basketball player Ben Gorham's shop has a chic, spare Scandi flair, befitting the unisex fragrance line he launched in 2006 with the concept of creating understated scents with simple compositions that translate memories into smells. Sample fragrances include Mojave Ghost and Rose of No Man's Land. Gorham also helped develop scents for & Other Stories.

Mäster Samuelsgatan 10, 111 44 Stockholm +46 8 525 026 10, byredo.com.

Dagmar

This Stockholm-based brand started by three sisters has a sophisticated point of view and interesting clothes, including inventive knits and faux fur outerwear.

Sturegallerian Stureplan 4, 114 35 Stockholm, +46 7 287 230 39, houseofdagmar.com.

Filippa K

Based in Stockholm, with stores throughout Europe, this contemporary brand was founded by Filippa Knutsson in 1993, and specializes in minimalist basics with subtle flourishes (jersey dresses with asymmetrical ties, sweaters with reverse seams).

Grev Turegatan 18, 114 46 Stockholm, +46 8 545 888 88, filippa-k.com, and additional locations.

Fran O Till A

Retail concept started in 2013 by denim designer Orjan Andersson, the store is four floors of cavelike rooms and a journey-of-discovery feeling. Andersson mixes established fashion brands with young designers in a playful way, combining them with second hand, vintage, and recycled products. In the store you can find designers such as as Marques Almeida, Acne, Altewaisaome, Haal, and Örjan Andersson.

Götgatan 105, 116 62 Stockholm, +46 8 644 1030, franotilla.com.

Grandpa

Flagship for the local chainlet of multi-label boutiques stocking the best of Swedish and Scandinavian fashion and design for men and women by Rodebjer, Hope Stockholm, Dagmar, Stylein, Back, Minimarket, and other brands (the edit is about clean lines, sporty details, and prices that won't cause too much pain). At this location, there's also a café, Sixten & Frans, with cocktails and seasonal dishes.

Fridhemsgatan 43, 112 46 Stockholm, +46 8 643 6081, grandpa.se, and additonal locations.

H&M

This fast-fashion gorilla is Sweden's biggest fashion import, and the world's

B. ÅKERLUND

STOCKHOLM SECRETS

She's worked with Lady Gaga, Madonna, Rihanna, and Britney Spears. Beyoncé's yellow Roberto Cavalli Lemonade *dress? That was all Åkerlund. The costume designer, stylist, and Stockholm native moved to Los Angeles at age fourteen to pursue her dream of working in film, fashion, and music. In addition to Beyoncé's* Lemonade *looks, Åkerlund cites Gaga's madcap fashion in the* Paparazzi *video as one of her proudest moments. Oh, and Åkerlund's personal style is pretty madcap, too.*

My passion for shopping drove me to the profession of styling. It feeds me with the instant gratification of making a purchase and discovering unique and rare things. In my hometown, Stockholm, I love the hidden gem **SAKER & TING**, a one-of-a-kind vintage shop where you can find anything from the turn-of-the-century to modern times. For interiors, I also love **SVENSKT TENN**, which carries traditional Swedish décor with Josef Frank prints. If you are looking for modern Swedish fashion, **ACNE**'s flagship store is in the middle of the mecca of Stockholm. The best spot for home-cooked Swedish food is **PA & CO.** Its menu never fails, and it's the best spot for hanging out with locals. I also love **MATTHIAS DALHGREN**. It's located next to the Grand Hotel, which happens to have the best spa and massage therapists anywhere.

SAKER & TING, Sturegatan 28, 114 36 Stockholm.

SVENSKT TENN, Strandvägen 5, 114 51 Stockholm, +46 8 670 16 00, svenskttenn.se.

ACNE, Norrmalmstorg 2, 111 46 Stockholm, +46 8 611 64 11, acnestudios.com.

PA & CO, Riddargatan 8, 114 35 Stockholm, +46 8 611 08 45, paco.se.

MATTIAS DALHGREN, Södra Blasieholmshamnen 6, 111 48 Stockholm, +46 8 679 35 84, mdghs.se.

GRAND HOTEL, Södra Blasieholmshamnen 8, 103 27 Stockholm +46 8 679 35 00, grandhotel.se.

second-largest clothing retailer, behind Spain's Inditex, with stores in more than sixty countries selling trendy items at rock-bottom prices. And it all started here, in Stockholm. The retailer has been around since the 1940s, and began to achieve international fame in 2004, when it collaborated with Karl Lagerfeld on a collection that sold out in some cities in less than one hour, helping to kick off the cheap-chic/designer collaboration craze. H&M has since collaborated with Stella McCartney, Jimmy Choo, Marni, Alexander Wang, Balmain, and others. This is the flagship and the head office.

Drottninggatan 53, 111 21 Stockholm, +46 3 314 0000, hm.com, and additional locations.

Herr Judit

A reference point for people anywhere in the world interested in men's vintage fashion, this store mixes gently used styles from the 1950s on with newer brands, plus interesting vintage furniture, toys, books, and watches. At 75 Hornsgatan, you'll find Judits, a women's secondhand store.

Hornsgatan 65, 118 49 Stockholm, +46 8 658 3037, herrjudit.se.

Jus

Avant-garde-meets-streetwear is the focus at this multi-brand boutique selling Ann Demeulemeester, Dries Van Noten, Rick Owens, Comme des Garçons, Maison Martin Margiela, and more for men and women.

Brunnsgatan 7, 111 38 Stockholm, +46 8 20 67 77, jus.se.

Monki

This H&M-owned brand merges Swedish design and Japanese street style. Monki customers—mostly members of Gen Z, who are referred to by staff as "our Monki friends"—are presented with a fable based around a cast of mischievous fuzz balls, the Monkis, who inhabit the colorful shops. The clothes are playful—think striped knit tops, snap-front suede miniskirts, and silk bomber jackets—and so are the fun phone cases and accessories.

Götgatan 19, 116 46 Stockholm, +46 8 640 0841, monki.com, and additional locations.

Nordiska Kompaniet (NK)

Swedish architect Ferdinand Boberg designed the art nouveau building for this luxury department store, established in 1915, and built around an atrium. Inside, you'll find Swedish and international fashion labels, cosmetics, design items, and food. There are ten restaurants on-site, including Korv & Glass for Swedish hot dogs, and a food hall in the basement.

Hamngatan 18-20, 111 47 Stockholm, +46 8 762 80 00, nk.se.

ONLINE SHOPPING TIP

Thanks to H&M, Swedish design has conquered the globe. Those sites, as well as Tiger of Sweden, Swedish Hasbeens, Rodejer, Dagmar, and Filippa K have comprehensive e-commerce sites with wide selections of merchandise shipping to many places in the world. To discover emerging designers, though, Aplace.com is both an online magazine and the website for a chainlet of brick-and-mortar stores in Stockholm dedicated to showcasing up-and-coming Scandinavian fashion designers. International shipping is available.

Rodebjer

Founded in New York in 1999 by native Swede Carin Rodebjer. After she was spotted on the streets of Manhattan wearing her handmade designs, she started selling to friends and stores in New York and Stockholm. Since then, Rodebjer has grown into a full-fledged, cool-girl contemporary collection available in the brand's two Stockholm boutiques, as well as in key stores around the world. Signature silhouettes include slouchy suits, drapey caftans, and easy-to-wear dresses and kimonos. The shoes are pretty rad, too.

Regeringsgatan 50, 111 56 Stockholm, +46 8 20 6614, rodebjer.com.

Swedish Hasbeens

This brand has taken a 1970s has-been, the clog, and elevated it to new fashion heights, with heels tall and small, Mary Jane, slip-on, sandal, and bootie styles, and in every color imaginable. The flagship is in Stockholm's trendy SoFo neighborhood.

Nytorgsgatan 36A, 116 40 Stockholm, swedishhasbeens.com, and an additional location in Bibliotekstan.

Tiger of Sweden

Founded in 1903 in the Swedish town of Uddevalla, by tailors Markus Schwarmann and Hjalmar Nordström as a classical menswear brand, Tiger of Sweden began to reposition itself in 1993 as younger and hipper, producing razor-sharp, mod-inspired suits in bold check prints. The slim-cut suits became a signature, amassing a loyal following of stylish men; womenswear was introduced in 2006. The brand has a slight rock 'n' roll vibe, through a pared-down, Scandi lens. Sold across Europe, Canada, and South Africa.

Biblioteksgatan 12, 111 46 Stockholm, tigerofsweden.com +46 8 200 3560, and addtional locations.

EURASIA

TURKEY
RUSSIA

ADNAN & HASAN

ISTANBUL

TURKEY

Aida Pekin

Istanbul-based jewelry designer Bihter Ayda Pekin launched her collection in 2005 and opened her store in Galata three years later. She has earned a following for her reasonably affordable, whimsically modern wire creations, which are crafted by artisans in the Grand Bazaar. Her designs are also sold at art museums around the world.

Serdar-i Ekrem 44/A, Galata, Istanbul, +90 212 243 1211, aidapekin.com.

Atelier 55

One of Galata's chicest boutiques, Atelier 55 stocks clothing, accessories, and jewelry by Turkish and international designers, including Bora Aksu, Nathalie Trad, David Koma, and VPL. It also has its own label and an espresso bar for refueling.

Şahkulu Mahallesi Serdar-i Ekrem Sokak Seraskerci Çıkmazı No: 55, Galata, Istanbul, +90 212 245 3255, atelier-55.com.

Au Vintage

Au Vintage started as an online shop, but the basement apartment is now a wonderland of perfect pieces from the 1920s to 1990s, mixed with a selection of items by contemporary designers, such as Mila Biju's whimsical throwback jewelry (pineapple earrings) and Burlap's handbags with beaded honeybees.

Küçükbebek Bebeck Cad. No: 34 apt. D:1, Bebek, +90 541 252 6836 auvintage.com.

Baston Vintage

"In the Galata neighborhood, on a small street across from the Crimean church, this store sells beautiful vintage leather luggage at reasonable prices," says Mickey Ashmore, founder of Sabah.

Şahkulu mah. Serdar-ı ekrem Cad No: 61/A, Beyoğlu, Istanbul.

Dilek Hanif

On the scene since the 1990s, this Turkish designer is known for her elaborate gowns and sophisticated ready-to-wear pieces incorporating Ottoman motifs and embroidery.

Macka Cad. Rally Apt. No: 37, Floor Tesvikiye, Istanbul, +90 212 219 3730, dilekhanif.com.

Fey

Owned by former fashion editor Fatoş Yalin Arkun, this boutique is a must-shop for its dreamy combination of

DILEK HANIF

vintage and contemporary clothing, accessories, and objets. You'll find circle skirts, classic shirts, bold vintage earrings, and more.

Mim Kemal Öke Cad. No: 9, Nişantaşı, Istanbul, +90 212 219 8724, fey.com.tr.

Gönül Paksoy

An Instanbul fashion stalwart, Paksoy reinterprets Ottoman designs for modern wardrobes, using vintage textiles to create breathtaking clothing and accessories that blur the line between fashion and art.

Teşvikiye Mah., Akkavak Sok. Demet Apt. 4/A, Nişantaşı, Istanbul, +90 212 236 0209.

Grand Bazaar

The centuries-old, labyrinthine complex with sixty-one covered streets and some 3,125 shops draws nearly 100 million visitors every year. Built approximately 554 years ago after Sultan Mehmed the Conqueror took Constantinople, the world's oldest shopping mall has been featured in several Hollywood films, including *Skyfall*, in which James Bond engages in a high-speed motorcycle chase on the Grand Bazaar rooftop. There are several stores that are musts, including Kafkas (No: 4-6) for fine jewelry, Adnan & Hasan for kilims (No: 89-92), Ottoamano for scarves and pashminas (No: 10), and Sivasli Istanbul Yazmacisi for fabric (No: 57). Shoe designer Paul Andrew calls the latter "one of the most inspiring stores for color and print that I've been to. The walls are stacked to the ceiling with bolts of fabrics in every color imaginable."

GRAND BAZAAR, Beyazıt Mh., Fatih, İstanbul, +90 212 519 1248, grandbazaar.org.

Haremlique

Luxury linens, towels, tunics, and pouches in exquisite fabrics. You can even order made-to-measure linens "for your home or yacht," as the website cheekily suggests.

Zorlu Center, Koru Sok. No: 2/194, Beşiktaş, İstanbul, +90 212 236 3843, haremlique.com, and additional locations.

Midnight Express

Owned by fashion designer Banu Bora and architect Tayfun Mumcu, this boutique offers a tight edit of clothing and accessories by regional designers including Nazli Bozdag and Selim Mouzzanar, alongside pieces from

EVREN DOGANCAY
HOMETOWN FAVES

Evren Dogancay is an Istanbul local and the buying manager for Beymen, one of Turkey's best luxury department stores.

My favorite department store in my hometown is **BEYMEN** at the Zorlu Center mall. It's a key location with a big variety of departments—home, shoes, bags, ready-to-wear, etc.—so it's very convenient. (Beymen carries international as well as Turkish designers, including Hakaan Yildirim, who has dressed Rihanna, Jennifer Lopez, and Lady Gaga in his couture-like creations.)

My favorite independent store is **SANAYI 313.** It's an architecture office in the middle of an auto repair shop that has a healthy fusion kitchen, the best coffee in town by Petra, and a lifestyle shop that sells everything stylish, from toothpaste, shoe polish, scented candles, and books to handbags and jewelry. They also make their own supercool slipper and pouch line.

SOUQ KARAKOY is a pop-up market started by *Vogue* Turkey editor Yaprak Aras. I love it because it has lots of personality. The vendors vary each time but are all local, up-and-coming, independent creatives. You can find literally anything here. Handmade bicycles, records, robes, activewear, sunglasses, dolls, and homemade healthy dishes are only a few items on the list.

Another Istanbul gem is the **GRAND BAZAAR.** The best part is the antique section. You can score rare vintage watches, silverware, and antique fabrics at great prices. I also love the variety of ikat fabrics and Turkish pottery.

BEYMEN, Zorlu AVM Levazım Mah. Koru Sok. No: 2, Şişli, İstanbul, +90 212 306 3300, beymen.com.

SANAYI 313, Maslak, 10. Sk. No: 313, Şişli, Istanbul, +90 212 286 3857, sanayi313.com.

SOUQ KARAKOY, Murakıp Sokak No.12, Karaköy, Istanbul.

GRAND BAZAAR, Beyazıt Mh., Fatih, İstanbul, +90 212 519 1248, grandbazaar.org.

BESTE & MERVE MANASTIR

ISTANBUL SHOPPING SECRETS

Inspired by their father's work as a revered leather artisan in Istanbul, Beste and Merve Manastir launched their handbag line in 2014, and gained worldwide attention after fashion editor Eva Chen posted several photos of the bags on her Instagram page. Manu Atelier is now one of the buzziest contemporary accessories brands on the market, following in the footsteps of Mansur Gavriel. The sisters combine time-honored leather-making traditions with pared-down silhouettes, creating such styles as the signature Pristine square flap-over bag, a favorite with girls in the know.

We really love **V2K DESIGNERS**, which is the coolest concept store in Istanbul and a part of the Vakko department store chain. This store is not only our first and only exclusive retailer in Turkey but also the very first fashion house in Turkey, founded in 1934. As for new attractions in Istanbul, we love **MAVRA CAFÉ DESIGN WORKSHOP** in Galata, which is located in old-city Istanbul, a historic place with traditional narrow cobblestone streets. You can have

DEVELI RESTAURANT, which serves traditional Turkish cuisine, just opened a location near our showroom in the Nişantaşı area. The interior is much more fine dining than traditional kebab restaurant. As for coffee, we consume a lot during the day and we prefer to go to **KRUVASAN BAKERY & COFFEE SHOP** or **MOC** (Ministry of Coffee), which is in the Nişantaşı area.

We love **FERIKOY FLEA MARKET** on Sundays. It is an antiques market, so the selection of antiques and gadgets is huge. It has enough stalls with mysterious objects to spend an entire day there. You can find clothes, jewelry, watches, books, cassettes, decorations, vintage tea sets, cameras and lenses, everything. On one side of the market are stalls with traditional Turkish pancakes, fresh fruit juice, and tea, so you can enjoy great food while you shop. In the Cukurcuma/Beyoglu area, there's **TURNACIBASI STREET**, where you can find lots of secondhand and antique shops, bookstores, music shops, and stores with all kinds of decorations. There are also some nice cafés such as **49 CUKURCUMA**, for example.

At **SOFA ART & ANTIQUES** you can find very unique art pieces, jewels, and gift alternatives for friends and family. You can also check their website (kashifsofa.com).

For cheap chic, we love **SENTETIK SEZAR.** They have two branches in Istanbul: one in the Europe side (Taksim/Beyoglu), one in the Asia side (Kadikoy). Taking into account the range of products and how amazing they are, the prices are cheap. If you love vintage, this place will become your favorite store in Istanbul.

V2K DESIGNERS, Abdi İpekçi Cad. No: 29, Şişli, Istanbul, +90 212 219 9487, vakko.com.

MAVRA CAFÉ DESIGN WORKSHOP, Hacımimi, Serdarı Ekrem Sok. No: 31/A, Beyoğlu, İstanbul, +90 212 252 7488.

DEVELI, A, Harbiye, Abdi İpekçi Cad. No: 61D, Blok. 3/4/5, Şişli, Istanbul, +90 212 514 8383, develikebap.com.

KRUVASAN BAKERY, Teşvikiye, Av. Süreyya Ağaoğlu Sok. No: 10, Şişli, Istanbul, +90 212 296 8656.

MOC ISTANBUL, Şakayık Sok. No: 4/A, Şişli, Istanbul, +90 212 234 4465, mocistanbul.com.

FERIKOY FLEA MARKET, Semt Pazarı No: 8, Cumhuriyet Mahallesi, Şişli, Istanbul.

49 ÇUKURCUMA, Kuloğlu Mh., Turnacıbaşı Cad. No: 49, Beyoğlu, Istanbul, +90 212 249 0048.

SOFA ART & ANTIQUES, NuruOsmaniye Cad. No: 53/A, Cagaloglu, Istanbul, +90 212 520 2850, kashifsofa.com.

SENTETIK SEZAR, Moda Cad., Leylak Sok. No: 20/aA, Caferağa, Kadıköy

Masscob, Zadig & Voltaire, and Jupe by Jackie, plus beautiful objects and books. Both Bora and Mumcu design pieces for the shop.

Küçük Bebek Cad. No: 3/A, Bebek, Istanbul, and Boorum, +90 212 263 2111, midnightexpress.com.tr.

Sevan Biçakçi

This master fine jeweler is known for being a Michelangelo of miniatures, creating incredible dome rings that celebrate the city's historical Byzantine and Ottoman sites, such as the Hagia Sophia encased in rose quartz. American designer Tory Burch is a collector. His atelier produces fewer than 1,000 pieces a year, which are priced from $3,000.

Sevan Biçakçi, Molla Fenari Mah., Gazi Sinanpaşa Sk. No: 16 Eminönü, İstanbul + 90 212 520 4516, www.sevanbicakci.com.

Ümit Ünal

The Istanbul-based designer sells his drapey, neutral-colored unisex creations worldwide. His atelier is on-site.

Nişancı Mah, Eyüp Nişanca Cad. No: 17, Eyüp, Istanbul, umitunal.com.

Vakko

One of Turkey's oldest fashion houses, Vakko started selling hats in the 1930s, and is now a successful manufacturer (clothing, accessories, swimwear, and more) and a retailer with a string of stores. It operates the edgy V2K, Vakkorama (which carries sportier brands such as Adidas, Swims, and Herschel Supply), Vakko Wedding, and Vakko Chocolate.

Abdi İpekçi Mah. 33, NİŞANTAŞI, Istanbul, +90 212 248 5011, vakko.com, and other locations.

V2K

This offshoot of Vakko next door sells well-known contemporary brands such as Alexander Wang, Sea, and Opening Ceremony, plus cool-girl Turkish handbag label Manu Atelier.

Harbiye, Abdi İpekçi Cad. No: 29, Şişli, İstanbul, +90 212 219 9487, vakko.com.

Yastik by Rifat Özbek

The cushion store to end all cushion stores, spearheaded by renowned Istanbul-born fashion designer Rifat Özbek, who had success on the runways in London and Paris in the 1980s.

Şakayık Sokak, No: 13/1, Teşvikiye, Şişli, Istanbul, +90 212 240 8731, yastikbyrifatozbek.com.

Yuka Studio

This local designer's simple, modern geometric jewelry shapes in bronze and brass make the perfect fashion souvenir.

Maçka Meydanı Sok., No: 18 /A Beşiktaş, +90 212 259 1099, yuka-studio.myshopify.com.

MOSCOW

RUSSIA

Air Moscow

This concept shop features cutting-edge clothing and streetwear with an emphasis on Japanese brands (all the Comme des Garçons labels, Undercover, and Bao Bao Issey Miyake are represented). Also present are Craig Green, Walter Van Bierendonck, Off-White, KTZ, Christopher Ræburn, ZDDZ, and the newest artist-fashion streetwear collabs from Adidas, Nike, and the like.

Teatralnyy pr-d, 3/4, Moscow, 109012, +7 (495) 621-78-91, air-moscow.com.

Aizel

Street-style star Aizel Trudel, whose social circle includes Christian Louboutin and Natalia Vodianova, is the proprietor of this must-shop, multi-label, three-story boutique, which shut down for Jennifer Lopez to enjoy a private shopping spree when she was in Moscow in 2016. You'll find top international labels, including Valentino, Gucci, Balenciaga, Dolce & Gabbana, and Delpozo, plus the very best of Russian fashion and accessories (Alena Akhmadullina, Katya Dobryakova, Walk of Shame), and an inspired selection of vintage.

Stoleshnikov per., 10/3, Moscow, 125009, +7 (495) 629-95-01, aizel.ru.

Alexander Terekhov

This Moscow-based designer is a go-to for cool, everyday pieces, including print shirtdresses, leather track pants, patchwork knit dresses, and liquid metallic trench coats.

ul. Petrovka, 24/2, Moscow, 127051, +7 (903) 721-66-07, alexanderterekhov.com/en, and additional locations.

Flacon

A former glass factory turned into a colorful urban space for creative businesses. One part functions as office space for media groups, PR agencies, design bureaus, and art workshops. The rest is filled with boutiques selling unique clothes and accessories by local designers, cafés, and bars, and temporary exhibition spaces.

ul. Bolshaya Novodmitrovskaya, 36, Moscow, 127051, +7 (495) 150-03-58, flacon.ru.

Freak Frak

One of the best vintage stores in town. In fact, this place may have introduced the concept of vintage to Moscow when it opened in 1997. It has the makings for any retro look you could

SV MOSCOW

dream up, including Soviet-era pleated skirts and schoolmarmish sweaters.

ul. Shabolovka, d. 25, k.1, Moscow, 119049, +7 (926) 251-52-78, freakfrak.ru.

KM20

Moscow's most famous concept store opened in 2009, and was the first in Russia to introduce Raf Simons, Lemaire, J.W. Anderson, Marques'Almeida, and Yeezy. The multi-label boutique is home to a ton of avant-garde brands, including Off-White, ZDDZ, and Commes des Garçons. Among the Russian designers showcased here are A.W.A.K.E., Gosha Rubchinskiy, Nina Donis, Tigran Avetisyan, and Walk of Shame. The space also functions as a gallery, and the greenhouse café is a popular hangout.

Kuznetsky Most, 20, Moscow, 107031, +7 (495) 623-78-88, km20.ru.

Leform

Opened in 1997, this may have been the first avant-garde designer store in Moscow. It's the place to find the latest from Dries Van Noten, Comme des Garçons, Maison Martin Margiela, and Simone Rocha as well as up-and-comers Nili Lotan and Simon Miller, plus edgy home furnishings, accessories, and apothecary items.

ul. Povarskay, 35/28, Moscow, 121069, +7 (495) 691-82-20, leform.ru.

Moussa Project

Founded by Elena and Victoria Moussa, this retail project lets shoppers rent clothing and accessories for a fraction of the retail cost, with the option of buying them later. Unlike similar services in the US, which focus primarily on formal wear, the Moussa showroom offers a range of dark and arty brands, including Haider Ackermann, Iris van Herpen, and Piers Atkinson.

Bol'shoi Patriarshy per., 8, Moscow, 123001, +7 (916) 166-19-03, facebook.com/moussaproject.

SV Moscow

In addition to stocking Comme des Garçons, Junya Watanabe, Ann Demeulemeester, Yohji Yamamoto, Damir

ONLINE SHOPPING TIP

Moscow multi-label concept boutique km20.ru ships worldwide for a $50 flat fee, and stocks Russian designers, including Nina Donis, Tigran Avetisyan, and Walk of Shame.

Doma, Rick Owens, and Maison Martin Margiela, this directional multi-label boutique was the first in Russia to carry Ashish, Haider Ackermann, and Vetements. SV has also added Raf Simons, Marni, The Row, Yang Li, and Undercover to the selection. Recently, it was the exclusive vendor for a Vetements hoodie dedicated to Zemfira Vetements and Balenciaga designer Demna Gvasalia's favorite Russian singer.

Malaya Molchanovka 6, Moscow, 121069, +7 (495) 215-53-51, svmoscow.com.

TSUM

A rival of GUM, the nearby TSUM department store has upped its fashion quotient in recent years, with a floor curated by street-style star Natasha Goldenberg.

ul. Petrovka, d.2, Moscow, 125009, +8 (495) 933-73-00, tsum.ru.

Tsvetnoy Central Market

A six-floor department store selling fashion, food, and interior design items, with high-end brands such as Self-Portrait, Marc Jacobs, and Peter Pilotto featured alongside Adidas, Reebok, and Maje, plus up-and-coming talents such as Yulia Yefimtchuk, a Ukrainian designer known for creating clothing inspired by her Soviet-era youth.

Tsvetnoy bulvar, 15/1, Moscow, 127051, +7 (495) 737-77-73, tsvetnoy.com.

Vintage Voyage

Moscow's premier vintage destination is full of treasures, including pristine Hermès bags, Chanel chain belts, 1980s Yves Saint Laurent dresses, and more.

ul. Neglinnaya, 9, Moscow, 107031, +7 (495) 968-11-79, vintagevoyage.ru.

OLYA THOMPSON

OLD-WORLD WONDERS OF MOSCOW

Olya Thompson textiles are sold through John Derian in New York and the Jules et Jim showroom in Paris. In addition to being an interior decorator and fabric designer, the Moscow resident (and Vogue *magazine favorite) recently launched a line of dresses inspired by Russian folkloric designs and '70s hippie looks that combine embroideries, handwoven silks, and vintage Uzbeki floral silks for a kind of "Russian Thea Porter" look.*

GUM (translates as the State Universal Shop) is the big city shop. The late-19th-century building, reminiscent of the Russian medieval boyar palace, is an architectural landmark, a multistory glass-covered arcade right on Red Square. There is a cozy art-house movie theater on the third floor. There is a historic wood-paneled powder room. There is a shoe repair place that will restore even the most weathered heels. It is a Moscow tradition to stroll the arcade, looking at the free exhibits, often featuring vintage fashion collections while having an ice cream cone. The best gelato-style ice cream comes from the **BOSCO CAFE CART**. Or head straight to **BOSCO CAFE**, grab a table on its sunlit terrace with a view of St. Basil's Cathedral, and enjoy a perfect porcini risotto. It can only compare to Caffé Florian in Venice with a view of San Marco! Among the shops, my favorite is the **IMPERIAL PORCELAIN FACTORY'S** (Lomonosov), where one can always find a lovely cup or teapot at a reasonable price.

I have become a big fan of the **YULIA YANINA COUTURE** atelier, hidden in the back of Tverskaya Street off Kamergersky Lane. These are truly red-carpet-worthy hand-embroidered gowns and cocktail dresses with the most delicate lace and layers and layers of tulle. Lady Gaga has discovered Yulia

Yanina, but somehow it is still a secret to the rest of the world!

GUM

GRISHKO is the place for Russian-made soft canvas ballet and pointe shoes of all shapes. It is the main Russian emporium for all things ballet. Tutus and costumes from many ballets are made to order here.

Located in a historic mansion featured in Tolstoy's *War and Peace*, **AXENOFF JEWELLERY HOUSE** is a gorgeously appointed showroom where one can find earrings, brooches, and tiaras in silver and gold and adorned with pearls, precious and semiprecious stones, and enamels inspired by the splendor of the Russian past.

The hat department in **TSUM** has a great selection of fur hats from Furland. They make perfect souvenirs from Moscow.

GUM, Red Square, 3, Moscow, 101000, +7 (495) 788-43-43, gum.ru/en.

BOSCO CAFÉ, GUM, +7 (495) 660-05-50, boscofamily.ru/en/restoration/bosco_cafe, and additional locations.

IMPERIAL CHINA, GUM, 1st line, 3rd Floor, +7 (495) 623-26-04, ipm.ru, and additional locations.

YULIA YANINA, ul. Tverskaya, 6 bldg. 6/1, Moscow, 125009, by appointment at +7 (495) 629-51-06, yaninafashion.com/en.

GRISHKO, 3-y Krutitskiy per., 11, Moscow, 109044, +7 (495) 287-45-77, grishkoshop.com, and additional locations.

AXENOFF JEWELLERY, ul. Povarskaya, 52/55-1, Moscow, 121069, +7 (925) 596-53-22, axenoffjewellery.com, and additional locations.

TSUM, ul. Petrovka, d.2, (across the street from the Bolshoi Theatre) Moscow, 125009, +8 (495) 933-73-00, tsum.ru.

LIANA SATENSTEIN

NEW WORLD WONDERS OF MOSCOW

New York–based Vogue.com news writer Liana Satenstein has been one of the magazine's resident experts on Russia for several years, using her experiences living abroad in Russia and Ukraine as an exchange student as a jumping-off point.

The concept store **KM20** is a must. They have Western-based labels like Hood by Air and Raf Simons, but they also offer up a great selection of Russian designers like Tigran Avetisyan and Nina Donis. Plus, they have a stellar vegan café with an amazing selection of fresh juices, kombucha, and salads.

I absolutely love the secondhand store **MEGASTYLE** (or Megastil). It's very sterile and somewhat eerie, but amazing. It's located about fifteen minutes outside of Moscow. There is so much bizarre deadstock shipped in from Turkey and Greece, as well as oddball bazaar-plucked pieces that look straight out of a provincial Russian town from the '90s. My biggest shopping score of all time was from Megastyle and it was less than $5. It was a semisheer shirt with a tiger printed on it. It's heinous and dated but weirdly chic in a cheeky-throwback way. I live in it.

My off-the-beaten-path shopping location is actually very commercial. I love the famed **ARBAT STREET**, which is a pedestrian tourist street in the heart of Moscow. There are so many soccer scarves and handmade linens in the souvenir stores.

I love the label **NINA DONIS.** It is one of the most established but low-key labels in Russia, as well as one of the most creative, mixing Soviet and Western motifs together. (It's available at KM20.) Another brand to watch is **AXENOFF** by Petr Axenoff. The jewelry is opulent and classic, right out of a Pushkin story. What makes it extra special is they use an old enamel practice called "Rostov finift" in their pieces even today.

I'd have to say living in Russia and Ukraine had a huge influence on how I dress. I came from a mall-rat American town (Amesbury, Mass.) where it was totally fine to roll up to class in a pair of pajamas. My senior year in high school, I decided to do an exchange year in Crimea. Though people there may not have had a lot of money, they still took great care of their appearance and clothes. Crimean women are perpetually well-heeled and have impeccable manicures.

KM20, Kuznetsky Most, 20, Moscow, 10703, +7 (495) 623-78-88, km20.ru.

MEGASTYLE, ul. Skladochnaya, 1, Moscow, 127018, megagiper.ru, and other locations.

UL. ARBAT, Moscow, 119002.

NINA DONIS, available at KM20, ninadonis.com.

AXENOFF JEWELLERY, ul. Povarskaya, 52/55-1, Moscow, 121069, +7 (925) 596-53-22, axenoffjewellery.com, and additional locations.

F21
FOREVER 21
防弾少年團
YOUTH
DMM
FX

ASIA

JAPAN
CHINA
SOUTH KOREA
INDIA

SHIBUYA CROSSING

TOKYO

AOYAMA/OMOTESANDO AREA

1LDK

"Almost all the brands they sell are available only there," says retailer Josh Peskowitz of this stylish but approachable place that redefines the workwear, military, and sportswear traditions in menswear. "They just opened a small store in Paris up the street from colette, so that's also a must for me." Across the street is the more spacious 1LDK Apartments location, with the Me boutique and editeD/Found café. Here you'll find women's clothing and decorative goods for the home alongside books and jewelry. Also worth mentioning: 1LDK's Depot in Jingumae and 1LDK Hotel in Minami-Aoyama.

#1A 1-8-28, Kamimeguro, Meguro-ku, Tokyo 153-0051, +81 3-5728-7140, 1ldk.com.

45RPM

The flagship for the cult Japanese denim-and-more brand is located inside a traditional Japanese house.

7-7-21 Minamiaoyama, Minato-ku, Tokyo 07-0062, +81 3-5778-0045, 45rpm.jp, and additional locations.

Bedrock

When in Tokyo, stylist and editor Lori Goldstein heads to this "high-end punk-rock gem," which is famously difficult to find (down a set of stairs in the back of the Forbidden Fruit café/smoothie shop). Thanks to chandeliers and cages, Bedrock resembles a rocker dungeon, and it stocks everything from vintage Givenchy to the owners' own brands, If Six Was Nine and Le Grand Bleu. Stylish Hong Kong restaurateur Bonnae Gokson is a fan, too.

Omotesando Hills, 4-12-10 Jingumae, Shibuya, Tokyo 150-0001, +81 3-3423-6969, maniac-co.jp.

Comme des Garçons

The granddaddy of all CDG stores, this one stocks all of the brands under Rei Kawakubo's umbrella. It also has the biggest range of sizes and styles in the city.

5-2-1 Minami-Aoyama, Minato-ku, Tokyo 107-0062, +81 3-3406-3951, comme-des-garcons.com, and additional locations.

Commes des Garçons Design Shop Good

"Rei Kawakubo's postmodern take on a dry goods store is stocked with all of the iconic designer's favorite things," says designer Brian Wolk. "Products range from the practical to practically luxurious spanning the gamut from Ms. Kawakubo's preferred flair-tip pen to a grandma-worthy metal-frame leather coin purse and everything else in between." In the same upmarket Gyre mall, you'll find the Comme des Garçons Play, Maison Martin Margiela, Visvim, and MoMA Design stores.

5-10-1 Jingumae, Shibuya-ku, Tokyo 150-0001, +81 3-3406-2323, comme-des-garcons.com, and additional locations.

Gallery Muveil

This contemporary womenswear line from Tokyo-born designer Michiko Nakayama launched in 2007, and is earning a reputation among those in the know for its quirky but feminine aesthetic, blending playful prints with whimsical details. Standouts include embroidered knitwear, beaded taffeta bomber jackets, romantic floral blouses, foil-print pleated skirts, and pearl-festooned ankle booties. Filled with vintage furniture and drawers of jewelry and accessories to explore, the store has the feel of a European apartment. Nakayama also designed the Muveil Work label and collaborated with Wes Anderson on a collection geared to the release of the film *Moonrise Kingdom*.

5-12-24 Minami-Aoyama, Minato-ku, Tokyo 107-0062, +81 3-6427-2162, gallerymuveil.com.

Garden

"An incredible store for underground-ish men's fashion," says retailer Josh Peskowitz. "It's not showy stuff, but progressive when it comes to silhouette and fabric. I hadn't heard of half the brands in there the first time I went, but I was blown away by the design."

4-8-12 Jingumae, Shibuya-ku, Tokyo 150-001, +81 3-3405-5075, gardenxxx.com.

Head Porter Plus

"Porter is a Japanese bag brand that is very famous locally and not really sold in the States," says designer Scott Sternberg. "They work with nylon and have stores throughout Japan; the Head Porter store in the Shibuya district is the most luxurious take on the brand."

3-21-112 Jingumae, Shibuya-ku, Tokyo 150-0001, +81 3-5771-2621 headporter.co.jp.

Issey Miyake

The sculptural creations of the iconic Japanese designer are as relevant now as at any other time. Keep walking on the same street, away from Omotesando Station, and you will come across several of the designer's other boutiques, including Issey Miyake Men and Pleats Please. At the end of the street is Reality Lab, which carries Miyake's most experimental collections, Bao Bao and In-Ei; and Me, featuring Miyake's collection of lightweight, compact, easy-to-wear,

HOW OLIVIA KIM DOES
TOKYO'S NARITA INTERNATIONAL AIRPORT

An Opening Ceremony buying department veteran, Kim helps Nordstrom stay on the cutting edge as the store's Director of Creative Projects.

My favorite magazine store is in Narita International Airport. Japanese magazines are my favorite—I learned how to apply makeup from them, how to take the best photos of food for social media, how to wear slouchy socks. I buy as many as I can fit in my carry-on! Also in the airport, there's an outpost of my favorite sock store, Tabio. I get all my socks there and all my last-minute presents and gifts for friends and family. I buy the same style of socks in navy and black, and I ask them for all the pairs they have and clean house on them. And then I throw in a few fun novelty pairs—some with sushi pieces or crocodiles or colored checks and lace.

NARITA INTERNATIONAL AIRPORT, Tokyo 282-004.

and easy-to-care-for clothing.

3-18-11 Minami-Aoyama, Minato-ku, Tokyo 107-0062, +81 3-3423-1408, isseymiyake.com, and additional locations.

Kigure

Celebrate nature in the heart of the city at this boutique featuring environmentally conscious clothing made of natural materials, vintage handmade pottery, and home workshop tools (*mingu*). "A really special store specializing in all sorts of Japanese folk crafts," says designer Kimberly Wu.

4-25-12 Jingu-mae, Shibuya-ku, 150 0001, +81 3-5414-5737, also in Marunouchi, kigure.com.jp.

North Face

"North Face Japan is a separate company, with its own design team and production," says designer Scott Sternberg. "The product is more specific, more interesting, and just cooler than the US version. They have two stores on the main drag of Aoyama; the smaller one houses the more interesting styles."

6-10-11, Jigumae, Shibuya-ku, Tokyo 150-0001, +81 3-5466-9278, goldwin.co.jp, and additional locations.

Quico

This design-oriented boutique around the corner from the MoMA Design Store stocks simple dresses, smocks, and work pants, sculptural jewelry, straw basket bags, kung fu shoes, beautiful pots and pans, organic towels, and more. Just try not to be charmed.

5-16-15 Jingumae, Shibuya-ku, Tokyo 150-0001, +81 3-5464-0912, quico.jp.

Sacai

If you've worn a T-shirt with a lace panel in the back, or a sweater with shirt cuffs, it owes a debt to Japanese designer Chitose Abe, who has made her haute hybrid designs into a booming business. The entire collection, plus the less expensive offshoot Sacai Luck, is stocked in this two-level boutique.

Minamiaoyama City House 5-4-44 Minamiaoyama, Minato-ku, Tokyo 107-0062, +81 3 6418-5977, sacai.jp.

Sou Sou

Started by a textile designer who used to work for Marimekko, this brand has a similar aesthetic, with whimsical, colorful *Ise-momen* fabric made into shirts, baby clothes, kimonos, tabi shoes, tote bags, and phone covers.

5-4-24 Minami Aoyama, Minato-ku, Tokyo 107-0062, +81 3-3407-7887, sousou.com.

Super A Market

Super A's tagline is "Fun with clothes," and you'll certainly have that here among the colorful styles by Dries Van Noten, J.W. Anderson, Tome, and Bless. "A concept store owned by the

JENN ROGIEN

SHOPPING VINTAGE LIKE A BROOKLYNITE IN TOKYO

When Girls *shot in Japan for season five, I got to do some serious shopping in Tokyo accompanied by Tony Crosbie, my Tokyo costume design counterpart and personal shopping guide.*

KOMEHYO (which is really a secondhand department store) specializes in designer accessories. Between the insanely good prices and the exchange rate, I bought myself my first Chanel bag (the small classic) and a red Louis Vuitton Epi weekender. The weekender was $200 because of a small blemish on the interior. Komehyo is serious about the authenticity and condition of its items.

CHICAGO, which operates several branches, felt like a Tokyo version of a Brooklyn thrift store but with kimonos. I bought amazing vintage *yukatas* (a cotton summer-weight version of a kimono) for all the ladies in my family as Christmas gifts. And I bought myself a killer pair of '90s vintage Levi's that fit like a dream. The rack was labeled "crashed denim" as all the jeans were "pre-loved." My pair has the best holes in the knees and wear and tear all over that make them brilliantly broken in. They were twenty bucks max.

RAGTAG is a chain that focuses on secondhand designer clothing and accessories. There were some amazing pieces at pretty great prices. The stores are basically thrift stores that feel like lovely boutiques. My co-designer and I shopped several pieces for the Japanese characters on *Girls* from Ragtags around Tokyo.

KOMEHYO, 3-5-6, Shinjuku, Shinjuku-ku, Tokyo 160-0022, +81 3-5363-9188, komehyo.co.jp, and additional locations.

CHICAGO, B1F Olympia Annex Bldg, 6-31-21 Jingumae, Shibuya-ku, Tokyo 150-0001, +81 3-3409-5017, chicago.co.jp, and additional locations.

RAGTAG, 1-17-7 Jinnan, Shibuya-ku, Tokyo 150-0041, +81 3-3476-6848, ragtag.jp.

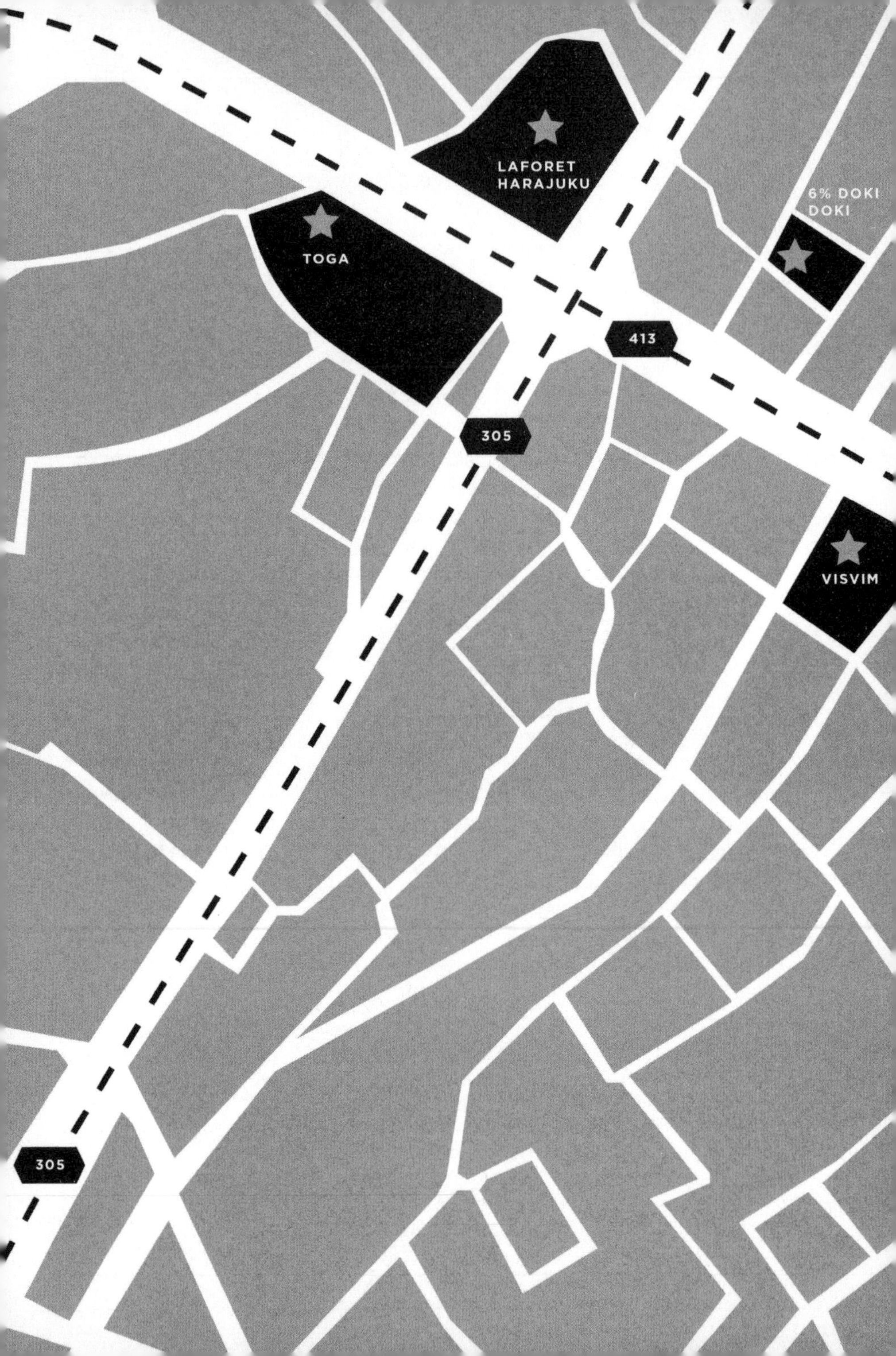
LAFORET
HARAJUKU
6% DOKI
DOKI
TOGA
413
305
VISVIM
305

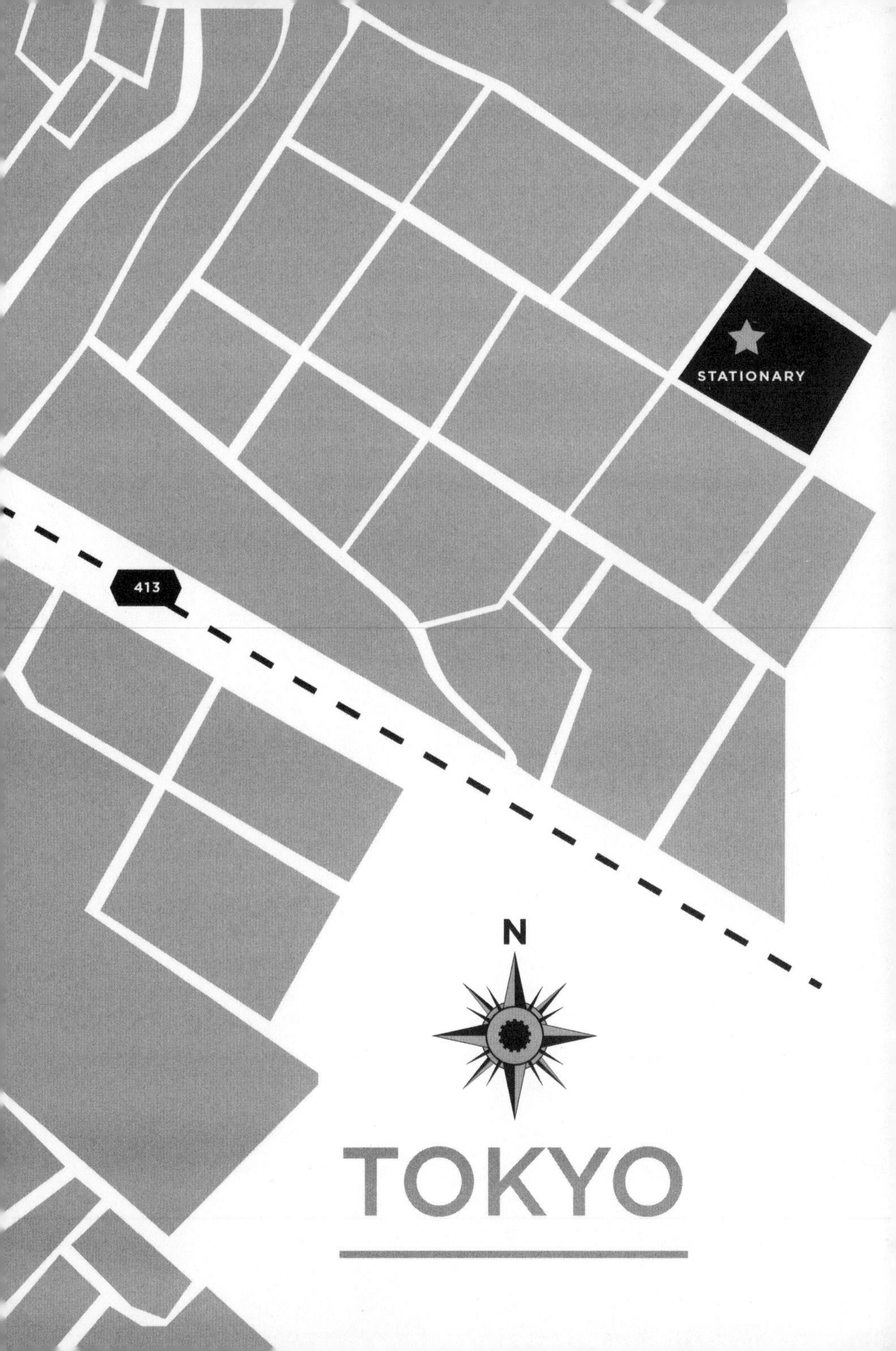
STATIONARY
413
N
TOKYO

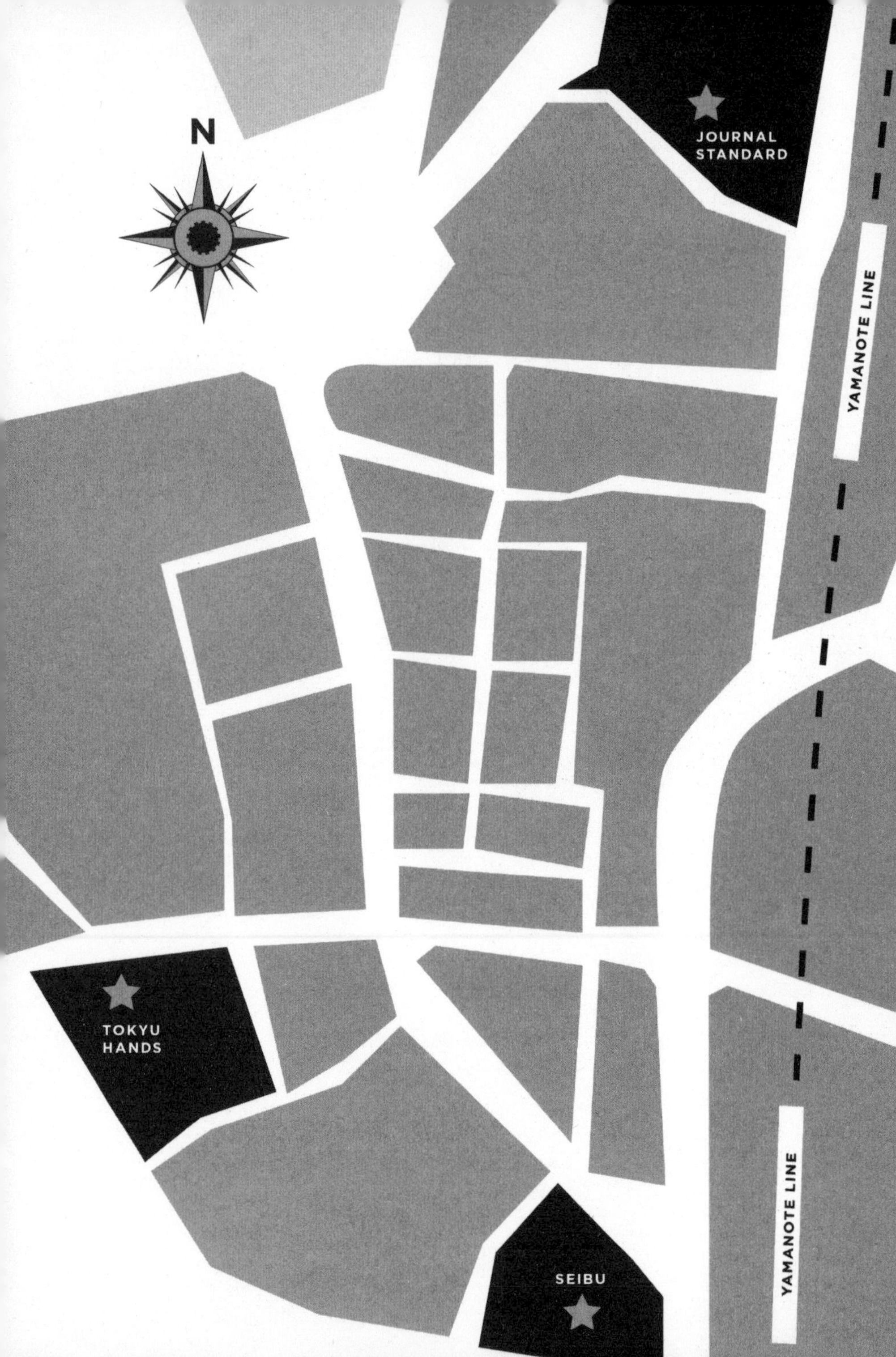
N
JOURNAL
STANDARD
YAMANOTE LINE
TOKYU
HANDS
YAMANOTE LINE
SEIBU

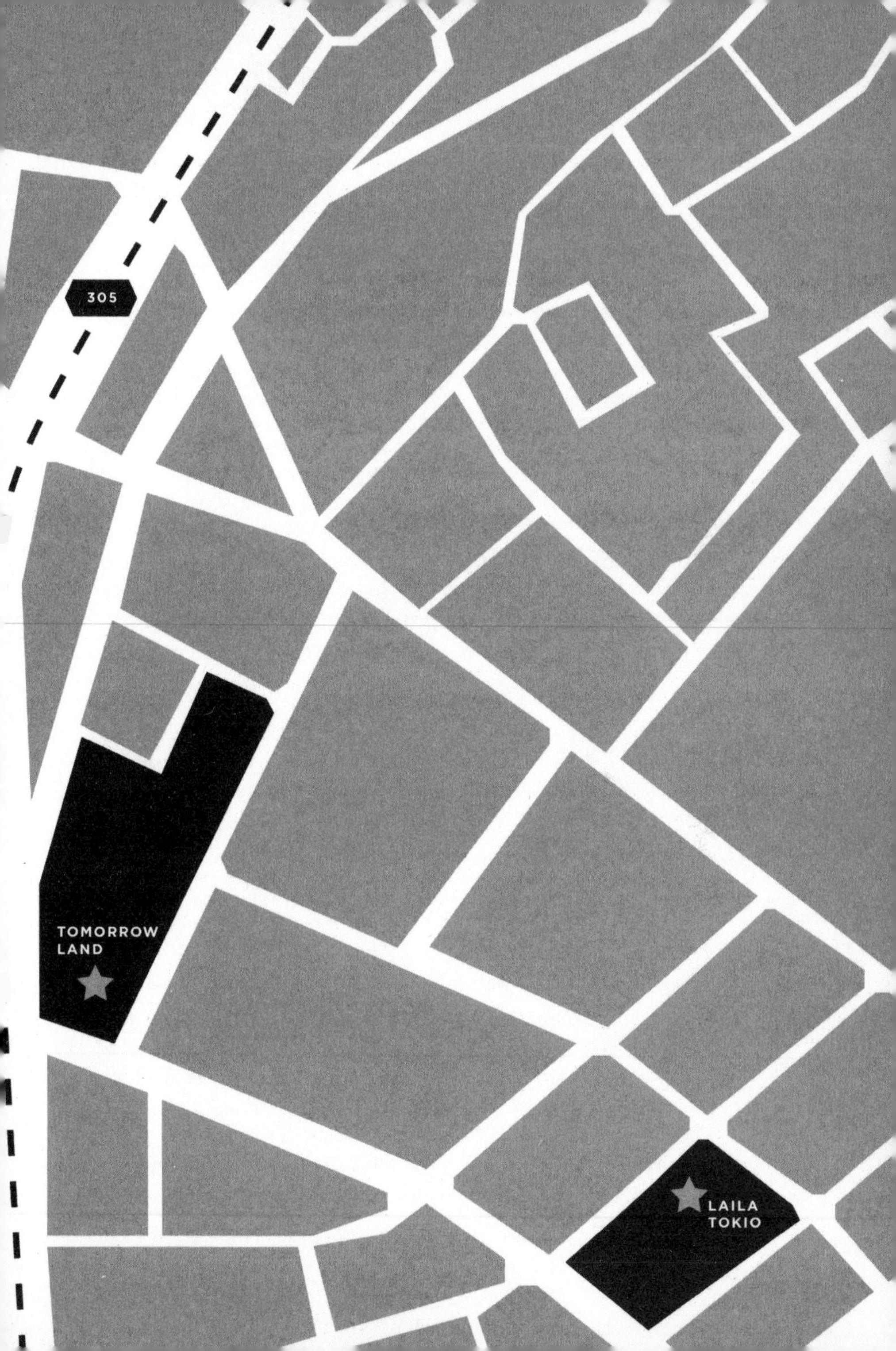
305
TOMORROW
LAND
LAILA
TOKIO

Japanese powerhouse Tomorrowland," says designer Lizzie Fortunato. "The store carries the best high-end fashion merchandised alongside playful jewelry, fragrances, housewares, menswear, and even buttons and rolls of ribbon. Another highlight of the store is the Bar & Grill restaurant at the back of the second floor—hidden and so cool."

3-18-9 Minami-Aoyama, Minato-ku, Tokyo, 107-0062, +81 3-3423-8428, superamarket.jp.

Tsumori Chisato

Popular both in Tokyo, where she has three stores, and beyond, Tsumori Chisato launched her label in 1990 and has earned a loyal fan base for her whimsical clothing and accessories that incorporate arty prints made from original illustrations, fun embroideries, and appliqués.

4-21-25 Minami Aoyama, Minato-ku, Tokyo, +81 3-3423-5170, tsumorichisato.com, and additional locations.

Undercover

The men's and women's flagship for the cult Japanese brand designed by Jun Takahashi, who creates edgy, streetwise clothing inspired by twisted fairy tales, lost innocence, and pretty punks.

5-3-22 Minami Aoyama, Minato-ku, Tokyo 107-0062, +81 3-3407-1232, undercoverism.com.

United Arrows

Founded in 1989, this multi-brand powerhouse has stores across Japan representing a diverse sensibility, from high-end to street, along with its own private label. It's worth stopping by to take a look at the latest pop-up (recently, it was Kith) or artist collab (Larry Clark, for example).

2-31-12 Jingumae, Shibuya-ku, Tokyo 150-0001, +61 3-3479-817, united-arrows.co.jp, and additional locations.

SHIBUYA

Journal Standard

Many Japanese brands take inspiration from American heritage brands and workwear, none more so than Journal Standard, which has four fashion lines and thirty stores around the world.

1-5-6 Jinnan, Shibuya-ku, Tokyo 150-0041, +81 3-5457-0700, journal-standard.jp, and additional locations.

Laila Tokio

The impressive all-white interior, with walls covered in 8,000 pyramid studs, is the canvas for hard-to-find designer archives, as well as up-and-coming labels, art books, and more.

2F, 1-5-11 Shibuya, Shibuya-ku, Tokyo 150-0041, +81 3-6427-6325, laila-tokio.com.

NINA GARDUNO
GETS INSPIRED BY TOKYO

A retail visionary, Nina Garduno is the founder and creator of L.A.'s pop-art-meets-commune Freecity store, which changes theme every few months. Her brand of sweats and T-shirts with feel-good sayings has gone global, with a store in Tokyo. And Tokyo, as it turns out, is one of the places that always inspires Garduno.

THE DAIKANYAMA TSUTAYA BOOKSTORE in Tokyo is completely obsessive-compulsive. So if it's race cars they're into, there's every video and small model car, books on vintage Mercedes and Porsches, and video footage of races. Or if it's *Star Wars*, they have every movie on VHS, Beta, and DVD, plus signed pieces of C-3PO. It's mixing media—old, new, vintage, cutting edge. And they have every magazine, and *every* issue of *W* and *National Geographic* ever printed. It's a library, too.

I love the **GOLDEN GAI,** which has three tiny roads of bars, each one a different genre. So you'll have one themed around 1930s geisha, and another one that's about samurai movies. These places are tiny, like four square feet, and you have to inherit spaces when others leave. Quentin Tarantino has a place he frequents that's inspired by French New Wave cinema. And they serve drinks that are of the place, so you feel like you are living it.

Then there's **TOYKU HANDS,** which has different worlds of craft, from letter making to stickers to candle making. It's floor after floor of dense, intense worlds and genres.

It's very real to step into these worlds, and it's very inspiring to me because it's what I do, too. My favorite purchase isn't anything I have bought—it's the experiences I have taken with me.

TSUTAYA BOOKS, 17-5 Sarugaku-cho, Meguro-ku, Tokyo 150-0033, +81 3-3770-2525, tsite.jp/daikanyama.

GOLDEN GAI, 1-1 Kabukicho, Shinjuku-ku, Tokyo 160-0021.

TOYKU HANDS, 12-18 Udagawacho, Tokyo 150-0042, +81 3-5489-5111, tokyu-hands.jp.

Seibu

One of Tokyo's biggest department stores, Seibu is spread out over two facing buildings and fourteen floors, two of them dedicated to an incredible food hall (a favorite of designer Trina Turk). Prada, Iris van Herpen, Muveil, and Yohji Yamamoto are just a few of the brands represented here.

21-1 Udagawacho, Shibuya-ku, Tokyo 150-0042, +81 3-3462-0111, sogo-seibu.jp.

Shibuya 109

This shopping mall may be to Tokyo what the Sherman Oaks Galleria was to Los Angeles. In the '90s, the Shibuya *gyarus* (gals) brought 109 into popular culture with their dyed blond hair, fake tans, miniskirts, and makeup. Nowadays, the mall is still a place to shop for fun fashion, including cutesy clothing (most in very small sizes), bedazzled phone cases, wigs, colored contact lenses, and more.

2-29-1 Dogenzaka, Shibuya, Tokyo 150-0043, +81 3-3477-5111, shibuya109.jp.

Tokyu Hands

"A department store like none you've ever seen," says designer Scott Sternberg of this eight-floor DIY heaven. "They carry everything you can think of, from bags and T-shirts to watches and appliances. The mix can be overwhelming, but if you step back and take your time, you'll find some of the best local oddities and deals." "Love all the gadgets and knickknacks. I always buy lots of stuff there: brushes, stickers, stationery, black earbuds, sushi erasers, shiso seeds, et cetera," adds publicist and retailer Valery Demure. Designer Erica Tanov describes Tokyu Hands this way: "An awesome living-ware store carrying items from traditional Japanese stationery, paper clips and perfect pens to fun bath and beauty products. I could shop there for hours. Cheap and cheerful, for sure."

12-18 Udagawacho, Tokyo 150-0042, +81 3-5489-5111, tokyu-hands.jp, and additional locations.

Tomorrowland

This elegantly preppy brand is the namesake label of the Tomorrowland retail and manufacturing group, but you'll also find other international fashion and accessories labels at the beautiful flagship, including Loewe, Isabel Marant, and Dries Van Noten.

F B1F, 1-23-16, Shibuya, Shibuya-ku, Tokyo 150-0002, +81 3-5774-1711, tomorrowland.jp, and additional locations.

ERICA TANOV

BOUTIQUE TREASURES IN TOKYO

MINÄ PERHONEN is the best-designed store I've ever been in (especially the dressing rooms). I love his work, he's a true original. Beautiful clothing, accessories, and fabrics. A feast for the eyes and heart.

FOG LINEN has a thoughtful mix of clothing and home goods in a natural, soothing color palette.

ARTS & SCIENCE is a beautifully curated clothing, accessories, apothecary, and housewares store. There are several locations, with each offering something unique. I admire how many of the stores in Tokyo require a map (which they print on their business cards) to locate them—you feel like you're on a treasure hunt.

MINA PERHONEN, Hillside Terrace G-1F 18-12 Sarugakucho, Shibuya-ku, Tokyo 105-0033, +81 3-6826-3770, mina-perhonen.jp, and additional locations.

FOG LINEN, 5-35-1 Daita, Setagaya, Tokyo 155-0033, +81 3-5432-5610, foglinenwork.com.

ARTS & SCIENCE, 6-6-20, Pacific Aoyama, Minami Aoyama, Minato-ku, Tokyo 107-0062, +81 3-3498-1091, arts-science.com, and additional locations.

HARAJUKU

6% Doki Doki

The capital of *kuwaii* (cute) Harajuku fashion, this place is a can't-miss for colorful dolly dresses, cosplay outfits, and candy-like jewelry. The salespeople dress the part and are worth the stop alone.

4-28-16 Jingumae, Shibuya-ku, Tokyo 150-0001, +81 3-3479-6116, dokidoki6.com.

Beams

Of all the stores owned by the Beams fashion empire (the chain has more than 100), the most luxurious is International Gallery Beams, which features the latest from Proenza Schouler, Jaquemus, and many other international labels, plus timely pop-up shops and limited-edition artist collaborations.

3-25-15 Jingumae, Shibuya-ku, Tokyo, +81 3-3470-3948, beams.co.jp, and additional locations.

Dog

"The first place I go to whenever I'm in Japan," says designer Pip Edwards of this hidden spot, a longtime favorite of Harajuku hipsters for reworked vintage. "You follow this winding path, then through a door and down a set of stairs. The store is all black, and it has the most amazing things, from vintage Mugler to new stuff."

3-23-3 Jingumae, Shibuya-ku, Tokyo 150-0001, +81 3-3746-8110.

Facetasm

Facetasm is Japan's latest fashion export. It was founded by Hiromichi Ochiai, who showed his collection in Paris for the first time in 2016 and picked up several international accounts, including Net-a-Porter. Inspired by pop culture and the Antwerp Six, the collection includes idiosyncratic takes on utilitarian styles (pleated hybrid skirt-pants and bow-embellished bomber jackets, for example).

#601 2-31-9 Jingumae Shibuya-ku, Tokyo 150-0001, +81 3-6434-9893, facetasm.jp.

Laforet

Tokyo's trend-setting teenage pop palace. Looking for the next Goth Lolita or Ganguro style? You're likely to find it here, where a lot of the Harajuku kids shop. "I walk each floor looking for anything that I can squeeze into," says author and street-style photographer Ari Seth Cohen. "I am totally Harajuku at heart. Laforet has floors and floors of independent little shops and designers with styles ranging from rainbow-streaked club-kid wear to French floral country grandmother. The whole place is a feast for the eyes."

1-11-6 Jingumae, Shibuya-ku, Tokyo 150-0001, +81 3-3475-0411, laforet.ne.jp.

Toga

Former costume designer and stylist Yasuko Furuta is a go-to at home and abroad (Katy Perry is a fan) for her avant-garde clothes and shoes, which mix feminine shapes and Western touches such as oversized silver buckles and silk fringe. **6-31-10 Jingumae, Shibuya-Ku, Tokyo 150-0001, +81 3-6419-8136, toga.jp.**

Visvim

"The way that designer Hiroki Nakamura approaches his brand is as an archivist, looking at the past and vintage to create something modern and authentic," says Nordstrom Director of Creative Projects Olivia Kim. "His flagship store in Harajuku is one of my favorite places to discover fashion—not only are the clothes there but his inspiration pieces are also on display—his photos of him and his

HARAJUKU GIRLS

family on the road in search of that inspiration. He also roasts his own coffee beans, Little Cloud Coffee, and brews one cup at a time. And on top of it all, Visvim makes the most delicious scented candles and room diffusers." **5-10-1 Gyre 2F Jingumae, Shibuya-Ku, Tokyo 150-0001, +81 3-5468-5424, visvim.tv.**

GINZA

Dover Street Market

Rei Kawakubo's hometown fashion fun house doesn't disappoint. There are seven floors of goodness, it's connected to the Uniqlo flagship, has a rooftop shrine, a branch of Rose Bakery, and Komatsu Bar. **6-9-5 Ginza, Chuo-ku, Tokyo 104-0061, +81 3-6228-5080, Ginza. doverstreetmarket.com.**

Muji

The mother of all Mujis, this flagship has everything you need to lead a serene and simple lifestyle, including apparel, furniture, home accessories, food, even a Muji prefab house you can tour and buy to build in Japan. There are aromatherapy and monogramming stations on site, plus a café

and a children's play area. In the same building, you'll find Loft, "a famous store for stationery, office, and art supplies, which is boring in the US but like Disneyland in Tokyo," says designer Scott Sternberg.

3-8-3 Marunouchi, Chiyoda-ku, Tokyo 100-0005, +81 3-5208-8241, muji.com, and additional locations.

Matsuya

"One of my favorite department stores because of its smaller size, design shop, and designer selections," says museum curator Sharon Takeda. On the third floor is "Le Place," which sells only local designer fashion; the two basement floors have an impressive selection of delicacies.

3-6-1 Ginza, Chuo-ku, Tokyo 104-0061, +81 3-3562-1111.

Oedo Antique Market

The largest outdoor antique market in Japan, Oedo is held the first and third Sundays of the month. "A wondrous array of Japanese antiques at reasonable prices," says designer Erica Tanov.

ONLINE SHOPPING TIP

Tokyu Hands, perhaps one of the most referenced stores by contributors to this book, ships internationally to many countries via BuySmartJapan. Look for the icon next to items on the tokyu-hands.co.jp website.

For Japanese design goodies in North America, there are Daiso dollar stores in Canada and the US, including California, Texas, and Washington, or order online at daisojapan.com. Websites for the popular Japanese brands Muji (muji.com) and Uniqlo (Uniqlo.com) also ship worldwide.

"I've found cherished items such as a favorite oil painting, handmade kitchen utensils, exquisite kimono fabric, and rustic ceramic vessels."

3-5-1 Marunouchi, Chiyoda-ku, Tokyo 100-0005.

Tansu-ya

This chain of vintage kimono stores is a hit with designer Elizabeth Kennedy, who says, "They sell beautiful vintage silk, *shibori*, and hand-painted kimonos. With a bit of luck, you can find a kimono on sale for as little as $35. Most start around $300 to 500, but they can cost up to $2,500!" The staff will teach you the traditional method of wearing a kimono, and there are stores all over the city.

3-4-5 Ginza, Chuo-ku, Tokyo 104-0061, +81 3-3561-8529, tansuya.jp, and additional locations.

Uniqlo

Standing twelve stories high, the Ginza flagship of the popular cheap-chic basics brand has a stunning glass facade and compelling displays inside, too, thanks to Wonderwall's Masamichi Katayama, famous for his innovative work with BAPE and colette in Paris.

6-9-5 Ginza, Chuo-ku, Tokyo 104-0061, +81 3-6252-5181, uniqlo.com, and additional locations.

SHINJUKU

Don Quijote

Designer Brandon Maxwell names Donki (as it's known) as his favorite store in the world. The discount chain is famous for its extended hours (this

TSUTAYA BOOKS

location is open twenty-four hours) and its distinctive jingle, it's "miracle shopping." "You can literally buy everything you ever imagined there. You can get a Kelly bag and a Rolex on the eighth floor and laundry detergent on the first floor!" Maxwell says.

1-12-6 Okubo, Tokyo 169-0072, +81 3-5292-7411, and additional locations.

Isetan

"Hands down my favorite department store in the world," says men's retailer Josh Peskowitz of this not-to-be-missed Tokyo hot spot that carries all the best fashion brands, local and international. "Honestly, there's nothing like it. Their windows at holiday time are the illest, most surreal examples of the craft that I have ever seen, and it extends to every point of the store displays." The champagne bars and basement food court come highly recommended, too, and the store always seems to be hosting a special event, designer appearance, or pop-up. "I have never been more impressed with a more manicured department store," adds fashion editor Karla Martinez de Salas. "The fruit department with $200 muskmelons is unforgettable."

3-14-1 Shinjuku, Shinjuku-ku, Tokyo, 160-0022, +81 3-3225-2514, isetan.mistore.jp/store/shinjuku.

Mannen-Ya

"A really special store specializing in

all sorts of Japanese workwear," says designer Kimberly Wu of this place, which is like an Army-Navy store for the hard-hat set.

3-8 Nishi Shinjuku, Shinjuku, Tokyo 160-0023, +81 3-3373-1111, mannen-ya.co.jp.

EBISU

Biotop

"Boutique, café, tree house, and nursery rolled into one" is how designer Kimberly Wu describes this innovative retail space, where you can stock up on emerging and established labels such as The Row and Rosetta Getty, and grab lunch at the Irving Place café upstairs, with views of the tree house outside.

4-6-44 Shirokanedai, Minato-ku, Tokyo, 108-0071, +81 3-3444-2421, biotop.jp.

Kapital

This cult brand of folksy, Japanese-meets-Americana denim and workwear cut, patched, and distressed to imperfect perfection is so beloved that David Sedaris wrote a *New Yorker* piece about it. There are several stores in Tokyo and they are all equal parts clothing and curiosities. "Best merchandising ever," says designer Ulla Johnson.

2-20-2 Ebisu 1F, Shibuya-ku, Tokyo 150-0022, +81 3-5725-3923, kapital.jp, and additional locations.

DAIKANYAMA

Okura

A treasure trove of all things indigo set up in a rustic house, Okura offers a glimpse into Japan's traditional hand-dye, batik, and block-print techniques on everything from sweatshirts to scarves. "It's all simple, classic style with wonderful Japanese tailoring," says Sabah founder Mickey Ashmore. "As at most Japanese institutions, the staff is very caring and attentive. I bought a double-breasted indigo suit here that I love." Downstairs, you can grab lunch and lotus baguettes at Bombay Bazar. Okura is owned by Seilin & Co., which operates several fashion stores and cafés around Japan, including the nearby Hollywood Ranch Market and High Standard.

20-11 Sarugakucho, Shibuya, Tokyo 150-0033, +81 3-3461-8511, hrm.co.jp/okura.

Tsutaya Books

Perhaps the most beautiful bookstore in

DON QUIJOTE

the world, Tsutaya sells new and used vintage books, DVDs, music, magazines, and more. It also has its own outdoor eatery and gallery. The two-story building complex was designed by Tokyo architecture firm Klein Dytham. "I could easily spend an entire day there browsing the art books and back issues of magazines and interacting with robots before sitting down in one of the swankiest lounges on the planet for a Manhattan made by a true cocktail master," says writer and retailer Lizzie Garrett Mettler.

17-5 Sarugaku-cho, Meguro-ku, Tokyo 150-0033, +81 3-3770-2525, tsite.jp/daikanyama.

White Mountaineering

Japanese designer Yosuke Aizawa's menswear and womenswear label is white hot. The premium brand may be inspired by the outdoors, but it has serious fashion cred, with reconstructed workwear and cozy, cool patterned knits.

2-7 1F, Sarugaku-cho, Shibuya-ku, Tokyo 150-0033, +81 3-6416-9110, whitemountaineering.com, and additional locations.

NIHANBASHI

Starnet

"The most beautiful ceramics," says handbag designer Kimberly Wu. "The Tokyo store is out of the way, though. Go to the Mashiko location for a really special experience—it's about a two-hour drive from Tokyo."

1-3-9 Higashi-Kanda, Chiyoda-ku, Tokyo 101-0031, +81 2-85-72-9661, starnet-bkds .com, and additional locations.

NAKAMEGURO DI

Cow Books

"A tiny, amazing rare bookstore in my favorite little neighborhood that is centered around a canal," says designer Scott Sternberg. "In April and May, it's cherry blossom season and the entire run of the canal is bright pink. It's stunning and charming."

1-14-11 Aobadai, Meguro-ku, Tokyo 153-0042, +81 3-5459-1747, cowbooks.jp.

Ganso Shokuhin Sample-ya

Plastic-food nirvana—you know, the stuff you see outside every Asian restaurant.

3-7-6 Nishi-Asakusa, Taito-ku, Tokyo 111-003, +81 120-171-839, ganso-sample.com.

SHOPPING THE WORLD FROM ETSY

For authentic Japanese workwear-style clothing, stylist Sarah Schussheim recommends the Etsy store **Sasakiyohinten**, located in Gunma, Japan. "It is run by the most lovely man, Mitsugu Sasaki. His pieces are a hodge-podge of techniques; the best way to describe them would be as remade from antique linen, Japanese cotton, sometimes dyed, sometimes not. Lots of boro-stitching and patchwork. My favorite pieces from here are a patched indigo chore jacket and a light-blue patched sweatshirt."

"One of my favorite shops on Etsy is **Embroidered Dream**," says Brigette Romanek. "It carries Ukrainian tunics and dresses. They're colorful garb with billowy oversize sleeves. I wear them day and night. I love them."

JOHANNA HO

HONG KONG

CHINA

Barney Cheng

"Great for a modernized cheongsam," says art dealer Pearl Lam of Hong Kong's premier designer for the social set. "Barney is greatly counterintuitive."

12/F, Worldwide Commercial Building, 34 Wyndham St., Central, Hong Kong, +852 2530 2829, barneycheng.com.

Cha Ling

This new LVMH-backed, tea-infused range of beauty products and fragrances includes cleansing powders, masks, steam tablets, and more.

Shop 3306A, 3/F, Gateway Arcade, Harbour City, Hong Kong, +852 3101 0708, cha-ling.com.

DelStore

"One of my favorite small-scale stores in the world," says retailer Josh Peskowitz of this multi-label menswear store, featuring indie brands such as Arts & Science, Kapital, Blue Blue, Yuketen, and Comoli. "The former menswear buyer at Lane Crawford opened it in a very out-of-the-way alley in the most fashionable neighborhood in Hong Kong and it's got such a well-thought-out aesthetic. Everything in the store from every brand could almost be made specifically for the store, they all meld so well into one whole."

3 Schooner St., Wan Chai, Hong Kong, +852 2528 1770, www.delstore.co.

Fang Fong Projects

Hong Kong designer Wu Lai-Fan makes contemporary-looking dresses in Asian-inspired fabrics.

69A Peel St., Central, Hong Kong, +852 3105 5557.

Initial

Founded in 2000, this chain of lifestyle stores with earthy furnishings and lulling soundtracks features its own romantic, vintage-inspired clothing for men and women. Inital has carved out an empire, opening several branches in China and even expanding into home (Initial Living) and dining (Initial Café).

Shop B13-15, Lab Concept, 93 Queensway, Admiralty, Hong Kong, +852 2623 2632, initialfashion.com, and additional locations.

Island Beverley Center

"An often-overlooked treasure of the Hong Kong shopping experience," local fashion expert Tania Mohan says of this trendy mall full of well-priced stores. "It has been a fashion-forward shopping experience since my late teens, and it remains a treasure with its four floors of quirky, independent street-forward fashion shops with a strong Japanese and Korean influence. You'll find everything from gorgeous dresses and well-cut blazers to laser-cut neon and PVC garments."

1 Great George St., East Point, Hong Kong, +852 2890 6823.

IT

"My husband and I stumbled upon this amazing store when we were in Hong Kong on our honeymoon," blogger Lainy Hedaya says of this multi-label monolith, which has eight locations in HK selling international and in-house brands. "We spent about five hours there and left with so many bags (it was also sale season). The curation of local designers and the quintessential luxury brands made for an amazing shopping experience."

2 Kingston St., Causeway Bay, Hong Kong, +852 2881 6102, ithk.com, and additional locations.

Jardine Crescent

"You can find anything from women's underwear to kids' clothing to cartoon pajamas," says fashion consultant and stylist Grace Lam of this narrow street market. "If you are looking for some essentials and fun local goodies, this is definitely the place to go."

Jardine's Bazaar, Causeway Bay, Hong Kong.

Johanna Ho

Hong Kong fashion designer Ho launched her brand in 1998 in London, and her first collection was quickly snapped up by Barneys New York. After continuing to build her business from Japan, she returned to Hong Kong a few years ago; in 2014, Ho opened her first flagship here, offering the quirky women's knitwear and whimsical men's tailoring that have made her a favorite of celebs such as Cantopop singers Eason Chan and Sammi Cheng and British actor Rosamund Pike. Popular in China, Ho has collaborated with numerous brands, including Birkenstock, Vans, and MAC.

Shop 315, 3/F, Windsor House, 311 Gloucester Rd., Causeway Bay, Hong Kong, +852 2722 6776, johannaho.com.

Joyce

"My all-time favorite boutique," says Hong Kong–based luxury marketing consultant Peter Cheung. "I have been shopping there since the '80s, and the founder, Joyce Ma, is truly the fashion and luxury pioneer of Asia. The boutique has been on the cutting edge of bringing the best in designer fashion

DIVIA HARILELA'S

FAVORITE HONG KONG BOUTIQUES

Harilela is a fashion media vet, having served as the fashion editor for Hong Kong's leading English-language newspaper, the South China Morning Post, *before founding her own luxury and fashion website the D'Vine in 2011. She is also a regular contributor to* Vogue China, Jing Daily, The Business of Fashion, *and* Departures, *to name just a few. Born and raised in Hong Kong, Harilela is often sought out as an authority on fashion in Asia.*

Hong Kong is full of big brand stores, but I prefer small, curated boutiques. One of my favorites is **VEIN,** which stocks hard-to-find Scandinavian brands (Ganni, Humanoid, Rodebjer, Wood Wood). **TABLA** is run by Tania Mohan and everything is handcrafted in India—think Western silhouettes with exquisite embroideries. You feel like you're buying an heirloom that you'll wear time and time again.

GRANA is relatively new; it started online à la Warby Parker. It's my go-to for everyday clothes. They cut out the middleman and offer great-quality basics such as T-shirts (comparable to Petit Bateau), denim made in Japan (the fit is almost as good as Uniqlo), and even cashmere. The prices are super reasonable as everything is direct-to-consumer. They just opened their first freestanding boutique in Hong Kong.

VEIN, 2 St. Francis Yard, Wan Chai, Hong Kong, +852 2804 1038, bvein.com.

TABLA, Princes Building, Central, Hong Kong, +852 2525 5590, houseoftabla.com.

GRANA, 108 Hollywood Rd, Sheung Wan, Hong Kong, +852 2755 8744

to Hong Kong, as well as searching the globe for young, up-and-coming designers to introduce to the Hong Kong market. One young Chinese designer that I love to purchase at Joyce is Xander Zhou. The store is such a beautiful haven in the busy Central district, it transports you to a world of calm and elegance that I don't think any other shop in town does." Designer Karen Erickson agrees: "Joyce Ma's legacy of avant-garde luxury is subliminal and perfect."

G/F, New World Tower, 232 Pacific Place, Central, Hong Kong +852 2810 1120, joyce.com, and additional locations.

Kapok

Founded in 2006 by Frenchman Arnault Castel with the goal of bringing future classics to the Asian market, Kapok has grown into a chainlet of lifestyle shops carrying Bensimon, Building Block, Clare V., Maison Kitsuné, Martiniano, Rains, and other pared-down basics, as well as its own unpretentious, casual Future Classics label.

Kapok, G/F, 5 St Francis Yard, Wanchai, Hong Kong, +852 2549 9254, ka-pok.com, and additional locations.

Landmark

One of HK's most prestigious malls, with Harvey Nichols spanning five floors, a wide variety of luxury brand boutiques, including Louis Vuitton, Céline, and Marni, and Michelin-star restaurants such as L'Atelier de Joël Robuchon. "I love combing through their edit whenever I am in Hong Kong," says fashion editor Joe Zee. "There are always items that are available only in Asia, and I particularly love their home décor department."

The Landmark, 15 Queen's Rd., Central, Hong Kong, +852 3695 3388, landmark.hk.

Lane Crawford

Founded in 1850, Lane Crawford is still Hong Kong's leading luxury fashion and lifestyle specialty store. "One of my favorite department stores," says shoe designer Paul Andrew. "They have a very progressive, well-curated assortment of collections in all departments, and they spend a great deal of energy supporting and nurturing emerging talent. It's really unparalleled in China. Beyond the selection, the store is beautifully designed and filled with great rest areas, including a café opposite the designer shoe salon that serves the best coffee and delicious cookies and pastries (traditional French recipes mixed with Eastern flavors and influences)." "Their selection is really well curated," says shoe designer Isa Tapia. "Especially the shoe and vintage shop. The vintage collection at the ICF mall is the best I've ever seen. This is the best place to buy vintage Chanel that you will wear forever."

IFC Mall, Podium 3, 8 Finance St., Central, +852 2118 2288, lanecrawford.com, and additional locations.

WHERE DESIGNER MARIE FRANCE VAN DAMME

FINDS INSPIRATION IN HONG HONG

Van Damme is the Montréal-born, Hong Kong-based founder of the travel-inspired luxury resort line that bears her name. Van Damme has five boutiques, and her collection is at upscale department stores worldwide.

Hong Kong is famous for its street markets. **CAT STREET MARKET** on Upper Lascar Row is antiques central—it's where I buy jade rings that I use as Chinese spoon rests.

A chef's dream, **SHANGHAI STREET** is fantastic for understated porcelain pieces that are great for dinner parties or decorating the home. I love to get little trinkets here. Many of these pieces, when situated correctly, can add an understated elegance to any space.

The **HONG KONG FLOWER MARKET** in Mongkok is a little oasis, with rows upon rows of stalls, shops, and stands brimming with fresh-cut flowers, exotic plants, and an abundance of foliage and color that is truly a treat for the senses. It can get very crowded, especially during Chinese New Year, when families come and buy auspicious plants that will bring them good luck and fortune.

SHAM SHUI PO, Hong Kong's material and trimmings bazaar, began in the mid-1970s; to this day, it still offers everything. It has street upon street of wholesalers selling fabrics in every color and pattern imaginable.

My favorite place to stop for tea is **TEAKHA,** located in Sheung Wan. It's a small, hidden spot where you can sit on the terrace. It has good pastries and treats, too.

CAT STREET MARKET, Upper Lascar Row, Tai Ping, Hong Kong, cat-street.hk.

SHANGHAI STREET, Yau Ma Tei, Hong Kong.

HONG KONG FLOWER MARKET, Flower Market Rd., Mong Kok, Hong Kong, flower-market.hk.

SHAM SHUI PO, Ki Lung, Nam Cheong St. and Yu Chau St., sham-shui-po.com.

TEAKHA, 18 Tai Ping Shan St., Hong Kong, +852 2858 9185, teakha.com

Liger

Local fashion icon Hilary Tsui and her business partner have three Liger stores in HK carrying a fun range of international and local brands, such as Alice McCall, Holly Fulton, Shrimps, Fenty, Stella Jean, and Johanna Ho, as well as the in-house label, Oh My God.

Shop A & C Vienna Mansion, 55 Paterson St., Fashion Walk, Causeway Bay; +852 2503 5308, ligerstore.com, and additional locations.

Lii Lii

"With the help of the fabulous staff, it is possible to have customized dream shoes handcrafted," says Hong Kong fashion expert Tania Mohan. "It's quite a phenomenal shopping experience and so easy to get lost in the choices of skins, colors, textures, finishes, and heel heights." Orders take ten to fourteen days.

Shop 75, 1/F, Admiralty Center, 18 Harcourt Rd., Queensway, Admiralty, Hong Kong, +852 2865 3989.

PageOne

"You can find the widest selection of fashion and travel magazines plus back issues," shoe designer Isa Tapia says of this local chain that has been struggling in recent years. "I found some issues of *Vitals* magazine there that I treasure to this day."

Shop LG 1-30, Festival Walk, 80 Tat Chee Ave., Kowloon, Hong Kong, +852 2778 2808, pageonegroup.com.

PMQ

"A wonderful place for discovering young and local designers," says luxury marketing consultant Peter Cheung of this creative complex (it used to be a school, then served as living quarters for young married police officers). "PMQ offers subsidized rental for local brands to have workshop and retail space. In the two building blocks, there are different shops, brands, and pop-ups. There's always something new."

35 Aberdeen St., Central, Hong Kong. +852 2870 2335, pmq.org.hk.

Qeelin

Owned by Kering, this Hong Kong–based luxury jewelry brand inspired by Chinese culture first caught the world's attention in 2004 when actor Maggie Cheung wore its curved, gourd-shaped Wulu earrings on the red carpet at Cannes. Since then, the brand has opened boutiques around the globe, including Paris, Beijing, and Shanghai, as well as wholesaling to stores like Neiman Marcus. The name Qeelin comes from the Chinese ideograms for male (*qi*) and female (*lin*), and symbolizes harmony, balance, and peace.

Festival Walk, 80 Tat Chee Ave., Hong Kong, +852 2787 2268, qeelin.com, and additional locations.

BONNAE GOKSON

HONG KONG'S CHICEST RESTAURATEUR, TAKES FIVE

The creative force behind Hong Kong's most fashionable restaurants and bakeries, Bonnae Gokson is also a fashion and style icon to boot!

My restaurant, **SEVVA,** at Prince's Building, has the best afternoon-tea experience, and **C'EST LA B CAFE** at Pacific Place has the best sweet treats in town. Book Samuel So at **MANDARIN ORIENTAL'S SALON** for the best pedicure you've ever had. It's a dying art, and So was trained by his famous father to use the sharpest knives and blades for the prettiest feet!

SEVVA, Prince's Building, 25/F, 10 Chater Rd., Central, Hong Kong, +852 2537 1388, sevva.hk.

C'EST LA B CAFÉ, Shop 202, 2/F, Pacific Place, 88 Queensway, Admiralty, Hong Kong, +852 2536 0173, msbscakery.hk.

MANDARIN ORIENTAL HONG KONG SALON, 5 Connaught Rd., Central, Central, Hong Kong, +852 2825 4888, mandarinoriental.com/hongkong/luxury-spa

ONLINE SHOPPING TIP

"I love Hong Kong designer Johanna Ho's online store johannaho.com. She has mega-cute and wearable womenswear and I like to support local designers," says Grace Lam. "Her knitwear collection is to die for and she ships internationally."

Marie France Van Damme

Clothes for the woman for whom every day is a holiday. The designer launched her namesake luxury resortwear collection in 2011, and it has since grown into a global lifestyle brand selling elegant yet relaxed swimwear, caftans, maxi dresses, and more that can take you from the beach to dinner.
IFC Mall, Podium 3, 8 Finance St., Central, +852 2882 9088, mariefrancevandamme.com, and additional locations.

Sasa

"You can find obscure Korean and Japanese skin care products and makeup here," accessories designer Fiona Kotur Marin says of this chain with more than a dozen locations. "I recently bought tattoos that you apply on your eyelids to resemble ornate makeup. It's great for unique beauty products."
G/F&2/F, Leighton Centre, 77 Leighton Rd., Causeway Bay, Hong Kong, +852 2555 0806, sasa.com, and additional locations.

Shanghai Tang

This international clothing company was founded in Hong Kong in 1994, and purchased by luxury conglomerate Richemont in 1998. There are forty-eight boutiques worldwide, selling brilliantly hued silk and cashmere ready-to-wear with a Chinese touch, cheongsams and mandarin suits, cardigans with silk linings, silk pajamas, lacquered boxes, and more. The stores also offer an Imperial Tailoring Service.
1 Duddell St., Central, Hong Kong, +852 2525 7333, shanghaitang.com, and additional locations.

SHANGHAI

CHINA

10 Corso Como

In 2013 the Milan-based concept store opened a Shanghai branch with four floors of art, design, and fashion, plus a bookstore, exhibition space, and an Italian restaurant.

1717 West Nanjing Rd., Jing'An District, Shanghai 200040, +86 21 6286-1011, 10corsocomo.com.

Alter

This multi-brand and lifestyle concept store opened in 2010, offering an alternative to luxury megabrands—its name is short for *alternative*—and has become a cornerstone of the city's new fashion scene. The stock is a cross section of eclectic women's fashion from Europe and Asia (Thakoon, Jason Wu, Simone Rocha, Charlotte Olympia), as well as apothecary items, all in a stunning space inspired by M.C. Escher's descending and ascending stairs.

Xintiandi Style, 245 Madang Rd., Lu Wan District, Shanghai 200021, +86 21 6302-9889, alterstyle.com

Dongliang

This is the place to get schooled about the best new Chinese designers. Located in a three-story lane house with lots of nooks and crannies to explore, Dongliang promotes homegrown talent, including Uma Wang, Yirantian Guo, Deep Moss, and He Yang, by supporting brands with marketing and mentorship, and organizing contingents of Chinese designers to travel to fashion weeks around the world. There's a second store in Beijing.

184 Fumin Rd., Jing'An District, Shanghai 200000, +86 21 3469-6926, dongliangchina.com.

Erdos 1436

China's answer to Loro Piana, Erdos 1436 is a luxury cashmere purveyor with a pared-back collection of ready-to-wear for men and women. It's no coincidence that Erdos lent its cashmere production supply services to the likes of Hermès, Burberry, and, yes, Loro Piana before launching its own brand in 2007. The company recently hired Graeme Black, a designer with luxury experience, to give it a more fashionable spin.

Shanghai Gulf, 1118 Pudong South Rd., Pudong New District, Shanghai 200120, +86 21 6888-1436, 1436erdos.com, and additional locations.

Grace Chen

Chen was hailed by the *South China Morning Post* in 2015 as "the power dresser . . . whom China's top-achieving women turn to." She worked as a designer in New York and Los Angeles before returning to Shanghai in 2009 to establish her own brand. Her made-to-order collection includes elegant evening gowns and cocktail dresses, chic day and business wear with an Asian spin. Her first boutique is located in Shanghai's former French Concession building, which also includes a gallery, library, movie theater, and fashion lounge to cater to China's high rollers, including the country's first lady.

1515 Hua Shan Rd. (French Concession), Changning District, Shanghai 200052, gracechenstyle.com

Guo Pei Xi

China's most famous couturier, Guo Pei, shot to international stardom when she dressed Rihanna for the 2015 Met Gala in a regal yellow cape gown with a train that went on for days. She opened this store for her (slightly) more accessible demi-couture wedding gown collection. Instead of a three-month lead-time, dresses can be made within two weeks. Prices are still high, but not as high as for her couture gowns, which can run in the $200,000 to $500,000 range, and are sold through her bespoke Rose Studio in Beijing or at her store in Paris.

South Bund 22, 22 Zhongshan Dong Er Rd., Huangpu District, Shanghai 200000, +86 21 5352-0796, guo-pei.fr.

Maison Charles Philip

The story of this made-in-China shoe brand started when founder Charles Philip had one of his blue-and-white-striped shirts crafted into a loafer by a Shanghai cobbler on Mao Ming Road. Now an international business, the brand produces chic loafers, smoking slippers, and sneakers in every color and pattern imaginable.

101 Gao An Rd., Suite B-2, Xuhui District, Shanghai 200031, +86 21 6422-6982, charlesphilipshanghai.com.

OOAK

This jewel box of a retail space showcases indie designers of costume jewelry, accessories, gifts, housewares, art pieces, and books, including Sharouk, Gentle Monster, Celestine, Delfina Delettrez, and Lizzie Fortunato.

No.30, 820 Nong, JingAn District, Shanghai 200000, +86 21 5424-8929, theooak.com.

One by One

Founded in 2003, One by One claims to be the first independent designer collection store in China. Designers Qiu Hao (winner of the 2008 Woolmark

GRACE CHEN

Prize) and Wang Chuqiao (her collection is Neither Nor) opened the store on Changle Road to showcase their minimalist avant-garde designs, alongside other top Chinese designers, including Masha Ma and Yun Linn. There are several branches in China, but the Shanghai store is the flagship.

Xintiandi Style, 245 Ma Dang Rd., Huangpu District, Shanghai 200000, +86 21 3331-2627, onebyonestudio.com, and additional locations.

Project Aegis

This two-story menswear temple combines contemporary labels (Kapital, Rag & Bone, Public School) with its own understated tailored brand. There's also a café. A must-see.

1 Taojiang Rd., Xuhui District, Shanghai 200000, +86 21 5403-9869, projectaegis.com and additional locations.

Shang Xia

China's first homegrown luxury brand, Shang Xia is backed by Hermès, and features furniture, decorative objects, clothing, accessories, and rotating exhibitions. The spare, blond-wood interior was designed by Japanese architect Kengo Kuma. Some of the items are reminiscent of Hermès products, including printed silk scarves, enamel bracelets, and bamboo pendants, but with an emphasis on materials and crafts native to China.

233 Middle Huai Hai Rd., Huangpu District, Shanghai 200000, +86 21 8017-9777, shang-xia.com, and additional locations.

Spin Ceramics

"A very chic ceramic store that I always find myself at to purchase tableware and kitchen accessories," says designer Tadashi Shoji of this destination for handmade vases, chopstick rests, and dim sum paperweights packaged in bamboo steamers. "It's not always cheap, but you can find great little treasures or bits of inspiration when visiting."

360 Kangding Rd., Jing'An District, Shanghai 200000, +86 21 6279-2545, spinceramics.com, and additional locations.

Triple Major

This destination for playful, indie fashion and design opened on Shaoxing Lu, a historic publishing street, in 2012, and eventually expanded from the ground floor to occupy the whole four-story building. In addition to Henrik Vibskov, Bless, Eatable of Many Orders, and other labels, you'll find home accessories, indie magazines, and artisan-made crafts.

25 Shaoxing Rd., Huangpu District, Shanghai 200000, +86 180 2100-2509, triple-major.com/shanghai, and additional locations.

Uma Wang

China's biggest international fashion success story, Wang is known for her oversized cuts, avant-garde draping techniques, and texture combinations. She studied in London at the prestigious Central Saint Martins and has shown her collections around the world. In 2012, Wang was selected to be the first Chinese designer to take part in the inaugural CFDA/China Exchange Program.

299 Fuxing West Rd., Xuhui District, Shanghai 200000, +86 21 6262-2032, umawang.com, and additional locations.

Xinlelu

Xinlelu highlights indie designers with the goal of creating what the website describes as a "new modern Shanghai girl." You'll find an edited collection of clothing, accessories, and gifts from China (Kun Man Ma, Sefhyir) and abroad (Alice & Trixie, Garance Doré for Rifle Paper).

414 Shaan Xi Bei Rd. (close to Plaza 66), Jing'An District, Shanghai 20000, +86 21 5213-3301, xinlelu.com.

Ziggy Chen

Shanghai-based designer Ziggy Chen established his namesake label in 2012, and has attracted international stockists based on his edgy but wearable menswear designs that incorporate prints on century-old Chinese and European silhouettes.

204/2F No. 6 Building, 123 Xing Ye Rd., Luwan District, Shanghai 200000, +86 21 3331-2968, ziggychen.com, and additional location in Beijing.

BEIJING

CHINA

Anchoret

This Beijing-based fashion boutique founded in 2011 is located in the heart of the Sanlitun shopping district. A multi-label boutique, it's been dedicated to bringing fashion to Beijing from the beginning. Yohji Yamamoto, Vetements, Yang Li, Lemaire, Undercover, Taichi Murakami, and more are represented.

Sanlitun Bei 25 Hao Lou, Beijing, +86 10 8400 2677, anchoret-beijing.com.

Brand New China

Opened by Chinese media veteran Hung Huang (known as "the Oprah of China"), and located in the basement of Tai Koo Li North, Brand New China brings together inventive clothing, shoes, bags, and accessories from a variety of local designers. A must-shop destination for cutting-edge talent.

NLG-09A, B/1F, Taikooli North, 11 Sanlitun Rd., Chaoyang District, Beijing, 100027, +86 10 6416 9045, brandnewchina.cn.

ONLINE SHOPPING TIP

Maison Charles Phillip Shanghai (**charlesphilipshanghai.com**) ships slippers internationally. Spin Ceramics (**spinceramics.com**) also has international shipping, as well as a brick-and-mortar store in New York City. **LaneCrawford.com** stocks a number of fabulous Chinese labels, including Shushu/Tong, Xiao Li, and Helen Lee, and ships internationally. **Modaoperandi.com** stocks several Chinese designers on the rise, including Huishan Zhang, known for his elegant, East-meets-West style.

Designer Tadashi Shoji, who splits his time between Los Angeles and China, recommends **world.Taobao.com**. "It's the largest online shopping market place in China. It's similar to eBay, but it is much more efficient, with extremely low prices."

SEOUL

SOUTH KOREA

Aland

Sometimes referred to as the Korean Urban Outfitters, this funky chainlet sells everything from new and emerging contemporary pop-culture-influenced Korean collections (SJYP, Stereo Vinyl Collection, Salad Bowls, Margarin Fingers, Fleamadonna) to vintage clothing and even iron-on patches, all at reasonable prices. There are several branches in Seoul and across Asia.

53-6, Myeongdong 2-ga, Jung-gu, Seoul, +82 2-3210-5890, and additional locations, alandglobal.com.

Beaker

This multi-brand shop is part of Samsung's Cheil Industries and stocks a wide range of contemporary brands, including Opening Ceremony, Our Legacy, Wood Wood, Rag & Bone, Melissa, Karen Walker, Building Block, and Common Projects, as well as hosting shop-in-shops for Korean brands.

78-6, Cheongdam-dong, Gangnam-gu, +82 2-543-1270, and additional locations, beakerstore.com.

Boon The Shop

"A fashion girl's mecca," says Olivia Kim of this Peter Marino–designed crown jewel of Seoul multi-label boutiques, which sells Céline, Rochas, Martin Margiela, Vetements, Balenciaga, and other top international labels. It also peddles Korea's own street-style-driven fun furs (KYE) and cheeky graphic separates (Kiok). "Located in the überchic neighborhood of Gangnam, Boon showcases the biggest brands in fashion as well as the coolest young, emerging brands to come out of Seoul, fashion's newest darling city. The level of service, the visual merchandising, and the great selection make this one of my faves," says Kim. Also has a café and a Japanese restaurant.

21 Apgujeong-ro 60-gil, Gangnam-gu, Seoul, +82 2-2056-1234, boontheshop.com.

Doota

In Dongdaemun, the retail and wholesale district that never sleeps, are several high-rise malls selling trendy clothing and accessories. The best is Doota, which has about 500 boutiques across a labyrinthine eight floors and devotes the basement to up-and-coming talent, some of whom eventually graduate to the Seoul Fashion Week runways. Open twenty-four hours, it's easy to lose track of time here. Consider yourself warned.

Doosan Tower, 18-12 Euljiro 6-ga, Jung-gu, +82 2-3398-3034, and additional locations, doota.com.

Ecru

"Located in the basement, it's not easy to find even with the small signs," says Minyeong Kim, brand director for Gentle Monster, of this boutique that stocks European and Japanese brands, including Acne, WTAPS, MSGM, Undercover, and its own in-house line. "It is quite like LNCC in London, but they carry uncommon things for Korea, so it's fun."

656-10 Sinsa-dong, Gangnam-gu, Seoul, South Korea, +82 2-545-7780, ecru.co.k.

Galleria

This department store has been described as the Korean version of Bergdorf Goodman. You'll find the crème de la crème of luxe labels, including Goyard bags, Tom Ford clothing, and Fred jewelry, alongside a great selection of contemporary Korean labels such as Low Classic, Pushbutton, Wooyoungme, and Lucky Chouette.

343 Apgujeong-ro, Gangnam-gu, Seoul, dept.galleria.co.kr.

Gentle Monster

This was the first flagship for the cool Korean eyewear brand, which has now expanded to several locations in Seoul and internationally. Set on two levels, one of which has a cactus garden, the store doesn't disappoint. Each Gentle Monster location has a different vibe.

192-10 Nonhyeon-Dong, Gannam-Gu, Seoul, +82 2-3443-2126, gentlemonster .com, and additional locations.

Goen J

Born in Korea, Goen Jong spent seven years in Paris before launching her own line in 2012. Her sculptural yet romantic pieces (ruffles, lace, and eyelet are mainstays, used in modern ways) have earned her an impressive roster of international retailers, including Barneys New York, Opening Ceremony, and Shopbop.com. This is her flagship.

546-18, Sinsa-dong, Gangnam-gu, Seoul, +82 70-4408-1754, goenj.com.

Gwangjang Market

While most people visit this traditional street market for food, it also has a bounty of textiles, traditional Korean *hanbok* outfits, used clothing, and accessories (if you have the patience to sift through the piles).

88 Changgyeonggung-ro, Jongno-gu, Seoul, +82 2-2267-0291.

Insa-dong

"One of the most memorable attractions in Seoul, it represents the focal point of Korean traditional culture and crafts," says fashion publicist Natalie Choy of this shopping district anchored by the main street of Insadong-gil, which connects to a multitude of alleys full of modern galleries and tea shops. "Stores in Insa-dong specialize in a wide variety of goods that can be purchased only in Korea such as *hanbok* [traditional clothing], *hanji* [traditional paper], traditional teas, pottery, and folk crafts." The street is closed to traffic on weekends.

62, Insadong-gil, Jongno-gu, Seoul.

Jardin de Chouette

Designer Kim Jae Hyun's young, fun collections (think, denim culottes, mixed plaid shirtdresses) have made fans of model Irene Kim and other Seoul tastemakers. Her lower priced Lucky Chouette label is also a hit, with printed backpacks, striped sailor shirts, velvet high top sneakers, and plenty of items featuring the brand's owl logo.

21-15 Cheongdam-dong, Gangnam-gu, Seoul, and other locations, +82 2-3444-1002, jdchouette.com.

Juun.J

One of the most important figures in Korean men's fashion, Juun.J debuted his first collection under the name Lone Costume in 1991, and launched his namesake label in 2007. Known for his directional collections, he describes his look as "street tailoring" (drapey trenches, reinvented zoot suits, and other oversized silhouettes). His collections are stocked at Dover Street Market, L'Eclaireur, and other influential retailers around the world. He has also collaborated with other brands, Adidas and Reebok among them.

4f, 343 Apgujeong Ro, Gangnam Gu, Seoul, +82 2-3449-4144, juunj.com.

Koon With a View

This Korean brand and high-end boutique sells J.W. Anderson, Alexander Wang, and other contemporary labels in a dynamic-looking space. A bit like Intermix but edgier.

21-12 Cheong-dam dong, Gangnam-gu, Seoul, +82 2-548-450, koon-korea.com, and additional locations.

Low Classic

One of the coolest contemporary brands to come out of Seoul, Low Classic is minimalist but whimsical (think Céline meets Tibi), with lots of asymmetrical wrap skirts, slip dresses, and sliced knits. For a recent collection, designer Lee Myeong Sin reflected on women's bodies by showing crisp white suits and slip dresses featuring ink sketches of female forms. Accessories are also strong, including square-toe mules and fold-detail bags.

554 Sinsa-dong, Gangnam-gu, Seoul, +82 2-516-2004, lowclassic.com.

IRENE KIM

NEW DESIGNER FAVORITES

Dubbed by Vogue *as an "ambassador to the buzzing South Korean fashion scene" and* Women's Wear Daily *as fashion's "It Girl," Irene Kim is the host of popular Korean fashion and beauty programs such as* K-Style*. She is at the forefront of the Korean entertainment establishment, and she represents the emergence of Korean talents who are influencing the marketplaces of East Asia and beyond.*

A great place to discover new talent is **COMMON GROUND,** a concept shopping venue made out of shipping containers with emerging new Korean designers, lifestyle items, accessories and Korean brands.

My favorite only-in-Seoul experiences are twenty-four-hour food delivery, Dongdaemun night shopping and the best fried chicken and beer in the world!

COMMON GROUND, 17-1 Jayang-dong, Gwangjin-gu, Seoul, +82 2-467-2747, common-ground.co.kr.

MIK247

Owned by stylist Chae Han-Suk, who works with some of K-pop's leading stars, MIK stands for Made in Korea. Suk exclusively stocks homegrown designers and collaborates with them on unique pieces, some of which are relatively affordable.

2/F, Shinwoo Building, 664-19 Sinsa-dong, Gangnam-gu, Seoul, +82 2-3446-8556, facebook.com/mik247.

MMMG

MMMG (Millimeter Milligram) puts the focus on the simple things in life by selling books and stationery and small quantities of clothing and accessories with a distinct point of view. A favorite of handbag designer Clare Vivier's.

240 Itaewon-ro, Yongsan-gu, Seoul, +82 2-549-1520, mmmg.net.

Monday Edition

Model/tastemaker Irene Kim loves the idiosyncratic jewelry from this local label, including ball-and-stick bracelets, twisted leather earrings, shell flower necklaces, and more.

1F, 57, Daesagwan-ro 11-gil, Yongsan-gu, Seoul, +82 70-4284-5923, Monday-edition.co.kr.

My Boon

Younger sibling of the Boon store, this space focuses on edgier brands, including Chrome Hearts, Visvim, Linda Farrow, Grenson, and Garret Leight, and stocks lots of gifts. It's inside the Shinsegae department store.

1F, SSG, Pie'N Polus, 4-1, Cheongdam-Dong, Kangnam-Gu, Seoul, +82 2-6947-1270, myboon.co.kr

Playnomore

This whimsical accessories brand turns out tasty treasures such as classic frame bags adorned with winking eye or red lip patterns.

60, Namdaemunggo, Jung-gu, Seoul, +82 2-3789-5526, playnomore.co.kr, and additional locations.

Queenmama Market

This seven-story concept store brings a bit of Los Angeles to Seoul. It was founded by Korean designers Kang Jin-Young and Yoon Han-Hee, who worked in New York and L.A. before returning to Korea to bring a taste of the laid-back West Coast lifestyle to the fashion retail scene. The building mixes nature and shopping, with clothes nestled among gardening tools and plants, housewares, stationery and candles, and a beautiful rooftop café, Manufact.

50, Apgujeong-ro 46-gil, Gangnam-gu, Seoul, queenmamamarket.com.

Rare Market

Opened in 2014 by lifelong friends Dami Kwon, sister of K-pop star

GENTLE MONSTER

G-Dragon, and Jessica Jung, Rare Market is a regular stop on the international fashion circuit for street-style stars (Miroslava Duma) and celebs (Rihanna) alike. The store specializes in the newest, coolest brands, whether that's Jacquemus, Marques'Almeida, and Faith Connexion from Europe, or KYE from Korea (a Rihanna favorite). It also has its own in-house label that launched in 2015 with a lookbook starring Leandra Medine.

95-5 Cheongdam-dong, Gangnam-gu, Seoul, raremarket.com.

Shinsegae

"You can spend the day there, it's a whole world," says Chrome Hearts designer Laurie Lynn Stark of Shinsegae, one of the best department stores in the world. Shinsegae carries every brand imaginable, has a rooftop park and restaurant, upscale food courts, and a cinema. "You are sitting on the roof having lunch, looking at the mountains with a trolley going up the mountain, and then there's a Jeff Koons Sacred Heart sculpture next to you. It's beautiful," she says.

52-50 Chungmuro 1ga, Seoul, +82 2-1588-1234, shinsegae.com.

SJYP

Husband-and-wife team Steve J and Yoni P are stalwarts of Seoul Fashion Week. The duo met in London at Central Saint Martins, and founded their label there in 2006. Now based in Seoul, they specialize in edgy denim and utilitarian pieces at contemporary prices. This is their flagship store.

1F, 685-12 Hannam-dong, Seoul, +82 70-7730-9988, steveyoniworld.com.

HOW AIMEE SONG DOES SEOUL

Instagram star Aimee Song, creator of the popular fashion blog **SONG OF STYLE***, has more than 4 million online fans who follow her tips on fashion, design, food, and travel. A frequent traveler to fashion weeks around the world, she is also the author of the book* Capture My Style.

BOON THE SHOP is like the Korean version of Barneys, but done even better. It's a super well-curated, multi-brand high-end fashion store with amazing interiors and futuristic architecture spanned across many levels. It's easy to get lost here and for any design lover, it's the best place to be lost! Even the elevators are super cool and well designed.

I actually found **MSMR SOCK STORE (also called Ladies and Gentlemen)** through a graphic designer I was following on instagram, @venusmansion. He did all of the labeling and design and I'm so happy I discovered it. They make the best customizable gift boxes. The whole experience is really fun—choosing the box and stickers to decorate it with. Not to mention all the unique socks. I never thought socks would make such a great gift until I came here!

There are a bunch of **GENTLE MONSTER** stores in Seoul and the surrounding cities. They're one of my favorite sunglasses brands and each store has a distinct concept. One I went to has a butcher shop theme. Another revolved around a traditional Korean spa with sinks, tubs, and amazing tile work. I love to see how they showcase the sunglasses and create unique experiences.

DONGDAEMUN DESIGN PLAZA

DONGDAEMUN DESIGN PLAZA is so stunning. It was designed by Zaha Hadid who is one of my idols. It's part museum, part exhibition space, and also where they hold Seoul Fashion Week.

INNISFREE is a great store for any K-beauty beginner. For the most part, getting good Korean beauty products in Korea is easy but for someone who wants a one-stop, this is a good place to start. They have great products for both men and women and what I like about this wallet friendly beauty store is that they carry products with ingredients sourced from Jeju island which is very unique to Korea.

BOON THE SHOP, 17 Apgujeong-ro 60-gil, Gangnam-gu, Seoul, +82 2-2056-1234, boontheshop.com.

MSMR SOCK STORE, 247-1, Itaewon-2-dong, Yongsan-gu, Seoul.

GENTLE MONSTER, , 192-10 Nonhyeon-Dong, Gannam-Gu, Seoul, +82 2-3443-2126, and additional locations, gentlemonster.com.

DONGDAEMUN DESIGN PLAZA, 281 Eulji-ro, Jung-gu, Seoul, ddp.or.kr.

INNISFREE, Myeong-dong Store, 64-2 Myeong-dong II(1)-ga Jung-gu, Seoul, +82 2- 776-0117, and additional locations, innisfreeworld.com

ONLINE SHOPPING TIP

Aland's website ships internationally (alandglobal.com). If you want to purchase merchandise from a Korean site that does not support overseas delivery, momokorea.com can help. An online middleman, it works with top Korean labels, including SJYP, Steve J and Yoni P, Stereo Vinyls, and more. Enter payment info on MomoKorea's website and it will do the rest. Another site of note: Peach & Lily (peachandlily.com). Founded by K-beauty star Alicia Yoon, it's a great resource for Korean and Japanese beauty brands.

Space Mue

This menswear concept store (a must for US avant-street designer Chris Stamp when he's in Seoul) caters to the K-pop set with trendy items from Lanvin, Valentino, and others, in an imposing gallerylike space.

93-6 Chungdam-dong, Seoul, +82 2-3446-8074, spacemue.com.

Slow Steady Club & Café

Dedicated to the values of "slow and steady," this store specializes in apron dresses, pullovers, simple coats, and other pared-down basics built to stand the test of time (think, brands like Champion, Common Projects, and Still by Hand). It also boasts a café and gallery.

130-1 Palpan Jongno-gu, Seoul, +82 2-725-1301.

Tom Greyhound

This multi-brand store, which has an outpost in Paris, stocks the best international designers alongside up-and-coming Korean labels. Interior designer Brigette Romanek calls it a "hipster haven curated with items you haven't seen before. They carry some collections you know, but they pick the pieces that other stores don't. It's fun in there."

10-3, Dosan-daero 45-gil, Gangnam-gu, Seoul, +82 2-3442-3696.

Worksout

With a spaceship-like silver facade, this three-story streetwear destination features more than forty labels from the US, Japan, and Korea, including Carhartt, Reigning Champ, Obey, and Vans.

20-4 Seolleung-ro 157-gil, Gangnam-gu, Seoul.

MUMBAI

INDIA

Tribe by Amrapali

One of India's most well-known jewelry brands, Amrapali was founded in 1978 by Rajesh Ajmera and Rajiv Arora. The brand is influenced by the country's varied cultural traditions, as interpreted by 1,200 craftsmen. Amrapali jewelry is available in more than 36 outlets. You can find everything from a pair of gold-plate floral jaali hoop earrings for less than $50 to a multicolored sapphire bangle for $10,000.

Juhu Rd., Mumbai 400049, + 91 22 26125001/5002, tribebyamrapali .com, and additional locations.

Anita Dongre

Inspired by Rajasthan's rich heritage, this designer brand showcasing Indian aesthetics with a modern sensibility was thrust into the international spotlight in 2016 when Kate Middleton wore one of Dongre's breezy, bohemian print dresses during the royal visit to India and Bhutan. (Demand for the style crashed the designer's website.)

Everest Classic, Linking Rd., Khar (West), Mumbai 400052, +91 22 67411504, anitadongre.com, and additional locations.

Anokhi

Beloved around the world for preserving the tradition of Indian hand-block printing. Through Faith Singh, Anokhi's British designer, this ancient textile art has been revived in modern designs and exotic patterns ranging from pastel florals to dramatic geometrics. Anokhi is involved with educational and social projects in Rajasthan, where the company is based and its products produced. Anokhi first appeared in London in 1970. Printing is done twice yearly in limited collections. At the shops, you can find everything from tunics and robes to pillowcases, scarves, place mats, and cosmetic pouches.

Rasik Niwas, Metro Motors Lane, Dr. A. R. Rangnekar Marg., Mumbai 400007, +91 22 23685761, +91 22 23685308, anohki.com, and additional locations.

Bombay Electric

"For eclectic fashion by local and regional Indian designers," says costume designer Arianne Phillips of this Indian concept store, which is also a favorite of fashion consultant/author Fern Mallis. Opposite the five-star Taj Mahal Palace and Towers and Gateway of India on "the Bond Street of Mumbai," and a stone's throw from a busy street filled with food stalls, Bombay Electric is housed in a historic heritage building. Restoration and redesign exposed antique interiors featuring original tree-size teak beams that were a gift from the king of Burma, coupled with sculptural white racks and industrial trunks. This is the place to find everything from Manish Arora's kaleidoscopic pop clothing to earrings shaped like Valium capsules, whimsical clutches, coffee-table books, and vintage Bollywood posters.

1 Reay House, Best Marg., Mumbai, 400001, +91 22 22876276, facebook.com/bombayelectric.

Bungalow 8

Mumbai's first concept store, Bungalow 8 specializes in unconventional Indian-inspired antiques and fashion finds, and is a must-shop in Mumbai for Fern Mallis, Divia Harilela (and Madonna and Sting). Maithili Ahluwalia's bungalow is devoted to spotlighting the best of Indian design, from handmade ceramics to salvaged factory lights and baroque picture frames. Think ABC Carpet & Home, only in India and underneath a cricket stadium.

Inside Wankhede Stadium, North Stand, E & F Block, D Rd., Churchgate, Mumbai 400020, +91 22 22819880/1/2, bungaloweight.com.

D Popli & Sons

Jewelry for all price points and occasions, all of it irresistible. In the front section of this unassuming store you'll find costume jewelry and silver pieces starting at less than $50. In the back is the finer stuff, contemporary-looking pieces set with diamonds, rubies, and semiprecious stones, including basic stud earrings and edgier three-finger rings.

Chhatrapati Shivaji Maharaj Marg., Apollo Bandar, Colaba, Mumbai 400001, +91 22 22021694.

Good Earth

"Love shopping for linens and china here," says Arianne Phillips of India's most famous home design company, founded in Mumbai in 1996. Good Earth is known for its crafts-focused approach to luxury and for reviving the authentic skills of the crafts communities of India, by producing handmade Kansa tableware, wallpaper, quilts, and more. The brand also has a line of clothing made of chintz textiles.

2 Reay House, Colaba, Mumbai, 400001, +91 22 22021030, goodearth.in, and additional locations.

Le Mill

"The colette of Mumbai," says Arianne Phillips of this iconic store, where global fashion brands (Balenciaga, Peter Pilotto, Sacai) sit alongside the new Indian voices of fashion (Dhruv Kapoor, Nimish Shah). "They have a great café and are upstairs from a delicious restaurant." (The restaurant is a branch of Indigo Deli, mentioned by Kavita Daswani.) The store is housed in a 1930s warehouse that was originally used as a rice mill. The founders have international experience at Bergdorf Goodman, L'Oréal, and Condé Nast.

1st Floor, Pheroze Building, Colaba, Mumbai, 400005, +91 22 22041926/27, lemillindia.com.

NEW DELHI

INDIA

Dili Haat Market

"A focal point for artisans from every region of India to come and showcase their beautiful handicrafts," fashion editor/designer Tania Mohan says of this open-air crafts bazaar. "You'll find everything ranging from exquisite silk embroideries to mirror works to reinterpreted threadwork to pashminas. The handicrafts are always changing, and the prices very fair. For my brand Tabla, which is wholly inspired by and made in India, this hub is a rich source of inspiration and the reason why I visit it at least a few times a year. It allows me to research such things as new weaves, techniques, and shawl compositions. I'd recommend a visit to everyone."

Sri Aurobindo Marg, Laxmi Bai Nagar, New Delhi 110023, +91 98 480 22338.

ONLINE SHOPPING TIP

PerniasPopUpShop.com is a comprehensive e-commerce site for jewelry, accessories, saris, tunics, and gowns by top Indian designers, including Sabyasachi, Manish Arora, Tarun Tahiliani, Amrapali, Anita Dongre, and more. It's curated by leading stylist and Bollywood costume designer Pernia Qureshi. Offers worldwide shipping.

KAVITA DASWANI

AN INSIDER'S GUIDE TO INDIA

Kavita Daswani is an Indian-American author who has published eight novels, which have been translated into seventeen languages. She is also a journalist covering fashion, beauty, travel, design, and celebrities for a range of global publications. A former fashion editor for the South China Morning Post *in Hong Kong and an Asian correspondent for* Women's Wear Daily, *both of which she still contributes to, she currently writes for the* Los Angeles Times, *and the international editions of* Vogue, Condé Nast Traveler, *and* Grazia.

In Delhi, India's top designers have made their homes in **EMPORIO MALL.** Next door to anchor brands like **LOUIS VUITTON** and **DIOR,** shoppers will find homegrown couturiers like **MONISHA JAISING** (shop number 331, monishajaising.com), known for svelte evening gowns, and **TARUN TAHILIANI** (shop number 351, taruntahiliani.com), who dresses Bollywood's biggest stars and is notable for his avant-garde approach to the traditional sari. While stoles and shawls are a dime a dozen in India, Delhi boutique **JANAVI** (shop 323, janavi.com) specializes in them: look for cashmere and merino wool shawls featuring modern motifs. Nestled amid all this beauty is **ZEST RESTAURANT,** popular for its multiple cuisines (Indian, Asian, European) and expansive terrace for a day when the smog is bearable.

Outside of Emporio, **OGAAN** is a multi-designer boutique chain with several outposts throughout the city. It's beloved by the fashion set for its curated offerings: stop in and find crisp linen shirts, flowing tunics, wide-leg pants, and elegant ethnic wear. End the day with a visit to the **AMBIKA PILLAI** salon, where Delhi's beautiful people go to be fussed over before a night out. You can get a blow-dry anywhere, but India is known for its lush, luxurious head massages using coconut, olive, or mustard oil. No matter

In Mumbai, stroll down **COLABA CAUSEWAY** for casual, locally made garments (cotton tunics, woven leather sandals). At **PALLADIUM MALL**, drop by **GLOBAL DESI** (second level), an India-based brand that fuses local fabrics and traditional patterns with a Western aesthetic and very appealing prices: breezy maxi dresses, cute dungarees with elephant prints, long tunics to be paired with jeans or belted and worn as a dress. Most items cost less than $50.

Similarly, **FAB INDIA**, with a flagship store in the trendy Kala Ghoda district, features clothing made by local craftspeople and modeled on Western wardrobe staples.

At the higher end, the city's socialites flock to the studio of **SABYASACHI MUKHERJEE**, whose extravagant pieces recall the nation's royal pedigree. Designer Tahrun Tahiliani's multi-brand boutique **ENSEMBLE** has long been a draw for brides-to-be compiling their trousseaux (even in modern India, this is a thing). There, seek out a hot favorite: **ANAMIKA KHANNA**, whose modern, almost architectural aesthetic has elevated Indian fashion to another level.

After a spot of shopping at **ENSEMBLE**, stop for lunch at **INDIGO DELI** for fusion offerings like pepper chicken stuffed into a paper-thin chapati-style wrap, or hop into a cab and adjourn to **THE DOME**, the rooftop bar at the Intercontinental overlooking the glittering lights of Marine Bay and the Indian Ocean.

DLF EMPORIO, 4, Nelson Mandela Marg, Vasant Kunj, New Delhi 110070, +91 11 461 6666, dlfemporio.com.

OGAAN FLAGSHIP STORE, H-2 Hauz Khas Village, New Delhi 110016, + 91 97 119 91998, +91 11 269 67595, ogaan.com.

AMBIKA PILLAI, South Extension, D-16 South Extension Part 2, 3rd floor, New Delhi 110049, +91 11 400 10000/400 10200, ambikapillai.com, and additional locations.

COLABA CAUSEWAY, Maharashtra, Mumbai 400005.

PALLADIUM MALL, 462, High St. Phoenix, Senapati Bapat Marg, Lower Parel, Mumbai 400013, +91 22 43339994, palladiummumbai.com.

FAB INDIA, Jeroo Building, 137, M.G. Rd., Kala Ghoda, Mumbai 400001, +91 22 22626539/40, fabindia.com.

SABYASACHI MUKHERJEE, Ador House, 6K Dubash Marg, Mumbai 400001, +91 22 22044774/75, sabyasachi.com.

ENSEMBLE, Great Western Building, 130/132 Shahid Bhagat Singh Rd., Mumbai 400023, +91 22 40564825/40564800, ensembleindia.com.

INDIGO DELI, Palladium Mall, Level 1, Senapati Bapat Marg, Lower Parel, Mumbai 400013, +91 22 4366 6666, and additional locations.

THE DOME, InterContinental Hotel, 135, Marine Drive, B Rd., Church Gate, Mumbai 400020, +91 22 39879999, ihg.com/intercontinental/hotels/us/en/mumbai/bomhb/hoteldetaili.

bambah

MIDDLE EAST

SAUDI ARABIA

UNITED ARAB EMIRATES

RIYADH

SAUDI ARABIA

O100°

"As you enter, you are taken through a tunnel of hanging Saudi roses, and your olfactory journey begins," says Marriam Mossalli, a Jeddah-based fashion consultant and editor. "Then a team of expert noses gives you a guided tour of the different offerings, from regional brands such as Tola to Histoires de Parfums."

Boutique # 10, Akaria Plaza, Olaya Street, Olaya, Riyadh 12244, +966 11 293 1119, O-100.com.

D'NA

In the heart of Riyadh, D'NA is an independent voice in the Middle East fashion scene. The space is a beautifully curated magazine come to life. Within its loftlike gallery space, you'll find specially commissioned pieces by designers and artists, including Jason Wu, Rodarte, Delpozo, The Row, Lisa Marie Fernandez, and Paul Andrew. "The best women's buy in the world," says Cameron Silver. D'NA is also a meeting place, where art exhibitions and film screenings are often held.

6611 Tukassisi St., Al Rehmania, Riyadh 12341, +966 11 419 9966, and an additional location in Doha, dnariyadh.com.

JEDDAH

SAUDI ARABIA

Life

This eclectic streetwear-inspired store stocks Yeezy, Comme des Garçons, Jeremy Scott, KTZ, Wildfox, and more.

Prince Sultan Rd., Al Andalus, Roshana Mall, Jeddah 23433, +966 12 284 4266, and an additional location in Riyadh.

Domvs

This lifestyle boutique (think Anthropologie), which includes a gallery and café, plays host to Homegrown Jeddah, a pop-up market for Middle Eastern designers on the first floor.

Al-Rawdah St., Jeddah 23432, +966 12 661 1447, domvs-ksa.com.

MARRIAM MOSSALLI

BUYING TRADITIONAL ARAB CLOTHING

Marriam Mossalli is the Jeddah-based owner of fashion consulting firm Niche Arabia and creator of the blog ShoesandDrama.com. In recent years, she has emerged as one of the Middle East's most revered fashion experts. As a fashion editor, she has fused cultural heritage with a modern edge, helping to define a new Arabic style. Since 2011, her consultancy firm has catered to high-profile clients, including Burberry, Carolina Herrera, TAG Heuer, and Harvey Nichols, helping them understand and thrive in the Middle Eastern market.

I love traditional clothing. Even as a youth, I would cross-dress and wear the men's *thobe* (a long, crisp white shirtdress that Arab men wear—it's the Bedouin equivalent to the Western business suit). **TOBY** by Hatem Alakeel is one of my favorite Khaleeji menswear brands; he's been called the "Tom Ford of Thobes" because his tailoring is so impeccable.

THAMANYAH from the Emirates is another chic brand; he brings an avant-garde touch to traditional wear—if Hatem is Ford, then Thamanyah's creative director, Ahmed Abdelrahman, is Rick Owens.

I also love *midas*, the traditional men's sandals. You've seen a lot of references to midas sandals from Christian Louboutin to Alexander Wang! My favorite place is downtown, in the old souk, **AL-BALAD,** where you can get custom leather ones made for less than $50.

I love going to downtown Jeddah. Historically, Jeddah was a major port city for ships traveling the Red Sea, which is why even today the traditional souks reflect a history of maritime trade and exchange. Jeddah continues to act as a vital gateway to Mecca (the holy city where Muslims come for pilgrimage), which is why you'll always find visiting Muslims selling their wares, from Russian dolls to Indian herbs and incense.

TOBY, Ameer SultanSt., after Naft Petrol Station beside Gardenia Flower Shop,

CARTEL

DUBAI

UNITED ARAB EMIRATES

Bambah

For three years, Bambah was Dubai's only high-end vintage boutique. It served as an inspirational spot for fashion influencers from all corners of the world. Rasheed has since debuted a vintage-inspired ready-to-wear collection.

The Boulevard, City Walk 2 in Building 13, Dubai, +971 55 224 1538, bambah.com.

Boom and Mellow

This high-end accessories boutique opened its doors in 2005, and has been a destination since for fine and costume jewelry, clutches, hats, bags, belts, shawls, small gift items, and lounge/beach dresses. Designers include Alexis Bittar, Goddis, Jennifer Behr, and Jacquie Aiche.

Town Centre Jumeirah, Ground Floor Shop 21, Jumeirah Beach Rd., Dubai, +971 4 344 4512, shopboomandmellow.com.

Boutique 1

"Dubai has become the Middle East's shopping hub, and while designer flagships are popping up in every corner of every mega-mall, Boutique 1 is a feminine, multi-brand boutique that gives the local fashionistas access to all the brands from London and Paris fashion weeks," says Marriam Mossalli of this destination with locations at Jumeirah Beach Resort and Mall of the Emirates. You'll find designs by Elie Saab, Alexander Wang, Rosie Assoulin, Proenza Schouler, The Row, and Victoria Beckham.

The Walk at Jumeriah Beach Resort, Dubai, +971 4 425 7888, boutique1.com, and additional locations.

By Symphony

Curated by Emirati entrepreneur Salama Alabbar, Symphony showcases designer brands from around the world alongside new and exciting rising stars. By Symphony aims to be a "home away from home," so you can take a load off and stay a while. Clothing by Gucci, Bottega Veneta, Delpozo, Simone Rocha, and Peter Pilotto is stocked alongside items by Dubai-based designer Madiyah Al Sharqi and Saudi designer Razan Alazzouni.

The Dubai Mall, Ground Floor Fashion Ave., Dubai, +971 4 330 8050, bysymphony.com.

cARTel

"Positioning itself as a purveyor of wearable art and showcasing regional designers, cARTel sits among Dubai's leading art galleries in Alserkal Avenue. It hosts pop-ups and screenings while producing its own in-house concept magazine," says Eileen Wallis.

6 Alserkal Ave., Al Quoz 1, St. 17, Dubai, +971 4 388 4341, thecartel.me.

Comptoir 102

"Created by two Parisiennes, this is a one-stop design destination housed in a traditional Dubai villa with an organic kitchen and café as well as housewares, jewelry, and fashion," says Eileen Wallis. Look for Raquel Allegra, Swildens, Jérôme Dreyfuss, Ileana Makri, Pippa Small, and more.

102 Beach Rd., Jumeirah 1, Dubai, +971 4 385 4555, comptoir102.com.

Dubai Mall

Dubai is a city with more than 100 shopping malls, a monthlong shopping festival, and a chain of luxury boutiques named Rodeo Drive (yes, really). The fashion capital of the region features the largest mall on the planet by area, and it has some off-the-hook attractions and amenities, including an indoor theme park, an Olympic-sized ice rink, the Dubai Aquarium and Underwater Zoo, an Armani hotel, a Shake Shack, a personal porter and private locker service for purchases, a walkway to Burj Khalifa (the tallest skyscraper in the world), and, oh yeah, some pretty great shopping, too, with 1,200 retail stores anchored by Galeries Lafayette and Bloomingdale's. There's also an area called the Souk that features gold jewelry, accessories, traditional Arab clothing, and handicraft stores, so you can experience an "authentic" souk in the comfort of a mall. "From glamour gowns to caviar to a huge variety of nice shops, just being in this mall is enough," says Hong Kong restaurateur Bonnae Gokson.

Financial Centre Rd., Downtown Dubai, +971 800 3822 46255, thedubaimall.com.

Etoile

"With a median age of twenty-eight years old, Saudi is a pretty young country in terms of demographics—and Etoile is the multi-brand boutique made for the millennial!" says Marriam Mossalli. "From Anya Hindmarch to Chloé, everything in there is an Instagram-perfect item ready to be hashtagged." Other labels stocked include Camilla, Dior, Nicholas Kirkwood, Prabal Gurung, and Roksanda.

Mall of the Emirates, Dubai, +971 4 341 4166, etoilelaboutique.com, and additional locations.

Global Shopping Village

The Disney World of shopping gives you the chance to shop the entire world in one place, with pavilions themed around all corners of the globe, from the Americas to the Far East. You can find everything from Japanese kimonos to Syrian baklava, and at relatively affordable prices, too. Open seasonally from November to March.

Sheikh Mohammed Bin Zayed Rd., Dubai, +971 4 362 4114, globalvillage.ae.

Gold Souk

Dubai's most famous and most visited souk is all about gold, and you're expected to haggle for it. Also on offer are beautiful textiles and Ali Baba shoes.

54 Al Khor St., Dubai.

iF Boutique

A villa tucked away near the beach in Umm Suqeim has one of Dubai's edgiest selection of designers: Yohji Yamamoto, Rick Owens, Limi Feu, Uma Wang, and Ivan Grundahl. "A true stylist's destination," says Dubai fashion expert Eileen Wallis.

26 Umm Al Sheif Rd., Dubai, +971 4 394 7260, ifboutiquedubai.com.

Level Shoe District

This may be the best shoe store in the world (sorry, Saks Fifth Avenue 1002Shoe), with 96,000 square feet and 400 in-store boutiques, stocking everything from Alaïa and Aquazzura to Sophia Webster, as well as offering shoe styling and restoration services and an on-site foot clinic. "The most comprehensive collection of fashion-forward shoes I have ever seen," says author and journalist Bronwyn Cosgrave. "There are also extremely opulent variations of every style of ultra-fine footwear: sneakers, flats, stilettos. I was particularly taken with the rainbow array of Manolo Blahnik Hangisi flats, which I swear by. Dubai is the only place I have seen this shoe with pearl-embellished buckles."

The Dubai Mall, Ground Floor, Dubai, +971 800 538 3573, levelshoes.com.

Mall of the Emirates

Features nearly 700 stores anchored by the British department store Harvey Nichols, plus Ski Dubai, the famous indoor ski slope, complete with chair lifts.

Mall of the Emirates, Dubai, +971 4 409 9000, malloftheemirates.com.

Mochi

As worn by Gigi Hadid, Kourtney Kardashian, and Chiara Ferragni, this Dubai-based brand is worth getting to know for its fun multiculti-inspired, colorfully embroidered jackets, off-shoulder tops, and fringed clutches. Founder Ayah Tabari, who was born in Palestine, raised in Riyadh and Amman, and studied in London before settling in Dubai, works with artisans all over the world, supporting the communities with job creation and incorporating stylish flourishes from Africa, India, and beyond into her designs.

Dubai Design District Building 9, Office 103, Dubai, +971 4 443 3451, allthingsmochi.com.

O de Rose

Set in a gorgeous residential-style villa far from the mall madness, this concept shop features fashion, accessories, and home décor items from regional designers and artisans.

999 Al Wasl Rd., Umm Suqeim 2, Dubai, +971 4 348 7990, o-derose.com.

Sauce

The trendiest concept boutique in Dubai, Sauce is a must-shop for its whimsical edit of local and international labels, including Zimmermann, Sea, Self-Portrait, Joshua Sanders, Lucy Folk, Sarah's Bags, and its own Made by Sauce collection. Look for banana-embroidered beach bags, flower-festooned sunglasses, and denim skirts with floral and bird appliqués. There are nine stores total, including locations in the Dubai Mall and Village Mall.

The Dubai Mall, Fashion Section, 1st Floor, Dubai, +971 4 339 9696, shopatsauce.com, and additional locations.

Souk Madinat Jumeirah

A re-creation of a traditional Middle Eastern souk, with craftsmen at work, rugs, cushions, Aladdin lamps, and Arabian coffee sets spilling out onto the walkways—only it's indoors and air-conditioned, bonus! This is the place for quality souvenirs.

Madinat Jumeirah Hotel, 6 Al Sufouh Rd., Dubai +971 4 366 8888, jumeirah.com.

Studio 8

Launched in May 2009, Studio 8 features an edited collection of designers from the Middle East and Asia, and is the brainchild of entrepreneur and fashion promoter Sarah Belhasa. If you are looking for the latest *jalabya* and *abaya* trends, Studio 8 offers a range by Khulood Bin Arab, Das Collection, Julea Domani, Sumaya Abdul Razak, and Amira Haroon, among others. You'll also find international designers, including Suneet Varma, Nikasha, Deepika Anand, Rahul and Anushka, Shaila Khan, Zeeshan Bariwala, and Rizwan Baig.

Villa 3, Jumeira Beach Rd., Dubai, +971 4 325 3258, studio8.ae.

ONLINE SHOPPING TIP

Up-and-coming Dubai-based brand Mochi's e-commerce site features a range of mirrored clutch bags, embroidered jackets, skirts, and shorts that can be shipped around the world (allthingsmochi.com). Zayan the Label also ships worldwide and has a comprehensive selection of items (zayanthelabel.com). Sauce also ships internationally and specializes in fearless, fun, Insta-friendly items (shopatsauce.com).

Ush Boutique

Founded by Fashion Arabia, Ush Boutique gave voice to a collection of avant-garde designers and created a welcoming space for shoppers looking for originality and craftsmanship. Ush became the vehicle for renowned Emirati designer Abeer Al Suwaidi, and her punk rock and contemporary takes on the traditional *abaya*. The store offers curated collections of the best *abayas*, *jalabyas*, caftans, dress shoes, bags, and accessories from some of the region's best-known and in-demand designers. The 3,000-square-foot villa also serves as a gathering place for events and fashion shows.

Villa C-125, 32B St., Al Wasl Rd., Jumeirah 1, Dubai, and also in Abu Dhabi, +971 4 344 0735, ushboutique.com.

Zayan the Label

This decidedly girlie label was created by Zayan Ghandour, cofounder of the multi-brand concept boutique Sauce, where she serves as creative director and head buyer. Following the success of Sauce, Zayan began developing her namesake brand, which debuted at Paris Fashion Week in 2011 to wide acclaim; she recently opened her first stand-alone in Dubai. The collection includes flutter-sleeve dresses, lace-edged joggers, and scallop-edged crop tops.

Galleria Mall, Shop 10, Al Wasl Rd., Dubai, +971 4 344 0104, zayanthelabel.com.

Organic
Neem
Black Soap
Organic
Peppermint
Black Soap
AFRICAN

AFRICA

MOROCCO

SIERRA LEONE

NIGERIA

KENYA

GHANA

SOUTH AFRICA

AKBAR DELIGHTS

MARRAKECH

MOROCCO

Atika

Loafers, drivers and sandals in every color of the rainbow await at this footwear feast for the senses.

34, rue de la Liberté, Marrakesh, Marrakech-Tensift-Al Haouz, +212 5244-36409.

Beldi

"A nicely curated market of shops, and a welcome break from the hustle of the main souks," says designer Stephanie von Watzdorf.

9-11 Soukiat Laksour, Bab Fteuh, Marrakech 40000, +212 5244-41076.

Lahandira

"My favorite rug source. I lose my mind every time I visit here," says designer Mara Hoffman, "you can witness this in my office, which is covered in beautiful carpets." "I love the baskets, the embroidered basket bags, the colorful vintage beaded bags with tassels, the babouches in every color. A feast for the eyes, with so much visual deliciousness to take in. I always buy hamsa hands, in metal, wood, glass, any material," says Stephanie von Watzdorf.

Foundouk Namouss "Draz" Sidi Ishaq Num 100 Errahba El Qadima, Marrakech, +212 6774 23353; lahandira.com.

ONLINE SHOPPING TIP

Maryam Montague's website (mmontague.com) has a beautifully curated selection of Moroccan goodies, including woven rugs, poufs, shell necklaces, baskets, Tuareg leather bags, indigo leather scarves, and vintage clothing, with items at all price points shipping to fifteen countries. A portion of proceeds benefits Project Soar, a nonprofit dedicated to helping prevent Moroccan girls from becoming child brides.

MARYAM MONTAGUE
MARRAKECH MUST-DOS

Designer, hotelier, and humanitarian Montague is also the founder of tribal-chic lifestyle brand M. Montague. Born in Cairo, raised in Tunis and New York, Maryam Montague has lived in Dakar, Kathmandu, and Windhoek. She and her architect husband moved to Morocco, where they pitched a tent on a working olive grove on the outskirts of Marrakech. There they designed, built, and decorated boutique hotel Peacock Pavilions, a favorite spot for travelers, and a shoot location for brands like J. Crew and Tory Burch.

I hang out at **33 MAJORELLE**, a big, beautiful concept store that carries everything from housewares to fashion—kind of like the Merci of Marrakech. The Technicolor Majorelle Garden, once owned by Yves Saint Laurent, is right across the street, making this an überstylish address.

For loungy fashions that channel Marrakech in the '60s and '70s, I'm a fan of **MAX & JAN**. I'm obsessed with their sarwal/harem pants, which are very cool without making you look like you're wearing a diaper, if you know what I mean.

For the very prettiest handblown Moroccan tea glasses, I head to **LE VERRE BELDI** at the Beldi Country Club. The glasses come in sets of twelve and are wrapped in brown paper packages tied up with string. No singing necessary but definitely one of my favorite things.

If I could afford it, I would buy most things at **AKBAR DELIGHTS**. This tiny jewel of a store in the Marrakech medina is filled with over-the-top hand-beaded tunics and coats—think, Marni meets Maasai warriors.

For color and pattern addicts, there is **POPHAM DESIGN**—the last word in Moroccan patterned cement tiles. My husband gets a look of fear when

I tell him I am making a trip there. For those not headed to Marrakech, the tiles are carried at Ann Sacks (US and London).

I also love the **SPICE SOUK**. Hidden among the spices are all kinds of local beauty concoctions. I recommend the supercheap rose cream, the homemade black olive soft soap, and argan oil for hair, skin, and nails. (Note that local chameleon sellers can also be found in the spice souk. Chameleons might be the coolest reptiles ever.)

I also have a tiny weird-jewelry obsession. In Morocco, people take genies and the evil eye seriously. Thankfully, the antidote is jewelry, especially amulets and talismans. For the real thing, there is no better place to shop than **JEWELS ARTS**. I have a single necklace made from fifty-two talismans—I think of it as supplemental life insurance.

AKBAR DELIGHTS

RUE MARJORELLE, 33 Rue Yves Saint Laurent, Marrakech 40000, +212 5243-14195, 33ruemarjorelle.com.

MAX & JAN, 14 Rue Amsefah, Sidi Abdelaziz, Medina, Marrakesh 44000 +212 5243-75570, maxandjan.ma.

LE VERRE BELDI, Km 6 route d'Amizmiz, Chrifia, Marrakech 40000, +212 5243-83950, verrebeldi.com.

ABKAR DELIGHTS, Square Bab Fteuh, Médina, Marrakech 40000, +212 671-661307, akbardelightscollections.com.

POPHAM DESIGNS, 7 Km Route d'ourika, Tassoultante, Marrakech 40065, +212 5243-78022, pophamdesign.com.

SPICE SOUK, Medina, Marrakech 40000.

JEWELS ARTS, 15 Souk Cherifia, Medina, Marrakech, +212 5243-85066, jewelsarts.com.

FREETOWN

SIERRA LEONE

Big Market

One of the oldest markets in Sierra Leone. "Great artisanal goodies: art, jewelry, textiles, et cetera," says designer Zainab Sumu. Vendors have been trading here since the days when slave ships docked in the nearby harbor, and the market's location eventually helped establish the city as a refuge for freed slaves.

Wallace Johnson St., Freetown.

LAGOS

NIGERIA

Temple Muse

Along with Alara, mentioned by Abrima Erwiah, Temple Muse is a leader in Nigeria's emerging high fashion scene. This luxury lifestyle concept store stocks top African labels such as Lisa Folawiyo, Pop Caven, and Ituen Basi, alongside European and American brands like Alexander Wang, Carven, Manish Arora, and Victoria Beckham, all in a gallerylike space featuring rotating art exhibitions and an in-house champagne bar.

21 Amodu Tijani Close, Victoria Island, Lagos, +23 708 726 4853, temple-muse.com.

TEMPLE MUSE

LAMU

KENYA

African Crafts

Sells art, crafts, ornaments, home décor, and jewelry made mostly from recycled materials, from throughout Africa.

+254 706 718562, facebook.com/Africancornerexportcom.

Aman Lamu

"Sandy Bornman's shop has a nice selection of her designs and a curated selection of items from smaller artisans from Southeast Asia," says designer Stephanie von Watzdorf of this spot on the island that's been referred to as "Africa's St. Barts." It stocks kurtas, Egyptian cotton shirts, African print pants, and more.

+254 733 455821, facebook.com/pages/Aman-Lamu.

Ali Lamu

"Goods made out of recycled materials, mostly sails, by local craftspeople," says Stephanie von Watzdorf. "They have great pillows, pouches, and totes. My best shopping score of late has been from Ali Lamu: an old canvas sail embroidered with a giant pink heart made out of recycled plastic sequins and Masai beading. It makes me think, *My heart is in Africa*, and it's

AMAN LAMU

just one of many amazing things that I have found while traveling."

+254 722 702510, alilamu.com.

Gallery Baraka

Well-curated selection of masks, jewelry, and crafts from Africa and the Far East.

+254 424 633399, +254 722 379934.

Slim the Silversmith

A true hidden gem. This guy makes beautiful jewelry, including his signature pieces: pendants fashioned from remnants of Chinese porcelain found embedded in Swahili houses in Lamu.

P.O. Box 58, Lamu 80500, +254 722 478878

ABRIMA ERWIAH
AFRICAN STYLE

In 2011, after a decade at Bottega Veneta, Abrima Erwiah partnered with actor Rosario Dawson to start Studio 189 (studiooneeightynine.com), a Ghana-based ethical-fashion label focused on creating jobs and supporting education and skills training. Erwiah also produces a private-label brand of breezy separates that highlights traditional African dyeing techniques. The two friends travel often in Africa to work directly with artisans and designers.

ALARA in Nigeria is the most beautiful store in Africa and one of the most beautiful stores in the world. Designed by famous architect David Adjaye and curated by Reni Folawiyo, the store looks like a contemporary art museum. It carries luxury brands from around the world mixed with innovative new African brands. It's a true lifestyle store including ready-to-wear, home, jewelry, accessories, bags, books, and even a stunning garden and restaurant.

In Ghana, **DUABA SERWA** is one of the most popular brands, worn by Ghana's fashion-savvy crowd. The designer, Nelly Hagan-Aboagye, creates refined, fitted, sexy dresses perfect for cocktail parties, weddings, the red

techniques into chic rafia bags in bright colors, available at **ELLE LOKKO.**

ZAINA LODGE, Ghana's first real eco-safari lodge, sets a new standard of luxury. Super relaxing, it's the only safari lodge in Mole National Park. It carries exquisite one-of-kind, locally made artisanal goods, like natural shea butter made by a woman in Larabanga village, black soap, and mud cloth pillowcases. You also get to enjoy incredible food and discover Ghana's wildlife—elephants, baboons, and more—from your cabin.

One of the largest festivals in Africa is **CHALE WOTE,** started by Mantse Aryeequaye and Sionne Neely a few years ago. It brings together Ghana's (and Africa's) most creative people. You can find one-of-a-kind clothing and art by many amazing young artists.

In Dworzulu, **HEEL THE WORLD** is a brand and social enterprise that works to empower Ghanian startup companies. You can order bespoke leather shoes, handmade by expert cobblers.

The Makola Market, known to locals as **THE BEND DOWN BOUTIQUE,** is where secondhand international wares end up. You can find all kinds of goodies and give them a second life.

Based in Senegal and with stores in Cape Town, South Africa, and Agadir, Morocco, **BANTU** is a swim, surf, and beachwear brand started by Yodit Eklund. The brand caters to Africa's fast-growing surfing and beach-going population, with swimwear, surfboards, and beach bags in prints that reference African art and textiles.

ALARA, 12A Akin Olugbade St., Lagos, Nigeria, +234 909 685 2076.

DUABA SERWA, Accra, Ghana, +233 26 210 1656.

A A K S, aaksonline.com.

ELLE LOKKO, N. F604/1, Lokko Rd., Accra, Ghana, +233 24 644 9944, ellelokko.com.

ZAINA LODGE, Mole National Park, Northern Region, Ghana, +233 54 011 1511, zainalodge.com.

CHALE WOTE STREET ART FESTIVAL, High St., James Town, Ghana, accradotaltradio.com/chale-wote-street-art-festival.

HEEL THE WORLD, Oxford St., Osu, Accra, Ghana +233 24 658 9160, +233 26 210 1656, htwshoes.com.

MAKOLA MARKET, Kojo Thompson Rd., Accra, Ghana.

BANTU, 368 Albert Rd Woodstock, Cape Town, 7295, South Africa, and KM 16 Route d'Essaouira, Agadir, Morocco, bantuwax.com.

NAIROBI

KENYA

Mille Collines

Founded by Spaniards Inés Cuatrecasas and Marc Oliver following a 2008 trip to Rwanda and an introduction to a local dressmaker, this fashion atelier focuses on both design and retail with an African spirit. Designs combine edgy tailoring and cool, African-inspired prints.

Village Market, Limru Rd., Gigiri, Nairobi 00621, +254 703 216541, and additional locations, millecollines.com.

Ngong House

"Home to the most amazing jewelry store," says designer Aurora James of this boutique inside the intimate luxury wildlife lodge Ngong House. "Penny Winter, the cofounder of Ngong House, has been designing jewelry for decades and has it all handcrafted in Kenya. Beautiful gems are fashioned into an eclectic and exciting mix of jewelry," such as horn cuffs and other pieces.

60 Ndovu Rd., Nairobi 24963, +254 422 434965, Ngonghouse.com.

West African Market

"It has no address and no sign," says Stephanie von Watzdorf. "You can find all kinds of African beads, beaded furniture, and shells. It's a real treasure trove."

MILLE COLLINES

ACCRA

GHANA

Christie Brown

One of the most well-known designers in Ghana, Aisha Obuobi learned her craft from watching her seamstress grandmother Christie Brown. Her women's apparel brand ranges from bespoke gowns to accessories, inspired by African culture and art. Think sophisticated, architecturally inspired sheath dresses, tailored tailcoats, and full skirts with hand-embroidered pockets, all making use of muted African prints. Obuobi has dressed everyone from Beyoncé's backup dancers on the Mrs. Carter Show World Tour to the stars of the Web series *An African City*, (the show has been dubbed the African *Sex and the City*).

809 Eleventh Lane, Viva Court, Osu, Accra, +233 24 441 8477, christiebrownonline.com.

Elle Lokko

A terrific boutique championing young African labels, including Osei-Duro, Raffia, Iamisigo, Monaa, Aaks, and Anago. Carries batik and batakari skirts, cool cross-body straw bags, beaded necklaces, sleek leather sandals, and more.

N. F604/1, Lokko Rd., Osu, Accra, +233 24 644 9944, ellelokko.com.

Kiki Clothing

Asymmetrical dresses, jumpsuits, off-the-shoulder tops, and other contemporary silhouettes in incredibly vibrant African fabrics.

Accra Mall, Shop G39A, Accra, +233 20 817 4362, kikiclothing.com.

La Maison

A superbly edited selection of art, home accessories, furniture, and decorative items from more than forty brands, many from Africa, plus jewelry and candles. La Maison was opened nearly two decades ago by Nada Moukarzel, who designed the interiors of Coco Lounge and Urban Grill, two trendy eateries near the store's second location, in the Icon House development in Stanbic Heights. La Maison is a part of the West African luxury group Yolo Experiences.

#F881/1 Annexe, 6th St., Osu R.E., Accra, + 233 30 278 9031, lamaisonghana.com.

Mina Evans

This up-and-coming Ghanian designer creates feminine pieces, from circle skirts to maxi dresses, in vibrant colors with print accents. They're a hit with

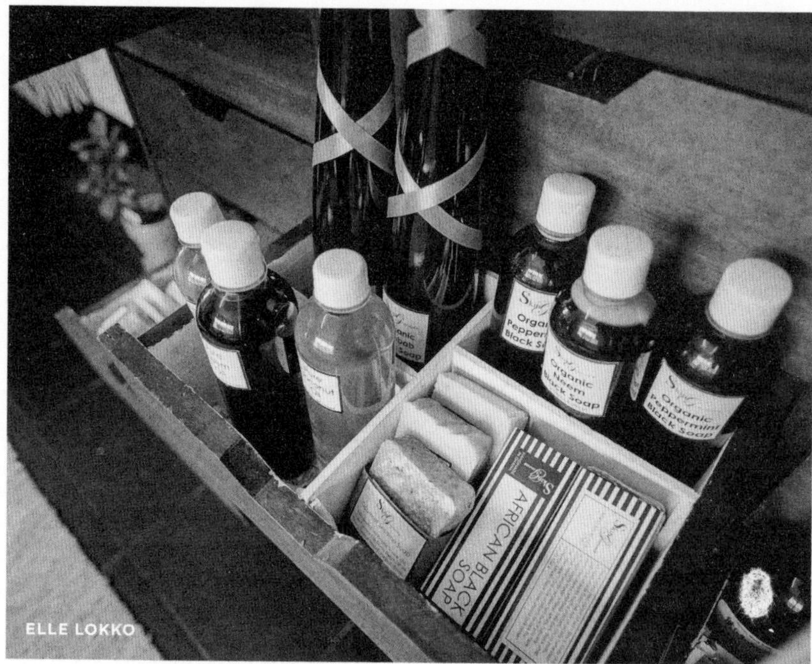

ELLE LOKKO

the local celebrity and style-blogging set. In 2015 Mina Evans won brand of the year at the Ghana Fashion Awards.
Ringway Link, Ringway Estates, Accra, +233 24 422 8120, mina-evans.com.

Poqua Poqu

A Ghanian fashion scene mainstay, this label specializes in cropped blouses, high-low dresses, and fluid gowns featuring combinations of textures, vivid colors, and African prints.
Osu Forico Mall, Mission St., Osu, Accra, +233 30 296 3909, +233 27 023 1261, poquapoqu.com.

Viva

Accra's top luxury fashion multi-label boutique sells a colorful selection of Dolce & Gabbana, Valentino, Antonio Marras, No. 21, MSGM, Self-Portrait, and more.
809, 11th Lane, Osu, Accra, +233 02 077 6629.

CAPE TOWN

SOUTH AFRICA

AKJP Collective

This concept store features the most exciting, cutting-edge designers on the men's and women's South African fashion scene, including Lukhanyo Mdingi, Rich Mnisi, Selfi's Celeste Arendse, and Drotsky's Elaine du Plessis.

73 Kloof St., Cape Town, 8001, +27 21 424 5502, www.adriaankuiters.com.

Chandler House

This charming shop is housed in an 18th-century Cape Georgian building that is also home to the Voorkamer Gallery. Walk inside and feast your eyes on gorgeous, locally made housewares, artisanal gifts, jewelry, antiques, textiles, and fine art. Michael Chandler opened the doors in December 2013 to showcase his own designs, and soon included other Cape artists and designers as well.

53 Church St., Cape Town, 8001, +27 21 424 4810, chandlerhouse.co.za.

Dear Rae

Dear Rae jewelry focuses on natural lines and simple forms translated into gold, silver, brass, and copper, with the occasional gemstone. Drawing on inspiration from her South African and German heritage, Karin Rae Matthee launched Dear Rae in 2010. Each Dear Rae piece—precious gold chain bracelets with palm-shaped charms, delicate half-sun brass bangles, rose gold heart rings—is designed and made by Matthee and her team at her Cape Town studio.

Shop 3, The Woodstock Foundry, 160 Albert Rd., Cape Town, 7925, dearrae.co.za, and other locations.

Glitteratti

This blogger-approved vintage emporium specializes in wares from the 1950s to the 1980s. There are several other vintage stores in the same complex.

Antique Arcade, 127 Long St., Cape Town, 8000, +27 82 819 5247, theantiquearcade.co.za/stores/glitterati.

Haas Collective

Haas (the Afrikaans word for rabbit) was created by Glynn Venter, Francois Irvine, and Vanessa Berlein. Their dream was to create a hub for edgy collectibles and one-of-a-kind quirky art pieces. They also operate Haas Coffee next door, which serves kopi

CHANDLER HOUSE

luwak, the most expensive coffee in the world, and an ad agency upstairs.

19 Buitenkant St., Cape Town City Centre, Cape Town, 8001, +27 21 461 1812 haascollective.co.za.

Klûk CDGT

A collaboration between Malcolm Klûk and Christiaan Gabriël Du Toit, this is one of South Africa's best-known fashion labels. Their glamorous dresses and coats emphasize lush embellishments and prints, making them a favorite with local celebs. Based in Cape Town, the designers also have a shop in Johannesburg and have showcased their designer collections as far away as New York and Paris. Their stores feature accessories and clothing by like-minded local designers alongside their collections.

43-45 Bree St., Cape Town, 8001, +27 83 377 7780, and 46 6th St., Parkhurst, Johannesburg, 2193, +27 83 377 7730, kluk.co.za.

Mememe

Owned by Doreen Southwood, another of Cape Town's most well-known designers, who shows at South Africa Fashion Week, this is the place to check out the best local talent, as well as Southwood's own collection of nostalgic, feminine designs.

117A Long St., Cape Town, 8000, and 54 6th St., Johannesburg, 2193, +27 21 424 0001, mememe.co.za.

Maison Mara

Upmarket concept store selling clothing and accessories from international labels, including J.W. Anderson (handbags), Acne (jeans), Balenciaga (coats), Petit Bateau (cotton T-shirts), and Costes (candles).

5 Jarvis St., Cape Town, 8001, +27 21 418 1600, maisonmara.co.za.

Merchants on Long

Amazing concept store housed in a striking building that was built in Edinburgh and shipped to Cape Town in 1903. Carefully curated selection of luxury and handmade brands, all sourced and made in Africa, including Bantu, Brother Vellies, Lalesso, MaXhosa by Laduma. Look for antelope-fur cuff bracelets, ostrich-feather bag charms, khanga-print beachwear, Xhosa-inspired knitwear, and men's shirts made of West African textiles, at this must-visit. Merchants is also home to the ethical African luxury handbag and accessories line Okapi.

34 Long St., Cape Town, 8001, +27 21 422 2828, merchantsonlong.com.

Missibaba

This colorful and playful luxury accessory label was established by designer Chloe Townsend, who is passionate about South Africa and supporting local industry. Townsend works from a studio in Woodstock, where she experiments with texture and color to craft boldly patterned bags and accessories with an exotic flair—leather appliqués in the shape of bananas and palm leaves, fun fringe, and patchwork details—which are sold at a flagship boutique on Bree Street, shared with jewelry designer Kirsten Goss.

229 Bree St., Cape Town, 8001, +27 21 424 8127, missibaba.com, and other locations in Johannesburg.

Mr. Price

The South African version of H&M, this chain of more than 400 stores offers value-priced trendy fashions for men, women, and kids, including off-shoulder tops, light-up sneakers, and printed varsity jackets. The retail group also includes Mr. Price Home, Mr. Price Sport, and Miladys.

Shop 146A, Lower Level, Victoria Wharf, Cape Town, 8001, +27 21 418 1499, mrp.com, and other locations.

Mungo & Jemima

Designers Kirsty Bannerman of Coppelia and Marian Park-Ross of Good opened Mungo & Jemima in 2008 to showcase the work of the emerging South African fashion scene. The flagship store in Cape Town's epicenter, Long Street, a second store in the Watershed at the V&A Waterfront, and the online shop, feature items from

KLÜK CDGT

Coppelia, Good, I Love Leroy, Selfi, Margot Molyneux, and more.
108 Long St., Cape Town City Centre, Cape Town, 8000, +27 21 424 5016, and B1&2 Watershed, V&A Waterfront, Cape Town, +27 21 418 1180, mungoandjemima.com.

Nap

This lovely store and South African chainlet was created by Carina Marescia and daughter Tamryn, who share a love for beautiful, and simple design, preferably raw-edged and neutral in color. Their motto is "believe in homegrown," and you'll find lots of locally produced goods, including resort clothing and subtle home accessories. Check the website for locations, since different stores have different specialties.
Nap Lifestyle & Apparel, Shop B3, Mainstream Centre, Hout Bay, Cape Town, 7806, +27 21 421 6482, napliving.co.za.

Neighbourgoods Market

Founded by entrepreneurs whose aim is to revive the public market as a civic institution, Neighborgoods features 100 specialty traders every Saturday, including local farmers, fine-food purveyors, artisan producers, and local designers such as Selfi (artsy, Marni-esque togs), and Chiumbo (cool printed harem pants).
Every Saturday 9 a.m.–2 p.m. at the Old Biscuit Mill, 373 Albert Rd., Woodstock, Cape Town, 7915, and Johannesburg, neighbourgoodsmarket.co.za.

Old Biscuit Mill

"One of my favorite places in the world," Fashionkind founder Nina Farran says of this mixed-use retail, fashion, and food destination. "From drinking fresh machete-cut coconuts to sampling food stands and discovering artisan talent in every nook and cranny, it is a must-go when in Cape Town. I discovered one of my all-time favorite artists there—Andile Dyalvane —who is now a dear friend. His ceramics tell the story of his country, his roots, and his soul. They are masterful demonstrations of the talent that exists around the world just wait-

ONLINE SHOPPING TIP

Luxury e-commerce is a relatively new frontier in Africa. Kisua.com and Oxosi.com are both great places to discover and order clothing and accessories by emerging African designers. Based in New York, Oxosi.com is a design-centered marketplace for African brands and enthusiasts, as well as a discovery platform for fashion, art, and design products made in Africa. South Africa–based kisua.com counts renowned Savile Row tailor Ozwald Boateng among its advisory board members.

ing to be discovered. To me, they are the true definition of luxury."

373-375 Albert Rd., Woodstock, Cape Town, 7915, +27 21 447 9120, theoldbiscuitmill.co.za.

Pichulik

Incredibly cool sculptural jewelry made of colorful cord and leather nods to traditional Masai and other African designs, but with a contemporary eye. Everything is made in South Africa by designer Katherine-Mary Pichulik, who has also collaborated with other labels on bags.

F36/F37 Watershed, V&A Waterfront, Dock Rd., Cape Town, 8001, and Johannesburg, +27 74 869 7979, pichulik.com.

SAM

Frustrated by the lack of a single beautiful space to find a variety of cool fashion and accessories, designers Berlinda White and Naomi Bossert created SAM (South African Market). It carries stenciled leather-detail clutches by Ilundi, jewelry by Pichulik, Bamboo Revolution watches, housewares, stationery, and art, too.

67 & 69 Shortmarket St., Cape Town, 8001, +27 83 690 6476, facebook.com/SouthAfricanMarket.

The Space

In 2000, the Space launched in Durban to partner with and showcase established designers and to provide a platform for promising young designers, giving them a chance to break into the fashion business. There are now ten Space stores in South Africa.

Shop L69, Cavendish Square, Claremont, Cape Town, +27 21 674 6643, thespace.co.za, and other locations.

A PRIMER ON THE JO'BURG SHOPPING SCENE

Thithi Nteta is a PR consultant and creator of style blog teeteeiswithme.com, which focuses on fashion in her home country of South Africa.

In the past five years or so, a variety of international retailers have landed on our shores. It started with Zara, then Topshop, H&M, and Forever 21 opened shortly after. When the stores opened, South African consumers were excited. I remember vividly how Zara was full every single day for six months after it opened. At the risk of sounding like an awful person, as someone who travels, the opening of these stores didn't excite me one bit. It kind of upset me because it meant South African designers and the boutiques housing South African designers had more competition.

I made a conscious decision years ago to spend my money buying from local designers and boutiques. If someone was traveling to South Africa and wanted somewhere to shop, have lunch, get a manicure, and have drinks, I would say go to **SANDTON CITY SHOPPING CENTRE** in Johannesburg, which is connected to Nelson Mandela Square.

It has everything in that respect, and is very convenient, but it's a mall, so no real ambience. A drink and sushi at **THE BIG MOUTH** or **TASHA'S** in the mall isn't a bad day out.

As someone who is passionate about local South African fashion, and it becoming an actual industry, I like to discover places where I can buy local. One favorite is **SUPERELLA**, which is South African fashion designer Ella Buter's stand-alone store/studio. She creates comfortable, everyday clothes, including geometric tops and apron dresses. **CONVOY** is owned by a group of South African designers. They stock wearable pieces that are unique and locally manufactured.

MAXHOSA BY LADUMA (for knitwear), **PICHULIK** (for jewelry), and **BLACK COFFEE** (for hand-dyed dresses) are some of my favorite stores to frequent in **WORK SHOP NEWTOWN**, a fashion, design, and lifestyle concept center.

It isn't new, but the **JOHANNESBURG ART GALLERY** is one of my favorite spaces in the city. I think a lot of people are still quite apprehensive to go into Johannesburg and explore, but it's a beautiful space with beautiful works of art.

Re cheap chic, I opt to shop for high-quality, unique pieces over cheap and mass-produced ones. We have a South African retailer called **MR. PRICE.** I always shop from their collaborations with local designers because that means money back in the designers' pockets.

My biggest shopping score is an Egyptian cotton shirt from **RICH MNISI** that can be worn two ways. The other day I discovered that I could also wear it as lightweight outwear, so that's three ways.

SANDTON CITY SHOPPING CENTRE, 0 2031 South, 163 5th St., Sandton, 2031, +27 11 217 6000, sandtoncity.com.

THE BIG MOUTH, Shop No. 13 & 14, Nelson Mandela Square, Johannesburg, 2031, +27 63 293 8869, thebigmouth.co.za.

TASHA'S, Shop No. 16, Atholl Square, Sandton Johannesburg, 2196, +27 11 884 0365, tashascafe.com.

SUPERELLA, 7th Ave. and 9th St., Melville, Johannesburg, 2092, +27 82 845 5551.

CONVOY, The Bamboo Lifestyle Centre, 9th St., Johannesburg, 2109, +27 83 548 5321.

MAXHOSA BY LADUMA, Newtown Junction, Lilian Ngoyi St., Johannesburg, 2000, maxhosa.co.za.

PICHULK, Unit S16, Newtown Junction, Newtown, Johannesburg, 2001, and Cape Town, +27 74 869 7979, pichulik.com.

BLACK COFFEE, 44 Stanley Ave., Milpark, Johannesburg, 2092, +27 11 482 9148, and 100 Carr St., Newtown, Johannesburg, 2001, +27 72 943 6192, blackcoffee.co.za.

WORK SHOP NEWTOWN, 100 Carr St., Newtown, Johannesburg, 2001, +27 79 676 1826, workshopnewtown.com.

JOHANNESBURG ART GALLERY, Cnr Klein and King George Streets, Joubert Park, Johannesburg, 2044, +27 11 725 3130, friendsofjag.org.

MR. PRICE, Shop 223 Carlton Centre, Commissioner St., Johannesburg, 2001, +27 11 331 9840, mrp.com, and additional locations.

RICH MNISI, +27 79 066 9515, richmnisi.com.

gorman
WALALA
gorman

AUSTRALIA

ZIMMERMANN

SYDNEY

AUSTRALIA

Akira

One of Australia's most important designers, Akira Isogawa draws inspiration from his Japanese heritage, creating soft and romantic silhouettes with natural fabrics in whimsical prints or distressed for a lived-in feel. He has received numerous awards, exhibited his work in museums, made costumes for the Australian ballet, and even had his face on a commemorative postage stamp. He has four stores in Australia.

The Strand Arcade, Shop 110, Level 2, 412-414 George St., Sydney NSW 2000, +61 2 9232 1078, akira.com.au, and additional locations.

bassike

Basic T-shirts that don't lose their shape after washing, in styles elevated by asymmetrical hems, contrast topstitching, and raw edges. Although there are several stores in Australia (and one in Venice, California), the two-story layout of the Paddington store makes it a top spot to see the breadth of Deborah Sams and Mary Lou Ryan's collection.

26 Glenmore Rd., Paddington NSW 2021, +61 2 8457 6882, bassike.com, and additional locations.

Berkelouw Bookshop

"You can have a herbal tea while you look at books and enjoy the view of Oxford Street in Paddington," says jewelry designer Jordan Askill. "They specialize in both new and vintage books."

19 Oxford St., Paddington NSW 2021, +61 2 9360 3200, and additional locations, berkelouw.com.au.

Camilla

Designer and artist Camilla Franks is synonymous with Australian fashion and resort lifestyle. She specializes in caftans, bathing suits, and maxi skirts characterized by vibrant-colored digital prints and delicate crystal details. In 2004 Franks opened her first boutique at Bondi Beach.

132a Warners Ave., Bondi Beach, NSW 2026, +61 02 9130 1430, Camilla.com.au.

Camilla and Marc

One of Australia's most successful women's fashion labels was launched in 2003 at Australian Fashion Week by Sydney-based brother-and-sister duo Camilla Freeman-Topper and Marc Freeman. The label mixes masculine tailoring with feminine draped silhouettes.

217 Glenmore Rd., Paddington NSW 2021, +612 9357 5822, camillaandmarc.com, and additional locations.

Cream on Crown

The Crown Street location of this vintage and repurposed vintage chainlet is beloved by locals, as much for the people-watching opportunities as for the shopping.

32/277-285 Crown St., Surry Hills NSW 2010, +61 02 9331 5228, creamonline.com.au, and additional locations.

David Jones

Australia's upscale department store, owned by South African retail group Woolworths Holdings Limited. At the Sydney flagship, you'll find a wide selection of Australian and international brands (Dries Van Noten, Dion Lee, Erdem, Phillip Lim, Paul Smith), plus a food hall.

David Jones Elizabeth St., 86-108 Castlereagh St., Sydney NSW 2000, davidjones.com.au, and additional locations.

Dinosaur Designs

Iconic resin jewelry and housewares line, founded in Sydney. "Working with resin is like working with paint," says Louise Olsen, who started the collection with her partner, Stephen Ormandy, when they were both art-school students. "My go-to place for a little accessory or gift," says Alyce Tran of The Daily Edited.

Shop 77, Strand Arcade, 412–414 George St., Sydney NSW 2000, +61 02 9223 2953, dinosaurdesigns.com.au, and additional locations.

Dion Lee

Since Lee established his brand in Sydney in 2009, he has been building a serious Hollywood fan club of leading ladies (Selena Gomez, Diane Kruger, Priyanka Chopra) who appreciate his sexy, red-carpet-ready clothing, which marries innovative construction and cuts with respect for the female form. Think fluid silk suiting and loop-woven dresses designed to enhance movement. After debuting at Australia Fashion Week, Lee presented collections in London before relocating to New York, where the brand has become a fixture on the New York Fashion Week schedule. He has six stores in Australia. "I'm a huge fan. Part of my uniform is a pair of Dion Lee cropped trousers (I have three of the exact same pair), and this is my favorite of his stores, with his full collection on display. The Strand Arcade is pretty great itself!" says Alyce Tran.

Shops 62–66, The Strand Arcade, 412–414 George St., Sydney NSW 2000, dionlee.com, and additional locations.

PIP EDWARDS

BONDI BEACH AND BEYOND

Aussie style star Pip Edwards is a designer and stylist who had roles at Sass & Bide and Ksubi before becoming design director of Australian brand General Pants. Based in Bondi Beach, she also has her own brand, P.E. Nation, which is a key part of the activewear stable at department store David Jones, and has been worn by Kendall Jenner, Bella Hadid, and Ruby Rose.

GENERAL PANTS is my love. I worked there at age eighteen, and so many people worked there when they were starting out. In Australian culture, we live in denim and this is where you go. General Pants is a partner in David Jones, too, so we have concept spaces within their stores.

In Bondi, **TUCHUZY** is amazing. You can get everything from Céline to Sir the Label, which is by two Aussie girls. Georgia Alice is another label to watch. Tuchuzy has its own in-house label, too. **SATURDAYS SURF** is also iconic.

I hardly ever shop in the city, but the **CORNER SHOP** at the Strand Arcade has all the brands, including Dion Lee and Romance Was Born, which is another favorite of mine.

GLEBE MARKETS, Saturdays 10 a.m.–4 p.m., and **BONDI MARKETS,** Sunday 10 a.m.–4 p.m., are fun, too if you're looking for a flea market experience.

GENERAL PANTS, Westfield Shopping Centre, 500 Oxford St., Bondi Junction NSW 2022, +61 2 8275 5145, generalpants.com.au, and additional locations.

TUCHUZY, Shop 11, The Beach House, 178 Campbell Parade, Bondi Beach.

NSW 2026, +61 2 9365 7775, tuchuzy.com.

SATURDAYS NYC, L08/ Bondi Beach (entry via Gould St.), 180-186 Campbell PARADE, Sydney NSW 2026, +61 2 8316 4518, saturdaysnyc.com.

CORNER SHOP, The Strand Arcade, 1/412-414 George St., +61 2 9221 1788.

GLEBE MARKETS, Glebe Public School, Corner of Derby Place and Glebe Pt. Rd., Glebe NSW 2037, glebemarkets.com.au.

BONDI MARKETS, Bondi Beach Public School, Campbell Parade, Bondi Beach NSW 2026, +61 2 9315 7011, bondimarkets.com.au.

Elleryland

Before making waves on the international fashion scene (she now shows at Paris Fashion Week), Australian designer Kym Ellery worked as an editor and stylist at Australia's *Russh* magazine. In 2007, she launched her own label, which features sophisticated clothing with dramatic slits, bell sleeves, and ruffled edges. Fans include Rihanna, Solange Knowles, Miranda Kerr, and Cate Blanchett. Her store is dubbed Elleryland.

2-16 Glenmore Rd., Sydney NSW 2021, +612 8068 2361, elleryland.com.

Gould's Book Arcade

An archive of used books, established in 1967. "A place of discovery where you could easily spend an entire day," says fashion designer Dion Lee.

32 King St., Newtown NSW 2042, +61 2 9519 8947, gouldsbooks.com.

Harrolds

"Amazing service. A lovely small-format store with lots of shop-in-shops with an interesting edit of great labels, Victoria Beckham, J.W. Anderson, and Vetements, to name a few," says Alyce Tran, cofounder of The Daily Edited, of this family-run department store, which started in menswear and expanded to women's in 2015.

Westfield Sydney, 188 Pitt St., Sydney NSW 2000, harrolds.com.au.

Hatmaker

"One of my favourites little stores in Sydney, located in a small shop front in the leafy streets of trendy Surry Hills," says Gary Pepper Girl blogger Nicole Warne. "The milliner Jonathon is a genius and creates the most spectacular hats for every season."

284 S Dowling St., Paddington NSW 2021, +61 2 9360 0041, hatmaker.com.au.

Incu

Established in 2002 by twin brothers Brian and Vincent Wu, Incu has twelve retail stores located across Sydney, Melbourne, and the Gold Coast, as well as a successful online business, selling understated clothing and accessories by Isabel Marant, Acne, Rag & Bone, Want Les Essentiels, Paul Smith, Outerknown, and the like. In 2014, Incu announced a retail partnership with French designer label A.P.C. and shortly after launched the brand's first Australian store, in Melbourne.

Shop RG 23-24 (women's) and RG 19-20 (men's), The Galeries, Sydney NSW 2000, +61 2 9266 0244, incu.com, and additional locations.

Jac and Jack

Originally established in 2004 as a knitwear business—with a focus on cashmere and luxurious yarns—the label has grown to encompass all aspects of the contemporary wardrobe for men and women. Designers and founders Jacqueline "Jac" Hunt and Lisa "Jack" Dempsey focus on creating effortless clothing and accessories, including incredibly chic, drapey silk "Hef" robes, polished T-shirts, ribbed knit flute skirts, and other modern essentials.

Shop 3, 82-92 Gould St., Bondi Beach NSW 2026, +61 2 8384 8062, jacandcak.com, and additional locations.

Lee Mathews

Established in 2000, contemporary Australian brand Lee Mathews creates collections with a quiet elegance: classic in design, considered in fabrication. Prints and textiles come from the namesake designer's interest in art, silhouettes from her passion for architecture, and color palettes from Australia's unique flora and fauna.

18 Glenmore Rd, Paddington NSW 2021, and additional locations, +6 12 9331 1699, leemathews.com.au.

Lover

Nic Briand and Susien Chong have seen their label, Lover, go from a humble stall at the Bondi Markets to a critically acclaimed ten-year anniversary runway show at the Sydney Opera House in 2011. They are a local fave for their beautiful lacy dresses and feminine floral prints.

Shop 69-71, The Strand Arcade, 412-414 George St., Sydney NSW 2000, +61 02 9232 7289, loverlabel.com.

Mode Sportif

"I don't like wearing an actual gym kit around, but I do love a relaxed luxe-sport look, and Mode Sportif does a great edit of relaxed designer pieces, highs and lows," says Alyce Tran of this store, which stocks Nike, Iro, Adidas by Stella McCartney, and other lifestyle collections.

24 Glenmore Rd., Paddington NSW 2021, +61 2 9331 7222, modesportif.com.

MUD

Australian fashion designer Dion Lee loves these handmade porcelain ceramics with a minimalist aesthetic, which come in a rainbow of glazes.

Shop 4, 1 Kiaora Ln., Double Bay, NSW 2028, mudaustralia.com, and additional locations.

Poepke

This upmarket boutique stocks Dries Van Noten, Comme des Garçons Girl, Marques'Almeida, Simone Rocha, and other arty-girl faves, alongside accessories from Maryam Nassir Zadeh, Martiniano, and Linda Farrow.

47 William St., Paddington NSW, 2021, +61 2 9380 7611, poepke.myshopify.com.

ERIN WEINGER

SYDNEY FASHION ESSENTIALS

Erin Weinger is a journalist and entrepreneur currently serving as the digital commercial editor of Vogue Australia, *where she's responsible for editorial and commercial content strategy across Vogue.com.au and its multi-platform subsidiaries. She previously served as digital style director of* The Hollywood Reporter, *where she launched and helmed the brand's digital style and beauty destination, Pret-a-Reporter.com.*

Shoebox-size boutique, **BLOODORANGE** has a selection of US and French labels I love—A.P.C., Alexander Wang, and Vanessa Bruno—along with my beloved Aesop hand soap and body oil.

DAISO is an amazing Japanese dollar store inside the Jean Nouvel-designed Central Park complex, which has amazing $2 collagen sheet masks and made-in-Japan pottery for exactly the same price.

I also adore **LOVEDUCK**, a jewel box of a shop in tony Paddington that's filled with a genius supply of vintage and vintage-inspired bohemian dresses of every variety—caftans, off-the-shoulder, and linen. Pay particular attention to pieces by Paddo to Palmy, the dreamy dress line started by former interior designer Heidi Carter in 2011.

The colette of Sydney if you will, owner Eva Galambos' high-end concept store **PARLOUR X** calls a circa-1845 Paddington church home and is filled to the, uh, pews with Valentino gowns, Céline bags, Balenciaga blouses, and Isabel Marant everything. This is also the place in Sydney to find Jennifer Meyer jewels and Vetements' latest creations—not to mention goods from Australian labels, including Ellery and Christopher Esber—as well as the chic-meets-utilitarian signature prints from Cecilie Copenhagen, a line every stylish Sydneysider seems to swear by.

In the heart of the Silver Lake-meets-Brooklyn enclave of Newtown, **PENTIMENTO PAPERIE** is the perfect place to pick up a Life notebook from Japan, Neil Perry's latest coffee-table-worthy cookbook, or a sleek, matte porcelain vessel from Mud Australia, the famed twenty-two-year-old Sydney-produced ceramics brand to which Pentimento has devoted an entire room.

A fairly obvious inclusion, but no stylish Australian—from Adelaide to Tasmania—would be caught dead without a pair of **R.M. WILLIAMS** bush-inspired, Chelsea-esque boots from the ninety-year-old homegrown brand, which sold a minority stake to one of LVMH's investment groups in 2013. Go for the Adelaide in calfskin, suede, or—for the more daring—kangaroo.

Walking into **THE SLEEVELESS SOCIETY,** a small but mighty vintage shop, I feel as though I've been transported to Los Angeles in the best possible way. That makes sense, as owner Jaimi Kost sources a bulk of her bounty Stateside. The perfect mix of mostly '80s and '90s label-less capes, caftans, and shirtdresses that you'd never want to lose combined with the odd Escada blazer and pair of Hermès trousers—at fairly reasonable prices, no less—makes this a must-visit for anyone who adores perfectly curated, unstuffy treasure.

Beachside contemporary boutique **TUCHUZY** mixes Australian designers—think, Kit Willow's KITX, Camilla and Marc, and Bassike—with the likes of Helmut Lang, Acne, and Common Projects. Because of its waterside location, the styling has that coveted, undone beachy vibe with a decidedly casual yet polished Australian aesthetic. You could walk in here shoeless and buy a $1,000 Sophie Hulme shoulder bag and no one would bat an eyelash.

Attached to the Rosebery headquarters and design studio is **ZIMMERMANN'S** famed outlet store, where everything from bikinis to children's clothes to garden-party-appropriate rompers to potential bridesmaid dresses can be found at 40 to 60 percent off retail. On my last visit, I spotted last-season off-the-shoulder floral dresses for $450 and silk jumpsuits for $190.

BLOODORANGE, 35 Elizabeth Bay Rd., Elizabeth Bay NSW 2011, +61 2 9357 2424, bloodorange.com.au.

DAISO JAPAN, 727 George St., Haymarket NSW 2000, +61 2 9212 6888, daisojapan.com, and additional locations.

LOVEDUCK, 222 Glenmore Rd., Paddington NSW 2021, +61 2 9361 4427, loveduck.com.au.

PARLOUR X, 261 Oxford St., Paddington NSW 2021, +61 2 9331 0999, parlourx.com.

PENTIMENTO PAPERIE, 249 King St., Newtown NSW 2042, +61 2 9565 5591, pentimentonewtown.com.au.

R.M. WILLIAMS, Westfield, Shop 4020, Level 4, 188 Pitt St., Sydney NSW 2000, rmwilliams.com.au.

THE SLEEVELESS SOCIETY, Shop 2, 181c Edgecliff Rd., Woollahra NSW 2025, thesleevelesssociety.com.au.

TUCHUZY, Shop 11, The Beach House, 178 Campbell Parade, Bondi Beach.

NSW 2026, +61 2 9365 7775, tuchuzy.com.

ZIMMERMANN OUTLET, 2E Hayes Rd., Rosebery NSW 2018, +61 2 8324 7323

BASSIKE

Reverse Garbage

Sydney's recycling institution, established in 1974 by a collective of teachers looking for inexpensive classroom materials, is dedicated to reusing stuff headed for the landfill. This place offers recycled materials for DIY, costume, and art projects, some of them donated by local theater companies. If you need sequin fabric, a road sign, a mannequin, or a flag that says SYDNEY, this is your place.

8/142 Addison Rd., Marrickville NSW 2204, +61 02 9569 3132, reversegarbage.org.au.

Sarah & Sebastian

Founded in 2011 by Sarah Gittoes and Robert Sebastian Grynkofki, this Australian jewelry brand quickly achieved fashion status. Designed and handmade in their Sydney studio, each piece is simultaneously modern and classic. Look for tiny bar and chain earrings, delicate multistone rings, and more.

12B, 32 Ralph St., Alexandria NSW, 2015, sarahandsebastian.com.

Scanlan & Theodore

Locals compare this chain to Club Monaco in the US, because of its mix of everyday basics with going-out dresses in lace, linen, or floral stripes, but at slightly higher prices.

122 Oxford St., Paddington NSW 2021, scanlantheodore.com, and additional locations.

Sneakerboy

Sneakerboy carries the best luxury streetwear and sneaker brands, including Raf Simons for Adidas, Buscemi, Fendi, Fear of God, DRKSHDW, Yeezy, and more. "A brick-and mortar/online hybrid. You go into one of their Australian stores to try the sneakers on, then they send them out to you," says Dion Lee, who counts sneakers as part of his daily uniform.

3 Temperance Lane, Sydney NSW 2000, +61 2 9279 4066, sneakerboy.com, and additional locations.

The Standard Store

Established in 2011 by Sydney-based husband-and-wife team Nicola and Orlando Reindorf, the Standard Store is their vision for fashion retail. With its unique mix of small but interesting and wearable labels from Europe, Scandinavia, and the US (Sea, Bellerose, Carven, Clare V., Humanoid, Rachel Comey), the Standard Stores in Surry Hills and Melbourne's Fitzroy feature a tightly curated selection of clothing, accessories, and lifestyle must-haves for men and women.

503 Crown St., Surry Hills NSW 2010, +61 02 9310 1550, thestandardstore.com.au.

Supply

"Has a great selection of skate brands like Richardson and Palace," says jewelry designer Jordan Askill. "It is right off the Main Street, but it is down a set of stairs, and a bit hidden."

Burton St & Riley St., Darlinghurst NSW 2010, +61 2 9361 0188, supplystore.com.au.

The Vintage Clothing Shop

"The store opened in the '70s, and at the time, there was nothing else of its kind. The owners have been collecting vintage for over forty years and are the main supplier for period film and television production in Australia, as well as loaning to fashion editors for editorial shoots," says Gary Pepper Girl founder Nicole Warne. "The store offers a wonderfully curated selection of good-quality vintage pieces at reasonable prices. It's my favorite place to pick up something that I know I won't see anyone else in."

St. James Arcade, 7/80 Castlereagh St., Sydney NSW 2000, +61 2 9238 0090.

Zimmermann

Sisters Nicky and Simone Zimmermann are behind the Zimmermann label, which is known for sophisticated feminine dresses in delicate laces and prints, swimwear, and resortwear worn by everyone from Beyoncé to Miranda Kerr. The Zimmermanns started their brand in 1991, and opened their first store in Sydney in 1992. Their airy, high-spirited pieces have made them synonymous with Australian style.

2/2 - 16 Glenmore Rd., Paddington NSW 2021, +61 02 9357 4700, zimmermann .com, and additional locations.

THIRD DRAWER DOWN

MELBOURNE

AUSTRALIA

Aesop

First established in Melbourne in 1987, Aesop is a beauty-turned-lifestyle brand of hair care, skin care, soaps, and fragrances infused with parsley seed, clove, rose, cardamom, and chai scents. Each store has its own version of a minimalist aesthetic (the details of which are broken down in a special "design taxonomy" section on the website), and the brand is into supporting the arts, collaborating with the *Paris Review* and publishing its own literary journal. There are stores around the world, but this is the brand's Australian flagship.

87 Collins St., Melbourne VIC 3000, +61 3 9650 3027, and additional locations, aesop.com.

Alpha 60

If there was ever a store that represented the "Melbourne look"—black, simple, chic silhouettes, more black—it is Alpha 60. Known for its fresh take on classic styles, visit for a piece of the brand's signature "sophisticated quirk."

201 Finders Ln., Melbourne VIC 3000, +61 3 9663 3002, alpha60.com, and additional locations.

Assin

Dark and minimalist, Assin houses a curated selection of men's and women's apparel and accessories by Comme des Garçons, Boris Bidjan Saberi, Daniel Andresen, Junya Watanabe, Nude:Masahiko Maruyama, Pearls Before Swine, and others, in addition to its own in-house label. The polished concrete interior matches the cooler-than-thou mood.

Basement 138 Little Collins St., Melbourne VIC 3000, +61 3 9654 0158, assin.com.au.

Bul

"Supersculptural, minimalist, and modern," Erin Weinger says of this label started by Virginia Martin, a designer who worked for Proenza Schouler and Cynthia Rowley in the US before moving home to Melbourne to start her business in 2010. There are seven stores across Australia.

241 Brunswick St., Fitzroy VIC 3065, +61 3 9415 8844, and additional locations, bul.com.au.

Christine

A treasure chest of accessories in a Flinders Lane basement. Blogger Nicole

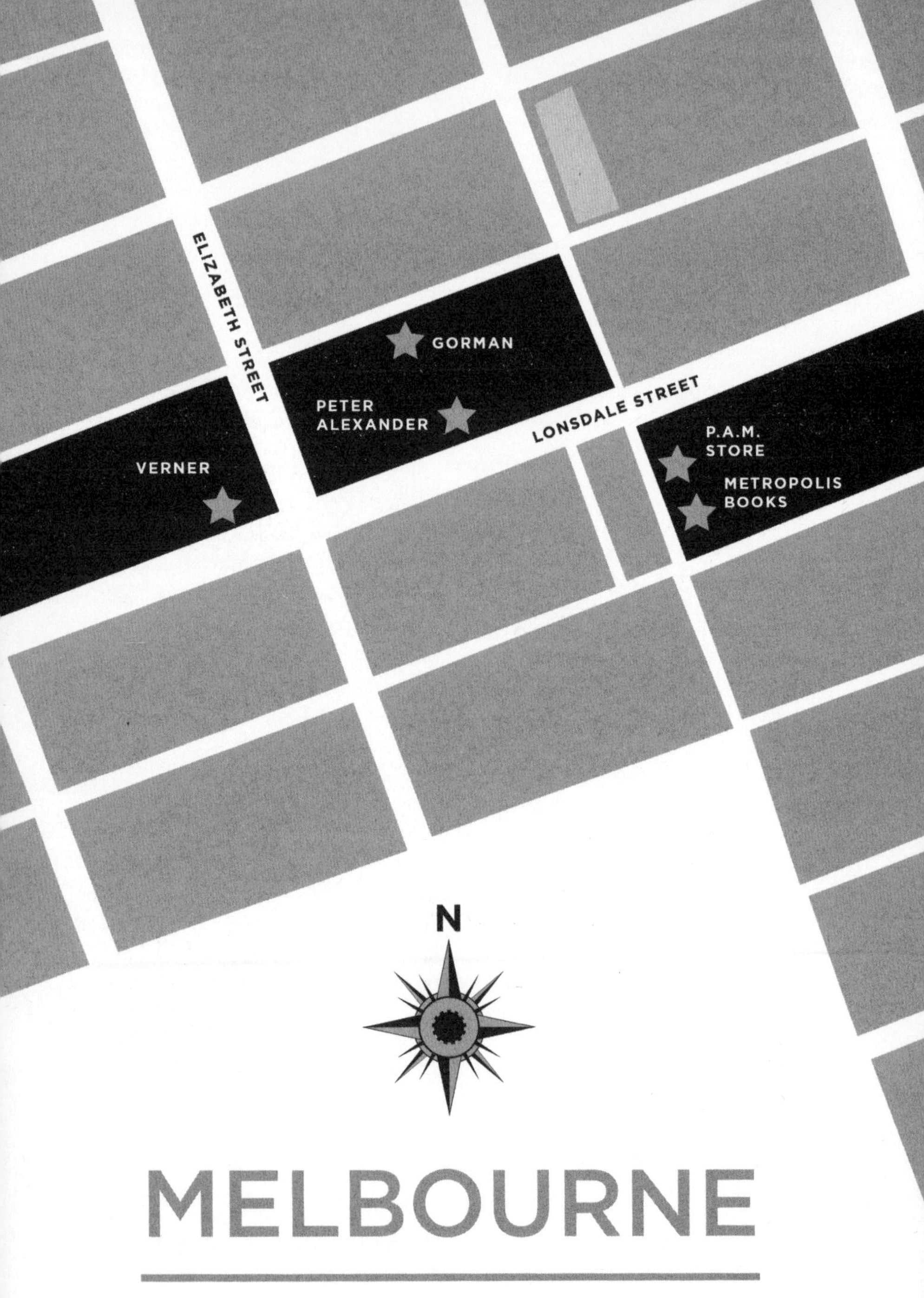
ELIZABETH STREET
GORMAN
PETER
ALEXANDER
LONSDALE STREET
P.A.M.
STORE
METROPOLIS
BOOKS
VERNER
N

MELBOURNE

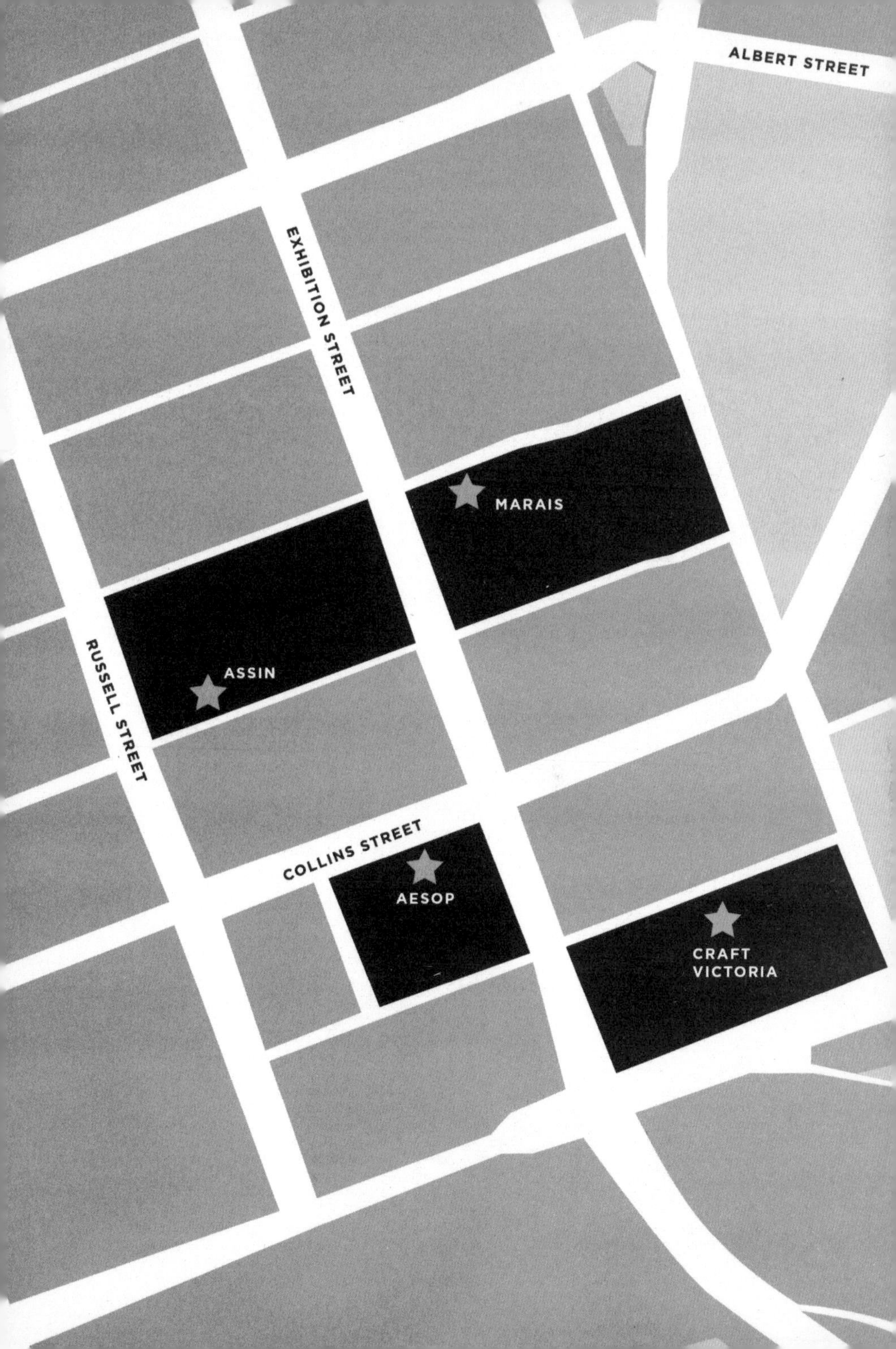
ALBERT STREET
EXHIBITION STREET
MARAIS
ASSIN
RUSSELL STREET
COLLINS STREET
AESOP
CRAFT
VICTORIA

ALBERT STREET
EXHIBITION STREET
MARAIS
ASSIN

GERTRUDE STREET

ALBERT STREET

Warne is a fan of owner Christine Barro's careful edits of elegant shoes, bags, gloves, and scarves.

Basement, 181 Flinders Lane, Melbourne VIC 3000, +61 3 9654 2011, christineaccessories.com.

Camberwell Market

Every Sunday, rain or shine, this market is the place to find secondhand designer labels and vintage furniture.

Market Place, Camberwell Victoria 3124, camberwellsundaymarket.org.

Cose Ipanema

This Melbourne institution stocks Dries Van Noten, Dolce & Gabbana, Jean Paul Gaultier, Comme des Garçons, Pauw, and more. From the people behind Assin.

113 Collins St., Melbourne, +61 03 9650 3457, www.coseipanema.com.

Country Road

A classic Australian chain with a simple, easy-to-wear aesthetic and a very affordable price point. "They do the best basics with a twist and use lots of natural fabrications so the clothing breathes and wears really well," says blogger Nicole Warne.

252 Toorak Rd., South Yarra VIC 3141, +61 3 9824 0133, and additional locations, countryroad.com.au.

Dejour

Nam Huynh, the man behind this cult custom-denim operation, has been making jeans for more than twenty years. His hole-in-the-wall shop has floor-to-ceiling shelves stocked with jeans in every size, shape, color, and design. They're made using wholesale denim from Bradmill, an Australian textile mill that's been operating since 1927. On weekends, expect to wait several hours to be helped. But with jeans at less than $100, including on-site alterations, it's worth it. While you're in Brunswick, try some Lebanese pastries, rose water, and pomegranate molasses from the Middle Eastern cafés on Sydney Road.

542 Sydney Rd., Brunswick VIC 3056, +61 3 9380 4884.

Fiorina

Melbourne-based silversmith and fine jeweler Fiorina Golotta specializes in a "modern tribal" aesthetic, creating pieces that cross historical periods, referencing everything from the Byzantine to the Victorian periods. Her chunky skull rings are particularly popular, as are her bracelets embellished with antique coins and tassels.

897 High St., Armadale VIC 3143, +61 3 9509 8883, fiorinajewellery.com.

Gorman

In 1999 Lisa Gorman launched her namesake label in Melbourne, with a collection titled Less than 12 Degrees.

GORMAN

The success of that first offering led to the Gorman label becoming an iconic part of the first Australian designer wave in the early aughts. Her stores are eco-friendly and cool, selling her funky gem-print dresses and shirts, smart knitwear, and clogs. She recently collaborated with Melbourne artist Mirka Mora on a collection featuring her famous snakes and birds. There are fifteen Gorman stores in Australia.

235 Brunswick St., Fitzroy VIC 3065, +61 3 9419 5999, gormanshop.com.au, and additional locations.

Kleins Perfumery

Established in 1993, Kleins Perfumery remains a favorite with locals and visitors alike. Located in Fitzroy, this beauty boudoir is decorated with vintage Australian wallpaper and Florentine chandeliers, and has a store cat. Kleins houses more than eighty different brands from Australia and beyond. The fig perfume, in particular, is a must.

313 Brunswick St., Fitzroy VIC 3065, +61 3 9416 1221, kleinsperfumery.com.au.

Kuwaii

Established in 2008 by designer Kristy Barber, Kuwaii makes beautiful, intelligently designed clothing and footwear for women. An alternative to mass-produced fashion, all Kuwaii products are made in Australia. Refined and romantic, the slip dresses are a must-have, as are the shoes made from stock leather remnants and the selection of vintage and locally designed jewelry.

37-39 Glenlyon Rd., Brunswick VIC 3056, +61 3 9380 5731, kuwai.com.au.

Le Louvre

This salon-like store with gilt mirrors and a glass staircase began more than ninety years ago as a place for Melbourne's society ladies to shop. Today it's a destination for the latest from Chloé, Saint Laurent, Lanvin, Gucci, Valentino, Roland Mouret, and other high-end designers, with an ample selection of eveningwear and bridalwear, too.

2 Daly St., South Yarra VIC 3142, +61 03 9560 1300; lelouvre.com.au.

Lost and Found Market

Vintage furniture, clothing, and bric-a-brac market on Saturdays and Sundays.

499-511 Lygon St., East Brunswick VIC 3057, +61 3 9383 1883, lostandfoundmarket.com.au.

Marais

"I don't think I'll ever get over their amazing windows. They do a serious sale at the end of each season, too," says fashion editor Alyce Tran of this multi-brand boutique that stocks Céline, Chloé, Lanvin, and more.

79/87-91 Bourke St., Melbourne VIC 3000, +61 3 8658 9555, marais.com.au.

Monk House Design

A local favorite that stocks a select range of creative items by established and up-and-coming designers. Check out the Witu bags—these neoprene totes are an Australian fashion essential.

102 Lygon St., East Brunswick VIC, Australia 3057, +61 3 9381 1191, monkhousedesign.com.

P.A.M.

This Melbourne streetwear brand known for putting its own high-fashion spins on track pants, jogging shorts, and bomber jackets for men and women, often using cool graphics, is housed in the historic Curtin House, a 1922 art nouveau building named after former Labor Prime Minister John Curtin. Also in the building: a live music venue on level two, and the Rooftop Cinema on level six.

Level 3, 252 Swanston St., Melbourne VIC 3000, +61 3 9654 6458, perksandmini.com.

Peter Alexander

Many a last-minute gift crisis has been solved inside the iconic Peter Alexander pink doors—an Australian institution for sleepwear. There is no better place in the world to buy soft men's-style flannel pajamas, colorful cotton sleep shorts, silky nighties, and the most coveted Australian fashion accessory of

VIRGINIA MARTIN
MELBOURNE

Martin is the owner and designer of Melbourne-based contemporary women's fashion label Búl. Her love of travel is the inspiration behind the label, with each collection based on a different world destination and referencing the individual landscapes, cultures, and architecture.

BÚL is my favorite, of course. The stores are unassuming and inviting, oases you can escape to from the hustle and bustle of the streets. **CRAFT VICTORIA GALLERY STORE** supports local artisans with exhibitions and retail programs. There's an outlet in the city where you'll find beautiful one-of-a kind pieces.

METROPOLIS BOOKSHOP is tucked away on the third floor of the iconic Curtin House building. It boasts an amazing range of specialist art and design books and hard-to-find editions. Explore the whole building to find great stores, bars, and restaurants. Make your way to the sixth floor to enjoy some cocktails and the beautiful view of the Melbourne skyline at **ROOFTOP BAR.**

NGV STORE (National Gallery of Victoria) is a design store that offers everything from books to fashion to housewares. They often have interesting collaborations with local artists, and editions relevant to the current exhibitions.

BÚL, Melbourne Central, Level 2, 211 Latrobe St., Melbourne VIC 3000, +61 3 9663 0139, bul.com.au, and additional locations.

CRAFT VICTORIA GALLERY, 31 Flinders Ln, Melbourne VIC 3000, +61 3 9650 7775, craft.org.au.

METROPOLIS BOOKSHOP, Level 3 Curtin House, 252 Swanston St., Melbourne, Victoria 3000, +61 3 9663 2015, metropolisbookshop.com.au, curtinhouse.com.

ROOFTOP BAR, Level 6 Curtin House, 252 Swanston St., Melbourne VIC 3000, +61 3 9654 5394, rooftopcinema.com.au.

NGV STORE (NATIONAL GALLERY OF VICTORIA), 180 St Kilda Rd., Melbourne VIC 3006, +61 3 8620 2243, ngv.vic.gov.au.

THRID DRAWER DOWN

all—the wool-lined Ugg boot.

Shop G045 Emporium 269 321 Lonsdale St., Melbourne, VIC 3000, +61 03 966 28024, peteralexander.com.au, and additional locations.

Shag

Showcases treasures from every era in a funky environment.

130 Chapel St., Windsor VIC 3181, +61 3 9510 8817, shagmelbourne.com.

Shifting Worlds

A luxury store located in the heart of the city, stocking clothing, accessories, and home goods from names such as Pleats Please, Bao Bao, and Maryam Nassir Zadeh—the shopping destination for

ONLINE SHOPPING TIP

Tuchuzy.com offers international shipping and a great selection of Aussie labels, including KITX, Georgia Alice, and Sir the Label (a favorite of Sydney-born model and Instagram star Mimi Elashiry). Top designer sites such as ellerlyland.com, zimmermann.com, and dionlee.com also include international shipping options.

obscure-label nerds!

187-193 Elizabeth St., Melbourne VIC 3000, +61 3 9600 0459, shifting-worlds.com.

Third Drawer Down

Curated objects from around the world, including home accessories, books, and jewelry, as well as items produced from the Third Drawer Down Studio. You'll find scarves and tote bags by artists, products from Tom Dixon, Lucy Folk, and other well-known interior designers, and more.

93 George St., Fitzroy VIC 3065 +61 03 9534 4088, Prahran, thirddrawerdown.com, and an additional location in Prahran.

Verner

Ingrid Verner first emerged on the Australian fashion scene as a TV star, before launching her namesake label in 2012. The brand has an upscale streetwear vibe; think, sweatshirts and sweatpants with artful cutouts. Sharing the space with the Verner store is Slow Waves, a concept store that collects small, independent labels. It's curated by Matli Atterton, who is focused on supporting the designers and getting the low-high balance right.

358 Lonsdale St., Melbourne VIC 3000, +61 3 9088 0760, verner.com.

CONTRI

B. ÅKERLUND is a costume designer, stylist, and Stockholm-to-Los Angeles transplant whose hand can be seen in everything: Television commercials for Dior, Absolut, and Nike; album covers for Lady Gaga and the Red Hot Chili Peppers; feature films (*Spun, Horsemen*); music videos ("Hold Up" from Beyoncé's visual album *Lemonade*); and Super Bowl halftime shows with the Black Eyed Peas (2011) and Madonna (2012).
Biggest score: A life-size Andy Warhol doll that I found at the Rose Bowl Flea Market.

JOSEPH ALTUZARRA launched the luxury women's line that bears his name in 2008, and has been raking in fashion industry accolades ever since. Recognitions include the CFDA/Vogue Fashion Fund award (2011), the CFDA Swarovski Award for Womenswear (2012), and the CFDA Womenswear Designer of the Year (2014). His strong, feminine dresses are worn by the likes of Lupita Nyong'o, Rihanna, and Zoe Saldana.
Style inspiration: Marlon Brando in The Wild One.
Words of wisdom:

If you're still thinking about a potential buy the next day, it's probably worth the purchase.

SOPHIA AMORUSO used a laptop computer and a love of vintage to build Nasty Gal into a retail empire. Her business memoir *#GIRLBOSS* hit the *New York Times* bestseller list in 2014, the same year she launched the GIRLBOSS Foundation, which awards financial grants to female creatives pursuing entrepreneurial endeavors. Her second book, *Nasty Galaxy,* was published in 2016.
Style icon: Bianca Jagger in her white suit.
Biggest score: A vintage Chanel jacket bought for $8 at the Salvation Army—and sold on eBay for $1,200.

PAUL ANDREW is a British-born, New York-based shoe designer who launched his namesake collection in 2013. In 2014, he became the first footwear designer to win the CFDA/Vogue Fashion Fund award; in 2016, he took home the CFDA Swarovski Award for Accessory Design. Among his celebrity fans are Cate Blanchett, Jessica Chastain, and Lupita Nyong'o.
Biggest score: A vintage Hermès Garden Party PM bag in navy-blue canvas and tan leather, purchased for $40 from Housing Works, a secondhand store in New York's West Village.
Words of wisdom:

Everything in life is about moderation, including the fun, frivolous, and impractical!

ROSE APODACA, the godmother of the L.A. fashion journalist set, has uncapped her pen on behalf of the *Los Angeles Times*, *Harper's Bazaar*, and *Women's Wear Daily* over the past several decades. She's penned a string of style-centric books about or with some

BUTORS

of the biggest names in the fashion business, including retailer Fred Hayman, stylist and designer Rachel Zoe, and burlesque queen Dita Von Teese. She also co-owns and operates the home goods emporium A+R with her husband, Andy Griffith.
Style icon: Nancy Cunard, and not only for her turbans, kohl-rimmed peepers, and limbs ringed in bangles. Those things only served to accessorize a maverick spirit of activism, intelligence, feminism, and conviction—and that is true lifestyle.
Words of wisdom:

Shopping is like a one-night stand: if there's any inkling you're going to end up regretting some part of it, then move on!

GABRIELA ARTIGAS AND TERESITA ARTIGAS, who originally hail from Mexico City, are the sister act behind Gabriela Artigas & Co., an L.A.-based jewelry business. Since the brand's launch in 2003, its everyday statement pieces have found favor with the likes of Tyra Banks, Emma Roberts, Chelsea Handler, and Carey Mulligan.
Words of wisdom: For everything that comes into your wardrobe, something must always come out. Extend the life of items you don't want anymore by reselling them. Someone, somewhere is going to appreciate the thing that you once appreciated. (Teresita)
Style inspiration: White clothes—tees, dresses, pants, shirts, everything—and red lips. There's a certain understated elegance when you have a white canvas. (Gabriela)

MICKEY ASHMORE, known to comfortably shod clients around the globe as "the Sabah Dealer," is a New York City–based former hedge fund manager who leveraged a six-month stint in Istanbul while working for Microsoft into a burgeoning business selling handmade Turkish slippers.
Words of wisdom:

Keep it simple. A few great items go a long way. I think one's choice of what to wear should take up minimal time each day.

Style icon: René Holguin, owner of RTH in Los Angeles.

JORDAN ASKILL is a New York City–based jewelry designer and sculptor who was born and raised in Sydney, Australia. He launched his namesake jewelry brand in London in 2010. In 2015 he won the British Fashion Award for Emerging Accessory Design—the first jewelry designer to win a BFA in more than five years.
Biggest score: A Tibetan bamboo cuff found at the gem market in Taipei.
Style icon: Elizabeth Taylor, because of her incredible collection of jewelry.

CONTRIBUTORS

BRIAN ATWOOD is a New York- and Milan-based FIT-educated model turned designer who holds the distinction of being the first American ever hired by Gianni Versace. He launched his namesake footwear collection in 2001. Atwood's fantastical footwear has appeared on the feet of such luminaries as Lady Gaga, Taylor Swift, Victoria Beckham, Jessica Alba, and Kate Hudson.
Biggest score: A vintage print of Chris von Wangenheim's Dior ad with Liz Taylor and a Doberman.
Words of wisdom:

Don't think an item will be there when you return. If you love it, buy it.

CHRISTENE BARBERICH is the global editor-in-chief and cofounder of the Webby award-winning lifestyle media company Refinery29. Barberich is also the *New York Times* bestselling co-author of *Style Stalking.* Prior to cofounding Refinery29 in 2005, she held posts at *Gourmet* magazine, *The Daily*, *The New Yorker*, and was the founding editor of the ASME-winning *CITY* magazine. Her fashion and design writing have appeared in the *New York Times*, *Travel & Leisure*, and *New York* magazine among other titles. She lives in Brooklyn.

VANESSA BELL's insatiable curiosity about her adopted hometown Buenos Aires led her to investigate its sleepy backstreets and unearth its most tucked away spots, emerging trends, and up-and-coming talent to create her blog cremedelacremeba.com. As a freelance writer, she is a regular contributor to *Wallpaper** and *Monocle*, and her work has appeared in *The Independent*, *Departures*, *Fathom*, Traveldo.se, and *Time Out.* She also operates the Crème de la Crème bespoke shopping service, which designs personalized itineraries in Buenos Aires for each client's shopping needs.

STACEY BENDET is creative director and CEO of the contemporary label Alice and Olivia, which she founded in 2002. Her ornamental fabrics and whimsical prints are a go-to for a stylish celebrity set that includes Jessica Alba, Eva Longoria, Anne Hathaway, and Heidi Klum. Bendet was named to *Vanity Fair*'s International Best-Dressed List Hall of Fame in 2014.
Style inspiration: A photo of my mother on her wedding day wearing this amazing Fred Leighton wedding dress with a pair of super-flare bell-bottom jeans underneath.
Words of wisdom:

Shopping is cheaper than a psychiatrist!

SOFÍA SANCHEZ DE BETAK is a Buenos Aires-born, New York-based fashion consultant, art director, and all-around fashion darling who has worked with Marni, Chloé, Tiffany & Co., Jimmy Choo, Belstaff, and Ermenegildo Zegna among others. In 2012 she turned her focus toward her home country and launched the website UnderOurSky.com to showcase Argentine design with a focus on handmade and one-of-a-kind accessories. In early 2016, the world traveler—she shares her globe-trotting adventures with her 92,000-plus Instagram followers (@chufy)—collaborated on a line of luggage with Globe-Trotter and the Luxury Collection Hotels.
Words of wisdom:

If you love it, get two!

AURÉLIE BIDERMANN is a Paris-based jewelry designer who launched her namesake collection in 2004. Her travels around the globe—to California, Bali, and India—inspire her collections, which are available at hundreds of boutiques worldwide. Celebrity fans of her

baubles include Céline Dion, Beyoncé, and Keira Knightley.
Style inspiration: I adore Charlotte Rampling. Her style is so timeless and elegant; she looks chic in anything she puts on and it always seems so effortless.
Biggest score: A vintage piece from Yves Saint Laurent's '70s-era Rive Gauche collection.
Words of wisdom:

Shop when you feel good.

ANINE BING is the Denmark-born, L.A.-based founder and creative director of the namesake Scandinavian-meets-American fashion line, which launched in 2012 and is currently sold in more than 300 boutiques around the globe. Her off-duty-model styles, including leather moto pants, studded boots, and lace bralettes, are faves with Kendall Jenner and Rosie Huntington-Whiteley.
Style inspiration: Jane Birkin.
Words of wisdom:

Less is more. That goes with everything I do in life, including shopping. I'd rather save up for one very nice thing than buy a bunch of stuff I'll only use one time.

CHRISTINA BINKLEY is the *Wall Street Journal*'s fashion and style columnist and author of the *New York Times* bestseller *Winner Takes All: Steve Wynn, Kirk Kerkorian, Gary Loveman, and the Race to Own Las Vegas*. Based in Los Angeles, she travels the globe, from New York to Milan and Paris, covering the twice-yearly fashion week circuit. She was part of a team that won a Pulitzer Prize for its coverage of 9/11.
Style influence: I don't even think of fashion that way. I just know what I like.
Words of wisdom:

Shop like a man. Demand great fit, and if the fabric doesn't feel good, walk away.

HELENA BORDON is a São Paulo-born blogger, entrepreneur, and designer who cofounded the Brazilian fast-fashion brand 284 in 2008. The daughter of Donata Meirelles, former creative director of Brazilian high-fashion boutique Daslu, Bordon documents her globe-trotting, style-centric adventures online at helenabordon.com. In 2013, she collaborated with LOOL on a limited-edition jewelry collection.
Biggest score: A vintage Lanvin coat from Casa Juisi in São Paulo.
Words of wisdom:

Go shopping with the same discerning eye a gallerist has at an art fair.

SONIA BOYAJIAN is an Antwerp-trained, Los Angeles-based designer of artful, eye-catching statement jewelry. She launched her namesake line in 2003 and opened an atelier/boutique in Hollywood in 2014. Her baubles have found favor with the likes of Scarlett Johansson and Natalie Portman.
Style inspiration: Women who look at ease in their clothing.
Biggest score: A Valentino bustier with a massive bow on it for $50 at a resale boutique.

CONTRIBUTORS

Words of wisdom:

In the words of Edith Head, "A dress should be tight enough to show you're a woman and loose enough to prove you're a lady."

JANIE BRYANT is a costume designer best known for her work on the AMC television series *Mad Men*, which earned her multiple Emmy Award nominations, two Costume Designers Guild Awards, a clothing collaboration with Banana Republic, and a book, *The Fashion File: Advice, Tips, and Inspiration From the Costume Designer of Mad Men* (co-authored with Monica Corcoran Harel). She also has an Emmy Award on her mantel for her work on the HBO series *Deadwood*.

Style inspirations: The rococo period, Jean Shrimpton, and Vivien Leigh as Scarlett O'Hara.

Biggest score: A 1960s white gold, mother-of-pearl, and diamond domed cocktail ring bought at Treasure Isle Flea Market in Naples, Florida.

Words of wisdom:

Buy pieces you are passionate about and always try on.

VICTORIA BRYNNER is a Swiss-born, Beverly Hills-based international creative consultant and the founder and president of Stardust Visions, a photo production company whose client list reads like a who's who of the luxury fashion world (Balenciaga, Prada, Giorgio Armani, and Valentino, among others). She is the daughter of Academy Award-winning actor Yul Brynner.

Style inspirations: My mother, Doris Brynner, Audrey Hepburn, early Balenciaga, and Valentino.

Biggest score: An original Arthur Elgort print of jazz tenor saxophonist Dexter Gordon—bought at a garage sale for $20.

TORY BURCH is the chairman, CEO, and designer of her namesake label. Launched in 2004 with a single NoLIta boutique, her company has since grown into a global bohemian-prep lifestyle brand that is a go-to for everyone from Kerry Washington, Jessica Alba, and Kiernan Shipka to the Duchess of Cambridge. In 2009 Burch launched the Tory Burch Foundation with the goal of empowering women and families through mentoring and microfinancing.

Style inspiration: My mom in a head-to-toe gold lamé outfit by Zoran.

Biggest score: A green tunic found at a Paris flea market. It would go on to inspire one of my first designs.

LIBBY CALLAWAY has contributed as a fashion journalist to the *New York Post*, *Elle*, the *New York Times*'s *T Magazine*, Style.com, *Travel + Leisure*, and *Glamour*, where she had her own fashion advice column. She is the media director for Nashville denim company Imogene + Willie. As a former wardrobe stylist and vintage clothing dealer, Libby is a noted secondhand shopping expert.

Style inspiration: I am a massive fan of '40s and '50s style, and I'd also have to say the wardrobe of Gialo horror films *Suspiria* and *Tenebre* by Dario Argento, and postmodernist architecture and design.

CHRISTINA CARADONA was born in New York and raised in France by a mother who was a professional model and a father who loved to travel. Christina is the model/actress who created the popular blog Trop Rouge in 2010. She has been featured in *Elle*, *Glamour*, *Cosmopolitan*, *Nylon*, and

Seventeen magazines, and her signature curly locks have appeared in campaigns for Paul Mitchell, H&M, Joe Fresh, OPI, and many other brands. She lives in New York City.

PETER CHEUNG is the Hong Kong–based founder and chief executive officer of Peter Cheung Asia Limited, a strategic branding and marketing firm. Cheung works with a range of luxury brands and celebrities, including Van Cleef & Arpels, Parisian couturier Gaspard Yurkievich, and model Philip Huang.
Style influence: Hong Kong in the 1980s. Luxury and fashion brands were just being introduced and the pioneer was Joyce Ma. Everyone dressed so perfectly for every occasion, at every destination—it was high-octane, put-together fashion!
Biggest score: A one-of-a-kind, full-length python trench coat purchased at the John Galliano boutique in Paris in 2005.
Words of wisdom:

Don't bother squeezing into it.

ALINA CHO is a New York–based journalist and editor-at-large at Ballantine Bantam Dell, where she develops fashion and lifestyle books. She is the host of the Metropolitan Museum of Art's lecture series "The Atelier With Alina Cho," for which she has interviewed fashion luminaries, including Anna Wintour, Donatella Versace, Alber Elbaz, Diane von Furstenberg, and Alexander Wang.
Style inspiration: The 1958 Willy Rizzo photograph of Yves Saint Laurent with models wearing clothes from his first collection for Christian Dior. It hangs in my bedroom and I look at it every day. It reminds me of a beautiful, feminine, formal style of a bygone era.
Biggest score: A floor-length ivory feather Lanvin coat found at Frock, a now-defunct vintage store in SoHo.

NATALIE CHOY was born in Providence, Rhode Island and moved to Korea at a very young age. As an adult, she moved to New York to study Photography and English Literature at the Parsons & Eugene Lang College, then Paris to pursue her degree in Fashion Styling at Istituto Marangoni. She has worked in event planning, styling and PR in London, Moscow and New York.

ARI SETH COHEN is the street-style photographer and creator of Advanced Style, a blog that's been documenting the fashion and style of the over-sixty set since 2008. He's also the creator of a documentary and two books based on the blog, *Advanced Style* (2012) and *Advanced Style: Older & Wiser* (2016).
Style inspirations: Nancy Cunard, Cecil Beaton's images of Edith Sitwell, the Marchesa Casati, the Seeberger Brothers street-style photos from the early 1900s, Liberace, Nudie's Tailors, Cary Grant, and Quentin Crisp.
Biggest score: A multicolored sequin kimono jacket from Etsy—a surprise gift from my boyfriend.
Words of wisdom:

You'll never regret buying a vintage treasure, but you may regret leaving it behind.

RACHEL COMEY is a New York–based fashion designer whose career kicked off with a collaboration with the band Gogol Bordello that earned her a place in the 2001 Whitney Biennial. Her namesake women's label launched in 2004. Known for arty textiles (foam, linen, pebble, crochet), modern silhouettes, and covetable shoes, it is sold at more than 100 high-end boutiques and department stores in sixteen countries as well as stand-alone stores in New York and Los Angeles.

CONTRIBUTORS

KENDALL CONRAD is a former model whose accessories design career began in 2000 when she couldn't find a handbag she liked. Today her Los Angeles–based namesake collection is available online and at brick-and-mortar boutiques in California, where the Santa Barbara native lives.
Style inspiration: California beach girl Lauren Hutton and Candice Bergen and Ali MacGraw mixed with a touch of European influence (Charlotte Rampling, Anouk Aimée, and Julie Christie).
Biggest score: Black satin YSL Rive Gauche sailor pants from the '70s purchased in the '90s from L.A. vintage store the Paper Bag Princess.
Words of wisdom:

Make sure it fits. Better to buy big, and tailor.

BROOKE TAYLOR CORCIA is the founder and CEO of Los Angeles–based online retail site The Dreslyn, which launched in 2012. She also served as the senior womenswear and accessories buyer for ssense.com, prior to which she was the associate fashion editor at *C Magazine*.
Style inspiration: Nineties minimalism was at its height during my formative years, so that inevitably had an impact on my way of imagining style. I still reference the timeless and understated costume design by Ellen Mirojnick for the film *A Perfect Murder*. It holds up after nearly twenty years.
Words of wisdom:

Less is more.

BRONWYN COSGRAVE is the director of Cosgrave Global Media, a London-based firm that focuses on luxury brand communications strategy. Her fashion CV includes serving as features editor of British *Vogue*, penning six fashion history books, serving as guest curator of the exhibition "Designing 007: Fifty Years of Bond Style" at the Barbican Centre, and contributing to a host of international fashion newspapers and magazines, including *Vogue* India, where she is a contributing editor.

EMILY CURRENT AND MERITT ELLIOTT are L.A.-based stylists, consultants, authors, and the design duo behind the Current Elliott denim brand, which they founded in 2008 and left in 2012. They are the creative directors of contemporary women's collection the Great.
Style influence: The Boxcar Children was our favorite childhood book. It's about children who are forced to be resourceful and imaginative, and create magical worlds in their minds. We love that childlike sense of discovery, and see it affect the way we create in our jobs.
Biggest score: A vintage sign that says SHIRTS AND TIES found at a vintage store in Ventura County that hangs in our office.
Words of wisdom:

Shopping can be a personal and emotional journey, and you should be led not by what you need or should get but what makes you happy.

KAVITA DASWANI is an international journalist and author, and the former fashion editor for the *South China Morning Post* in Hong Kong and Asian correspondent for *Women's Wear Daily*, both of which she still contributes to. She also currently writes for the *Los Angeles Times* and international editions of *Vogue*, *Condé Nast Traveler*, and *Grazia Italia*. She has published seven books, including the 2012 Harper Collins' India title *Bombay Girl*, set in the high-society world of one of India's most sophisticated cities.

JESSICA DE RUITER started her career more than decade ago working as a fashion editor with a range of Condé Nast titles, including *Vogue*, *Teen Vogue*, *W*, and *WWD*. She works as a stylist to the stars, and her list of A-list clients includes Jennifer Lawrence, Michael Fassbender, Emily Blunt, Robert Pattinson, Diane Kruger, and Angelica Huston. She's also worked with a range of commercial clients, including Ferragamo, James Perse, Bebe, and Madewell. She lives in Ojai, California.
Style influence: Carolyn Bessette Kennedy, for her easy elegance and classic, clean style.
Words of wisdom:

Sleep on it.

ANNA DELLO RUSSO is a Milan-based fashion journalist, fashion-show front-row fixture, and enthusiastic collector of apparel and jewelry. She spent nearly two decades at Condé Nast Italia, including roles as fashion editor at *Vogue* Italia and editor of *L'Uomo Vogue*. She is editor-at-large and creative consultant for *Vogue* Japan. In 2012, she collaborated with Swedish fast-fashion brand H&M on a line of accessories and jewelry.

VALERY DEMURE founded her namesake jewelry-focused PR agency in London in 2005. In 2012 she launched e-commerce site valerydemure.com, which curates jewelry and accessories from around the globe. In addition, she serves as an industry consultant to a range of brands and is an adviser for the fashion jewelry and accessories curriculum at London College of Fashion.
Biggest score: A pair of black suede and gold metallic open-toe Chanel booties, lusted after for years and eventually scored during a 2 a.m. eBay session.
Words of wisdom:

It's not about needing it.

EVREN DOGANCAY is the chief buyer for the department store Beymen and former head buyer for the Kirna Zabête boutique in SoHo. Based in Istanbul, she can be found trotting the globe, from Milan to Paris and beyond, to find the right mix of merchandise to stock the store.
Style influences: Lee Radziwill and Catherine Deneuve.
Biggest score: Thigh-high Alaïa boots that I got at Kirna Zabête in New York. I was working as the buying director at the time. The boots were from the previous season and there was only one pair left.

JACEY DUPRIE is a style blogger and the editor of Damsel in Dior, a website she launched in 2009 that encompasses fashion, lifestyle, travel, and home décor. The website has been featured in the Huffington Post, *Vanity Fair*, *WhoWhatWear*, *Forbes*, and *E! News*, and Duprie has appeared in ad campaigns for Saks, GAP, and Nordstrom. She lives in Los Angeles.

ALISON EDMOND is one of the most highly regarded editorial stylists in the fashion industry and has worked with the who's who of Hollywood, including Beyoncé, Gwyneth Paltrow, and Angelina Jolie. A native Brit, she has worked all over the world styling, art directing, and consulting for magazines, advertising, TV commercials, and design houses. She is currently fashion director at *C Magazine* in Los Angeles, also covering C Men, C Home, and C Weddings.

PIP EDWARDS is a stylist and veteran of the Australian fashion scene. She serves as design director for the multi-brand retailer General Pants Co. She is the cofounder of the retro-inspired activewear label that bears her initials—P.E. Nation—which launched in early 2016. She lives a stone's toss from Sydney's Bondi Beach.

CONTRIBUTORS

Style inspiration: Seventies denim and '90s street.
Biggest score: At One of a Kind, the London vintage shop where Kate Moss shops, I found an original Vivienne Westwood Pirate collection dress. I can wear it, but I don't, it hangs on my wall. It cost a fortune, and my baby daddy bought it for me. I buy not necessarily to wear but to appreciate.

CRISTINA EHRLICH is a former professional ballet dancer who works as a New York–based stylist. Her list of A-list clients includes Margot Robbie, Priyanka Chopra, Anna Kendrick, Uzo Aduba, Gugu Mbatha-Raw, Julia Louis-Dreyfus, and Tina Fey. She has worked with photographers such as Patrick Demarchelier, Mert Alas & Marcus Piggott, Peter Lindbergh, and Peggy Sirota. She was awarded "Celebrity Stylist of the Year" at the 2012 Style Awards in New York City and has partnered with Pandora to serve as a brand ambassador.
Style inspiration: Jean Seberg in *Breathless*. It was all about her effortless street style, her flats, jeans, T-shirts. She was the absolute French gamine.

Words of wisdom:

Take risks but be realistic.

MIMI ELASHIRY is a Sydney-born model and fashion blogger who leveraged a cult Instagram following into a career working with brands like Diesel, Free People, and Glue Store. In 2014, she was tapped to be the official style ambassador of MTV Australia. She is currently based in Los Angeles.
Style inspiration: Cher in the '70s had an incredibly eclectic style—from the neon mesh to the heavily beaded cutout gowns, Indian-inspired two-pieces, and very little makeup or accessories—that has always influenced and inspired me.

MERITT ELLIOTT (see Emily Current).

KAREN ERICKSON is cofounder and designer of New York–based Erickson Beamon, a vintage-inspired jewelry brand founded in the early '80s. She has accessorized high-profile A-list clients from Lady Gaga to Michelle Obama, with Gwyneth Paltrow, Beyoncé, Madonna, and Nicole Kidman in between. A go-to runway collaborator for luxury fashion labels such as Alexander McQueen, Givenchy, Donna Karen, and Zac Posen, Erickson launched a collaboration with Target in 2009.
Style inspiration: I became fashion-aware in the '70s, and I thank my lucky stars the '70s remain fashion insiders' most referenced decade. The designers in the '70s were inspired by the '20s and the '40s, so with one decade I get three. My fashion icon is a decade.

ABRIMA ERWIAH is cofounder and co-creative director of the Ghana-based Studio One Eighty Nine, which she created in 2013 with actress and activist, Rosario Dawson. Their social enterprise helps promote and curate African and African-inspired content and brands through worldwide distribution and manufacturing of their private label, Studio One Eighty Nine, as well as through support of other brands. Erwiah is a veteran of the fashion and luxury industry, with more than sixteen years' experience at Bottega Veneta, Hermes, John Lobb, and other brands.

NINA FARRAN is the founder of e-commerce site Fashionkind.com, which features a curated mix of ethically produced and sustainable luxury products from labels such as Coclico, A Peace Treaty, Ryan Roche, and Rialto Jean Project. Her background is in developing new opportunities that make a positive impact. While at the University of Pennsylvania, she launched a humanitarian fashion effort that built schools in sub-Saharan Africa and, more recently, she initiated and successfully built an impact-investing program at a national investment and wealth management firm. She's based in New York.

CARLA FERNÁNDEZ is creative director of the Mexico City–based fashion label that bears her name. Launched in 2000, her ready-to-wear collection takes inspiration from traditional Mexican textiles and geometric patterns, and is created in collaboration with artisans across Mexico.
Words of wisdom:

I always tell my kids that shopping is like the warning they give you on an airplane. Place the oxygen mask on yourself before helping others; shop for yourself first and then shop for the rest of the family and friends!

SAMUEL FERNSTRÖM is the managing director of fashion brand & Other Stories, and works out of ateliers in Paris and Stockholm. He's been on board since day one, cofounding the brand together with a small group of creatives. Samuel worked at H&M for ten years before he started to develop & Other Stories. Most of his years at H&M were spent in the concept development group at the new business department in Stockholm.

ERIN FETHERSTON was raised in the San Francisco Bay Area, and studied fashion design in Paris, where she first launched her namesake women's collection in 2005. She relocated to Los Angeles in 2016, and launched a home collection.
Words of wisdom:

Before I make a purchase, I always ask myself, "Will I love it years from now?"

ANNABELLE FLEUR is a Latvia-to-Los Angeles transplant who helms the fashion blog Viva Luxury. The Victoria's Secret ambassador has worked with a range of beauty and fashion brands, including Olay for the Grammys, RED Valentino, Stuart Weitzman, Bergdorf Goodman, 7 for All Mankind, Pandora, and Express.
Biggest score: An in-season Marc Jacobs Trouble bag bought at a 70 percent discount from the sale section of TheCorner.com.
Words of wisdom:

Regardless of how beautiful something looks on a hanger, the only thing that really matters is how good it looks on you.

HEATHER JOHN FOGARTY writes about the things she loves, whether that's a well-executed gin and tonic, a Case Study house, a Rodarte chiffon coat, her favorite hotel swimming pools, or a Jambon-Beurre sandwich slathered in buckwheat honey butter. Her work has appeared in publications such as Australian *Vogue*, *Marie Claire*, *Los Angeles Magazine*,

C Magazine, *Playboy*, *Robb Report*, the *Los Angeles Times*, and *Bon Appétit*, where she was wine and spirits editor from 2004 to 2011. She is currently working on her first novel.

BILLY FONG has served as executive director of the Texas Association of Museums since 2016, prior to which he held posts at prestigious museums around the country. He's also a stylist and writer, and penned a style column for *PaperCity* magazine for nearly two years. He lives in the Dallas/Fort Worth area.
Biggest score: My first-ever pair of Gucci loafers purchased in 1995 for $395 from the brand's Boca Raton boutique. Twenty-five pairs later, they're still displayed in a place of honor—and still in the original box.

LIZZIE FORTUNATO is the designer and cofounder (with twin sister Kathryn) of the Lizzie Fortunato jewelry line, which launched in 2008 and added leather goods in 2011. Her artful modernist accessories with an exotic flair have adorned the fashion world ever since. The sisters have expanded their line, offering a range of artisanal home goods discovered on their travels to India, Morocco, Mexico, and Peru.
Style influence: Angelica Huston modeling Alexander Calder's curvy "feathered" brass necklace with a high chignon and black turtleneck. Her look is so classically chic and the jewelry makes such a statement. It's an image I think of a lot when getting dressed.

LISEANNE FRANKFURT is native Californian whose career as a jewelry designer began when she started selling her work during her sophomore year at UCLA. She launched LFrank Jewelry and opened a retail store in Venice, California, in 2007. In 2015, Frankfurt expanded the line to include a lingerie collection.
Biggest score: An incredible red leather trench coat from Alber Elbaz's last collection for YSL at the Barneys Warehouse sale. It was originally around $10,000. I was pregnant with my daughter at the time, with a toddler running around and a renovation at home, so it was far too indulgent. I found it at the sale for $199. I felt faint, and as it turned out, went into the hospital the next day in premature labor!

NINA GARDUNO launched the L.A. brand FREECITY in 2002 with a simple T-shirt that read FREECITY NEIGHBORHOOD. The idea blossomed into a lifestyle movement, which is brought to life in the brand's 3,000-square-foot Highland Avenue store in Los Angeles. The inspirational retail environment has a different theme each season, which translates to the artwork on the walls, the tunes played in the store, and the words on the clothing.

LIZZIE GARRETT METTLER is a Los Angeles-based freelance writer and creator of the-reed.com, an online destination that's part blog, part travelogue, and part carefully curated e-commerce experience. Her first book, *Tomboy Style*—based on her blog of the same name—was published in 2012.
Style influences: Coco Chanel's rebellious attitude, Diane Keaton's nonconformist nonchalance, Katharine Hepburn's "I don't give a damn, I'm wearing pants anyway" mantra all help me out on days when I don't know what to wear.

ROSETTA GETTY is a former model turned designer whose namesake collection of modern, sophisticated, and uncomplicated clothing launched in 2014, and is carried by some of the top boutiques and department stores worldwide including A'Maree's in Newport Beach, Ikram in Chicago, and Harvey Nichols and Selfridges in London. She lives in Los Angeles.

Style influences: Louise Bourgeois, Betty Parsons, '90s Helmut Lang, Prada, and Jil Sander.
Biggest score: A Wolfgang Tillmans photograph—one of the first purchases in my collection. I bought it from Shaun Regen.

ROBIN GIVHAN is the Pulitzer Prize–winning fashion editor of the *Washington Post* and the co-author of *Michelle: Her First Year as First Lady*. Her first solo book, *The Battle of Versailles* (2015), is being made into a movie for HBO Films co-written and directed by Ava DuVernay. In 2006, she won a Pulitzer Prize in criticism for her fashion coverage. She is based in Washington, DC.
Style influence: My mother from her heyday in the 1960s and '70s. She was always polished. Never fancy, but pulled together. I hear her voice telling me not to go out in wrinkled clothing. It's because of my mother that I am incapable of traveling in sweatpants. She would be appalled.

BONNAE GOKSON is the Hong Kong–based style icon, restaurateur, and creative force behind Sevva, C'est La B, and Mrs. B's Cakery. Prior to focusing on foodstuffs, the "queen of cakes" worked in the fashion space helping luxury brands Prada, Giorgio Armani, and Chanel build their presence in Asia. Her edible works of art are the subject of an award-winning coffee-table book *Butterflies and All Sweet Things* (2014)
Style influence: Grace Kelly.
Words of wisdom:

Quality over quantity always.

LORI GOLDSTEIN is a New York–based stylist who enthusiastically embraces the philosophy that "everything goes with anything." She's worked for a who's who of the celebrity set on both sides of the camera. In 2009, she added designer to her résumé with the launch of LOGO by Lori Goldstein exclusively for QVC. She's also the fashion editor-at-large for *Elle* magazine and the author of *Lori Goldstein: Style Is Instinct* (2013).
Style influences: Everyone from my grandmother GaGa Gladys, who wore head-to-toe leopard, to Marilyn Monroe. Everything Liz Taylor did and wore was heaven. Cher, Bowie, Barbra in every movie, *The Thomas Crown Affair*, *Valley of the Dolls* . . . I'm stopping now.
Words of wisdom:

If you can't stop thinking about it, get it.

NJ GOLDSTON is the Beverly Hills–based founder and editor-in-chief (and The Brunette) of the Webby-award-winning fashion and style blog The Blonde & The Brunette. She's also the chief creative officer of advertising, branding, and digital agency, The UXB, and a managing partner of her twin sons' L.A.-based footwear brand Athletic Propulsion Labs.
Biggest score: A *Sergeant Pepper*–style jacket from the Christophe Decarnin days at Balmain. It was hidden in the back at Browns in London. I still wear it at least once a year, on Michael Jackson's birthday.
Words of wisdom:

Don't buy something with an occasion in mind. Buy something because you love it, and it will be ready to go when the moment arrives.

LIZ GOLDWYN is a Los Angeles–based writer, filmmaker, artist, and an enthusiastic collector of vintage clothing. Her works include the nonfiction book *Pretty Things: The Last Generation of American Burlesque Queens*, the HBO documentary based on it (which she also directed), and the novel *Sporting Guide: Los Angeles, 1897* (2015).

Biggest score: A Rudi Gernreich kabuki dress bought at a serious discount from Cameron Silver the week he opened Decades.

Words of wisdom:

I crib Janis Joplin's ethos—"If you buy it today, you don't wear it tomorrow." Preach.

MARY ALICE HANEY is a celebrity stylist and fashion editor (*Marie Claire*, *GQ*) turned designer who launched her namesake Los Angeles–based luxury women's label Haney in 2013. Celebrity fans of her sexy, red-carpet-ready creations include Jennifer Lawrence, Chrissy Teigen, Kate Hudson, and Taylor Swift.

Style inspiration: Old Hollywood. It's the inspiration for my collections, too.

STEFANIE HANSSEN is the founder and creative director of Berlin-based perfume brand Frau Tonis Parfum. In addition to creating a suite of fragrances that use the city of Berlin as a theme, she has partnered with other brands, from the Ritz-Carlton Hotel to concept stores and fashion magazines, to create bespoke scents.

Style influence: Diana Vreeland! I love her style and her idea of beauty. Her book *The Eye Has to Travel* is my bible.

DIVIA HARILELA is a thirteen-year veteran of the fashion media, having served as the fashion editor for Hong Kong's leading English-language newspaper, the *South China Morning Post*, before founding the luxury and fashion website the D'Vine in 2011. Born and raised in Hong Kong, she's often sought out as an authority on fashion in Asia.

Biggest score: An incredible jacket I found in Berlin made from a hand-painted vintage kimono. It's been deconstructed and put back together again all by hand—even the stitching is a detail in itself. The back looks like a piece of art, and people always stop me when I wear it.

KEMAL HARRIS is the New York–based half of the bicoastal styling team known as Kemal and Karla (the other half, Karla Welch, is based in L.A.), who have created red-carpet looks for the likes of Olivia Wilde, Felicity Jones, Hailee Steinfeld, and Zooey Deschanel, as well as tour wardrobes for Justin Bieber, Pink, and Idina Menzel. Harris added costume designer to her CV in 2015 when she was tapped to design wardrobe pieces for longtime client Robin Wright's character Claire Underwood on the Netflix series *House of Cards*.

Words of wisdom:

Trust your gut but also watch out for repeat offenders. I own approximately twenty-five biker jackets—nobody needs that many.

JOHNSON HARTIG is the cofounder and designer of the Los Angeles–based Libertine label that launched in 2001. His book, *Libertine: The Creative Beauty, Humor and Inspiration Behind the Cult Label*, was published in 2015.

Style influences: I'm a "more is more" guy: Tony Duquette, Mario Buatta, Mark Hampton, Madeleine Castaing, and Jean Cocteau. Last year I visited Cocteau's house in Milly-la-Forêt, outside

Paris. Much of his place is still as it was when he died, and I continually reference it as inspiration. It's well worth the day trip; I recommend it if one has an extra day in Paris.
Biggest score: I just found a Birkin and a classic '70s Gucci bag for $24 each. I'm not going to tell you at which Goodwill I found them, because then I'd have to kill you.

LAINY HEDAYA is a model, writer, brand consultant, and the founder/creative director of the New York City fashion blog the Haute Inhabit, which she launched in 2011. She's worked with a range of fashion- and style-focused brands, including Chanel, Tiffany & Co., H&M, and W Hotels, and has appeared in the pages of fashion magazines (*Marie Claire*, *Elle*, and *W*, to name but a few).
Biggest score: A J. Mendel gown for $100 at a sample sale. It had a bloodstain on it.
Words of wisdom:

Unless you know you're going to wear it until it's destroyed, it's not worth a penny to you. Clothes are meant to be a part of your memories, not stuck in a closet collecting dust.

BRETT HEYMAN is the founder of Edie Parker, a brand of vintage-inspired clutches and handbags based in New York City. The aesthetic of the brand and its signature acrylic clutches, which have been carried by nearly every star in Hollywood, sprang from Heyman's love of midcentury style.

MARA HOFFMAN is a New York-based fashion designer who launched her namesake label in 2008 with a women's swimwear collection. In the years since, it has expanded to include a colorful kaleidoscopic range of colorful women's ready-to-wear, bridal, activewear, accessories, and a kids' collection.
Biggest score: My vintage Levi's boys jacket, from Narnia Vintage near my place in Williamsburg, that has drawings of all *The Simpsons* characters that (I assume) were done by a guy named Nick R. Ferrara, which is the name scribbled inside the jacket.
Words of wisdom:

Pay attention to where the things you're buying were made and what they were made from . . . and don't over-consume.

EMILY HOLT is a fashion and lifestyle writer turned retail entrepreneur based in San Francisco. She launched her latest project—a high-end boutique called Hero Shop—in 2016. She's also the creative director in residence for Fab.com, and her previous fashion industry experience includes a four-year stint as the fashion news editor at *Vogue* and a five-year run as the editor of *W* magazine's party pages.
Style influences: Sophia Loren and Monica Bellucci, two of those great Italian film stars who, to me, epitomize what it is to look like a woman. I can't say I dress like them except for the rare occasion, but I do think about them a lot, so the intention's there.

CONTRIBUTORS

AURORA JAMES's fashion industry career included stints as a model and a creative consultant before she founded footwear brand Brother Vellies in 2013 with the goal of preserving the shoemaking craft in Africa. As the label's creative director, she travels to Africa every two to three months to work with artisans to develop the collection. She lives in Brooklyn.
Style inspiration: Donyale Luna was a magical and inspiring soul. I try to channel her creativity and spirit into my collections every season. I am also profoundly influenced by traditional African attire and the artisanal skills passed down through centuries of the people in my workshops in Africa.
Words of wisdom:

It's on sale for a reason.

ULLA JOHNSON is a Manhattan fashion designer who founded her namesake women's label in 2000 just out of college. Celebrity fans of the brand include Jennifer Lawrence, Mila Kunis, Kate Hudson, Anne Hathaway, Amber Heard, and Kate Bosworth. Johnson lives in Brooklyn.
Style influence: Georgia O'Keeffe.
Biggest score: An antique hand-loomed Moroccan vest covered in sequins and fringe and silk tassels that I picked up in Marrakech. It's just beyond.

MINYEONG KANG is the creative manager of the Korean eyewear brand Gentle Monster. The brand has already amassed a huge following in Asia, but is quickly finding fans in the US. The flagship stores feature a gallery showcasing the work of local artists, which Kim herself curates.
Style influence: The Beatles.

SHALINI KASLIWAL is the president and CEO of Sanjay Kasliwal Jaipur-New York, the Stateside outpost of India's famed jewelry business, making her the ninth generation of the Kasliwal family involved in the gem trade, a lineage that can be traced back to the crafting of megawatt bling for the maharajas of the Mughal empire.
Style influence: Carolina Herrera is so very elegant. She visits my shop and I love what she is wearing every single time.
Words of wisdom:

Don't think too hard about something that makes you happy.

RAVEN KAUFFMAN is a luxury lifestyle consultant and accessories designer who launched her namesake line of fantastical clutches, handbags, and jewelry in Los Angeles in 2007. Fans Jennifer Lopez and Sarah Jessica Parker, among others, love Kauffman's one-of-a-kind custom pieces and limited-edition series, which incorporate all things organic, from peacock feathers to laser-cut metal snakes on clutches.
Biggest score: Paul Smith used to have a beautifully curated collection of vintage in his Los Angeles store. I got the most divine 1930s brocade tapestry coat with Middle Eastern motifs in gold bullion. I adore this coat—it instantly makes me feel like an eclectic marchesa, even when I'm wearing it with jeans.

ELIZABETH KENNEDY launched her namesake exclusive-to-Bergdorf-Goodman luxury collection of couture, ready-to-wear, and eveningwear in 2011 after a decade-long fashion industry career that included stints at Isaac Mizrahi, J. Mendel, Donna Karan, and Max Mara. Her list of A-list clientele includes Mariah Carey, Molly Sims, Sharon Osbourne, and Mindy Kaling, the latter of whom wore one of Kennedy's gowns on the 2016 Academy Awards red carpet. The collection is produced in New York City's Garment District.

Style influence: For personal dress, the '90s; as an eveningwear designer, the '50s and '60s and Charles James.
Biggest score: A squash blossom necklace I found on eBay.

HILLARY KERR is the cofounder and co-CEO of content and commerce company Clique Media Group, parent of the celebrity-focused fashion and shopping website Who What Wear, which she and Katherine Power launched in 2006. The site was so successful that in 2013, the duo added sister sites focused on beauty and home (Byrdie.com and MyDomaine.com, respectively). Kerr is also co-author (with Power) of three books, most recently *The Career Code: Must-Know Rules for a Strategic, Stylish, and Self-Made Career* (2016).
Words of wisdom:

Know your measurements. I do 95 percent of my shopping online and it makes all the difference if you can find the garment's measurements.

IRENE KIM is a Seattle-born, Seoul-raised, FIT-educated model, YouTube sensation, TV star, and social media standout who has served as a global beauty contributor for the Estée Lauder cosmetics brand since 2015.

OLIVIA KIM is the Seattle-based vice president of creative projects for Nordstrom, where, since 2013, she's been switching up the traditional brick-and-mortar shopping experience by staging a series of themed, curated pop-up shops. Prior to joining Nordstrom, she spent a decade at Opening Ceremony.
Style influences: Esprit, Benetton, Generra, Contempo Casuals, anything '80s that moves into early-'90s grunge.
Biggest score: My favorite pair of vintage jeans from Metropolis on Third Avenue in NYC. On my way out, I saw the jeans hanging there and was all, "WHOA WHOA WHOA. What are those?" I had never dreamed that a pair of vintage jeans could look like those did. After I saw them, I couldn't imagine a day in my life without them.

DESIREE KOHAN opened the doors of her namesake Los Angeles boutique in 2005. In the decade since, the converted 1920s Miracle Mile warehouse on Cloverdale Avenue has become a must-visit retail destination for the stylish set thanks to its highly curated assortment of apparel, footwear, accessories, gifts, and home goods representing established luxury brands and up-and-coming designers, as well as a range of vintage Chanel, Gucci, and Hermès pieces.

GEORGE KOTSIOPOULOUS is a Los Angeles–based fashion editor, consultant, stylist, and former co-host of E!'s *Fashion Police*. He's also the author of *Glamorous by George: The Key to Creating Movie-Star Style* (2014).
Style influence: Late '50s, early '60s, when Steve McQueen ruled with his style and swagger.
Words of wisdom:

If it's clothing, one should ask, "Where am I wearing this?" If there is no answer, then don't buy it. If it's furniture or décor, one should ask, "Where am I putting this?" Again, if there's no answer, don't buy it.

FARAN KRENTCIL is a contributing editor at ELLE.com and Yahoo News. She is the founding editor of Fashionista.com and served as *Nylon*'s first-ever digital director. In 2015, she illustrated her first book, *The Craft*, by rock stylist Lou Teasdale.

GRACE LAM is a Hong Kong–based fashion director, stylist, and consultant. In 2005, she moved to Shanghai as part of the team that launched *Vogue* China.
Style influence: I still like singer Faye Wong's style. She has a model's figure, therefore she can carry lots of different and diverse styles. She is not afraid to try new looks. She doesn't care what other people think of her, which is extremely rare in Chinese entertainment culture.
Words of wisdom:

Don't wear heels unless you can walk gracefully in them.

PEARL LAM is a Hong Kong–born art dealer and collector and is the owner of Pearl Lam Galleries. A pioneer in the Chinese art world, Lam opened her first permanent gallery space in Shanghai in 2005, in the early years of its rise as a center for contemporary art. Focusing on design, Lam used the gallery to introduce Chinese collectors to the international art market. Lam also manages a design workshop that produces custom furnishings and lighting for her galleries and apartments. She lives between Hong Kong, Shanghai, and London.

OLYMPIA LE-TAN founded her Paris-based namesake collection of storybook-inspired handbags and minaudière in 2009 and expanded to include women's ready-to-wear in 2013. Her collaborative projects include key chains for Uniqlo (which was also a partnership with the United Nations' refugee agency UNHCR), candles with Diptyque, and a range of clutch purses featuring the artwork of Keith Haring.
Style inspiration: Bettie Page always and forever.
Biggest score: I once bought a pink-and-white Alaïa coat with the Tati print from Etsy, it was super cheap and in perfect condition. I love it and wear it all the time.

DION LEE is a designer hailing from Sydney, Australia, and launched his eponymous label in 2009. Known for sensual silhouettes, dissected to enhance the body's movement and shape, Lee's designs have been worn by Selena Gomez, Miranda Kerr, Cara Delevingne, and many other celebrities. After debuting at Australia Fashion Week, Lee presented collections in London before relocating to New York, where the brand has become a fixture on the seasonal schedule.

LORI LEVEN is a veteran retailer and the director/designer of Love Adorned, a fine jewelry and lifestyle store that focuses on vintage, one-of-a-kind pieces and artisanal goods informed by years of traveling and collecting. It has attracted a celebrity following that includes Leonardo DiCaprio, Christy Turlington, and Paul McCartney.
Style inspiration: Carol Beckwith and Angela Fisher's "African Wedding Rituals," published in 1999 by National Geographic. These ladies' photos influenced me to open New York Adorned.
Words of wisdom:

Always ask if there are other things not on the sales floor.

ALIZA LICHT is a fashion industry veteran and founder/president of Leave Your Mark, where she works as a strategic consultant to brands at the intersection of fashion and technology. Her fashion CV includes serving as the longtime SVP of global communications for Donna Karan International (where she created the popular DKNY PR GIRL social media presence). She's also the author of the bestselling book *Leave Your Mark: Land Your Dream Job. Kill It in Your Career. Rock Social Media* (2015).

Style inspiration: A fashion editorial styled by Carlyne Cerf de Dudzeele for American *Vogue*. She had supermodels in Chanel ball gowns on motorcycles. I love the juxtaposition of feminine and tough.

Words of wisdom:

Don't buy for a future size.

ANDREA LIEBERMAN was born and raised in New York City and her career has included styling stars like Gwen Stefani and Jennifer Lopez (including the memorable plunging green Versace number Lopez wore to the 2000 Grammys). She launched her L.A.-based A.L.C. women's clothing label in 2009.

Style inspiration: The iconic images of Veruschka in the desert styled by Giorgio di Sant'Angelo. They were hanging on the wall of his studio when I worked there in my first job out of college.

Words of wisdom:

Never try to rationalize an emotional purchase. If you are completely swept away by something and it brings you joy, go for it!

CHRISELLE LIM is a stylist, digital influencer, and founder/creative director of Chriselle. In 2011, she launched the Chriselle Factor, a blog and YouTube channel where she chronicles her personal style. The luxury brands she's worked with include Dior, Gucci, Fendi, Louis Vuitton, Valentino, Cartier, Elie Saab, Miu Miu, Maison Margiela, and Stella McCartney. Her influence—and more than 2.2 million social media followers—has earned her the title of one of Fashionista.com's eight most successful bloggers for 2016.

Words of wisdom:

Invest in the classic pieces and experiment with trends wisely.

CHLOE LONSDALE is the founder and chief creative officer of London-based M.i.h. jeans, which launched in 2006 and has celebrity fans in Rachel Weisz, Jennifer Lawrence, and Julianne Moore. Lonsdale's parents were influential in the denim revolution of the '70s, which affords her the ability to draw on a personal design archive that spans nearly half a century.

Words of wisdom:

Pick things up on your travels. It's far more special to have something unique to a place and time, to a memory, than something that was bought in an anonymous environment. It's always worth it. I drove home with an eight-foot surfboard

CONTRIBUTORS

from Cap Ferret last weekend!

MELISSA MAGSAYSAY is a Los Angeles–based style and beauty writer and creative consultant whose work currently appears in a range of publications, including the *Hollywood Reporter* and the *Los Angeles Times*. She is also author of *City of Style: Exploring Los Angeles Fashion From Bohemian to Rock* (2012).
Words of wisdom:

Never shop while in a hurry or after having consumed more than two glasses of wine.

MARYAM MALAKPOUR is an Iranian-born, Los Angeles–based fashion editor, stylist, and shoe designer who has worked with a celebrity set that includes Rolling Stones frontman Mick Jagger (as well as the band itself for several world tours) In 2009 she and sister stylist Marjan Malakpour launched the minimalist footwear line Newbark.
Biggest score: At Scout LA I found three Valentino couture silk blouses [in] beautiful prints. All three were the perfect size, no alterations needed.
Words of wisdom:

If you're not having fun, then you're doing it wrong.

MARY ALICE MALONE is the creative director and **ROY LUWOLT** is the managing director of the London-based women's luxury shoe brand Malone Souliers, which they cofounded in 2014. Since then, their shoes, handmade in Italy, have shod the feet of such famous folks as Lupita Nyong'o, Solange Knowles, Kylie Jenner, and Kim Kardashian, who was spotted sporting a pair during her honeymoon.
Words of wisdom:

Fussy, uncomfortable, or wrong for you should never make the cut.

FERN MALLIS is a New York–based fashion consultant, author and the creator/organizer of New York Fashion Week during her decade-long tenure as executive director of the Council of Fashion Designers of America (CFDA) from 1991 to 2001. She has also served as senior vice president of fashion for IMG and is currently president of her own international consulting firm. Her book *Fashion Lives: Fashion Icons with Fern Mallis*, was published in 2015.
Words of wisdom:

The last thing you want is to spend years regretting not buying something.

BESTE AND MERVE MANASTIR, daughters of a leather craftsman, founded their handbag label Manu Atelier in Istanbul in February 2014. Their distinctive designs, handmade in Turkey, including the rectangular Pristine bag with a flap top, have been featured in *Vogue*, *Business of Fashion*, and *Women's Wear Daily*, and on the arms of such fashionable women as Eva Chen and Bella Hadid. Manu Atelier is available at Net-a-Porter, Selfridges, and other stores around the world, as well as at ManuAtelier.com.

SHEA MARIE is a globe-trotting fashion influencer, designer, stylist, creative consultant, and editor of PeaceLoveShea.com. Her website and various social media accounts generate more than

8 million impressions a day. She's appeared in the pages of fashion glossies including *Glamour*, *Marie Claire*, *Harper's Bazaar*, and *Vogue*. In 2015 she launched the luxury swimwear label Same Swim.
Biggest score: I found a pair of zippered Balmain booties in a teeny vintage store in London for a couple hundred dollars. They had been worn maybe once. Definitely the best vintage piece I ever found for the price.
Words of wisdom:

Work hard so you can shop harder.

FIONA KOTUR MARIN launched her accessories label Kotur in 2005. Celebrities seen clutching Kotur clutches over the years include Iman, Ginnifer Goodwin, Jennifer Lopez, Emma Roberts, Kendall Jenner, and Selena Gomez. Martin splits her time between New York City—where she was born and raised—and Hong Kong where her business is based.
Biggest score: When I was a student visiting Paris's Porte de Clignancourt flea market, I found a beautiful vintage leather doctor's bag that I vowed would be an integral part of my collection should I start a handbag company—and it has been!

JJ MARTIN is the founder and editor of the shoppable online magazine and creative agency LaDoubleJ.com. The site sells vintage clothing, makes new clothing with vintage prints from hidden Italian archives, promotes Italian talent and style, and wraps it all up in a colorful, fun, humorous package. Martin grew up in Los Angeles and now lives in Milan, where she's one of the city's most stylish women. She has been chronicling the fashion and design industries for more than fifteen years as an editor and writer at publications including *Harper's Bazaar* and *Wallpaper* magazine, where she is currently editor at large, Italy.

VIRGINIA MARTIN's passion for clothing was nurtured by her mother, who taught her to sew. After finishing high school Virginia threw herself into design, and at nineteen years old, stores throughout Australia took up her first collection. Virginia eventually took a break and moved to New York, further growing as a designer while interning at Proenza Schouler, Cynthia Rowley, and Heatherette. She returned to Melbourne eager to establish her own label. The ocean and the coast acted as inspiration and motivation for launching her line of sculptural basics, búl, in 2010.

KARLA MARTINEZ SALAS is a longtime fashion editor who currently serves as editorial director at *Vogue* Mexico and Latin America. She grew up in El Paso, Texas, spent a dozen years in New York City, and currently lives in Mexico City. In addition, she's the cofounder of luxury loungewear label Piamita (with designer Cecilia de Sola), which launched in 2011.
Style influence: Dolores Guinness and her old-world glamour.
Biggest score: Mink coat by Revillon from the '70s from a store in El Paso called Vintage Mode.

ANN MASHBURN, a former assistant and editor at *Vogue* and *Glamour* who, along with her equally fashionable husband, Sid, opened their first Sid Mashburn men's store in Atlanta in 2007, followed by an Ann Mashburn women's store in 2010. Today they sell apparel and accessories bearing their names at four sets of connected men's and women's shops in Atlanta, Houston, Dallas, and Washington, DC as well as at a stand-alone Sid Mashburn store in Los Angeles. She lives in Atlanta.
Style influence: Every single photo of Jackie Kennedy wearing short, flared white jeans and a black crewneck T-shirt. I wore this outfit for like ten years straight as a young housewife in paradise.

Words of wisdom:

If you really love it, buy a backup.

BRANDON MAXWELL is a stylist turned designer who earned early name recognition for his work with Lady Gaga, for whom he's been fashion director since 2012. He launched his namesake collection of luxury eveningwear in 2015, which finds favor with Jennifer Lawrence, Reese Witherspoon, Kate Hudson, Uma Thurman, and Michelle Obama. His industry recognitions include the Fashion Group International Rising Star award for Womenswear and the CFDA Swarovski award for Womenswear, both in 2016.
Style influence: Everything Jackie Kennedy, always.
Words of wisdom:

If the shoe fits, buy it in every color.

PATRICK MCDONALD's sartorial flair—spotted in the front rows of New York Fashion Week for decades—has earned him a reputation as "the Dandy of New York" as well as countless street-style photo ops. His adventures in high style include modeling and stints at Fiorucci and Barneys as well as penning *Paper* magazine's Highbrow column for several years. Formerly a fixture on the New York fashion scene, he currently hangs his distinctive top hat in San Francisco.
Style influence: Silent movies from the 1920s with Rudolph Valentino.
Words of wisdom:

Fashion finds are everywhere—explore, find, create your own style. Be original!

LEANDRA MEDINE is the founder of the Man Repeller, a fashion-meets-humor website launched in 2010. It has since grown into a multimedia business that has earned Medine spots on all kinds of power lists including *Forbes'* "Top 30 Under 30," *Time*'s "25 best blogs," and *Adweek*'s Fashion Power 25." In 2013 she published her first book *Man Repeller: Seeking Love, Finding Overalls*. She lives in New York City.
Biggest score: I got a yellow Valentino military jacket for $2 from an Outnet.com sale. When they were just starting, they used to host these ridiculous $1 and $2 sales once a year and I scored access to the $2 sale, *et voilà*.
Style influence: A photograph of Jane Birkin in the South of France holding a straw basket and wearing a T-shirt and high-rise jeans that hit just below the ankle—this photo is an important reference for my frame of mind. No matter the time of year, or what I'm doing, I always want to feel like I'm carrying a straw basket in the South of France.
Words of wisdom:

If you wouldn't buy it at retail, don't buy it on sale.

JENNIFER MEYER is a Los Angeles native who worked in communications for high-profile fashion brands including Ralph Lauren and Giorgio Armani before launching her namesake jewelry collection in 2005. In 2012 she was awarded runner-up in the CFDA/Vogue Fashion Fund; the following year she was nominated for the CFDA's Swarovski Award for Accessories Design. Her delicate, personalized pendants have become a Hollywood staple, spotted on the likes of Amy Adams, Claire Danes, Alicia Vikander, Kerry Washington, and Emma Roberts.
Style influence: Jane Birkin really paved the way for the chic casual look

that works so well living in California. Diane von Furstenburg has also been an inspiring style icon for me, in every way.

ELIZABETH MINETT is a Canadian model turned lifestyle influencer and creator of the website HautAppetit.com—a guide to satisfy an "It" girl's appetite for life—which she launched in 2011. A frequent fixture at fashion weeks around the globe, she has collaborated with a range of international fashion and beauty brands. She splits her time between Los Angeles and Paris.

Style influence: Masculine power dressing from the '80s (think Grace Jones), juxtaposed with the feminine bombshell vibe of the '60s (think, Brigitte Bardot).

Words of wisdom:

Retail therapy does, in fact, mend a heavy heart.

REBECCA MINKOFF is a New York–based fashion designer who launched her namesake collection in 2005. Today she helms a global lifestyle brand that also includes footwear and jewelry as well as men's clothing and accessories under the Uri Minkoff label (named after her label cofounder and brother), sold globally through 900 retail doors as well as stand-alone stores in the US and internationally. Her industry recognitions include the 2011 Breakthrough Designer Award bestowed by the Accessories Council.

Style influence: Anything Bianca Jagger wore at Studio 54.

Words of wisdom:

My best pieces are the ones that made me a little uncomfortable. Push yourself into something uncomfortable.

TANIA MOHAN is a Hong Kong–based fashion expert who has retail in her blood—her family founded the Mohan's department stores in India in the 1950s—who served as the first fashion editor of the *Hong Kong Standard* newspaper in the 1990s. In 1999 she launched Tabla, an India-inspired luxury brand.

Style influence: The regal elegance and grace of Maharani Gayatri Devi fused with the timeless essence of Coco Chanel. Indian majestic regal charm, polo, tiaras, maharanis, and jodhpurs.

Biggest score: My first designer bag, the Louis Vuitton Speedy, was purchased during my first international trip to Paris. The bag is forever linked to my memories of sitting in Les Deux Magots relishing in all the beauty and romance of the City of Light. The bag is now almost twenty years old, I use it regularly.

MARYAM MONTAGUE is about as much of a global citizen as you can be: born in Cairo, raised in Tunis and New York, she did humanitarian work in Dakar, Kathmandu, and Windhoek before alighting in Marrakech, Morocco, where she and her husband designed, built, and decorated a boutique hotel, Peacock Pavilions, that's been the backdrop for fashion shoots for a range of brands, including J. Crew and Tory Burch. Her blog, My Marrakesh, launched in 2007, led to the creation of the M. Montague Souk, an online shop focusing on tribal-inspired and Moroccan home décor. She's also the author of *Marrakesh by Design* (2012).

Biggest score:
I was in Yemen on a humanitarian aid assignment, when I found in the souk an antique hand-embroidered dress, once worn by a Yemeni woman. More than 100 years old and less than $199, the dress fits like it was made for me.

CONTRIBUTORS

CLAUDE MORAIS AND BRIAN WOLK are the globe-trotting fashion designers behind the L.A.-based Wolk Morais fashion label. Before launching their namesake label in 2015, they made a name for themselves with the critically acclaimed New York cult label Ruffian.
Biggest score: A Napoléon-era letter-carrying bag (*portefeuille*) from the legendary (and since-shuttered) Old England department store in Paris.

JENNIFER MORRISON is an actress/director/producer/model and lover of fashion best known for her roles as Dr. Allison Cameron on *House*, and as Emma Swan on the adventure fantasy *Once Upon a Time*. She catalogs the brands she wears and riffs on the labels she likes via the website jennifer-morrisonstyle.com. Her directorial feature film debut, *Sun Dogs*, is scheduled for a 2017 release.

SASHA CHARNIN MORRISON is a freelance stylist and editor but is probably best known for a nine-year run as the fashion director at *Us Weekly* magazine (2006–2015). She is also the author of *Secrets of Stylists: An Insider's Guide to Styling the Stars*. She is based in New York City.
Style influences: My parents, Genii and Martin Charnin—they are the bomb and my first stylists and style icons. We wore the greatest looks—yes, we wore "looks" as a family. I also love Theda Bara. Look at her. Her style in 1917 was so ahead of its time. The hair, the lined eyes, and the clothing.
Words of wisdom:

Buy the shoes.

MINNIE MORTIMER is a New York City to SoCal transplant and cofounder of the members-only cosmetics website Vainité, which launched in 2016. Her other adventures in the fashion space include launching a namesake women's sportswear line in 2009, a 2010 collaboration with W Hotels, a 2013 capsule collection with Three Dots, and a consultation/collaboration partnership with Boast USA.

MARRIAM MOSSALLI is the Jeddah, Saudi Arabia–based founder of luxury consultancy firm Niche Arabia, which she launched in 2011, and has a client list that includes Burberry, Versace, and Prada. That's the same year she launched her blog, Shoes & Drama. Her fashion CV includes stints as executive editor at Style.com Arabia, fashion editor at Destination Jeddah, and editor-in-chief at *Design* magazine.
Style influence: Catherine Deneuve—I was lucky enough to be on set with her in Malaysia (my mom and sister both had small parts in the 1992 film *IndoChine*) and I remember being memorized by her elegance and dominance. She was assertive, unfriendly, and unapologetic. It was her confidence and diva-ness that drew me in, and I memorized everything about her. Her wardrobe on set was very Coco Chanel and Jeanne Lanvin. Off set, she wore crisp white men's shirts with long maxi dresses, her hair in a messy bun. I recall seeing her Louis Vuitton trunks (which encouraged me to call dibs on all of my mother's trunks and luggage as soon as we returned home).
Words of wisdom:

"Charge it!" I remember watching Troop Beverly Hills *(1989), and there was this scene in the beginning where Shelley Long is shoe shopping and says, "That one, and that one . . . out! I'll take the*

rest!" I would mimic that scene over and over. As a result I was the most obnoxious five-year-old ever!

KATE AND LAURA MULLEAVY are the cofounding sisters of the Los Angeles-based luxury women's label Rodarte, which they launched in 2005. Their collections have earned them numerous industry recognitions including multiple CFDA award nominations and wins. The costumes they designed for the film *Black Swan* earned them a Broadcast Film Critics award nomination. Enthusiastic collaborators, they've worked on special projects with Frank Gehry, Gustavo Dudamel, Benjamin Millepied, Target, and the Gap among others. Their pieces are in the permanent collections of the Costume Institute of the Metropolitan Museum of Art, and the Los Angeles County Museum of Art, among others.

IRENE NEUWIRTH is a Los Angeles-based jewelry designer who launched her namesake collection of fine jewelry in 2003. Her industry recognitions include the CFDA's Swarovski Award for Accessory Design in 2014 and her list of celebrity clientele includes Reese Witherspoon, Claire Danes, and Scarlett Johansson. She opened a stand-alone flagship boutique on Melrose Place in West Hollywood in 2014.
Style influence: Frida Kahlo, need I say more?
Words of wisdom:

Invest in something you know is colorful, fun, unusual, and will separate you from everyone else.

PAOLO NIEDDU is the two-time-Emmy-nominated costume designer for the television show *Empire*. He began his costume design career as an assistant costume designer to Pat Field on the 2008 big-screen version of *Sex and the City*, and his other screen credits include *Sex and the City 2* and *Confessions of a Shopaholic*. He grew up in the suburbs of Detroit and currently calls the New York City area home.
Style influence: I'm obsessed with the book *Those Glorious Glamour Years: Classic Hollywood Costume Design of the 1930s*, by Margret J. Bailey. It inspired me as a kid and still does today.
Biggest score: My super-thin Lanvin jacket. I saw it in the Paris men's store—I didn't buy it 'cause it was 2,700 euros. I saw it in Bergdorf's later that season and it was on sale for $1,000, but they didn't have my size. The salesperson took my info and believe it or not, someone returned my size!

LENNY NIEMEYER is a Rio de Janeiro-based landscape architect turned swimwear designer who launched her namesake label in 1993 out of an Ipanema storefront, and went on to become Brazil's bikini queen—now her collection is stocked in stores around the globe. Among the high-profile folks who've worn her wares are Nicole Kidman and Lady Gaga.
Words of wisdom:

Learn how to appreciate a piece and not necessarily consume it.

THITHI NTETA is the creator of the popular style blog TeeTeelsWithMe.com. Nteta works as a freelance stylist, consultant, publicist, and graphic designer in Cape Town, South Africa. She posts regularly about fashion, beauty, lifestyle, and events in South Africa and beyond.

MONIQUE PÉAN is a former investment banker turned fine jewelry designer who launched her namesake, socially responsible and sustainable fine jewelry line in 2006. She has guest lectured at Harvard Business School, the University of Pennsylvania, the Smithsonian Institution and Parsons the New School for Design. She is based in New York City.

ERICA PELOSINI is a jet-setting, globe-trotting, Florence-born model, stylist, art director, and contributor to *Vogue* and *L'Officiel Paris*. She is also the cofounder (in 2012) of the shoe business that bears the name of her husband, Louis Leeman. A recent Paris-to-Los Angeles transplant, she can frequently be found at fashion weeks around the world.
Style influence:
Marchesa Casati was an early-20th-century Italian muse and patron of the arts. It's always intrigued me how she used to walk through the streets of Venice with her cheetahs and their diamond-studded leashes wearing her furs and piled on jewelry.
Biggest score: My monogrammed Louis Vuitton luggage.

SALLY PERRIN is a Minnesota-born, Seattle-raised model turned handbag designer for the French luxury leather goods brand Perrin Paris, which dates to 1893. The brand has stand-alone stores in New York, Beverly Hills, Hong Kong, Kuwait, and Paris, the last of which is also home to the design studio and showroom. The Perrins (her husband, Michel, is the family-owned company's CEO) call Los Angeles home.
Biggest score: A black tulle Yves Saint Laurent dress from the '80s with bright color pom-poms. I mentioned to vintage guru Cameron Silver of Decades at a dinner an article I had read about him in *Elle*, with a photo of this very dress, and how it caught my eye. The very next day he had it delivered to my house. It fit as if it were custom-made for me. I have two daughters, they will have to work out a time share.

JOSH PESKOWITZ is the cofounder of Magasin, a multi-brand men's concept store in Culver City, California that opened its doors in 2016. His style-centric CV also includes stints as men's fashion director at Bloomingdale's, men's style director for Gilt Groupe, fashion editor for men.style.com and market editor for *Vibe* magazine. He currently hangs his knit cap in Los Angeles.
Biggest score: Probably the thing that I've worn the most over the years is a cable-knit shawl collared cardigan from RRL. I found it at the Polo Ralph Lauren outlet in Las Vegas (hey, seemed better than losing money at the craps table). This was in, like, 2004, so no one in Las Vegas was checking for RRL, and I got the sweater for $18. Retail on something like that is north of $700, so I was feeling like I was the only person to beat the house in Sin City that day.
Words of wisdom:

If it doesn't fit in the store, it's never going to. Keep it moving.

Also, if you're still thinking about it thirty minutes later, go back and buy it. You may never see it again. Especially if you're traveling. Which brings me to my most important point: Unless the deal is so good you can't pass it up, never buy something abroad that you could buy at home. My clothing is sort of like travel slide show, and I'm far more interested in the local market than the mall. Leave extra room in your suitcase and budget to go shopping a little bit. Nothing's worse than showing up back at the hotel room from Istanbul's Grand

CONTRIBUTORS

Bazaar and realizing you've got no room for that robe you just bought.

ARIANNE PHILLIPS is a stylist whose client list includes Madonna, Lenny Kravitz, Courtney Love, and Justin Timberlake, and a costume designer whose film work earned her a pair of Academy Award nominations for *Walk the Line* and *W.E.* She also designed costumes for Tom Ford's two films, *A Single Man* and *Nocturnal Animals.*
Style influence: Does film history count? Does *Yentl* count? David Bowie, Charlotte Rampling in *The Night Porter*, the Duke and Duchess of Windsor, Sally Bowles from *Cabaret*, Amelia Earhart, Peggy Guggenheim, Lee Miller, Marie Antoinette, and more.
Biggest score: I found a rare 1960s Rudi Gernreich dress in perfect condition at a thrift store in St. Louis for $3 and sold it at Decades for $1,200.

KATHERINE POWER (see Hillary Kerr).

JEN RADE is a costume designer, stylist, and self-described "wicked witch of the wardrobe" whose list of A-list clientele stretches nearly as long as an awards-show red carpet and includes Angelina Jolie, Abbie Cornish, Cher, Jenna Fischer, Pink, Marilyn Manson, Dave Matthews, and Tina Turner. Her industry recognitions include a pair of Costume Designers Guild awards for excellence in commercial costume design for her work with Apple and Target.
Words of wisdom:

Something has to grab you.

NICOLE RICHIE is a Los Angeles-based former television star turned designer whose House of Harlow 1960 brand launched in 2009 as a collection of jewelry, expanding over the years to include ready-to-wear, eyewear, footwear, and handbags, sold at high-end department and specialty stores around the world.
Style inspiration: I love moon manicures from the 1920s, the dark lipstick and glamour of the 1940s, the freedom of the 1960s and '70s. The '80s . . . not so into the '80s.
Biggest score: This year it was a vintage YSL oversized coat. I found it at Shabon, one of my favorite vintage stores in L.A.

LOUISE ROE is a model, digital influencer, writer, and television host whose fashion-focused résumé includes serving as the news editor for Vogue.com in London, writing for *Elle* UK, *InStyle* UK, and *People Stylewatch*. Her first nonfiction book, *Front Roe: How to Be the Leading Lady in Your Own Life*, was published in 2015.
Biggest score: A bright-red printed Gucci silk scarf from the '80s from Ebth.com (Everything but the House). They auction estate sales online and have an incredible selection.
Words of wisdom:

Imagine it worked into three outfits you already own before buying it. Then you know you'll wear it.

JENN ROGIEN is a Brooklyn-based costume designer whose work can be seen on Netflix's *Orange is the New Black*, and HBO's *Girls*, the latter of which earned her a 2013 Costume Designers Guild Award nomination. She was also nominated for an Emmy for her work on *The Good Wife*. In addition, she's collaborated with a range of brands and retailers including Sorel Footwear, TJ Maxx, the Gap, and Aerie Lingerie.

Words of wisdom:

Try. It. On. Hanger appeal is a real thing. Some garments are a disaster on the hanger but will be the best thing you've ever had on. Some things look great on a hanger and are an utter disaster once you've got them on.

BRIGETTE ROMANEK is an L.A.-based former actress/singer turned handbag designer turned interior designer. Her line of luxury handbags has graced the shelves of Barneys, the pages of *Vogue*, and the arms of celebrities like Kate Moss and Gwyneth Paltrow.
Style influence: My style icon hands down, is Nina Simone. Almost any image I find of her is strong and powerful. She always looked like a warrior. She was an African American doing bold things during a time that wasn't easy. She's my icon on many levels.
Words of wisdom:

Know yourself, what makes someone else look cool, may not be the look for you.

CHARLOTTE RONSON is a London-born, New York City–raised designer whose fashion career began with the launch of C. Ronson women's apparel in 2000, a label that would evolve, five years later, into the Charlotte Ronson brand. A frequent collaborator, she's partnered with a range of brands including Urban Outfitters, Uniqlo, JC Penney, Sephora, Luxottica, and even Starbucks.
Biggest score: A Hermès Kelly bag, it's less a shopping score and more of a "lucky me" loving gift score from my mother and stepfather. But, I am too scared to wear it, so it remains in the box in my closet.
Words of wisdom:

In the words of my mother: "Do you love it? Now, are you sure you love it?"

SHIVA ROSE is an actress and activist whose holistic lifestyle blog, The Local Rose, eventually resulted in the launch of a namesake line of toxic-free products and eventually expanding to include body scrubs, eye creams, body oils, and candles. She lives in Pacific Palisades.
Style influences: Georgia O'Keeffe and Frida Kahlo, because they were able to look chic and original no matter what the style of the day was.
Words of wisdom:

For me, dressing is a bit like storytelling. I feel I can be whatever character I want in whatever script I choose.

AMANDA ROSS is a fashion director, stylist, costume designer, and consultant who muses on all things life and style through the website ARossGirl.com, which also serves as a platform for see now, buy now seasonal designer collaborations. Her prior fashion industry CV includes serving as the fashion director for *Departures* magazine, fashion market director for *Harper's Bazaar*, and global fashion director to

CONTRIBUTORS

W Hotels. She is currently based in New York City.
Style influence: My favorite style icons are my grandmothers and my mother and stepmother.
Words of wisdom:

Shop to explore. Be curious. Only buy what you love.

KARA ROSS is a New York-based jewelry designer whose latest project is Diamonds Unleashed by Kara Ross, a jewelry brand with the goal of promoting and supporting women's empowerment that launched in 2015. She launched her namesake jewelry collection, Kara Ross New York, in 2003 with fine jewelry that incorporated materials like jet, lava, wood, and titanium, later expanding to include handbags made from exotic skins. Industry recognitions include Fashion Group International's "Rising Star" Award for Jewelry Design in 2008 and the GEM Award for Design from the Jewelry Information Center in 2014.
Words of wisdom:

You need to love it, not just like it.

CATHERINE RYU is the South Korea–born, Canadian-raised, L.A.-based creative director for the Citizens of Humanity brand, which she joined in 2012 after design stints at AG Adriano Goldschmeid, Gap, Calvin Klein, Urban Outfitters, and Club Monaco.
Style influence: Françoise Hardy and Carolyn Besette Kennedy.

LIANA SATENSTEIN is a news writer at Vogue.com, where she specializes in the Eastern European and Central Asian markets, as well as tracksuits (for real). She fell in love with all things Eastern European while on a high school exchange program in the Ukraine. She has written for *Vogue*, *Vogue* Ukraine, British *Vogue*, Elle.com, and *Fashionista*, and is based in New York City.

LEE SAVAGE is a Savannah-to-New York City transplant who transitioned from a career in interior design to handbag design with the launch of her namesake line of art-and-architecture-inspired clutches in 2013. Designed in New York and manufactured in Italy, her bags have become a go-to red carpet accessory found in the hands of famous ladies including Naomi Watts, Julie Bowen, Kate Hudson, Diane Kruger, and Jessica Alba.
Style influence: Lee Radziwill. One image of her that stands out is a Mark Shaw photograph from the 1960s in which she is in a mustard yellow Nina Ricci gown and blue cape. It's such a stunning simple gown, but impeccably tailored and chic.
Words of wisdom:

Always ask, "How long do I see myself wearing this?"

SARAH SCHUSSHEIM is a stylist, consultant, and contributing West Coast fashion editor at *Elle* magazine who has lent her considerable talents to the betterment of Penelope Cruz, Octavia Spencer, and Uma Thurman (all for *Elle* covers), and to glossy editorial spreads in *Details*, *DuJour*, *Teen Vogue*, and *Vanity Fair*. She lives and works between Los Angeles and New York City.
Style influence: I like the Town & Country look of Ralph Lauren, Céline Dion in Dior at the 1999 Oscars, Barbra Streisand's frumpy/sexy style in *The Mirror Has Two Faces*. Kanye's style over Kim for sure.
Words of wisdom:

If it feels right, it probably is.

CONTRIBUTORS

JEREMY SCOTT is a Los Angeles–based fashion designer who launched his namesake line in Paris in 1997 and was quickly embraced by a celebrity set that included Björk, Madonna, Kylie Minogue, and Britney Spears and later, Miley Cyrus, Rihanna, Nicki Minaj, and Katy Perry. In 2013, he was tapped to serve as the creative director of Italian luxury label Moschino, injecting a new energy into the brand. He's the subject of the documentary film *Jeremy Scott: The People's Designer*, released in 2015—the same year he became the first fashion designer to be immortalized with a pair of handprints pressed into the wet cement in front of the TCL Chinese Theatre on Hollywood Boulevard.
Style influence: The film *Blade Runner* for fashion, architecture, and design. The mix of futuristic and vintage, the old and the starkly new mixing together to create a volatile cocktail.
Words of wisdom:

If you think about it for more than five minutes, you should probably just get it.

KENDRA SCOTT is the Austin, Texas–based designer and CEO of Kendra Scott Designs, the jewelry and accessories company, which she launched in 2002 with $500 and has since grown into a multi-million dollar business, known for drop earrings and Color Bars, which allow customers to customize designs.
Style inspiration: In 2005, I had the honor of meeting Oscar de la Renta and collaborating with him to design the jewelry for his Spring 2006 runway show. The detail and elegance with which Mr. de la Renta dressed women is an incredible inspiration to me.
Words of wisdom:

Every woman needs a great statement piece.

CHLOË SEVIGNY is an award-winning American film actress, fashion designer, and former model. Some of her most notable roles were in *Kids* (1995), *Boys Don't Cry* (1999), *American Psycho* (2000), and the HBO television series *Big Love*, for which she received a Golden Globe in 2010. Recently, she's had roles in *Hit & Miss* (2012) and *American Horror Story: Hotel* (2015–2016). She has designed several fashion collections with Opening Ceremony, and in April 2015 published a self-titled book about her style with Rizzoli.

VANESSA SEWARD was born in Argentina, and grew up in London before moving to Paris at age twelve. After studying at Studio Berçot, she worked for nine years as an accessory designer for Chanel and Tom Ford at Yves Saint Laurent before becoming second-in-command at the house of Loris Azzaro. Following Azzaro's death in 2003, Seward became artistic director. She left Azzaro in 2011, and for two years created capsule lines for French contemporary brand A.P.C. before launching namesake fashion label in 2014, which is known for its *Charlie's Angels*-meets-Parisian sense of cool.

DARIA SHAPOVALOVA is founder and creative director of Mercedes-Benz Kiev Fashion Days, founder of the Russian-language fashion website Fashion Week Daily (fw-daily.com), and an influential champion of up-and-coming designers in her native Kiev.
Biggest score: We could dedicate an entire book to my best scores. I have an amazing dress bought from the L.A. vintage store the Way We Wore, made by Karl Lagerfeld for Chloé. I was wearing it at a Chanel runway show in Paris, and was approached

by the seamstress who made it. She remembered it from all those years ago.
Words of wisdom:

Work harder to shop harder.

SUSIE SHEFFMAN is a Toronto-based stylist and contributing fashion editor at *Fashion* magazine. The list of celebrities she's worked with over her three-decade career includes Ashley Olsen, Jennifer Hudson, Claire Danes, Taylor Swift, Britney Spears, and Rihanna. She's also served as fashion director for a range of brands, including Joe Fresh and Hudson's Bay.
Style influence: I'm a bit of a tomboy, so Steve McQueen and Paul Newman in American classics, and Pablo Picasso in a Breton shirt.
Biggest score: I became obsessed with finding a horn necklace like the one worn by Diana Vreeland. As I sat at Brioni's spring 2011 Milan show, there it was, around the necks of the models marching down the runway before me! I hunted down the sample and styled it as the signature piece on one of my favorite fashion magazine stories. To my delight, I was later gifted it by Brioni as a thank-you for the shoot. It's become my own signature and I'm rarely without it.
Words of wisdom:

If you love it, buy two!

And whether it's a tux, a watch, a brogue, or a cashmere V-neck, it's always better from the boy's department.

TADASHI SHOJI is the founder and chief designer of the women's apparel line that bears his name. His gowns have been worn on the red carpet by Florence Welch and Octavia Spencer, but the bulk of Shoji's business is in sales of tasteful, figure-flattering cocktail dresses and evening gowns for women who want to feel like celebrities in their own lives. He was born and raised in Sendai, Japan, moved to Los Angeles in the 1970s and launched his label there in 1982.
Style influence: Joan of Arc because of her iconic strength and dedication to what she believed in.
Biggest score: My Tibetan bamboo cuff that I got at the gem market in Taipei. The cuff has a historical importance in Taiwan and the legend is that it provides both safety and protection.

CAMERON SILVER is the co-owner of the Decades luxury vintage boutique he opened in Los Angeles in 1997. Since that time, he has enthusiastically worn, sold pieces from, consulted for, and partnered with enough big-name brands to stock a store sixteen times over. His book *Decades: A Century of Fashion* was published in 2012. The latest feather in the cap of the globe-trotting vintage clothing impresario came in 2015 when he was tapped to serve as the fashion director of the H by Halston and H Halston brands.
Biggest score: In the late 1990s, Paris flea markets and auctions were amazing and I have the Hermès collection to prove it!
Words of wisdom:

Would Cary Grant or Liberace wear this today?

TARA SOLOMON is a journalist-turned-PR guru and the founder of Tara, Ink., a boutique public relations, marketing, and special events firm in Miami Beach with clients including Dior, Chanel, Louis Vuitton, *Vanity Fair*, Art Basel, The Delano, Shore Club, STK, Soho Beach House, and W Hotels. In the 1990s, she chronicled Miami's nightlife scene as the Queen of the Night columnist at the *Miami Herald*, before going on to become a syndicated advice columnist for the publication.

CONTRIBUTORS

TATIANA SOROKKO is a Russian-born, San Francisco-based model, fashion journalist, and collector of haute couture and antique jewelry whose treasures were featured in the 2010 Moscow Art Museum exhibition, "Extending the Runway: Tatiana Sorokko Style." Her fashion CV also includes styling photo shoots featuring the likes of Elizabeth Taylor and Joan Collins and serving as a contributing editor for *Harper's Bazaar*.
Style influence: Virginia Oldoini, Countess of Castiglione, is one of my most important style influences from history. La Castiglione, as she was known, was a mistress of Emperor Napoléon III and renowned for her immense beauty and elaborate court style.
Biggest score: A haute couture "sari" dress from Cristobal Balenciaga's spring 1964 collection, found at a vintage store in Paris when I was working there as a model. The brocaded lamé dress, with Lesage bead embroidery, was photographed by Richard Avedon for the October 1963 issue of *Vogue*. I had only ever seen one other, but it was in pale green, with a slightly different construction. In 2011, the Kerry Taylor Auction house in London held a sale of haute couture that included a version of my dress, owned by Elizabeth Taylor, which she wore to the New Review Lido premiere in Paris, in December 1964. Identical to mine in every way, the dress fetched £30,000.
Words of wisdom:

No cheap booze or cheap shoes.

LAURIE LYNN STARK is the co-owner and co-designer of the Los Angeles-based Chrome Hearts luxury line of jewelry, leather goods, and home furnishings that counts Cher, Steven Tyler, and Elton John among its clientele. She's also an accomplished photographer, art director, and creative director of photography of *Chrome Hearts Magazine* published in Japan and distributed internationally. She lives in New York and Los Angeles.
Words of wisdom:

Don't buy things just because everyone else is buying them.

SCOTT STERNBERG founded and served as creative director of the Los Angeles-based Band of Outsiders brand in 2003 and expanded it over the course of a decade to include complete men's and women's apparel and accessories collections and bricks-and-mortar retail stores in Tokyo and New York City. The cookie-and Polaroid-film obsessed designer left the label in 2015 and has since served as a much sought after consultant to a variety of brands and businesses in the fashion space.

ELIZABETH STEWART is a high-profile Hollywood stylist whose clients include Cate Blanchett, Jennifer Lawrence, Jessica Chastain, Julia Roberts, and Salma Hayek, to name just a few.
Style inspiration: The excess of Marie Antoinette. Also, I remember the first image that influenced me, a *Vogue* Patterns picture of a model in a wrap skirt on a tarmac. The wrap skirt was very easy and effortlessly glamorous. I felt the love!

ZAINAB SUMU is the Boston-based designer of the Primitive Modern label, which she launched in 2015 with a capsule collection of Mali-inspired, African-made scarves (singer Alicia Keys is a fan). Originally from Sierra Leone and educated in the UK, France, and the US, Sumu's fashion industry experience included a stint at Comme des Garçons.

CONTRIBUTORS

TARA SWENNEN started her career working for Andrea Lieberman and Rachel Zoe before establishing herself as a go-to celebrity wardrobe stylist whose A-list clientele has included Kristen Stewart, Heather Graham, Kate Beckinsale, Mila Kunis, and Kaley Cuoco. Her work has also appeared in the pages of *InStyle*, *Nylon*, *Teen Vogue*, and *Esquire* UK. She lives in Los Angeles.

Style inspiration: The Dior post-war era is still truly one of the most influential times for me! The designs were structural, architectural, and the tailoring was impeccable.

Words of wisdom:

If you're on the fence about something, put it on hold.

SHARON TAKEDA is the senior curator and head of the Department of Costume and Textiles at the Los Angeles County Museum of Art (LACMA). Sharon has curated a number of exhibitions including *Reigning Men: Fashion in Menswear 1715–2015*; *Kimono for a Modern Age*; *RODARTE: Fra Angelico Collection*; and *Breaking the Mode: Contemporary Fashion* for the Los Angeles County Museum of Art.

ERICA TANOV has her name on a collection of women's apparel, accessories, and home goods—launched in 1990 in New York City—and a quartet of multi-brand boutiques located in San Francisco, New York City, Berkeley, and Marin. She currently resides in the San Francisco Bay area.

Style inspiration: I do love sculptor Louise Nevelson's style. She had such a raw, fearless glamour that I find timeless, ageless, and beautiful.

Biggest score: An antique, ornately embroidered, fur-trimmed kimono dress that I bought at a tiny (and, unfortunately, since closed) antiques store in Winters, California.

ISA TAPIA is a Puerto Rico–born, Manhattan-based designer of women's footwear who launched her namesake line in 2012. A member of the 2014–16 CFDA Fashion Incubator program, she spends most of her time traveling throughout South America, Europe, and Asia.

Words of wisdom:

From Carrie Bradshaw, "I have this little substance abuse problem. Expensive footwear."

OLYA THOMPSON is a Moscow-based textile designer whose style sense—and fabric designs inspired by everything from Ballets Russes costumes to Tartar robes—has earned her a reputation as Moscow's most stylish woman.

Style inspirations: Paris of 1913, Paul Poiret caftans, and Leon Bakst costumes for the Ballets Russes. Russian ballerina Tamara Karsavina in a *kokoshnik*, an ornate folkloric headdress.

Words of wisdom:

Support rare artisanal and unique individual brands. Be consistent with your style and you will be rewarded not just with purchases.

RICCARDO TORTATO is the New York–based fashion director for TSUM Moscow. Tortato can be found dressed in a bespoke suit, sitting in the front rows of fashion shows around the world.

ALYCE TRAN is the cofounder and creative director of

(TheDailyEdited.com). Tran established the Australian online store and corresponding collection of customizable and personalized leather accessories collection with Tania Liu in 2014. The business has grown enormously in two short years, and in January 2016, they launched their first permanent retail space in David Jones Sydney, where their accessories are now monogrammed on the spot.

TRINA TURK launched her namesake women's contemporary clothing line in 1995, and, in the decades since, she and husband Jonathan Skow have built the L.A.-based label into a full-fledged California-flavored lifestyle brand that include accessories, swimwear, jewelry, home goods, textiles, a Mr. Turk menswear line, and a dozen stand-alone stores across the country. When not traveling the globe, Turk splits her time between Palm Springs and L.A.'s Silver Lake neighborhood.
Biggest scores: I love the macramé lion and rhino "trophies" we found at Studio 111 in Palm Springs (the gallery has since moved to Cathedral City).

TRACY TYNAN is a costume designer whose career has spanned more than thirty years and includes films (*The Big Easy*, *Great Balls of Fire!*, *Blind Date*) and TV movies (*Tuesdays With Morrie*, *The Witches of Eastwick*). In 2010 she was awarded the Women's Film & Television Showcase International Visionary award for her contributions to costume design. Her memoir, *Wear & Tear: The Threads of My Life*, was published in 2016. Originally hailing from the UK, she now calls downtown Los Angeles home.
Words of wisdom:

Check the return policy just in case.

ILARIA URBINATI is a Rome-born, Paris-raised, Los Angeles–based stylist whose client list has included Bradley Cooper, Ryan Reynolds, Ty Burrell, Ben Affleck, Shailene Woodley, Marisa Tomei, Lizzy Caplan, and Laura Dern, among others.
Style inspiration: People often refer to *Annie Hall*, but I've always preferred Diane Keaton in *Manhattan*—all those little shirts buttoned to the top, tucked into those high-rise pants. She's perfect.
Words of wisdom:

Shopping is good for the economy.

MARY FRANCE VAN DAMME is the Montréal-born, Hong Kong-based founder of the travel-inspired luxury resort line that bears her name, which she launched in 2011. Her three decades of experience in the fashion industry include stints heading up a company that created private label brands for Macy's and Lord & Taylor and starting a manufacturing company (in Hong Kong) that developed and manufactured apparel for retail brands that include Monoprix, Marks & Spencer, and Saks Fifth Avenue.
Words of wisdom:

Only buy the best.

SUSANA MARTÍNEZ VIDAL is a fashion journalist based in Madrid and Mexico City. Over the past twenty-five years she's held posts as director of *Elle* Spain and *Elle Décor* Spain, founder of *Ragazza* magazine, and, most recently, contributor to the Huffington Post. Her coffee-table book *Frida Kahlo: Fashion as the Art of Being* was published by Assouline in 2016.
Words of wisdom:

To shop well, you must be prepared to return home empty-handed. If not, you will spend money on things you don't really want and won't end up wearing. And finally, as Frida Kahlo demonstrated, how one wears something is more important than what one wears.

DANIELA VILLEGAS is a Los Angeles–based jewelry designer known for translating her love of nature into wearable creations that combine 18-karat gold, gemstones, and a range of organic elements that include (but aren't limited to) beetles, porcupine quills, and feathers. Since launching her namesake jewelry collection in 2008, those spotted wearing her wares have included Demi Moore, Katy Perry, Salma Hayak, Christina Aguilera, Halle Berry, and Miley Cyrus.
Words of wisdom:

It's not about how much you pay, it's about how happy it makes you feel.

CLARE VIVIER was inspired in 2008 to launch her namesake Clare V. line of handbags and accessories after being unable to find a stylish and functional laptop case. Founded in 2008, the Los Angeles–based label that melds SoCal cool and Parisian chic currently sells a range of leather goods that includes clutches, totes, wallets, and luggage tags—and the occasional roll-up backgammon set—through retailers around the globe as well as a half-dozen US stand-alone stores.
Biggest score: My friend found white suede Prada platform brogues on the side of the road in Big Sur. She grabbed them and realized they weren't her size—but they were mine!
Words of wisdom:

It's okay to shop to make yourself feel better. And pay attention to where things are made!

DITA VON TEESE is a Los Angeles–based burlesque dancer whose high-end striptease act—which often involves Von Teese performing in a giant martini glass—has been performed to sold-out crowds around the world. She is also a designer, with her own line of lingerie, eyewear, and a fragrance collection. She has published three books, the most recent of which is *Your Beauty Mark: The Ultimate Guide to Eccentric Glamour* in 2015.
Biggest score: A Christian Dior New Look 1954 three-piece tweed circle skirt suit, with the Christian Dior Paris label bearing the red serial numbers. It has a silk lining and garters attached to the blouse, from Relic Vintage in San Francisco.
Words of wisdom:

I always dress well to shop and never buy anything that isn't better than what I have on.

STEPHANIE VON WATZDORF is the founder and creative director of the New York–based women's luxury label Figue (pronounced fig), which she launched in 2012. The collection of ready-to-wear, handbags, shoes, and jewelry has a gypsy vibe inspired by both her passion for travel and her upbringing; she was born on the outskirts of Paris to a German-French father and a Russian mother and her grandfather Leonide Massine was a renowned choreographer of the Ballets Russes.

CONTRIBUTORS

Style influence: Anita Pallenberg and that effortless, very cool style of the late '60's and early '70's. Anouk Aimée has exquisite style, that perfect French look.

EILEEN WALLIS is the managing partner of the Portsmouth Group in Dubai, and has more than seventeen years of PR experience in the Middle East. Under her direction, The Portsmouth Group develops and manages regional communications strategies for clients in the retail, luxury, arts, entertainment, and hospitality sectors. The agency has worked with a number of brands, including Christie's, Rocco Forte Hotels, Swarovski, and Van Cleef & Arpels.

NICOLE WARNE started her Gary Pepper Girl website in 2009 as a hobby to sell clothes, and it has since grown into one of Australia's most successful lifestyle blogs. She became the first digital influencer to sign with IMG's Talent Division, and has graced the covers of *Harper's Bazaar* Singapore and Malaysia, *Elle* Australia, *Miss Vogue* Australia, *Lucky*, *Nylon*, and Net-A-Porter.com's The Edit. She counts premium brands Chanel, Valentino, Chopard, Dolce & Gabbana, L'Oreal Luxe, and Net-a-Porter.com among her list of clients.

SOPHIA WEBSTER is the London-based creative director of the namesake footwear and accessories label she founded in 2012 and which is now stocked by more than 200 retailers around the globe.
Style influence: Gwen Stefani. She has always stayed true to her unique sense of style and I love that about her. My favorite look of all time has to be from the "Just a Girl" video, classic Gwen.
Words of wisdom:

You can never have too many shoes!

ERIN WEINGER is a journalist and entrepreneur currently serving as the digital commercial editor of *Vogue* Australia. She previously served as digital style director of the *Hollywood Reporter*, where she launched and helmed the brand's digital style and beauty destination, Pret-a-Reporter .com. Her career in fashion writing began as a staff writer for the *Los Angeles Times* Image section. Her editorial contributions have appeared in *Entrepreneur*, *Vanity Fair*, Elle.com, InStyle.com, *Paper*, *Departures*, and other publications. She lives in Sydney.

ALEXANDRA WILKIS WILSON is a serial entrepreneur who cofounded luxury, members-only e-commerce site Gilt.com in 2007 and home-blow-out business Glamsquad in 2014. She and Gilt cofounder Alexis Maybank are the authors of the *New York Times* bestseller *By Invitation Only: How We Built Gilt and Changed the Way Millions Shop* (2012).
Biggest score: A Valentino coat that I bought through Gilt. We didn't even photograph it, I paid $500, it was a $10,000, black suede with a Swarovski belt, a little bling, lined in fur.
Words of wisdom:

When you're traveling, you can be impulsive. Carpe diem!

BRIAN WOLK
(see Claude Morais).

KIMBERLY WU is one half of the Building Block sister act. Kimberly and her sister Nancy Wu launched their L.A. brand of industrial design-minded leather accessories in 2011. After graduating from Pasadena's Art Center College of Design, where she studied industrial design, Kimberly went to work for Honda's Advanced Studio in Tokyo, where she also discovered the hardware store to end all hardware stores, Tokyu Hands. There, she started to collect electrical sockets and cords that inspired the bags of Building

Block, which are sold in stores around the world, including their own in downtown Los Angeles.

KATE YOUNG is a New York–based stylist who started her career as an assistant to *Vogue* magazine's Anna Wintour and Tonne Goodman, a job that led to the honor of styling the first-ever cover of *Teen Vogue* in 2003. Her list of red-carpet clients has includes Margot Robbie, Natalie Portman, Michelle Williams, Rachel Weisz, Dakota Johnson, Sienna Miller, and Selena Gomez. She's also worked with A-list designers and has styled ad campaigns for Dior, Joie, Guerlain, and Carolina Herrera, among many others.
Biggest score: I bought tons and tons of vintage YSL from Resee.com when it first launched. My best score ever.

JOE ZEE is the Los Angeles–based editor-in-chief and executive creative officer at Yahoo Style, prior to which he logged seven years as the creative director of *Elle* magazine. He is the author of *That's What Fashion Is: Lessons and Stories From My Nonstop, Mostly Glamorous Life in Style* (2015).
Style influences: Kurt Cobain and John F. Kennedy Jr. A bit of an oxymoron when it comes to style, but they represent two very distinct sides of me.
Words of wisdom:

Wear it now. If you love it enough to splurge on it, then use it. Before it's too late.

RACHEL ZOE is a Los Angeles–based stylist, fashion designer, TV personality and editor whose list of A-list clients over the years has included Nicole Richie, Jennifer Garner, and Jennifer Lawrence. She was the focus of Bravo's reality TV series *The Rachel Zoe Project*, which debuted in 2008 and aired for five seasons. The debut of her namesake collection of ready-to-wear, jewelry, and footwear, and the launch of her media company Zoe Report was in 2011. She has two books to her credit, the *New York Times* bestseller *Style A to Zoe* (2007) and *Living in Style* (2014).
Style influences: Brigitte Bardot, Jane Birkin, Coco Chanel, and countless others. I'm so influenced by the '60s and '70s in terms of my own taste and the aesthetic of my collection, and I will forever be inspired by these amazing and beautiful women.
Biggest score: One of my favorite most unforgettable shopping experiences was when I first met William Blanks Bailey, of William Vintage Shop in London, and visited his extraordinary store. This was my first time really "shopping" in over a year—my longest time without a purchase since my son Skyler was born. I ended up spending six hours in the store—Skyler got comfortable and took a nap! I found some unbelievable Christian Dior haute couture pieces and a Jean Patou vintage gown that I wore on the cover of my second book. It was hands down the best shopping day I have ever had.
Words of wisdom: This took me about twenty years to learn, but I promise these are words to live by:

Shop with a purpose. Try to not always be driven by trends and only buy something if you can picture a moment in your life that you will wear it.

ACKNOWLEDGMENTS

I would like to thank my friends near and far for helping me compile this guide, particularly Kelly Cutrone, Heather John Fogarty, Lizzie and Kathryn Fortunato, Jane Lim, Fiona Marin, Ann Mashburn, Lisa Parrish, Frances Pennington, Bryan Smith and Erin Weinger for being such generous connectors, and Ruth O'Neill for her extraordinary research skills. Thank you to my husband, Adam Tschorn, for his clever turns of phrase, and for all the long hours (years?) spent patiently waiting for me outside stores; to my parents Richard and Susan Moore for supporting me in every way; and to my sister Kathleen Moore for always being willing to tag along on a shopping excursion. Thanks to Missy Anderson and Billie Huff, two world-class shoppers in their own very different ways who taught me the thrill of the hunt, and to Judith Regan and Mia Abrahams for their guidance and determination.

BOOTH MOORE

has been an Olympic-level shopper since she was a schoolgirl in New York City. After graduating from Duke University, she began her career in that city of the sensible suit, Washington, DC, at *The Washington Post.* Moore joined the *Los Angeles Times* in 1996, where she logged tens of thousands of miles as the paper's fashion critic, covering the runways in New York, London, Milan, and Paris (and stopping to shop along the way). She left the *Times* in 2015, is now the senior fashion editor at *The Hollywood Reporter*, and has contributed to the *New York Times*, *Wall Street Journal*, *Town & Country*, and *Condé Nast Traveler*, among other publications.

She lives in Los Angeles with her husband, two cats, and an overflowing closet room that could one day be a pop-up store.

PHOTO

NORTH AMERICA

Tommy Boudreau/Bodega, 12 (top left), 43; Chosen Vintage, 12 (center left); FREECITY workshop, 12 (bottom left), 46; Ari Becker Photo, 12 (bottom right), 71; Want Apothecary, 12 (center right), 147; © 2016 Madison Hall, 12 (top right), 134; Draper James, 13 (top right), 126, 130; 13: Photo courtesy of Trashy Diva/Brittney Werner, 13 (top center); Gus Powell, 13 (top right), 24; Billy Farrell/BFA, 13 (bottom right); Courtesy of Ann Mashburn, 13 (bottom center) 116; Courtesy of Secret Location, 13 (bottom left), 148, 150; Love Adorned, 14; Courtesy of Journelle, 19; Courtesy of the author, 34, 240, 243; Amy Dickerson, 37, 324; Courtesy of Concrete & Water, 38; Lucas Allen, 39; Nancy Pearlsteen, 40; John Phelan, Wiki Commons, Creative Commons License, 41; Courtesy of the Vermont Country Store, 42; Courtesy of Faran Krentcil, 45; Courtesy of Irene Neuwirth, 52; Courtesy of Reformation, 54; Ali Mahdavi, 59; Autumn de Wilde, 67; Ben Ritter, 73; Sharon Suh, 77; Xander Bennett, Flickr, Creative Commons License, 79; Courtesy of Trina Turk, 80; Patrick Aguilar, 82; Tom Schwartz, 85; Leslie Santarina, 87; Alana Hale, 90, 333; Franco Folini Flickr, Creative Commons License, 93; Courtesy of Nordstrom, 97, 323; Jaclyn Campanaro, 98; Liz Gross, 101; Avant Toi, 102; Jay Carroll, 103; Courtesy of Allens Boots, 104; Photo courtesy of ByGeorge, 106; Courtesy of Kick Pleat, 107; Nathan Schroder, 108; Courtesy of Stanley Korshak, 111; Betty Newton, 112; Ben Gately Williams, 115; Christopher Ziemnowicz, Flickr, Creative Commons License, 117; Courtesy of the Webster, 118; J Stephen Young, 124; Caroline Allison, 128; Giampaolo Sgura, 131; Courtesy of Space 519, 135; Tender, 136; Shinola, 137; Luke Truman, 138; Courtesy of Susie Sheffman, 141; Sarui Ghah Remanpour, 182; Marc Cramer and Saucier + Perrotte Architects, 146; Brian Bowen Smith, 151;

MEXICO & SOUTH AMERICA

Courtesy of Comme il Faut, 152 (top left), (center right), 185; Courtesy of Uxuacasa, 151 (center left), (bottom left), 171; Holly Wilmeth, 152 (bottom right), 160; Courtesy of Fernanda Yamamoto, 152 (top right), 174; Courtesy of Gabriela and Tere Artigas, 156; Courtesy of Yakampot, 159; © 2016 Caravana Tulum, 162; Alejandra Photography, 163, 281; Gustavo Garcia Villa, 165; Paulo Troya and Renan Teles, 167; Courtesy of Lenny Neimeyer, 169; Courtesy of Ana Kozak, 172; Michell Zappa, Flickr, Creative Commons License, 173;

EUROPE

Courtesy of La Commercial, 188 (top left), 284, 288; Courtesy of Caffé Giacosa, 188 (top right), 275; © & Other Stories, 188 (center right), 296; Courtesy of 10 Corso Como, 188 (bottom right), 253; Betty Newton, 188 (bottom left); Courtesy of Prada, 188 (center left), 254; Al Higgins, 189 (top left), 218; Courtesy of Frau Tonis Parfum, 189 (center top), 293, 294; Pablo Recio, Flickr, Creative Commons License, 189 (top right), 216; Marc Dantan, 189 (bottom right), 222; Luisaviaroma – Luxury Shopping Worldwide Shipping, 189 (bottom center), 273; Jaclyn Campanaro, 188 (bottom left), 282; Courtesy of Roksanda, 190; Jamie Kingham, 203; Anna Bauer, 206; Carmen De

CREDITS

Witt, 209; Alikhan & Radik, 211; Courtesy of Liberty London, 212; Stella Gehrckens, 215; Blanaid Hennessy, 220; Roland Halbe, 232; Les 3 Marches de Catherine B, 235; Pierre Bailly, 238; Sunshinecity, Flickr, Creative Commons License, 269; Alberto Zanetti, 270; Courtesy of Erica Pelosini, 274; Zoltán Vörös, Flickr, Creative Commons License, 276; Doug Inglish, 277; Eric Titcombe, Flickr, Creative Commons License, 279; ANNA-KARIN KARLSSON Campaign shoot "DECADENCE" by Ekaterina Belinskaya, Head piece Agnieszka Osipa/ Sunglasses ANNA-KARIN KARLSSON/ Rings Loree Rorkin, Lynn Ban & Yeprem/ Fur collar Jh Nocturnal/ Outfit Patrik Guggenberger, 299;

EURASIA

Courtesy of Axenoff, 302 (top right), 317; Courtesy of Dilek Hanif, 302 (top right), 306; Adnan & Hasan, 302 (center right), 304; Lelis Noroditky, 302 (bottom right), (center left), 312; Kemal Olca, 302 (bottom left); Courtesy of Evren Dogancay, 307; Cemre Mert, 308; Charles Thompson, 314; Martin de Lusenet, Flickr, Creative Commons License, 315; Kathryn Wirsing, 316;

ASIA

Courtesy of Johanna Ho, 318 (top left), 342; Courtesy of Marie France Van Damme 318 (top right), 319 (bottom middle); Kate Shanasy, 318 (center right), 335; Elise Bergerson, 318 (bottom right), 336; Nestor Lacle, Flickr, Creative Commons License, 318 (bottom left), 363; Courtesy of Daikanyama Tsutaya Books, 319 (center left), 318 (left top), (center top), 338; Seth Powers/KolcaiStudios, 319 (top right), (bottom left), 353; Lisa Eisner, 331; Dick Thomas Johnson, Flickr, Creative Commons License, 340; Courtesy of Divia Harilela, 345; Sabrina Sikora, 347; Courtesy of Bonnae Gokson, 349; Justin Poland / The Society Management, 359; Courtesy of Gentle Monster, 361; Aimee Song, 362;

MIDDLE EAST

Courtesy of Bambah, 370 (top left), (center); The cARTel Dubai/Peter Richweisz, 370, (top right), (bottom right), (bottom left), 374; Roy Ghattas, 373;

AFRICA

Sandy Bornman 380 (top left), 387; Courtesy of Chandler House, 380 (top right), 394; Akbar Delights, 380 (center right), 382, 385; Amfo-Akonnor Kwadwo (Amfo Connolly), 380 (bottom right), (bottom left), 392; Toby Murphy, 380 (center left), 396; Delphine Warin, 384; Courtesy of Temple Muse, 386; Emmanuel Andre @TBWA, 388; Ines Cuatrecasas, 390; Keagan Kingsley Carlin, 398;

AUSTRALIA

Courtesy of Saturdays NYC, 400 (top left), (center); Alpha60, 400 (top right); Gorman, 400 (bottom left), 419; Camille Walala, 400 (bottom right); Andrew Baker Photographer 401 (top row); Courtesy of Peter Alexander, 401 (bottom right); Shantanu Starick, 401 (bottom left), 412, 422; Courtesy of Zimmermann, 402; Courtesy of Pip Edwards, 405; Courtesy of Erin Weinger, 408; Terence Chin, 410; Kate Ballis, 421;